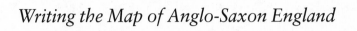

Writing the Map of Anglo-Saxon England

NICHOLAS HOWE

Writing the Map of Anglo-Saxon England

ESSAYS IN CULTURAL GEOGRAPHY

Yale University Press
New Haven &
London

Published with assistance from the Louis Stern Memorial Fund.

All photographs are by the author.

Set in Sabon Roman type by Keystone Typesetting, Inc, Orwigsburg, Pennsylvania.
Printed in the United States of America by Thomson-Shore, Inc., Dexter, Michigan.

Library of Congress Cataloging-in-Publication Data

Howe, Nicholas.
Writing the map of Anglo-Saxon England : essays in cultural geography / Nicholas Howe.
p. cm.
Includes bibliographical references and index.
ISBN 978-0-300-11933-6 (cloth : alk. paper)
1. Anglo-Saxons. 2. Great Britain — History — Anglo-Saxon period, 449–1066.
3. Civilization, Anglo-Saxon. 4. Civilization, Anglo-Saxon, in literature.
5. English literature — Old English, ca. 450–1100 — History and criticism.
6. Great Britain — History — Anglo-Saxon period, 449–1066 — Historiography.
7. Cultural geography — Great Britain. 8. Manuscripts, Medieval — England.
I. Title.
DA152.2.H69 2008
942.01 — dc22

2007016407

A catalogue record for this book is available from the British Library.

10 9 8 7 6 5 4 3 2 1

For Georgina, as always

Contents

Preface

To the writing of place in Anglo-Saxon England there is, I have learned, no end. Choose a topic or genre, trace out the possible senses of place that each displays, and you will discover far more than can easily be accommodated in even a full-length study. I could assemble several tables of contents to place beside the range of materials surveyed in this book, alternatives that would feature very different works and questions. Thus, from the start, certain exclusions have been necessary, starting with works that were driven by an alien political culture, such as the Domesday Book, or that date from after the end of Anglo-Saxon England, such as those by William of Malmesbury. Another deliberate exclusion, perhaps the most important, was the aim of writing a definitive or encyclopedic account of the subject. The chapters of this book are, as its subtitle notes, essays in cultural geography, that is, explorations from various starting points rather than exhaustive coverage of the subject. The map of Anglo-Saxon England offered by this book is not coterminous with the subject it surveys: it provides some routes across the terrain, some means for locating the major features of the landscape, but it is considerably less completely featured than the subject itself.

Perhaps the most useful of these routes lies in the sequence of chapters that follow. I open with the most local and immediate senses of place that an Anglo-Saxon might have known, such as those determined by the terrain underfoot and by the ways in which the idea of home was constructed. Beginning with specific sites in Anglo-Saxon history or the boundary clauses of legal charters expresses my conviction that probing such matters is far more likely to yield insight into how the Anglo-Saxons thought about their world than is the alternative method of positing some theologically derived sense of place that will then be used as a master narrative to interpret all sites and texts. I would argue that beginning with the local and immediate and then moving through historically and culturally inflected senses of place, often having to do with the presence of Rome in Anglo-Saxon England, prepares us for the more complex and multivalent visions of place that we can find in the great Anglo-Saxon manuscripts I call "books of elsewhere": British Library, Cotton Tiberius B v and Vitellius A xv, as well as Oxford, Bodleian Library, Junius 11.

In the course of this progression from place as that which rests beneath one's feet to place as the final destination of the Christian soul after death, there is space to consider all sorts of evidence: linguistic, textual, archaeological, visual, geographical, historical, and material. Exploring this range of materials has been part of the pleasure of this project, especially when doing so took me to fields I had rarely considered before. But doing so has also imposed constraints on how much of the scholarship on any given matter can be cited. To have listed all the available scholarship on any manuscript, text, or site would quickly have overwhelmed this book with references. I have thus cited only those works that are immediately relevant or that directly shaped my thinking on the matter at hand. If this practice helps to counter the bloat of references that characterizes much recent scholarship in Anglo-Saxon studies, I will not be unhappy.

As its title suggests, *Writing the Map of Anglo-Saxon England* is about the world as it was known and imagined by the English before A.D. 1100 or so and, more exactly, as it was written by them in both the vernacular and Latin. It argues across many genres and topics that mapping entailed for the Anglo-Saxons not a visual field but a verbal technique, that it used many of the methods they inherited from Biblical narrative and Roman geography to make sense of the world by describing it, cataloguing it, compiling itineraries, and (sometimes) inventing it. By design, this book ranges across as much of the representative evidence as I have been able to locate in order to offer not a single Anglo-Saxon sense of place but, instead, many such senses of place. This claim is perhaps the most necessary that the book has to offer: the Anglo-Saxons had many different ways of looking at the world and were not content to impose a single template on the world and call it mapped. *Writing the Map of Anglo-Saxon England* can be taken, in that regard, as a sequel to my *Migration and Mythmaking in Anglo-Saxon England,* that is, as a series of answers to the question that book posed implicitly but did not pursue: What do you make of the place where you find yourself once you have migrated there from elsewhere? What stories accrue to the place where you find yourself after being transplanted? *Writing the Map of Anglo-Saxon England* can also be taken as a historical parallel to my *Across an Inland Sea: Writing in Place from Buffalo to Berlin,* which documents the shaping of life through places where I have lived, spent time, and read. Like that project, *Writing the Map of Anglo-Saxon England* raises large questions about how place as fact and idea operates within a culture.

A brief preface is not the occasion to define or otherwise delimit a fact and idea as complex as place. The scholarly and imaginative literature on the subject is very large and contains interesting cultural contradictions about what is place and what is space. The French and Anglo-American schools tend to use these terms in distinctly opposing ways. While I have learned much from Henri Lefebvre's *The Production of Space* and Marc Auge's *Non-Places: Introduction to an Anthropology of Supermodernity,* to cite two obvious examples, I have found the precise analysis that characterizes the Anglo-American tradition, as cited in many of the chapters below, to be more illuminating for examining a specific place. If this study as a whole were to have an epigram, it would be a sentence by the contemporary American architect Donlyn Lyndon: "Places are spaces that you can remember, that you can care about and make a part of your life." He writes in the present tense here of the places we move through and live in, but his observation comes from a book cowritten with another architect, Charles W. Moore, called *Chambers for a Memory Palace.* Place in its relation to memory, as mediated through the canons of rhetoric; memory in its haunting of place, as recorded by words and the shaping of the earth; place and memory as ways of understanding the past, as we look at it across the centuries — these themes constitute the project of this book. The places I write about are those from Anglo-Saxon England that, once read or visited, have remained in my memory and become part of my life.

Acknowledgments

One tragedy of this book is that its author did not live to see it published; another is that he never wrote the acknowledgments that he had planned. At the time of Nick's death, on September 27, 2006, at age 53, the book itself was finished. He had submitted the manuscript to Yale University Press earlier that year. Then his health took a turn for the worse, and he was in the hospital for six weeks, from the end of April until early June. During his stay, the two readers' reports arrived from the press. The two authors' lively engagement with Nick's manuscript and their many comments and suggestions inspired him to get out of the hospital and back to work. Over the summer he made the necessary revisions and assembled the images he wanted to use as illustrations. In August, when his health began again to decline, he had many conversations with me and others about the problem of writing acknowledgments, the difficulty of finding the right way to thank all the people who contribute in so many different ways to a writer's project. Then on September 13 he was admitted to the hospital. He died two weeks later.

Among his papers I found notes mentioning people he intended to thank, a simple list of names and, in some cases, initials. I am sure that this was not a complete list. I am also sure that he would have wanted to identify each person's particular contribution with his usual graciousness. Sadly, I cannot express Nick's appreciation in the way he would have, and so I merely list the names here, in the hope that the people named, and the people omitted, will forgive the inevitable oversights.

He would have expressed his gratitude for the conversations and friendship of scholars such as Roberta Frank, Drew Jones, Roy Liuzza, Dale Kinney, Ursula Schaefer, Roxann Wheeler, Joyce Hill, Simon Keynes, the late Patrick Wormald, Catherine Karkov, Katherine O'Brien O'Keeffe, Andy Orchard, Fred C. Robinson, Seth Lerer, George Brown, and Carol Neuman de Vegvar. Nick took great pride in the accomplishments of his former students, who also helped the project along: Stacy Klein, Tom Bredehoft, Cynthia Zollinger, and Dana Oswald. During the last stages of work on the book, he was assisted by two research assistants whose fine work he wished to acknowledge: Eleanor Johnson and Karen Williams. The responses of audiences at venues from Manchester to Dresden and Utrecht to Miami were also appreciated. Nick carried out much of the research for the book during his tenure of a Guggenheim Fellowship in 2002–3. Parts of some chapters — everything has been extensively rewritten — appear in his Toller Memorial Lecture (2000), in *The Journal of Medieval and Early Modern Studies* (2004), in *Reading Medieval Culture* (2005), and in *Postcolonial Approaches to the European Middle Ages* (2005).

I would like to express special gratitude to the Yale editor, Ann-Marie Imbornoni, for her skillful work: Nick could not have wished for a more loving or attentive reader. Among many other kindnesses, Yale University Press arranged for an external professional to compile the index. Asked by Nick to see the book through the publication process if he was unable to do so himself, Roberta Frank and Drew Jones answered editorial queries, read sets of proofs, and checked the index. To all who helped Nick bring this book to light, my warm personal thanks.

Georgina Kleege

Introduction: Book and Land

In his *Lives of the Abbots of Wearmouth and Jarrow*, Bede relates this episode from the career of Ceolfrith:

> Dato quoque Cosmographiorum codice mirandi operis, quem Romae Benedictus emerat, terram octo familiarum iuxta fluuium Fresca ab Aldfrido rege in scripturis doctissimo in possessionem monasterii beati Pauli apostoli comparuit.

> For eight hides of land by the River Fresca he exchanged with King Aldfrid, who was very learned in the scriptures, the magnificently worked copy of the Cosmographers which Benedict had bought in Rome.[1]

The monastery of St. Paul's at Jarrow was Bede's home from his boyhood until his death in A.D. 735. Situated above the River Tyne, some three miles from where it empties into the North Sea, the monastery has come to be celebrated as the center for the great flowering of Latin learning that made the north of England a center of western Christendom in the seventh and eighth centuries. Its stone church with glass windows and wall paintings, its library with numerous manuscripts brought by Benedict Biscop from Rome, its succession of powerful and charismatic abbots — all of these features are well known through the writings of Bede and others.

There is, in other words, a secure context for reading this passage about the exchange between Ceolfrith and Aldfrith. Yet most of its details remain frustratingly uncertain: Where is the otherwise unidentified River Fresca? Might *fresca* be Bede's form of *frisca,* meaning "fresh, i.e., not salt," and thus designate a type of river rather than a specific one?[2] What sort of land were those eight hides? Where were their boundaries? What were the contents of this eight hides? Where were their boundaries? What were the contents of this compendium of cosmographers? Indeed, does that term refer to those who wrote about the shape of the cosmos and its creation or, more modestly, to geographers who expounded the places and peoples of the known world?[3] Was the book supplied with maps or otherwise illustrated? Is the reference to Aldfrith's great learning meant to remind readers of his literacy in Latin, a skill acquired in his youth at Malmesbury and Iona?[4] In the face of so many questions, one is tempted to turn away from the passage as being too vague to yield much of substance. Doing so would be, I suggest, a mistake because there is more in Bede's sentence that can be puzzled out or at least treated to reasonable surmise.

To start with, there is the fact of an exchange between an abbot and a king that involved a book of cosmography and a parcel of land. In some rough measure of economic worth and readerly desire, eight hides of land and a book about the shape of the world or cosmos could be seen as equivalent, at least to those two men at that one moment in the late 680s in Northumbria. The most pragmatically local sense of place one can imagine—that of the earth underfoot—and the most intellectually abstract—that of the order of the created earth—come together in this moment. This exchange may thus be read as suggesting some of the varying senses of place that were available in Anglo-Saxon England, from the most immediate and physical to the most distant and abstruse. And yet that transaction between Ceolfrith and Aldfrith demonstrates that these senses were not mutually exclusive binaries but rather were closely related and could become, on occasion, mutually entangled.

This book of cosmographers was certainly written in Latin, having its origin in Rome, and may perhaps have included maps or diagrams to accompany its text. Such may be the meaning of Bede's claim that it was elaborately worked. Its contents may possibly have recorded that Britannia was a province of the old Roman Empire and may even have specified Hadrian's Wall—the northernmost demarcation of that same empire—which was not far distant from the monastery at Jarrow. Or the manuscript may have been, like those that displayed "the wonders of the east," entirely concerned with other regions of the known world and silent on the subject of northern England. That the manuscript was acquired in Rome, the capital of Anglo-Saxon England as I have called it, and found its way to the northern frontier of Christendom does sug-

gest that there is a dynamic at work here that uses the model of center and periphery to organize knowledge about places. Whatever its contents, though, we
can be certain that this Roman manuscript used writing to relate information
about the larger world or cosmos. Its sense of cartography was primarily textual rather than visual, and its contents are best categorized as a written map.

The parcel of land exchanged for this manuscript would have had to be
demarcated in one way or another for the purposes of this transaction, so that
each party could be secure in his knowledge of what he was giving up and
what he was gaining. No charter survives for this transaction, if indeed one
ever existed, but contemporary examples of the genre from the south of England designate a parcel of land being transferred either by its name, suggesting that its boundaries were common knowledge in the neighborhood, or by a
reference to its "well-known boundaries," indicating another form of local
familiarity.[5] Occasionally a rough set of topographical features will be used to
describe the relevant boundaries in the early charters, but they are not as
specific or as detailed as the boundary clauses that characterize charters from
later in the Anglo-Saxon period. Bede's phrase "iuxta fluuium Fresca" might
even be a trace of such a description, since rivers have a self-evident utility for
marking out property bounds.[6] By whatever means Ceolfrith and Aldfrith
demarcated those eight hides of land, however, they must have used language
in the form of oral or written text. That there was some text—whether a
simple estate name or a fuller list of boundaries—suggests that a place is
known in its local setting through language in ways that bear comparison with
those found in a book of geographers. That is, to state the obvious, a sense of
place was far more likely to have been created, transmitted, and preserved in
Anglo-Saxon England through the use of language than through any type of
visual representation. Only one visual map on a large scale survives from
Anglo-Saxon England, that in British Library, Cotton Tiberius B v, and the
preponderance of evidence indicates that it was very rare. Having come from
Rome, though, this book of cosmographers might have had some visual maps
in it. Aldfrith may even have prized it for that very reason.

If this sentence from Bede's *Lives of the Abbots* remains vague about the
location of the eight hides and the contents of the book of cosmographers, it
does provide a glimpse into the ways the Anglo-Saxons thought about places
and the ways they represented them. That a parcel of land could have some
equivalence with a learned treatise suggests that any exploration into how the
Anglo-Saxons wrote the map of their world must include both the literal and
the abstract, the immediate and the distant. The transaction also recapitulates
the twofold basis for the *stabilitas* of monastic life in Anglo-Saxon England: it
required land to sustain itself agriculturally and economically as well as manu-

scripts to sustain itself intellectually and spiritually. Ideas of place must therefore embrace the settings of domestic life and agricultural production as well as offer some means to comprehend the mysteries of the created universe. Or, in terms of genres, this study can draw as profitably on the boundary clauses of land charters as on the body of Latin geographical learning that was transmitted to England with the conversion to Christianity in the years after 597. Or, to consider thematic representations of place, it must balance what we can know about how the Anglo-Saxons knew of home in the sense of earthly habitation with what they thought of home as the promise of Heaven from listening to homilies and their own vernacular biblical poetry.

The evidence for this study is largely drawn from written texts, as well as a very few diagrams of holy sites and a single map of the known world found in British Library, Cotton Tiberius B v. The sophisticated Roman tradition of mapmaking, based at least partly on the work of Ptolemy, left very few visible traces in Anglo-Saxon England, though some features of the Cotton map may derive from it.[7] Whatever other traces there might have been, however, are far less significant than the mass of surviving evidence for the influence of Latin geographers as well as the exemplars for writing about place to be found in the Bible. All of these sources of geographical knowledge and forms of place writing will be explored in the following chapters. They focus for the most part on texts as they provide models of cartographical narrative, ways of moving across the earth consecutively by means of itineraries and other genres of sequential representation. This Anglo-Saxon tendency to use writing rather than drawing to create maps of the known world and beyond may seem alien to us in the twenty-first century when visual maps are a ubiquitous fact of life. Implicit in this book's argument will be, however, the suggestion that written maps have their own cultural logic and necessity as well as some quite marked advantages over visual maps.

The word *map* has in these last few sentences grown perilously metaphoric in designating a construct or schema of knowledge about places and the directions that knowledge takes rather than "the accepted concept of a map—a conventionalized depiction of spatial distributions viewed vertically," to cite the definition in Monkhouse and Wilkinson's manual for mapmakers.[8] My concept of map edges further into ethnographic and historical reportage than usual because it worries the question of what it means to live in or visit the place set on a map's geographical field.[9] Figuring the map as a representation of the world in words rather than images leads to asking about the discipline of geography in a culture where maps did not use visual display as their primary form.[10] Denis Cosgrove suggests a more expansive sense of mapping when he writes: "To map is in one way or another to take the measure of a world, and more than merely take it, to figure the measure so taken in such a way that it may be communicated between people, places or times. The measure of mapping is not restricted to the mathematical; it may equally be spiritual, political or moral. By the same token, the mapping's record is not confined to the archival; it includes the remembered, the imagined, the contemplated."[11]

If we define cartography as the craft or science that produces representations of geographical knowledge, then we can ask if there might not have been a pre- or nonvisual cartography in early medieval England. I use pre- or nonvisual cartography here to parallel how medievalists speak of pre- or nonliterate textuality. Scholars like Brian Stock and Katherine O'Brien O'Keeffe have shown that access to textuality is not limited to the literate and can often take forms very different from our own experience of reading a book silently and alone.[12] There is thus no reason to restrict textuality to a single form, such as appears in manuscript. To complete, and thus perhaps to suggest the value of, this analogy between cartography and textuality, I would assert that the fact that almost no visual maps survive from the Anglo-Saxons does not mean they had no geographic imagination or, yet more strongly, felt no imperative to map the world.[13] If the past is indeed another country, then its sense of how to map that country might well also have been different from ours. Or, as the historian of medieval maps P. D. A. Harvey acknowledges, "When people in the middle ages did draw maps it was thus something quite unusual, something quite alien to their normal way of thinking."[14]

What then would not have been alien to the normal way of thinking among Anglo-Saxons? That we have only the one map from pre-Conquest England does not rule out the possibility the Anglo-Saxons made ephemeral maps, such as we do, by sketching a route in the air with a finger or in the dirt with a stick.[15] Or that they were not in the habit, when speaking, of chaining together narrative instructions: from where we are here, go first to that landmark you see over there, and from there go to the next landmark, and so on until you reach your destination or, if you get lost, until you find someone else to ask for directions. That such descriptions existed in spoken discourse is strongly suggested not simply by common sense but also by the survival of similar sequences of landmarks in Anglo-Saxon documents, where they take the familiar form of boundary clauses in hundreds of land charters. This practice of writing a landscape by beginning with a set point and then following a fixed series of landmarks is in practice little different from the technique of a Latin writer such as Pliny, for whom cartography is essentially a narrative rather than a visual technique.[16] These writers locate places not by pointing to them on an illustrative map or by setting their coordinates on a grid, but by writing them in an ordered sequence that typically begins with a well-defined and isolatable site and then moves outward to such other regions as Britain.[17] Without a system of abstract demarcation, such as the grid of longitude and latitude, places cannot be mapped with an absolute location but exist instead in a contiguous and sequential relation to each other. Our convention of longitude and latitude allows a mapmaker to depict a given territory on a single sheet in an atlas that one can examine as it lies on a desk, and yet also enables viewers to locate that same territory on a world map hanging on a wall: one has only to note the coordinates of longitude and latitude on the atlas map and then transfer them to the wall map. The classical and early medieval technique of sequential mapping has as its temporal counterpoint a genealogy that moves from the founding generation through all of the intervening ones to reach its end point. To locate where a place is in this form of cartography, one must relate the sequence of places that lead to it. Or, in the idiom of American jokes about places, you cannot get there from here unless you go through all of the places in between.

With this idiom comes the possibility of narrative. An ordered sequence of places for Pliny or Bede is not simply a list of station names such as appear on the subway map of a modern city, like that done by Henry Beck in 1933 for the London Underground.[18] Instead, this narrative sequence contains an implicit history that must be interpreted by the reader. Perhaps the most striking and self-aware expression of this logic that I have encountered in any Anglo-Saxon text appears in a letter Bede wrote about 716 to Acca, bishop of nearby Hexham in Northumbria. Anglo-Saxonists tend to quote Bede whenever a theorized statement about anything — time, history, cartography, hermeneutics — is necessary because he had an unusually well-defined sense of abstract thought and intellectual practice. We are, in that regard, very much like Bishop Acca when he turned to Bede for assistance in reading the list of resting places occupied by the Israelites as they made their exodus from Egypt into the promised land (Numbers 33:1–49). Acca seems to have wondered if there was a significant relation in this biblical passage between the forty-two resting places and the forty-two years of the journey. More specifically, he wondered if this meant that each was occupied by the Israelites for a year. Was there a kind of divinely ordained congruence of time and place? Bede explains that there was no such neat symmetry and then turns to the matter that intrigues him:

> Ubi diligentius intuendum quare legislator tanta solertia trium annorum conscripto catalogo reliquas maluerit praeterire silentio, ita ut tanto temporum vel potius saeculorum spatio distincta mansionum loca sub contextu continuae narrationis quasi mox subinvicem succedentia connectat: Egressique de Hebrona castra metati sunt in Asiongaber. Inde profecti venerunt in desertum Sin, haec est Cades. Egressi de Cades, castra metati sunt in monte Hor.

Here we ought to consider more carefully why the lawgiver [Moses] who had so diligently composed a catalogue of three of the years preferred to pass over the rest in silence, in such a way that he fastened the distinct locations of the resting-places of such greater periods of time (or rather ages) into the form of a continuous narrative, as though they were following in turn, one right after another: *And departing from Abronah they encamped at Ezion-geber. Going on from there, they came into the desert of Zin (that is, Kadesh). Departing from Kadesh, they encamped at Mount Hor.*[19]

By reading this passage in Numbers as a series of place-names that yields forth a continuous or unbroken sequence, Bede offers an exemplary instance of narrative cartography. His reading is notable for being foregrounded so explicitly, for being (in our terms) so precisely theorized within the larger context of biblical hermeneutics. Under the pressure of doing exegesis, of instructing a superior in the ecclesiastical hierarchy, Bede sets out a means for understanding places so that they form a sequence within providential history. The passage in Numbers is neither a jumbled list of names from a badly read map nor the fixed points on an itinerary; instead, it serves to order the great biblical story of the flight from oppression and the entrance into the chosen land. That there should be a sequence of locations concluding in the desired place is, of course, the narrative significance of the exodus. It is not at all surprising that Numbers 33 should have produced so theorized a reading of its geography, for rarely does a sense of place so profoundly underlie both the literal and the allegorical Christian meanings of a biblical passage as it does with this written map of the exodus. Nowhere in his letter to Acca does Bede explicitly relate this passage, and its larger context of the Israelites' migration, to the ancestral experience of his own people. To have done so would probably have taken him beyond the terms of Acca's original query. But one also remembers that the great mythmaker of the Anglo-Saxon migration and its map of cultural geography was Bede in his *Ecclesiastical History.*[20]

This technique of mapping by moving from one place to the next was not reserved in Anglo-Saxon England for accounts of a biblical people or Roman treatises on geography. It can also be found in works from Anglo-Saxon England about the travels of the English. The *Anglo-Saxon Chronicle* notes in a single sentence that in the year 990 Bishop Sigeric was ordained archbishop and traveled to Rome for his pallium, the ceremonial stole of office that signifies papal blessing: "Her was Siric [*sic*] to arcebiscope gehadod. Her siþþan ferde to Rome æfter his pallium."[21] An entry of this sort is very common in the *Chronicle* because the journey to Rome was a necessary aspect of ordination. As it happens, we have very precise knowledge of the route that Sigeric took back from Rome to the English Channel because an itinerary of his journey survives in British Library, Cotton Tiberius B v, along with much other geographical material, including the map of the world noted earlier.[22] The itinerary of Bishop Sigeric, from the last decade of the tenth century, records seventy-nine *submansiones,* or stopping places, from his departure in Rome to his arrival at the Channel: "Iste sunt submansiones de Roma usque admare; I, urbs Roma" through to the rather puzzling location of "Sumeran," or Sombres.[23] This averages out to about twelve miles between stopping places, probably a good day's travel, especially when crossing the Alps. Some of Sigeric's intermediary stops are familiar to this day, though their names are often rather different in form: Lucca, Vercelli, San Remigio, Orbe (German Orbach), Besançon, Rheims, Thérouanne-sur-Lys, near Calais. This itinerary is simply a list of place-names without any elaboration; it is a string of locations very much like those that appear in eighteenth-century strip-maps of familiar roads or the "Trip-Tiks" produced by the American Automobile Association for drivers who prefer to follow a set route. Sigeric's itinerary inscribes a path for returning home from Rome, one that could be followed by an ordinary pilgrim or by a bishop who had received his pallium. It also inscribes, by its very nature, the route for going to Rome, because the reader has simply to work backward through the list of (frequently) monastic stopping places to reach the holy city.

Sigeric's itinerary is perhaps the simplest geographical text one can imagine, but it is no less eloquent for that simplicity because it reflects the various reasons an Anglo-Saxon would have for going to Rome, whether to receive the pallium or to venerate the relics and holy places of the capital city of western Christendom. As a map, it provides a sequence of stages for a journey that is at once a crossing of natural and cultural terrain. That the sequence of Sigeric's itinerary is homeward bound suggests the injunction that such journeys, as they begin by looking south, must be completed by returning north. That is to say, the meaning and purpose of his journey was to return to England as an archbishop and to practice his pastoral duties there. Sigeric's itinerary can be read as an implicit reminder that the journey to Rome for the pallium was a necessary rite of passage and not a frivolous distraction from such duties if, but only if, the recipient made his way from Rome back to England.[24]

As will be apparent, the argument of this book proceeds for the most part within the familiar conventions of literary and historical interpretation. Its methodology does not depart markedly from that of my earlier work, especially *Migration and Mythmaking in Anglo-Saxon England,* and for that reason requires little prologue or explanation. What does prompt some prologue is the way in which my thinking about ideas of place in Old English and Latin texts has been shaped by visiting the surviving structures and landscapes of Anglo-Saxon England. The trips I made to Northumbria, Mercia, and Wessex, to use the Anglo-Saxon names for these regions, were often rushed, usually limited to a single visit, and always driven by the need to take notes and photographs while the light held and the rain held off. Even so, these visits were deeply illuminating, often in quite precise ways having to do with the dimensions of churches or the distances between sites and always in the more general sense of setting a context for these structures and landscapes. The experience of walking through the Anglo-Saxon church at Escomb or looking out from behind the Anglo-Saxon earthen wall along Offa's Dyke does not, however, stand by itself; it must be translated into precise and documentable claims about that church or wall — as well as about the people who built it. I have never been graced, when looking at a site or landscape like Escomb or Offa's Dyke, with mystical inspiration simply by virtue of being there. When looking at an Anglo-Saxon church, one may be inexpressibly moved by the sheer fact of its survival or the beauty of its setting, but such responses likely have more to do with ourselves than with the Anglo-Saxons. Getting one's boots muddy while clambering around an early medieval earthen fortification or setting a church in its landscape tends to yield more specific considerations about place.

Even a brief visit to a short length of Offa's Dyke, that earthen construction running along much of the Anglo-Welsh border, can make clear something about its reasons for being that is not immediately evident from photographs. If one stands on the Dyke at Sedbury Park, very near where it reaches the Bristol Channel, it is difficult today to see it as a defensive fortification (Figure 1). Even allowing for erosion of the wall and silting in of the accompanying ditch, it seems never to have presented a formidable obstacle to anyone intent on crossing it. Nor does it seem especially well suited for defensive purposes, except perhaps on a small scale that would delay but not prevent incursions. At points along this stretch, it may have been as much as ten or twelve feet high above the ground on the Welsh side, though by its very nature an earthen wall must have some slope to it and thus cannot present a sheer face to the outside. The dimensions of the Dyke will seem curiously shrunken to anyone who has visited similar fortifications at Cadbury or Wareham. Manning the Dyke, almost 150 miles in total length, would have been a formidable challenge on a standing basis, though perhaps local forces could be rallied to specific points along it to ward off sporadic attacks. Studying the dimensions of Offa's Dyke on site and the way it generally follows established political boundaries sug- gests that its defensive intent may have been more symbolic than literal, though no less purposeful for that. Taken as the marker of territorial borders and a very visible assertion of a ruler's power over the land, Offa's Dyke offers a form of defense by asserting the presence of its builder. Just as place-names

Figure 1: Offa's Dyke, near Sedbury Park.

record a pattern of habitation, so earthworks assert the presence of power.[25] If Offa's Dyke is a brilliant form of political display meant to remind all concerned of its maker's might, then we need to adjust our accounts of the Anglo-Saxon landscape to include the ways it embodied and manifested a political sense of place.

No lingering aura about these structures and landscapes can offer a key to understanding them or to interpreting Anglo-Saxon texts. My experience of visiting sites has been far more valuable for the questions it provokes than for the answers it provides. Walking through the stone circle at Avebury and marveling at the genius of its makers is a deeply human emotion, and one that I have felt on several occasions, but it should not be confused with walking through that same stone circle and registering its close proximity to the site of a church that still retains elements of Anglo-Saxon stonework in its fabric (Figure 2).[26] For that observation can yield some productive questions about how the Anglo-Saxons might have looked at their own historical landscape and thus how they might have created a sense of place for themselves. What might an Anglo-Saxon mason building a church at Avebury have made of the stones across the nearby landscape? Were they a useful source of rubble for filling the spaces between masonry walls? Were they marked by some lingering

Figure 2: Avebury, Wiltshire, with a stone from the prehistoric circle in the foreground and the tower of the Norman church, with Anglo-Saxon elements, in the
background.

trace of mystery or sanctity, some memory that this had once been a sacred site and thus was not to be disturbed?[27] Were they simply familiar features of the landscape like the trees and dwellings he could also see as he looked out from his scaffold? Did these stones make him think at various times and in various degrees of each of these possibilities? Anglo-Saxon masons being a notably laconic breed, we have no record of what this one made of his surroundings at Avebury. Nor should we attempt to fill the historical record by confidently assuming that his responses to the site were self-evidently the same as our own. Instead, we can begin by registering as fact the proximity of church and stone circle on that piece of the Anglo-Saxon landscape. Where we go from there will depend on many conditions, not least the limits of our evidence. Yet noting that fact of proximity matters to re-creating some of the senses of place that were current in Anglo-Saxon England.

The experience of looking at an Anglo-Saxon landscape today can rarely be separated from the available textual sources, both historical and scholarly, because they are usually what sent us to look at a site in the first place. We visit somewhere like the Isle of Athelney in the Somerset Levels, where a beleaguered and almost-defeated King Alfred sought refuge in the marshes with his followers in 878, because we have read about it in the surviving texts of Anglo-Saxon England. Without that historical resonance, the Isle of Athelney would simply seem a gentle but otherwise unremarkable rise of ground visible from a lay-by just northeast of Lyng off the A361 (Figure 3). Likewise, the textual account gains greatly when complemented by a visit to the site, and sometimes in surprising ways. Athelney is a case in point precisely because we have an evocative description of it from a contemporary source. In his *Life of King Alfred,* Asser relates the events of the year 878:

> Eodem tempore Ælfred . . . cum paucis suis nobilibus et etiam cum quibus-dam militibus et fasellis, per sylvestria et gronnosa Summurtunensis pagae loca in magna tribulatione inquietam vitam ducebat. Nihil enim habebat quo uteretur, nisi quod a paganis et etiam a Christianis, qui se paganorum sub-diderant dominio, frequentibus irruptionibus aut clam aut etiam palam sub-traheret.

> At the same time King Alfred, with his small band of nobles and also with certain soldiers and thegns, was leading a restless life in great distress amid the woody and marshy places of Somerset. He had nothing to live on except what he could forage by frequent raids, either secretly or openly, from the Vikings as well as from the Christians who had submitted to the Vikings' authority.[28]

A few paragraphs later, Asser adds the telling detail of location by noting that Alfred "made a fortress at a place called Athelney" but adds nothing there

Figure 3: The Isle of Athelney, Somerset.

about the topography of the site, presumably because he did not wish to digress in his triumphalist narrative. Only later, once he has seen Alfred through to victory over the Vikings, does Asser tell his readers about the lay of the land at Athelney. Significantly, he does so in the course of recounting the monasteries Alfred later built for the good of his soul:

> Unum monachorum in loco, qui dicitur Æthelingaeg, quod permaxima gronna paludosissima et intransmeabili et aquis undique circumcingitur, ad quod nullo modo aliquis accedere potest nisi cauticis, aut etiam per unum pontem, qui inter duas [alias] arces operosa protelatione constructus est.

> One of these was for monks and was located at a place called Athelney, which is surrounded by swampy, impassable and extensive marshland and ground-water on every side. It cannot be reached in any way except by punts or by a causeway which has been built by protracted labor between two fortresses.[29]

Topographical descriptions of such detail are relatively uncommon in Anglo-Saxon narratives, and even this one requires a certain amount of adjustment to accommodate subsequent changes in the landscape. Today, after centuries of drainage works, the ground at Athelney is not as swampy or impassable as Asser describes it. The Isle is now pasturage belonging to a neatly kept farm on the site. Yet one can still see sheets of groundwater dotted with aquatic birds in the immediate area and can thus, with a minimum of topographical imagining, place the rise of land at Athelney in something like its Anglo-Saxon landscape.

One can also learn at the site something that goes unremarked in Asser's *Life:* the Isle of Athelney is very small, perhaps one half mile long and several hundred yards wide, at least as it can be demarcated today. Relatively few people—counted in the hundreds rather than the thousands—could have found refuge there, especially if their animals are factored in. The sadly reduced state of Alfred's force at that moment becomes palpably evident from looking at the site. Asser says that Alfred's force was small, but it is at once illuminating and sobering to look directly at the landscape evidence to judge how small it must have been. It is, in that respect, more historically useful to gain some sense of Athelney's size than it is to be reminded yet again that it was where, in a later and probably apocryphal story, Alfred burned the cakes.

Placing Alfred at that site in the Somerset Levels can also prompt one to think more expansively about the role that places played in his life. For the conventional pieties about Alfred at Athelney miss a telling point about him: he was not simply some Anglo-Saxon tribal king or (less charitably) warlord on the run in Somerset, chased by and in turn chasing Danes through the swamps. He was also a man who had visited Rome while a boy in 853, who had seen that the longevity of a Christian city could be measured in centuries. Asser tells us very little about the visit Alfred made to Rome when he was five years old, presumably because he was not one of the large party of Anglo-Saxons who accompanied him. But he does note, suggestively, that "Quo tempore dominus Leo Papa [quartus] apostolicae sedi praeerat, qui praefatum infantem Ælfredum oppido ordinans unxit in regem, et in filium adoptionis sibimet accipiens confirmavit" (At this same time the lord Pope Leo [IV] was ruling the apostolic see; he anointed the child Alfred as king, ordaining him properly, received him as an adoptive son and confirmed him).[30] The exact nature of this ceremony has proved controversial among scholars; it may have been nothing more than an attempt to impress the English visitors with the sacramental and political power of the papacy by predicting that Alfred would become king in due course.[31] That something happened to the young Alfred in Rome, and more precisely, in an ecclesiastical precinct, seems reasonably certain. When he took refuge in Athelney, Alfred was well traveled for an Anglo-Saxon king. He had seen the great city of western Christendom in all of its stone-built glory; he knew that there was more to the world than what he could see on his native island and thus that there was all the more reason for him as a Christian king to defeat the pagan marauders from the north.

Just as Alfred would later identify certain books as necessary for his culture's survival and arrange for their translation from Latin into the vernacular, so he would have known from his own experience that certain sites embodied that culture and could be recollected at times of peril.[32] To think about Athelney as a historical site requires us to make a series of interpretive moves: imagining the marshes that once surrounded it, registering its limited dimensions, tracing the topographical refuge it provided — and then asking how Alfred might have related these facts to his memory of Rome as an enduring capital city. From such collocations of the local and the foreign, the hillock amid the marshes and the stone-built churches of the distant city, one can make some sense of Alfred's life. This kind of interpretive work allows for a productive balance between the distinct acts of reading texts as cultural documents and visiting sites as topographical features. That balance informs much of this study, even if it by necessity draws more heavily on texts to trace the means by which the Anglo-Saxons conceived their maps of the world.

In the course of visiting Anglo-Saxon sites in Wessex, I was reading Iain Sinclair's *London Orbital* (2002), a book about walking the outlying districts of London ringed by the M25 motorway. A series of English locations less like those of pastoral Wessex could hardly be imagined, but as Sinclair made his way through the far reaches of the city, he articulated the essential point about walking and seeing sites historically: "The nature of any walk is perpetual revision, voice over voice. Get it done, certainly, then go home and read the published authorities; come back later to find whatever has vanished, whatever is in remission, whatever has erupted."[33] Living as I do far from the sites I walked and looked at, I started by reading the "published authorities," then visited, and finally went home to reread the authorities and study my slides. The point remains the same: it is the interchange between looking as one walks and rereading that yields understanding.

After looking at landscapes and reading texts from Anglo-Saxon England, I am reluctant to use a phrase such as *reading the landscape* because of the historical conditions that defined and also limited literacy in that culture. If the Old English word *rædan* originally meant "to solve a riddle" or "to offer advice aloud" and only later came to mean "to process written text," then the phrase *reading the landscape* seems particularly misleading in this historical context.[34] For the use of such figurative language tends, more or less implicitly, to treat landscape and text as belonging to the same category of evidence and thus as subject to the same interpretive strategies. I would resist this commingling for various reasons. The most pressing is that we have so little evidence of any kind from Anglo-Saxon England and thus would do well to respect the particularity of each kind we do have in the hope that they can, in their acknowledged differences, illuminate each other. A phrase like *reading the landscape* seems more and more a means to elide difficult questions by reducing all forms of experience to a text. The temptation to do so reflects the contemporary scholar's place in a highly literate and hermeneutically nervous culture. We read written text visually so that we can interpret; it is our accustomed starting point.

For all that the Anglo-Saxons — or at least some of the clerics among them — had learned the interpretive strategies of the patristic tradition, there is little evidence to suggest that they as a people looked at places as if they were reading books in the same way that we do, silently and visually. That is not to say their understanding of places, especially those distant in geography and chronology, was not deeply shaped by textual representations. Indeed, I argue, the Anglo-Saxon tradition of cartography was far more narrative than visual; it wrote maps far more often than it drew them. The Anglo-Saxons, as a result, learned more about places by hearing texts read aloud than by seeing them displayed on a cartographic sheet. In a culture where people can program the global positioning systems in their cars to find the most efficient route between any two locations, this Anglo-Saxon reliance on narrating places seems clumsy, if not alien to the imagination. As such, it is only one of the radical differences between their cultural and intellectual practices and those of our postmodern society that must be registered and respected.

The view across an inhabited landscape is a form of cultural knowledge, as much a part of belonging to a community as is membership in its religious and political life.[35] The view may be very localized because it is hemmed in by the contours of topography and the limited opportunities for travel available to those who live there; but even when tightly circumscribed it offers a way of being set in place and of setting one's position in the world. In a largely agricultural and rural society, such as that of Anglo-Saxon England, the view across the landscape would most immediately yield evidence of production: cultivated fields of grain, intensively managed woodlots and fishponds, pasturage grazed by animals.[36] Other evidence of human occupation would also be visible: paths worn into the earth through regular use; timber or wattle-and-daub structures; stone churches shining in the sunlight because of their whitewash; remains of earlier cultures, such as megalithic circles or the stone walls and streets made by Roman legionnaires. Writing of the Anglo-Saxon landscape, Oliver Rackham makes the crucial point: "The landscape is earlier than we used to think; much of it is inherited from the Roman period; and a good deal was already there when the Romans came."[37] This landscape was full of history and yet we know very little about how its inhabitants thought of that history. Using an evocative trope found elsewhere in Old English poetry, the poet of *Maxims II* speaks of a city made of stone that was visible from afar as the "work of giants":

> Cyning sceal rice healdan.   Ceastra beoð feorran gesyne,
> orðanc enta geweorc,   þa þe on þysse eorðan syndon,
> wrætlic weallstana geweorc.

> A king should hold the kingdom. Cities may be seen from afar, those that are on the earth, the skilled work of giants, the artfully crafted work of wall stones. (ll. 1–3a)[38]

Such descriptions of the inhabited landscape are all too rare in texts from Anglo-Saxon England, especially in suggesting the presence of structures built during an earlier period. One wishes that the poet of *Maxims II* had lingered to describe more about the site he envisions. From what distance is the site visible? What do its structures look like? Who, if anyone, was living in it at the time he saw it? What sense of historical knowledge did he derive from it? From what angle or perspective did they actually see the burg in its landscape and history?

This last question about the angle of vision or perspective by which the Anglo-Saxons viewed their landscape raises a caution against relying unthinkingly on the use of aerial photographs. They have revolutionized our understanding of the historical landscape in Britain by enabling archaeologists to locate sites of lost villages and pathways and by allowing agricultural historians to trace shifting patterns of land use over centuries.[39] Without such photographs, much would remain uncertain, if not unknown, about the distribution of settlements and populations. Yet just as aerial photographs enable one to see what survives beneath the surface of the earth, so they can obscure an understanding of that same surface by introducing a perspective and a way of imaging that were not possible in the eighth or the eleventh century. The classic aerial perspective, as in the Luftwaffe photographs of Britain taken in the late 1930s in preparation for a bombing war and later used by British historians and archaeologists for peaceful purposes, is not at all the same as the traditional bird's-eye view in terms of angle of vision or elevation. Most problematically, aerial photographs introduce an illusory element of omniscience into representation; they not only impose greater clarity and order on the scene than may actually be discernible on the ground, but they also convey a godlike view of the earth in doing so. By virtue of being photographs, they have in our culture the power of the authentic rather than the manipulated image: what they show is what we will see there, or so we are likely to conclude. Even skeptics who have learned to distrust photography's claims to absolute accuracy are likely to accept aerial photographs because they seem so utterly mechanistic in origin and without opportunities or motives for artistic manipulation. What greater proof for the truth value of these images can one cite than the destruction they have enabled through aerial bombardment?

Consider, however, an aerial photograph of a site like Cadbury Castle in Wessex. This hill fortification of some six hundred feet in elevation was used as a stronghold over the centuries from the early Roman era through the wars of the early eleventh century and beyond. Climbing to its top and looking around from its earthen walls allows one to learn the great fact about the place: it is the highest spot around for miles. Seen in an aerial photo, however, Cadbury Castle loses its prominence and thus its historical importance, namely, that no one could have the advantage of looking down on its occupants during time of war and siege. An elevation in the hundreds of feet, as at Cadbury Castle or Burrow Mump near Athelney, can give a very long view across an otherwise level landscape, yet that measure of elevation is flattened out, and even sometimes erased, in aerial photographs. From them, it would be difficult to know, for instance, that Burrow Mump would have been an obvious landmark for those journeying southwest from Cadbury through the marshes toward Athelney, some two miles away.

There must be, to make my point straightforwardly, a kind of historicist concern for the visual representation of landscape. Whatever claims we might make about how the Anglo-Saxons looked at the landscape should follow from what one can see at ground level or from atop a high hill or ridgeline. If an aerial photograph helps us locate an otherwise lost Anglo-Saxon settlement, we should remember that those who lived in it knew perfectly well where to find it because it was home. This argument is not Luddite; it does not deny the value of aerial photography for research, nor would it banish such images from books. The point to be made is rather more subtle, namely, that excessive reliance on modern technologies of flight and photography can make us forget that the Anglo-Saxons did not use them to look at their landscapes or to inform their own senses of place.

The issue of photographic representation is relevant to this study in another, equally important manner. As those who have browsed through books about Anglo-Saxon England know, photographs of sites and buildings from the culture are typically presented in such a way as to emphasize those elements that can be dated securely to the period, with earlier or (more usually) later elements often deliberately excised. A classic instance of this historical selectivity can be found in photographs of Odda's Chapel in Deerhurst, a late eighth-century structure that is frequently cited in textbooks as one of the three or four most authentic Anglo-Saxon churches extant. To make this claim more visually persuasive, photographs will show images of the chapel's west

Figure 4: Odda's Chapel, Deerhurst, Gloucestershire, from the south.

front or south façade with a very tight cropping that eliminates as many traces as possible of the half-timbered house built directly onto the east end of the chapel in the late medieval period (Figure 4). From a strict historicist point of view, this photographic editing shows the chapel in something like the form that Anglo-Saxon worshippers would have known when it was constructed. One suspects, at times, that some advocates of this position would prefer to raze the later addition as an excrescence, though doing so would doubtless anger devotees of fourteenth- and fifteenth-century architecture who would see that as an act of violence on the half-timbered style. The complicating irony is that the Anglo-Saxon structure probably survived largely intact because it was incorporated into the later building as a storeroom or barn and was thus preserved until its original function as a chapel could be recognized by antiquarians in 1885.[40] The desire to remove later additions and accretions to an Anglo-Saxon structure, either in images or in reality, may well relate to the tendentious idea that there is a period style that is alone authentic and characteristic of the culture. The Anglo-Saxons never knew, however, that there was such a thing as an authentic or pure Anglo-Saxon style.[41] That is a later construction meant to satisfy purists.

The desire to photograph Anglo-Saxon buildings in order to place them squarely within their own period has its internal contradiction, however, for many of the extant stone churches from the culture incorporated elements artfully or, at least, knowingly from much earlier Roman sites. And these stones cannot be excised as easily from photographs as can half-timbered additions. It is an awkward historicism, after all, that allows the past of a building to be seen but banishes its future. Anglo-Saxon masons used Roman *spolia* with great technical skill and stylistic elegance.[42] The incorporation of a Roman arch to divide nave and chancel at the Church of St. John at Escomb is the paradigmatic instance, as I argue below with reference to the postcolonial legacy of Rome. To see that use of spolia is worth a trip in itself, especially if the church at Escomb is taken as an exceptionally adept instance of a reasonably common practice.

A less aesthetically notable and more functionally routine use of spolia can be found in the Church of the Holy Cross at Daglingworth, one mile or so off the old Roman road between Cirencester and Gloucester. The church is beautifully situated on a rise and may well have been placed there so as to be visible from the road and draw worshippers. Among its many attractions, including some Anglo-Saxon sculptural panels and a sundial, the church has a two-light window on the north wall of the (nineteenth-century) vestry made from the stone of a Roman inscription (Figure 5).[43] Its text was no longer readable by me in 2002, partly because it has weathered badly and partly because it is tucked away above a metal tank for storing fuel oil. From the original carving of the inscription to the installation of the tank may run as many as two thousand years. The length of this interval is remarkable, but its real lesson is to remind us that the history of Anglo-Saxon structures and sites has always been marked by use and re-use, extending far beyond the close of the period. Why not use the earth that previous generations have moved for walls or tombs, as at Cadbury or Sutton Hoo?[44] Why not pillage Roman sites for dressed stone and ornamental pieces that can be turned to Christian uses, as at Escomb or Daglingworth? Anglo-Saxon sites then, in turn, become available for later uses, as with the churches at Deerhurst or Bradford-on-Avon, which were turned to a variety of utilitarian purposes in later centuries. What happened to these Anglo-Saxon buildings after their original ecclesiastical function was forgotten is part of their story, especially because these changes occurred when no one would have had a textbook knowledge of how an Anglo-Saxon church differed stylistically from a Norman one. Sites and buildings, like poems, have an afterlife that is part of their history.

Looking for Anglo-Saxon England means at times encountering a site with visible remains that date to earlier and later periods and then wondering if there was ever anything there from the seventh or tenth century. In some instances, this question arises from the ways in which a richly stratified site is

Figure 5: Church of the Holy Cross, Daglingworth, Gloucestershire, with Roman spolia.

presented today to the visiting public by those charged with preserving it. A case in point would be the Roman fort at Birdoswald along Hadrian's Wall. The most apparent constructions there are the remains of the Roman structures and wall as well as the large eighteenth-century house by which one enters the site. In the midst of all this visible history, at once inescapable and easy to date, is the ground plan of a vanished structure that is delineated by two shades of gravel and wooden posts about five feet high (Figure 6). These posts are set within the outlined foundations of a larger structure, a Roman granary, and demarcate the floor plan of a timber hall that was built over the site in the sixth or seventh century by those left to survive in the postcolonial void created by the withdrawal of Roman troops in 410.[45] If the site had been designed to foreground the former presence of the timber hall, another arrangement could have emphasized that fact more strikingly. As it stands, the sixth- or seventh-century presence on the site is a footnote to the history of Roman occupation, a minimal acknowledgment of what it might have meant to make a place for oneself after the Romans' departure. Birdoswald as it is recreated today teaches less about early timber halls as structures in themselves than it does about the ways in which they were built on an occupied landscape of use and re-use.

Figure 6: Birdoswald, with wooden posts showing foundation outline of Anglo-Saxon hall built over existing Roman structure.

A more complex instance of this phenomenon — what one might call the lost or obscured Anglo-Saxon presence on a site — appears at Knowlton, some fifteen miles southwest of Salisbury in Dorset. Having seen it only from aerial photographs, where it looks like a level circle with a dot in the middle, I had trouble locating it on the landscape at ground level.[46] For the photograph obscured how dramatically the ruined tower of the Norman church rose above the prehistoric circular earthen rampart there; it gave no sense of scale for the site, no sense of the church in its setting. By flattening the scene, it failed to represent the reason for building the church there: so that it could be encircled (though not obscured) by the existing earthen wall and thus demarcated spatially (Figure 7). This site with its stratified history is quite extraordinary, for it suggests the ways human beings, despite all of their cultural differences, continue to use an otherwise unspectacular site over a very long period of time.

When I visited Knowlton on a cold day, almost bleak, with a heavy but photographable sky that threatened to rain but never did beyond a sprinkle, the weather seemed fitting for a site where so much has happened, been forgotten and barely commemorated. It seemed one of those places that haunt us because they hold stories, even if these same stories are lost, barely recovered,

Figure 7: Knowlton, Dorset, with earthen mounds and ruined Norman church.

invented. In a certain way, the site at Knowlton evades chronological history because it shows the prehistoric earthwork and the Norman church with nothing visible to fill the interval: no trace of Celtic or Roman or Anglo-Saxon, though it seems likely that any or all of them might have used the site for a bivouac or the like. Textual records indicate that the Anglo-Saxons chose the site for meetings of the local Hundred, and there is reason to suspect that the Norman church replaced an earlier Anglo-Saxon one.[47] The interval between the visible traces on the earth is not, in other words, a vacuum, though its patterns of use and re-use are more obscure than one might wish. Yet Knowlton teaches that our own sense of the past must learn to contain the past's sense of its own past—not as a grammatical past perfect, a completed past in the past, but as a sense far less fixed or perfected and thus much more fluid.[48] If this sense in Anglo-Saxon England was rarely bounded by fixed dates, it was often contained within the fixities of place. This sense suggests that something has been on that site for as long as anyone can remember and thus has been naturalized onto the landscape, so much so that it may provoke no notice or need for explanation. As Iain Sinclair observes in his *London Orbital:* "History leaks."[49] That is, it does not remain safely in its containers, the periods we imagine as defining and limiting and bounding it. It is fluid, and as such gives life, indeed, is necessary for life.

Clambering over the site at Knowlton, trying to find angles to capture the

Figure 8: Knowlton, with earthen mounds, ruined Norman church, and recycling truck.

minimalist monumentality of the site in photographs, I kept moving to avoid a truck parked in the background while its driver had his sandwiches and tea on a quiet October day. Finally, I realized that I would have to stand immediately in front of the truck if I wanted to excise it and its unwelcome modernity from my viewfinder. Only then did I notice the name of its owner: Perry's Recycling (Figure 8). That the truck parked at Knowlton was not a cement mixer or fuel tanker but a recycling truck was probably unremarkable to anyone who knew the site; it was a pleasant spot for a driver on his regular rounds to park for lunch and a nap, especially when no visitors were there. The task of the moment was to realize that the presence of this truck was of a piece with my understanding of the place as a site of use and re-use.

That a sense of place grows out of some relation to the past, whether conveyed through folk tradition, poetic celebration, or scholarly research, is a necessary working assumption for this study.[50] For an American who has grown up in landscape that its advocates celebrate as unspoiled, virgin soil, untouched by human hand, this insistence that a sense of the past defines a sense of place comes hard, though also with a certain relief at being freed from one's own national myths. The geography that the Anglo-Saxons inherited with their conversion to Christianity was heavily laden with history, both imperial and biblical. Indeed, geography more than chronology served as the guiding principle of most secular histories written in the early Middle Ages. Even Bede, who was the first to use anno Domini dating for the course of an extensive work, thought of his history's scope as determined by the inhabitants of a place: *The Ecclesiastical History of the English People.* Geography serves as the anchoring principle of history when conventions of chronology have not yet been fixed, when it is easier to define one's subject as concerned with what happened *there* in a given place rather than with what happened *when* in a given time. For a writer like Bede whose sense of there was bounded by England's status as an island with easily recognized boundaries, at least by the standards of the period, geography was a way of shaping the history of his narrative.

Writing in 1570, at a moment when the Eurocentric conventions of traditional geography had been radically shaken by recent encounters with parts of the world previously unknown to its practitioners, Abraham Ortelius offered as his motto "Historiae oculus geographia." As a mapmaker, Ortelius had every reason to think of geography as the eye of history because, in Walter Goffart's phrase, it "allowed history to be visualized" by anyone looking at a cartographic sheet.[51] Visual display is to a map as narrative is to a text: each is a way for the content of the medium to be ordered and comprehended. We respect the visual conventions of a historical map just as we respect the narrative conventions of a historical text, while also recognizing that they are culturally specific rather than generically universal. Historical maps printed in the European tradition typically have north at their top, and historical narratives in that same tradition typically proceed sequentially from earlier to later. During the Anglo-Saxon period in England, when visual maps were relatively rare, geography did not disappear as a discipline or as a body of knowledge. Instead it took on different conventions and found expression most commonly in narrative texts, that is to say, in texts that were arranged using a sequence of places to do their work.

The geographical lore of the Anglo-Saxons took the form of a written map that could guide the traveler or reader from point to point just as a visual map does. If today I relate my sense of place to a friend by pointing to a location on a map and saying that is where I live and belong, I am relying on a form of geographical representation. That representation contains scientific knowledge, but it also evokes a shared means of communication — pointing to a map — that is part of our cultural practice. Gesturing in this way depends upon a shared map and a shared desire to use that map. It also assumes that an act as significant as defining one's place in the world can be achieved with a visual map. And yet most of us would, I suspect, take the act of pointing to the map

as an initial and partial act of self-identification. There would follow, to augment the bare factuality of the map reference, some talk about why we have
such a sense of place, and that talk would have, if we were willing to think
beyond the current moment, a sense of history to it and thus an embryonic
narrative.

In diverse, often contradictory, and sometimes confusing ways, the Anglo-
Saxons used words to talk about places and to understand them. These oral
accounts were ephemeral by their very nature, though some notion of what
was said in them may be deduced from what survives in written documents.
The practice of stringing together landmarks in spoken discourse has, for
example, some correspondence to the technique used in the boundary clauses
of charters. In Constance Bouchard's vivid phrase, medieval land charters
were texts for "organizing eternity," that is, they ordered the surface of the
earth by demarcating it and allotting it for all of human time.[52] Anglo-Saxon
charters also organized eternity by being written records of spoken transactions that could survive the forgetfulness of generations. In another way, however, charters organized eternity not by relating the shape of the cosmos but
rather by specifying the legal status of land as it was looked at, walked over,
and labored on by those who lived there. They placed the topographically
local within the religiously eternal. They are the most literal and immediate
statements of place that survive from Anglo-Saxon England and thus provide
the necessary starting point for this study.

PART I

Local Places

Writing the Boundaries

Scholars interested in medieval senses of place have typically begun with the large scale: the Christian map of the world with Jerusalem at its center; the transmission through Christian encyclopedists of ancient geographical lore from Pliny, Strabo, and others; the travels of pilgrims and merchants across the known world and beyond its edges. These are all necessary variations on the theme of place, but each examines the subject from above, and each neglects senses of place that were more immediately present, that is, more local or more ingrained as a setting for daily experience. This scholarly emphasis on the global or, at least, the continental scale has as much to do with disciplinary habits as with the availability of sources. While there are various Anglo-Saxon sources that speak directly to the large scale, as will become evident later in this book, there are fewer that provide local descriptions and virtually none that can be said to offer personal accounts of places.

Such generic categories as local description and personal account may well be ill-suited to interpreting the available evidence from Anglo-Saxon England. Certainly one cannot, as is often the case with later periods, cite writers from the period that use local description as a medium for personal accounts, as do Gilbert White in Selborne and Henry David Thoreau at Walden in later centuries. Yet before rejecting these categories altogether, one might ask if some trace of their qualities and effects cannot also be detected in Anglo-Saxon texts. Doing so requires one to read obliquely, or across the grain, a technique that risks anachronistic over-interpretation but can also yield unexpected results.[1] These results are unexpected, one hastens to add, within the terms of long-held disciplinary habits that have settled what our sources contain and thus what they can tell us about a given subject. These habits will require some reexamination in response to various types of evidence presented in this book, but first one might ask how it is that a place can be described as being local or as ingrained with lived experience.

The need to recognize the local is all the more pressing in a traditional society where movement, while not impossible, is often restricted by terms of labor service, customs of land use, and a general uncertainty about the nature and dimensions of the outside world. The Anglo-Saxons, or at least some of their elites, could be great travelers, but even they were familiar with the circumstances and obligations of the local. Some of them may have been pilgrims to Rome or Jerusalem, others may have been missionaries or traders to ancestral regions of Germania, while others attended closely to the bounds of the estates that sustained their economic life and to the range of the episcopal sees that organized their religious practice. Trying to comprehend the relation between the local and the distant is, as I have suggested, the point to be drawn from visiting Athelney and thinking about Alfred's time there. The local, as distinct from the more general or universal, contains information about the names and locations of places, the people who live there currently or did so in the past, and the topography that shapes communities over the turn of generations.

The local is also by its very nature closed off or only partially accessible to outsiders. Most place-names, then as now, are not known beyond a restricted orbit, as likewise are facts about the past such as who lived in this hamlet or who built that dyke or path. To those on the ground, such knowledge is largely transparent; it has been known and shared in that community for generations without reference to a wider world or outside audience. Such local knowledge can be placed within the terms and practices of religious and legal systems, as when Anglo-Saxon charters record a grant of land. Yet the relation between such systems and local facts is often difficult to define beyond such generalities as observing that a grant of land was often made for the good of the donor's soul and often carried penalties for anyone interfering with it. Those who drafted boundary clauses for charters did not invoke the deeply learned Christian traditions of law and geography, nor did they require their audience to know them. Such traditions were the source for other writings about place in Anglo-Saxon England, especially those by learned clerics such as Bede. His ideas about place are notable for never being completely circumscribed by the local, even though he is unusual for an Anglo-Saxon writer in noting the sites where he was born and lived as a monk in Northumbria.[2]

Local senses of place also have about them a strong element of lived experience. Those who formulated boundary clauses in charters knew the necessary landmarks because they had walked the landscape. By contrast, one suspects that many of the scribes who inserted such clauses into charters — especially those who set English clauses into Latin charters — would be as hard-pressed to retrace those boundaries as we are today. Such scribes probably worked in a central office for writing charters and had no personal knowledge of the property being transferred. Under this interpretation, such scribes would write all of the charter except for the boundary clause, which would then be inserted by a local figure who knew the territory. This practice of writing the legal sections of a charter in a central registry and then recording the local facts on site may well also explain the presence of two distinct scribal hands in many of the charters.[3] Historians such as Nicholas Brooks and Simon Keynes have drawn fruitfully on charters for a variety of purposes: to understand the intricate workings of the Anglo-Saxon legal system, to track the dates and movements of kings and nobles, to determine the revenue sources of monasteries and other ecclesiastical bodies.[4] Landscape historians such as W. G. Hoskins, Oliver Rackham, and Della Hooke have concentrated on the boundary clauses of charters — the verbal descriptions that demarcate the grant of land — to trace the topography of Anglo-Saxon England and to inventory the relevant Old English terminology.[5] When read at a slant, however, these boundary clauses still have much to say about the ways Anglo-Saxons thought about place, and not just as it was construed as property. As Jacques LeGoff has observed more generally, "In form as well as content even the most prosaic of charters may yield traces of the imagination."[6] To understand these traces, one needs some working familiarity with the intended purposes and generic conventions of charters.

Charters have not been much considered by literary scholars, though they make up a substantial proportion of the extant documents from Anglo-Saxon England. The standard handlist by Peter Sawyer inventories over 1,800 examples of the genre.[7] At the most basic level, charters record the transaction by which a grant of land was made; their legal status is as a written record of the oral ceremony that effected the transfer and made it binding. The charter is not itself the primary means of transfer, as is a deed in later property law. Charters exist, to quote the opening of one early example from 781, because "Tempora temporibus subeunt et vicissitudinum spatiis evenit ut prisca jam dicta inrita fiant nisi scriptis confirmemur" (Seasons follow seasons, and it happens in periods of change that things said in former times may be made void unless we confirm them with writings).[8] As Dorothy Whitelock puts it, charters were "evidentiary" and served as "a precautionary record of an act performed before witnesses, an act valid and complete whether a charter was made or not."[9] The majority of extant examples record grants to ecclesiastical foundations rather than to secular individuals, though that may well have less to do with actual patterns of transfer than with the survival of vellum texts. Individual Anglo-Saxons, unlike monasteries, rarely had secure means of preserving legal documents inherited from earlier generations.

If one moves carefully and very tentatively through these charters one can learn something about those who lived on the land and worked it, who did not travel far, and whose horizons were shaped less by written texts than by the landscape where they were born, labored, worshipped, and died. In the absence of firsthand accounts by those who were tied to the land, or eyewitness reports by outside observers, charters provide some evidence of how Anglo-Saxons attuned to local circumstances thought of the landscape in which they lived. To quote W. G. Hoskins in a similar vein, "We catch a sight of an earlier world in the bare words of this charter."[10] The point to remember is that charters give only a partial glimpse and never the complete picture. As a genre, Anglo-Saxon charters tend to fall into four sections: first, an opening statement of several sentences or more that evokes God or Jesus Christ or both as the authority by which the person in question (such as a king or lord) grants the property in perpetuity; second, a clause demarcating the bounds of the property in question so that there will be no confusion about the extent of the transaction; third, a certain amount of legal boilerplate concerning what will happen (none of it good) to anyone who dares to interfere with the transaction; and fourth, a list of those who witnessed the transaction complete with their titles and signatures.[11]

The choice of available languages—Latin or English or both—must always be considered when reading Anglo-Saxon charters. Many early charters are entirely in Latin, but it became increasingly common by the tenth century or so to draft bilingual charters according to a reasonably predictable pattern: the boundary clauses are in English and the other three sections are in Latin.[12] That some charters are in Latin from start to finish, especially in the earlier period, weakens the appealing argument that those who drafted charters had to write about the landscape of England in English, as a kind of geo-linguistic essentialism.[13] Those who drafted charters may well have found it easier to use English, especially when relying on types of flora to designate boundaries; vernacular names for trees and hedges may have been more available to them than Latin ones. Certainly, the practice of writing boundary clauses in the vernacular becomes more common later in the period.[14] But when necessary, charters could be drafted without recourse to the vernacular. So why then was English used to write the map in these charters?

The answer, I would argue, lies less in the problem of composition, which was a formulaic matter because of the relatively finite set of features for denoting boundary points, and more in the problem of reception. The vernacular was used to present information that was of immediate importance to those who could not comprehend Latin by eye or by ear: the actual bounds of the territory. Those who lived in the area and worked the land would not have needed to know all the names and titles of those who witnessed the transfer; they probably assumed that it was given forever. And they certainly knew it was to be fooled with at their own risk. What touched their lives, what altered the map of their world, was who owned that parcel of land as a result of the transfer. For that could mean changes in patterns of labor and potential loss of traditional rights of use and would certainly mean a new landlord to whom rents or service might be owed.[15] The choice of language for a boundary clause has further implications that will become clear after an analysis of specific examples.

In an early charter from A.D. 679 we find the most rudimentary possible statement about the boundaries of a grant and thus the one least useful for the historical record:

> In nomine domini nostri salvatoris Jhesu Christi. Ego Hlotharius rex Cantuariorum pro remedium animæ meæ dono terram . in tenid . quæ appellatur . Uuestan.ae tibi Bercuald . tuoque monasterio cum omnibus ad se pertinentibus campis pascuis meriscis . siluis modicis . fonnis piscaris omnibus ut dictum est ad eandem terram pertinentia . sicuti nunc usque possessa est . juxta notissimos terminos a me demonstratus [*sic*] et proacuratoribus meis . eodem modo tibi tuoque monasterio conferimus.

> In the name of our Lord and Saviour Jesus Christ. I, Hlothhere, king of the people of Kent, grant for the relief of my soul land in Thanet which is called *Westan ae* [i.e., "west of the river"] to you, Brihtwold and to your monastery, with everything belonging to it, fields, pastures, marshes, small woods, springs, fisheries, with everything as has been said, belonging to that same land. As it has been owned hitherto, by the well-known boundaries indicated by me and my reeves, we confer it in the same way to you and your monastery.[16]

The enumeration of topographical features on this property — its fields, pastures, marshes, small woods, springs, fisheries — becomes all the more interesting as one observes that the charter makes no attempt to delineate its boundaries. It says simply that they are very well known ("notissimos terminos") to the possessor of the property and his reeves and have been so in the past. The knowledge of place here is at once local, because it is limited to those who know the property from personal experience, and immediate, because it could not be re-created or retraced by someone from outside the community in future years. The location of this parcel on the small island of Thanet — itself a very defined territory — may perhaps explain this reliance on local knowledge. Yet one also comprehends, on reading this text, why charters are more likely to make some attempt, no matter how vague and impossible to retrace today, at demarcating the property so as to avoid misunderstanding when they might be read in a more distant location or generation. Writing may preserve the memory of the grant over these distances, but without some demarcation of its bounds, all that will survive in memory is the act rather than the dimensions of the transaction.

Achieving greater specificity in delineating boundaries is not necessarily a consequence of the genre developing over time. An example from a charter drafted within a decade of Hlothhere's grant to Brihtwold makes some attempt at least to name the properties in question. This grant from Œthelræd to the Abbess Æthelburh refers to "terram quae appellatur . Ricingahaam . Budinhaam . Deccanhaam . Angenlabeshaam . et campo in silua quae dicitur Uuidmundesfelt" (the land which is called Ricingahaam, Budinhaam, Deccanhaam [Dagenham], Angenlabeshaam, and the field in the wood which is called Widmund's field).[17] Naming in a society like that of Anglo-Saxon England is, of course, another form of local knowledge because it reflects conventions that are shared by those who live in the place and thus allows for greater precision than does the phrasing of Hlothhere's charter. (By contrast, one suspects that only the most notable places in England would be known by those who lived at a distance.) At the very least, those living near Ricingahaam, Budinhaam, Deccanhaam, and Angenlabeshaam could have had some sense of their locations and boundaries without necessarily holding an official position like that of reeve. That all four of these place-names combine what appears to be a tribal or personal name with either *-haam* or *-ham,* meaning "estate," "homestead," or "dwelling," is further demonstration of the local nature of this information. These are the places of neighbors who can be identified, whether they are the current residents of the site or those who founded them and lived there in the past. If one believes that all of this charter is contemporary to Œthelræd, probably from the years 686–688, then it is also notable for offering an explicit avowal of its purpose and a brief boundary clause:

> Et ut firma et inconcussum sit donum . Termini sunt autem isti huius terre cum quibus accingitur . ab oriente Writola burna . ab aquilone Centinces triow . et hanc Hemstede . ab australe flumen Tamisa.

And that the gift may be firm and unshaken, the boundaries of this land with which it is surrounded are these: on the east *Writolaburna* [perhaps the river Bean], on the north Centing's tree and *Hanchemstede,* on the south the river Thames.[18]

Even if this passage is datable on scribal grounds to the second half of the eighth century, as seems likely, the fact remains that its drafter still had no choice but to rely heavily on local terminology, such as "Centing's tree," to designate bounds.[19] That the River Thames is world famous today does not necessarily mean that it was at the time significantly better known in a distant region of England like Northumbria than was "Writolaburna," or that it could be located precisely by those living far away.

That local knowledge must be the inescapable means for designating the bounds of a property becomes — paradoxically but tellingly — clearest when we turn to a Latin charter that does not use the vernacular for its boundary clause. A charter recording King Cynewulf's grant of land to St. Andrew's Church in Wells (probably from 766) enumerates a variety of topographical features, including some that it explains are designated according to the names used by local residents: "in collem quem incolæ appellant Thornhill" (the hill which the natives call Thornhill); "rivuli quem incolæ vocitant Sealtbroc" (a stream which the natives call Saltbroc); and "sambucin quam vocitant Ellentrow" (the elder which they call Elder-Tree).[20] That a scribe, probably a cleric, writing in Latin and charged with demarcating the property being granted should have resorted three times to a phrase like "the natives call" or "they call" rather than "we call" in a relatively short clause suggests that he was not of the place and instead relied on local terminology to accomplish his task. Such phrasing also suggests that this clause was written very much to be read by local people because it makes every effort to ensure that the "natives" will know exactly what are the bounds of the property now in the possession of the church in Wells, located some distance away.[21]

Local knowledge in boundary clauses can extend beyond matters of nomenclature to include evidence of the most mundane local history. In a charter of 846 by Æthelwulf of Wessex we find the grant being demarcated by references to various ditches, such as "heottes dic" (Heott's ditch); "fyxan dic" (the vixen's ditch); and, most intriguing, "ðone dic ðær Esne ðone weg fordealf" (the ditch where Esne dug across the road).[22] Such a landmark could have been specified only by a local resident who had some memory of the ways a neighbor had modified their Devon landscape, even perhaps in violation of the customary standards of road maintenance. On a large-scale map of Anglo-Saxon England, Esne's ditch is less than insignificant; in the charter and the local culture it preserves for later generations, it is one of the necessary designations by which the landscape is mapped and its human-made history recorded. The sense of the past displayed by charters and especially their boundary clauses is that of the locality itself — so much so that, as Dorothy Whitelock observes, charters containing more encompassing historical material from Bede or the *Anglo-Saxon Chronicle* are suspect as later forgeries.[23] There is something quite appropriate in treating extraneous historical material as grounds for skepticism when judging the authenticity of an Anglo-Saxon charter. It is the immediate sense of place and its mundane history of ditches dug and the like that characterizes the genre, not its knowledge of world geography and history.

By the tenth century, as boundary clauses become longer and are more often written in English, they give a closer sense of the landscape. The localizing force of the vernacular in these clauses becomes all the more evident when set in their larger Latin context. An especially vivid example is provided by the charter in which King Edgar grants a parcel of land at Staunton, Herefordshire, to his retainer Ealhstan in 958. For the sake of brevity, I quote here only the second and third sections of the charter:

> Quapropter ego Eadgar divina favente gratia totius regni Merciorum monarchiam optinens . tribuo et libenter concedo . Ealhstane . fideli meo ministro quoddam rus pro suo placabili pecunia hoc est . XL . mancusis de auro obridzo . in pago . Magesætna . hoc est. VI . manentium . in loco qui ab illius loci incolis dicitur . Stanton . ut habeat et semper æternaliter possideat cum omnibus bonis ad illam terram rite pertinentibus et quicquid exinde facere voluerit . potestatem habeat faciendi.
>
> Est autem hæc terra istis circumcincta terminis . Ærest of myle forda ondlong erge þæt in wæsceford . of wæsceforda ondlong erge ymb holaneige ufeweardre . of holaneige ufe weardre . on þa ac ecge ufe weardre þæt ond land þære ac ecge ufe weardre þæt on snæd weg foreweardre: of snæd wege ymb heanlege on æcnabrycge up ondlong broces þæt in ða dic . ondlong dices in tanes bæce . of tænes bæce ondlong mærgeardes . þæt on lionhina gemære . ondlong leonhiena gæmeres þæt on aðelwoldes hege . of æðelwoldes hege in hean oldan . of hean oldan in mærðorn . of mærþorne ondlong geardes in ðæt hlid get . of ðam hlidgete ondlong stræte on dicesgeat of dicesgeate in ðæt ðridde geat . ðæt ondlong stræte þæt eft in myleford.

> Therefore I, Edgar, by the favour of the divine grace obtaining the monarchy of the whole kingdom of the Mercians, bestow and willingly concede to my faithful thegn Ealhstan for his acceptable money, namely 40 mancuses of refined gold, a certain estate in the province of the *Magonsæte,* i.e. six hides in the place which is called by the inhabitants of the place Staunton, that he may have it and always possess it eternally, with all benefits duly belonging to that land, and that he may have the power to do with it whatever he shall wish to do.
>
> And this land is surrounded by these boundaries: First from the mill ford

along the Arrow, then to *Washford;* from *Washford* along the Arrow round the top of *Holaneig;* from the top of *Holaneig* to the top of the oak edge, then along the top of the oak edge, then to the front of the *snæd* way, from the *snæd* way round *Hanley* to *æcna*-bridge, up along the brook, then to the dyke, along the dyke to *Tanesbæc,* from *Tanesbæc* along the boundary-fence, then to the boundary of the community of *Lene,* along the boundary of the community of *Lene,* then to Æthelwold's hedge, from Æthelwold's hedge to *Heanoldan,* from *Heanoldan* to the boundary thorn, from the boundary thorn along the fence to the swing-gate, from the swing-gate along the paved road to the dyke-gate, from the dyke-gate to the third gate, then along the paved road back to *Milford.*[24]

Latin, the language of the elite orders that could give and receive such grants of land, serves here to assert claims of authority, to issue injunctions against interference, and to record signatures of witnesses; English, the language of the order or class that worked the soil, serves here to demarcate the boundaries of the land parcel in question.[25] The Latin text establishes necessary measures of authority and eternity; English maps the parcel being given as it can be seen in the here and now. If this seems to be a satisfying or inevitable explanation for the ways charters use the two languages to represent authority and landscape, one must note again that many Anglo-Saxon charters were written entirely in Latin and used that language to demarcate the relevant parcel of land. By shifting the focus from the composition of these bilingual charters to their likely audiences, however, one may speak more productively about contemporary ideas of place and community.[26]

Those who lived on the landscape and worked it would need to know one particular aspect of a legal transaction involving property: the dimensions and boundaries of the parcel of land that now belonged to the recipient named in the charter. What they had to know was exactly what had passed to the new owner, for changes in the demarcation of the landscape could bring with them changes in land use. If the designation of the parcel in question was given in Latin, it would not be immediately accessible to those who worked it or lived near it because they possessed no access to that language. If, however, the boundary clause was written in the vernacular and then read aloud, those concerned would be able to satisfy their need to know about shifts in ownership. When read aloud to those who lived in the area, a charter with a boundary clause in English would become the basis for a textual community, that is, in Brian Stock's sense of that term, a group bound together by an interpretation of a text that is both correct and shared.[27]

The probability that such clauses were written in order to be read aloud is evident from their compositional mode, for many features demarcating the landscape appear twice, first as a point of arrival and then as a point of departure, or first as the place to which one goes and then as the place from which one goes: "of ðam hlidgete ondlong stræte on dicesgeat of dicesgeate in ðæt ðridde geat" (from the swing-gate along the paved road to the dyke-gate, from the dyke-gate to the third gate) and so on. Repetition of this sort increased the possibility that listeners would remember the sequence of landmarks that bound a parcel. If we consider that such clauses were intended to invent a place for legal purposes, that is, to give it specificity and definition, then this strategy of repetition would aid in fixing that invention in memory. This conjunction of memory and invention will not surprise anyone familiar with medieval rhetoric.

A personal anecdote may help illustrate this claim that boundary clauses mark places and in doing so allow the nonliterate to hold them in memory. In the summer of 1998, my wife and I were eating dinner in a restaurant in the small, rural town of Harriman, Tennessee. We had driven for hours, and it was pleasant to sit over a beer and casually eavesdrop on our neighbors. (My wife, a novelist, calls it "doing research.") Two middle-aged couples at the next table were talking about a much older woman who belonged to their church. She could barely read or write, I gathered, but she could, as one of them said, "walk the lines of her property" as accurately as any surveyor could mark them. This ability "to walk the lines" is perhaps the most immediate sense of place a person can have because it marks out her ownership of a piece of this earth, her parcel of ground from which all other notions of place might emerge. Writing of his character Betty Higden in *Our Mutual Friend,* Dickens celebrates this form of identity by evoking "the track in which her last home lay, and of which she had last had local love and knowledge."[28] This sense of place seems increasingly difficult to cultivate today because it depends upon one's immediate relation to the land over time as well as patterns of local ownership. Walking the lines today seems to verge on antiquarianism; it has less and less evidentiary value in a legal culture that sets a sense of place through written deeds and surveyor's measurements. Metes and bounds, not walking the lines, tell us where we live because our maps are drawn rather than written. We must rely on specialists to tell us where those boundaries might be.

The English clause in Edgar's charter of 958 offers a wide range of features for tracing boundaries. Some are natural elements of the landscape, such as the oak edge, brook, and hedge, but most are man-made features, such as the boundary fence, the swing-gate, the paved road, and the dyke-gate. Some seem more enduring, such as fords and dykes, while others seem quite ephemeral, such as the various gates. These are not, admittedly, the most ephemeral feature one finds in Anglo-Saxon charters; that distinction may well belong to the *ealdenemyxan,* or "old manure-heap," noted in a charter of 709 that is, alas, a later forgery.[29] Still, what is one to make of a document, like Edgar's grant to Ealhstan, that demarcates the landscape for eternity (or at least until the day of judgment) and then fixes its borders through features of the landscape that are unlikely to outlast a single human generation? Are we to imagine that the Anglo-Saxons were unable to distinguish between the eternal and the ephemeral, between the promise of a future home and the fact of a current home? If we make such an assumption, there are certain further corollaries for our practice as readers that we may not wish to accept: allegory becomes disabled because distinctions of time do not hold; the great elegies of the language such as *The Wanderer* and *The Seafarer* will seem no more than overwrought travelogues; the Anglo-Saxons will appear dim-witted.

Instead, we should recognize the limitations facing the Anglo-Saxons as they tried to delineate landscapes for legal reasons and thus, of course, for the fundamental purpose of using the land to grow what was necessary to feed, clothe, and shelter themselves. The features that delineate the landscape are to be read in these charters as falling within a perambulation, a walking of the circuit, and not simply as features isolated in or scattered randomly across a landscape. They are signs and should not be confused with what they signify: the section of the landscape that must be described or invented as a discrete unit in order to ensure its transfer from one holder to another. More immediately, these are boundary clauses, that is, they appear in charters that never describe the parcel itself in any detail but only track its edges or boundaries.[30] These clauses give us the periphery in as much detail as possible or necessary, but they do not describe the center of the parcel, except perhaps to offer a brief statement that it is pasturage or tillable land or woodlot. This practice of thinking about landscape divisions in terms of boundaries explains the presence in Old English of the word *snæd,* meaning "a piece of land within defined limits, but without enclosures; a limited, circumscribed woodland or pasturage."[31]

In the charters, landscape is not a vista to be contemplated but a sequence of signs to be walked.[32] The course around the boundaries matters; the periphery is, in this case, more central than what fills the center. These documents speak of landscape as bounded, as contained by human-defined purposes. Indeed, within most such parcels, the terrain would self-evidently determine its use: a water-meadow would be used to grow hay for winter feed, woodlands would be managed for fuel and building materials, and so on. From the most practical point of view, the problem posed by place in a society that does not practice communal ownership but instead allows private or restricted ownership is how to divide and bound land in order to prevent disputes and preserve ownership through the turn of generations for individuals and through the course of recorded history for religious foundations. The immediate questions are: "What is mine (or ours), and what is not mine (or not ours)?"[33] The landscape is thus invented as a series of markers that guide local inhabitants from point to point — "from the swing-gate along the paved road to the dyke-gate, from the dyke-gate to the third gate" — and thus resolve the problem posed by the landscape.

To the extent that these charters refer to human-made features like ditches and swing-gates to do their work, they also convey a sense of the past during which the place was created by its residents. The record of property boundaries, one notices, is in no small measure the record of human intervention on the landscape.[34] These clauses implicitly set the parcel of land within a kind of unchronologically differentiated flow of time that derives from a very local sense of the past. When a ditch was dug, or a dyke raised, or a swing-gate set in a hedgerow was not precisely datable to a given year, even when a personal name was attached to any of these features. Yet that does not mean it was not associated with the past. When a boundary clause refers to a feature that possesses a more specific or more recoverable past, then that clause can be said to belong within a more comprehensive (or less local) sense of history. Or, at least, it can be said to do so for a modern reader alert to such larger resonances.

To illustrate the ways in which boundary clauses can contain a more formally historicized past than seems present in references to Esne's ditch and the like, I will focus on a grant of sale by King Athelstan to his thegn Ealdred in 926. This charter is not necessarily representative of the genre from the historian's point of view, but it does exemplify how valuable reading charters can be for those studying the ways place was demarcated and constructed in Anglo-Saxon England. It concerns a parcel of land in Bedfordshire that Ealdred had bought earlier from "pagans" at the order of King Edward, the immediate predecessor of Athelstan. These pagans were of course Danes living in the Danelaw. Whether or not one agrees with Dorothy Whitelock's assertion that Edward had a policy of urging his followers to buy up properties in the Danelaw before he set out to conquer the region, it is clear that this charter is deeply imbued with a sense of the island as a place fundamentally and necessarily Christian.[35] This charter may thus be read within a political and spiritual context of West Saxon attempts to conquer or convert regions of the homeland that had been ceded to Danes under the treaty signed by Alfred and Guthrum after the battle of Edington in 878.

The full charter is too long to quote in its entirety, so I offer only the opening section on the eternal authority of God by which Athelstan grants the property in perpetuity and the third section on the bounds of this parcel:

In nomine domini nostri Jhesu Christi cuncta quae humanis optutibus ca-
ducarum molimina rerum liquide videntur decidunt. Que vero abdita invisa-
que sunt eterni arbitris moderamine perpetualiter constare . haut dubium est
his que illa adipisci largiflua Dei largiente gratia atque mercari posse meren-
tibus divina scripturarum documenta pollicentur . . . *Mete de Chelegrave* . —
Ðær se dic sceot in wæclinga stræte anlanges wæxlinga stræte ðæt in ðane
ford þæt anlang broces in þanne oðerne ford þonne of ðæm forde up on þane
welle 7 þanan in ðæt dele þanan of ðæm delle in ðone dic of ðæm dic in ðone
oþerne dic þone of ðæm dice in þone borc þonne of þæm broce to cynburge
wellan þanne anlang dices. to east coten þat þanan in þane ealdan broc up of
þam ealdan broce . on æfem ðæt riþig þæt up rihte in ðiod weg æftær ðiod
wege in þone dic . æft dice wæxlingga strate.

In the name of our Lord Jesus Christ: All acquisitions of transitory things that
are plainly visible to men's eyes fall to ruin. There is no doubt, however, that
things which are unseen and hidden last forever by ordinance of the eternal
Judge, and the teachings of Scripture promise to those who so merit that, by
bountiful favor of God's grace, they are able to acquire and purchase those
[eternal goods] by means of the [transitory]. . . . These are the boundaries of the
aforesaid land: Where the dyke runs into Watling Street, along Watling Street
to the ford, then along the brook to the other ford, then from that ford up to the
spring, and thence into the valley, thence from the valley to the dyke, from the
dyke to the second dyke, then from that dyke to the brook, then from the brook
to Kimberwell, then along the dyke to *Eastcote,* then thence to the old brook,
up from the old brook parallel with the little stream, then straight up to the
highway, along the highway to the dyke, along the dyke to Watling Street.[36]

No Modern English translation can convey the linguistic and cultural sophis-
tication of this charter because that language alone cannot register the use of
Latin to establish the authority under God by which the grant is made and the
use of Old English to demarcate its boundaries.[37] Together these two languages authenticate the transaction on the two dimensions of time and space
by which human beings conduct their lives. The dual nature of these bilingual
charters is stylistically apparent in this example because its Latin revels in an
ornate pomposity favored by Athelstan, and its English strings together pre-
positional phrases austerely to move from one local point to the next.[38] Later
sections of the charter that aim the rhetoric of hellfire at those who might
violate its terms seem particularly bombastic after the laconic boundary
clause. These stylistic differences suggest that a place can also be demarcated,
at least in part, by the style one uses to write about it.

The vernacular passages in charters convey almost entirely what a cultural
anthropologist would call "local knowledge," that is, information that re-

quires some prior familiarity or enculturation if it is to be understood and used.[39] Athelstan's grant contains references to topographical features, such as dykes, brooks, springs, and the like, that would be most familiar to those who worked the land and traversed it regularly. The modern reader going through such a section usually feels disoriented: What ditch and dyke? What brook? How far apart are they? How could anyone find, let alone agree, on these landmarks? Even those who retrace boundary clauses today often admit bewilderment in this regard. It is thus a relief for the reader to move from such vague features in the clause to the reference to Watling Street, the old Roman road that has been naturalized in the charter as "wæxlingga strate" and that was one of the main lines of division between Anglo-Saxons and Danes under the terms of the Danelaw.[40] Because it was paved with stones by Roman legions, this road had a physical specificity that defined its presence; it appears in the mapped landscape of this charter as a named thoroughfare and not as an obscure pathway or animal track. Watling Street may also be read as a marker that moves from local knowledge (as one border for this parcel of land) to the larger history and politics of the kingdom in which this parcel is mapped (as a reminder of the Roman imperial presence on the land). This reference begins with the local and immediate, which can be traversed by foot or eye, and goes on to the more distant in time and place, which can be demarcated only in language. To put it another way, this vernacular boundary clause moves from the visual, which can be seen, to the textual, which must be written.

The use of the vernacular boundary clause here, as in previous examples, established a textual community that had the matter of property as its most immediate concern, but it could also have asked what it meant to exist within a larger community that used the same language to inhabit the same space. One example of how such a community might define itself comes from another text in which Athelstan's name features prominently, *The Battle of Brunanburh*:

> Her Æþelstan cyning,   eorla dryhten,
> beorna beahgifa,   and his broþor eac,
> Eadmund æþeling,   ealdorlangne tir
> geslogon æt sæcce   sweorda ecgum
> ymbe Brunanburh.

> In this year, king Athelstan, lord of men,
> ring-giver to warriors, and his brother also,
> prince Edmund, won at battle
> long-lasting glory with their sword-edges
> at Brunanburh. (ll. 1–5a)

In this poem, identity derives from the successful defense of the island's territory against the incursions of outsiders; the homeland is preserved intact in a victory greater than any won, according to what books say, since the time when the Angles and Saxons came across the sea to Britain (ll. 65b–73).[41]

Writing about the cartularies of high medieval monasteries in France, Constance Bouchard has described these collections of charters as "a new way of organizing and thinking about both a monastery's past and its possessions."[42] The title of her study puts the claim vividly: "Monastic Cartularies: Organizing Eternity." Although the circumstances surrounding French cartularies were often quite different from those surrounding Anglo-Saxon charters, the claim that a legal document concerning a grant of property or that a set of such documents addresses not simply the future but all of time in God's creation is possible because each text also records the past of that same property. To have authority in the future, the document must be fixed in that moment when the grant was made and the property came into the possession of the monastery or other owner. But then, one must ask, how does a text connect a fixed and legally defined moment of transfer with all eternity? If a grant is to be valid for all posterity, as so many Anglo-Saxon charters proclaim themselves to be, then it must accomplish its work through that which is itself immune, at least in theory or belief, from the destructive workings of time. It must, in other words, demarcate the site through a boundary clause that implicitly records its past. In a remarkable act of geographical transubstantiation, to coin a phrase, the charter turns a site with its human history into a fixed, unchanging entity that exists under the warrant of divine authority.

That such clauses perform this work by tracing evidence of the human-made landscape as well as the evidence left by the natural turn of the years (fallen trees, stumps, and the like) would have presented no great theological paradox to the Anglo-Saxons. Whether such language would also have altered the ways in which local residents or natives felt about the place inscribed in such a clause is fascinating to consider, though direct evidence for that possibility eludes us. We can speculate, however, that a boundary clause spoke not only to the legal ownership of a parcel of land but also to its ultimate place within God's creation. In that way, some vital connection could be traced between a highly abstract doctrine of divine cosmography and a matter-of-fact sense of place that works by stringing together landmarks into a chain of description. The local must find its place in the eternal.

This designation of an immediate place within a Christian sense of eternity can also be found in wills written by private individuals in Anglo-Saxon England. The number of such documents extant is very small, but one at least speaks eloquently of this process of connecting the local with the eternal by evoking a distant pilgrimage site:

þis is seo feorewearde þe Vlf 7 Madselin his gebedda worhtan wið [Gode] 7 wið
sce PETER. þa hig to Ierusalem ferdon. þat is þat land æt Carlatune into Burh.
æfter heora dæge heora saule to alysendnesse. 7 þæt land æt Bytham into Sce
Guthlace. 7 þat land æt Sempingaham. into sce Benedicte to Ramesege.

This is the agreement which Ulf and his wife Madselin made with [God] and
with St Peter when they went to Jerusalem. That is, the estate at Carlton to
Peterborough after their death for the redemption of their souls; and the
estate at Bytham to St Guthlac's; and the estate at Sempringham to St Benedict's at Ramsey.[43]

The motives for giving these grants to three separate monastic bodies would
have been immediately evident to an Anglo-Saxon reading this will, for it
would have assured that three separate monastic communities would pray for
the salvation of the donors' souls. The phrase "to Ierusalem" signals the occasion of a pilgrimage undertaken for the good of the donors' souls, and their
bequests acknowledge the danger of such a journey and the possibility that
they might well not return to their English home. The earthly pilgrimage to
Jerusalem was also meant to prefigure the soul's journey to heaven, so Ulf and
Madselin's will may also be read as the necessary divestiture or renunciation of
all that fixed their bodies in place as corporeal and economic beings. To dis-
pose of property for the good of the soul is to loosen, if not sever, one's sense of
place on earth and look instead toward the final home of salvation. Such is, as I
will argue in the next chapter, the evident consolation of Old English poems
like *The Wanderer*.

In Ulf and Madselin's will we can see that a local sense of place manifested in
actual estates and land has been loosened in preparation for journeying to the
place that will be their home after death. In that process, names like Carlton,
Bytham, and Sempringham locate the couple's earthly being, while the reference to Jerusalem sets in place their spiritual migration toward salvation. This
process is explicitly announced in Ulf and Madselin's will through the reference to Jerusalem and the statement that their bequests are intended for the
redemption of their souls. The process that is explicit in this particular will is
implicit in other Anglo-Saxon wills by individuals that donated estates to
ecclesiastical bodies. Offering land on earth for the redemption of one's im-
mortal soul in heaven was very much within the normal practices of Anglo-
Saxon Christianity and should not be construed as a mercenary attempt to
gain divine favor. H. D. Hazeltine puts the matter succinctly: "Rights in ter-
restrial possessions are exchanged for rights in the heavenly mansions; and
these rights are exchanged by grants which at the same time are contracts."[44]
The knowledge of local place prepares for the experience of an eternal place
and thus underwrites the contract.

That Anglo-Saxon wills can define place in contractual terms, that is, establish it as property, explains why their sense of earthly place is almost indistinguishable from that in land charters. Both types of texts were meant to preserve bequests against the passing of time as well as the forgetfulness and deceit of human beings. For the most part, Anglo-Saxon wills designate the estate in question simply by a name, as when Thurketel of Palgrave gives "Simplingham" to his wife and "Wingefeld" to his nephews. On occasion, wills designate the size of the bequest, as when the same Thurketel gives fifteen acres and a *toft*, or homestead, to Leofcwen.[45] Estate names, as they designated the grant of land, must have been common currency in the immediate area and thus seemed to need no further demarcation because their boundaries would have been known. Whether used in wills or diplomas, place-names would have had the same advantage of being locally recognized as well as the disadvantage of being somewhat ill-defined and potentially open to dispute. One surviving Anglo-Saxon will does have a boundary clause that delineates the grant in question:

> þis sind þa landmearca to Byligesdyne of ða burnan. æt Humelcyrre. fram Humelcyrre . . . Heregeresheafode. fram Heregeresheafode æfter ðam ealdan hege to ðare grene æc. þonne forð þæt hit cymð to þare stanstræte. of þare stanstræte ⁊ lang scrybbe þæt hit cymð to Acantune fram Acyntune þæt hit cymð to Rigendune, fram Rigindune æft to þara burnan. ⁊ þær. Is. landes fif hida.

> These are the boundaries of Baldson: from the stream at *Humelcyrre;* from *Humelcyrre* to *Heregeresheafod* from *Heregeresheafod* along the old hedge to the green oak; then on until one comes to the paved road; from the paved road along the shrubbery until one comes to Acton; from Acton until one comes to Roydon; from Roydon back to the stream. And there are five hides of land.[46]

This clause works through a variety of features such as naming the estate and marking its boundaries through additional place-names and topographical features, both natural and human-made.

Absent from this particular list of features, as well as from boundary clauses in general, are references to buildings on the landscape. As Eric Ferne has observed, "Even the wills which start to appear [late in the Anglo-Saxon period] are singularly unforthcoming about standing property."[47] Anglo-Saxon wills refer to all sorts of portable property, including weapons, books, ecclesiastical vestments, and the like as well as to real estate, most usually using the Old English word *land*. This practice suggests that the Anglo-Saxons conceived of the land itself and all that grew on it as more enduring than anything human beings could build on it and thus as more useful for legal purposes. The absence of references to houses and other buildings in most wills and land charters reflects, of course, the fact that wealth in Anglo-Saxon England was derived from agriculture, from working the land by planting crops or grazing animals.[48] That land was the source for producing wealth made it the object of enduring value and thus worthy of being bequeathed. By contrast, in an industrial or postindustrial economy, much land is valuable not for its productive capacity but as the site for buildings that by their presence render it useless for agriculture.

Wills and charters speak vividly to the notion that the Anglo-Saxons thought of their earthly home as the land rather than the buildings. In other words, the land on which a house sat was home for them, not the house itself. These documents also strongly suggest *why* the Anglo-Saxons thought of land itself as the earthly version of home. Gifts of land from secular owners to ecclesiastical foundations, usually monasteries, had to be for perpetuity by their very nature. Otherwise, they could not have the desired effect of enabling the donor's quest for eternal salvation. There is another way, perhaps less legalistic though certainly as binding, to conceive of this exchange. The land given by human beings to religious bodies so that their members would pray for the good of the donor's soul after death was never the absolute possession of the human beings who gave it, nor was it their true home. As the poet of *The Wanderer* reminds his audience, all things on earth are *læne,* that is, they are transitory, because they are loaned or given by God. To give land to a monastery, for instance, is thus to return it to God's keeping and also to acknowledge that one's true home is not here on earth. Rather it is in the heavenly realm that cannot be apprehended directly or even described by those on earth. On this matter, at least, those who composed poems and legal documents in Anglo-Saxon England seem to have agreed. Home is, finally, the place that lies beyond direct human experience or apprehension. It can be entered only by those who knew well how to live on earth in a transitory house of wattle and daub, that is, who knew that insubstantial buildings are the appropriate dwelling for those awaiting salvation.

2

Home and Landscape

The dwellings that Anglo-Saxons built and the landscapes they set them within offer other clues as to how lived experience may have shaped their ideas of place. From the timber-built and thus impermanent nature of their houses, one can appreciate why the Anglo-Saxons tended to define home more through the enduring presence of land than the transient existence of buildings. In the vernacular poetry, correspondingly, that notion of the earthly *ham* moves by its own internal logic toward a more religiously inspired vision of the heavenly home. This awareness of earthly transience, as it gains pathos from its accompanying faith in heavenly permanence, runs through many of the vernacular poems and deeply influenced the ways in which their poets imagined and represented places. Setting the course of human events in place provided the vernacular poets with a measure for ordering experience. Time as it shapes the human-made landscape must therefore be a theme of this book, whether on the local scale of the boundary clause or on the universal scale of God's creation as unfolded in the biblical poems of the Junius Book.

The representation of local experience in the extant texts of Anglo-Saxon England never goes untouched by larger perspectives of time and place. The land given in any grant had its history; the forms of domestic dwellings contained a link to the premigratory home of the Anglo-Saxons; the identification of home with land offered a way to set one's place in God's creation. The

landscape of Old English poetry — and here one moves into a more psychologically inflected sense of place — could also serve to depict states of interiority
that otherwise go largely unexpressed by figures within a heroic code of reticence. To make this interpretive move is to recognize that representations of
place in Anglo-Saxon texts often testify to their makers' beliefs and allegiances. Places are not, in other words, merely décor. Establishing the bounds
of a grant of land or setting one's sense of home on the land gives geographical
identity to the idea of community; each is a way to announce being and
belonging. These forms of being and belonging are not objective facts in themselves but rather inner conditions of belief. Both relate to the ways people are
able to conceive of themselves, for example, as a figure in a productive landscape, as a believer in search of a final home, as a poet exploring the inner
condition of speakers unable to reveal themselves confessionally. To value
representations of place in Anglo-Saxon texts only for their abstract or figural
significance, as if the local made no claims on those who created them, is to
misunderstand both the terms of representation and the people that used them
to make sense of their world. A sense of local allegiance among the inhabitants
of a place registers the specificity of a culture, its ways of knowing and doing.
It signals the ways people have of being in place.

Yet anyone looking casually through the definitive three-volume *Anglo-
Saxon Architecture* by H. M. Taylor and Joan Taylor could well be forgiven for
concluding that the English in the years before 1100 lived in the open air or, if
lucky, in tents and caves because the work offers no discussion of domestic
architecture.[1] By limiting themselves to stone churches, the Taylors reflect a
common practice among Anglo-Saxon architectural historians in concentrat-
ing on buildings that still stand above ground — in whole, in pieces, or incorporated into later structures — for all to see. In that regard, they differ from
archaeologists of the period who have more readily asked questions about
domestic structures such as houses, halls, and barns that were characteristically
built in wood.[2] Yet there remains a quietly apologetic tone to some of this
discussion, as in C. J. Arnold's *An Archaeology of the Early Anglo-Saxon
Kingdoms:* "Carpentry was also extensively used to build the houses, barns and
byres which were more common and fundamental to everyday life. The skills
required were no less than for the intricate metalworking and jewelling skills of
the period, but the effort and raw materials were on an altogether different
scale."[3]

That most Anglo-Saxon structures were made of wood has had obvious
consequences for archaeologists. Such buildings had a predictable lifespan of a
generation or two and were ephemeral features on an enduring landscape.
They certainly would not have outlasted the metal implements and objects

used within them. Nor would they have outlasted, in the usual run of affairs, a charter written on vellum that might have delineated the territory on which they were built. The transitory nature of Anglo-Saxon structures also had, as I shall argue later in this chapter, considerable influence on the ways in which the Anglo-Saxons may have defined that most intimate sense of place, that which goes by the name of home. But first the material conditions of dwellings need to be considered, if only briefly and in general terms.

The Anglo-Saxons were so accustomed to building in wood, rather than stone, that the usual verb in their language for "to construct" or "to erect" was *getimbran* or *getimbrian,* literally, "to timber." This verb was used for all types of buildings and cities, even those rare ones made from stone. Consider, for example, this passage from the *Anglo-Saxon Chronicle* for the year 626:

> Ðis wæs ge don on Eoforwic. þær he ær het getimbrian cyrican of treowe, seo wæs halgod on sancte Peteres naman. þær se cining sealde Pauline biscop setl. 7 þær he het eft timbrian maran cyrican of stane.

> This was done in York, where before he had commanded that a church be built of wood, which was consecrated in the name of St. Peter. There the king gave Paulinus a bishop's throne and there he later commanded a greater church be built of stone.[4]

That (*ge*)*timbrian* can be used for the building of a wooden and a stone church alike makes clear its standing in the language as the general verb of choice for any form of construction. A more historicized example of the verb being used in this way appears in the *Chronicle* for the year 409 (410): "Her wæs brocen Romana burh from Gotan ymb .xi. hundra wintra 7 .x. wintra. þæs þe heo ge timbred wæs" (In this year the *burh,* or stronghold, of the Romans was destroyed by the Goths, 1,110 years after it was *getimbred,* or built).[5] To speak of the foundation of Rome, the center of imperial and then papal power, in this way suggests the verb's general currency, for that city was the exemplar of stone and masonry construction for the Anglo-Saxons, as I shall detail in the following two chapters. That the Anglo-Saxon English built their domestic buildings in wood and other perishable materials means that nothing like a house survives from the period. The archaeological record for domestic structures is largely limited to postholes, foundation trenches, cellar pits, and other subsurface evidence. We can enter into the three-dimensional reality of an Anglo-Saxon house only by visiting a reconstructed dwelling at a site such as Bede's World at Jarrow in the north of England.[6] But such visits, while piquing one's curiosity, do not allow one to view domestic buildings with some of their original fabric intact, as one still can at later medieval sites. That the physical evidence for Anglo-Saxon houses is now largely to be found below the surface has its interpretive analogue, as I shall argue, in the depictions of place offered by Old English poems, which reveal the interior life of their characters and speakers.

The dwellings of Anglo-Saxons may have been built of impermanent materials, but they were marked by a historical sense of place that reached beyond the immediate and familiar experience of home. Their domestic architecture was not purely native or insular in origin but rather was influenced by styles and practices brought from the continental homelands by the Angles, Saxons, and Jutes when they migrated to Britain in the fourth and fifth centuries A.D. Adaptations were certainly made to reflect local conditions, but the line of continuity remained and provides compelling evidence for the ongoing presence of continental culture in postmigration England. To the extent that they were built to an older model that was modified to suit the climatic conditions of England, Anglo-Saxon domestic halls represent a form of cultural adaptation to a new locale. They suggest the ways in which a migratory people can hold to its old-country traditions while also accommodating the different conditions of the new homeland. This process of cultural adaptation to new places, as it was displayed in the timber halls of the period, is a reminder that the island was the postmigratory home of continental tribes that did not forget their origins in Germania and indeed used those memories to form cultural myths of identity.

The enduring fact of migration is that it is remembered as a transit between two places, between a home that has been left behind and the one that has been found or, more likely, seized on arrival. The interpretive model used by the Anglo-Saxons to remember their migration from northwest Europe to the island of Britain was drawn from the Old Testament story of the Israelite exodus.[7] Like the Israelites, the Anglo-Saxons were a people that, according to their own myth of migration, had been chosen by God to possess a promised land. Home was thus not simply a site of long settlement, a matter of remembered territory or geography, it was also — for both Israelites and Anglo-Saxons — a place blessed by a divine covenant. More specifically, the Anglo-Saxons had left regions in Germania where they knew spiritual captivity as pagans to cross the North Sea and arrive at a homeland that over time became the setting for their conversion to Christianity. The Anglo-Saxons' myth of migration endured for centuries because it helped to explain within providential history how it was that they were able as pagans to seize the island from its Christian inhabitants. The migration myth served, in short, as a warrant for the Anglo-Saxons to possess the land and make it home.

More precisely, it was the land itself that fell within the covenant the Anglo-Saxons believed they had with God. Home for the Anglo-Saxons was the land itself, the work of God's creation, as I argued in the previous chapter, far more than it was anything built on the land. Human beings sentenced to live within time built such structures, and thus all of them—not excluding their stone churches and rare stone halls—were fated to be victims of decay and destruction. The Anglo-Saxons historicized their sense that everything built on the earth was ephemeral, that is, they interpreted this knowledge that nothing human-made endured by setting it within the temporal sequence of human history. In poems such as *The Ruin* and *Maxims II,* the Anglo-Saxons described the remains of stonework construction they saw on their landscape as "enta geweorc" (the work of giants) or "orðanc enta geweorc" (the skillful work of giants) that had distantly preceded them on the island.[8] That such structures were most likely the work of Romans rather than giants is our knowledge, our form of periodization, and does not alter the Anglo-Saxons' belief that this stonework was left behind by a race that had occupied the land in an earlier time. If nothing else, these buildings spoke to a different sense of home than the Anglo-Saxons knew, one that was physically enduring and yet spiritually vacant.

Introductions to Anglo-Saxon archaeology typically note that while there were differences across England during these centuries, there were also, generally speaking, two common forms of wooden domestic buildings: halls and *Grubenhäuser.*[9] The halls in question were certainly not all of a royal scale and magnificence such as Heorot in *Beowulf,* though the excavations at Yeavering in the north of England suggest that some at least were of considerable size and were set in quite elaborate compounds that could include numerous outbuildings as well as a grandstandlike structure.[10] Most halls in Anglo-Saxon England were modest in scale and functioned within a working agricultural landscape that included barns and other outbuildings. As a term and as structures, *Grubenhäuser* have generated a good deal of controversy among archaeologists who are not at all agreed on whether they should be translated and reconstructed as "pit houses," "grub huts," or "sunken featured buildings."[11] There is, moreover, considerable debate about whether they were used as dwellings at all or simply as workshops and storerooms.

The well-excavated site of West Stow in Suffolk, which dates from the fifth and sixth centuries, presents a good example of an early Anglo-Saxon village containing both wooden halls and sunken featured buildings. The seven halls on the site vary in size from 16 by 32 feet to 23 by 46 feet, that is, from 512 to 1,058 square feet, and none presents evidence of internal subdivisions or walls. The thirty-four sunken buildings at West Stow are typically much smaller, 8 by 10 feet.[12] Each hall stood separate from the others, though each was surrounded "by a small cluster of sunken featured buildings."[13] According to Martin Welch's interpretation of the site, "it seems likely that families lived, cooked, ate and slept in the seven halls" while "the sunken featured buildings provided for a similar range of ancillary functions such as stores and workshops."[14] Weaving was among the likely purposes for such buildings because it would benefit from the dampness of a partially sunken structure.[15] Later halls in Anglo-Saxon England were more likely to have internal subdivisions, presumably to wall off sleeping quarters from the main area of the building. Thus, in King Edwin's hall at Yeavering perhaps one-quarter of the area is thought to have been used for that purpose.[16]

From a settlement in Cowdery's Down near Basingstoke (Hampshire), archaeologists have been able to gather considerable evidence about the techniques of wood construction used for building halls in Anglo-Saxon England. The site preserves evidence for various types of timber buildings, including those using "earthfast uprights both in individual 'post-holes' and in wall trench foundations." In each case, oak planks were pegged together to frame the walls and then were "infilled with wattle panels made from interwoven thin branches and windproofed by being daubed by clay."[17] These daubed panels may have been painted, and some of the timbers may have been ornamented with carvings. This form of construction allowed the Anglo-Saxons to minimize the amount of dressed lumber necessary for a given structure and thus would have made it less costly in terms of labor and materials. Roofing was of either thatch or thin wooden shingles. The halls at Cowdery's Down have been reconstructed in various ways by modern scholars, but the basic principles are clear: they were built solidly of immediately procurable materials using the available carpentering skills. Oliver Rackham makes the larger point: "Anglo-Saxons were carpenters rather than masons."[18] By drawing on local skills and materials, especially wood that would have been grown on the site or very nearby, such structures were themselves expressions of the place. That they have been reconstructed in quite different ways, as the sketches available in Leslie Webster's study of Cowdery's Down indicate, serves as a useful caution against assuming too much about Anglo-Saxon domestic architecture.[19] While noting this caution, one can see that such buildings were vulnerable not only to fire, being constructed of highly inflammable materials, but also to damp and rot, being built directly on or below the ground without water-resistant foundations of stone or masonry. The average life of such a hall could hardly have extended far beyond two or three generations and would have required regular maintenance to last that long.

The reconstructed floor plans of Anglo-Saxon halls suggest that even at their largest they were considerably smaller than continental versions. Lest this difference be taken as evidence that the Anglo-Saxons were somehow less prosperous or sophisticated than their continental relations, one may note that local conditions were a factor in this regard. More specifically, halls in the Germanic homelands were built to accommodate not only people but also animals in byres: "In these at least half of the building was subdivided into stalls, designed to keep cattle and other livestock in good condition through the relatively severe winters of these regions."[20] The milder English weather made such byre-houses unnecessary. The halls that were built in England for people seem not to have been especially cramped or confining; they were smaller because they had one less function to perform. Houses without attached stalls for animals were probably more salubrious and pleasant to the nose, though that response may be a modern prejudice born of too much soap and disinfectant.

The archaeological evidence for Anglo-Saxon settlements suggests a typical pattern of small clusters, or local groupings of dwellings, in an agricultural landscape.[21] In addition to the houses at such sites, the buildings used for a craft such as weaving or for storing the year's produce would have also tied the inhabitants to the land. That conjunction of God's creation and the human-made dwelling suggests the balance of the permanent and the impermanent that underlies most senses of place in Anglo-Saxon England. That balance finds expression, though sometimes only as an undercurrent, in many texts from the culture. One would like to know a great deal more about how the Anglo-Saxons thought of their houses as human constructions in a landscape created by God.

Literary texts supply a few telling clues, though hardly as many as one might want. The catalogue poem conventionally known as *The Gifts of Men* presents a wide survey of the abilities and talents that God is said to have given to human beings. These range across intellectual, athletic, martial, political, and artistic endeavors. Together they form a compilation or index of those skills that were valued in Anglo-Saxon England. Among them, and it is unusual in being inventoried twice in this relatively short poem, is house building:

> Sum mæg wrætlice   weorc ahycgan
> heahtimbra gehwæs;   hond bið gelæred,
> wis ond gewealden,   swa bið wyrhtan ryht,
> sele asettan,   con he sidne ræced
> fæste gefegan   wiþ færdryrum.

One can artistically plan the construction of each lofty building; his hand is skillful, wise and controlled, as is right for a worker, in order to erect the dwelling; he knows how to join fast the wide building against sudden collapse. (ll. 44–48)[22]

The last line of this passage reflects the practice of using wood for construction because making tight joints is essential to insure the stability of buildings and to protect them against collapse. Having glossed what it might mean to excel at raising a building, the poet can offer a brief restatement of this skill later in the poem: "Sum bið bylda til / ham to hebbanne" (One is an excellent builder at erecting a home; ll. 75b–76a).[23] The statements of the *Gifts* poet are intriguing because they dovetail so neatly with the archaeological evidence. The attention in the poem to craft, to the planning of the dwelling suggests the degree to which such work was valued in the culture; indeed, the poet cites setting gems for jewelry as belonging, like house building, to the praiseworthy human talents. Yet this praise of the housewright's craft is, by another reading, an admission that he works in a material that will not endure. It is, after all, a human skill.

The most widely quoted depiction in Old English poetry of home and homecoming appears in another poem offering traditional lore, the so-called *Maxims I*. The poet's technique for evoking the desired order of the world is to issue a series of normative statements interrupted by an occasional vignette that seems almost to open into high drama. Even at this moment, however, the poet ignores the built structure of the home to portray home as the place of return:

> Scip sceal genægled,   scyld gebunden,
> leoht linden bord,   leof wilcuma
> Frysan wife,   þonne flota stondeð;
> biþ his ceol cumen   ond hyre ceorl to ham,
> agen ætgeofa,   ond heo hine in laðaþ,
> wæsceð his warig hrægl   ond him syleþ wæde niwe,
> liþ him on londe   þæs his lufu bædeð.

> The ship must be fastened with nails, the shield bound, the light linden board; and the beloved man (must be) welcome to the Frisian woman when his boat stands in; his ship has come and her husband as well to home, her own provider, and she invites him in, washes his dirty garments and gives him fresh clothes, lies with him on land as his love urges. (ll. 93–99)[24]

For all that this passage speaks movingly of homecoming and the domestic life shared by a man and woman, it is not without interpretive difficulties. Most immediately, why does an English poet speak of a Frisian woman? Is she somehow to be imagined as the ideal of the welcoming wife just as Frisian men were reputed to be venturesome sailors? Are they meant to balance each other as homebody and adventurer? Most intriguingly, why does *this* poet represent the marital home as part of the desired order of the world when so few others of his peers do so? How are we to understand the surprising nature of this passage within the larger context of Old English poetry? Why should a scene of tender homecoming — of care given and desire gratified — seem so unusual as a means of representing place in this poetry?

Readers of the *Odyssey* might for a moment recognize in this passage from *Maxims I* a brief version of Penelope welcoming Odysseus on his return to Ithaca. The comparison is valuable chiefly for identifying the differences between this Greek epic and all of Old English poetry, for the *Odyssey* is filled with places represented as scenes of returning and departing, of being welcomed as a castaway by a young maiden and her friends or of fleeing the unwelcome hospitality of a one-eyed giant. Just as the theme of *philoxenia*, the welcome owed to the stranger, makes us understand what home as a physical setting meant to the Greeks of the *Odyssey,* so the relative absence of sentiments about home life and domesticity in Old English poetry make one want to read the episode of the Frisian woman as deeply revealing of its culture. It may be, however, that one puts too much interpretive weight on this passage simply because it is so unusual in depicting home. The poetry of the Anglo-Saxons is far more likely to urge thoughts of journeying to the heavenly home than it is to celebrate the return to the earthly home.

The surviving texts of Anglo-Saxon England pay little explicit attention to home as a physical structure, a building with walls and a roof, a setting of family life. The structure that appears repeatedly and centrally in the heroic poetry of the period is the royal hall, the site of public ceremony where lord and retainers — and even some women — gather to celebrate life and thereby hold off the darkness that lies around them.[25] But a hall in Old English poetry is not truly a home, at least not in the sense of being a place where men and women live day in and day out with their children and members of their extended family. As Anita R. Riedinger has argued in a valuable study, *Beowulf* and its halls have distracted modern readers: "Yet everywhere in the background of most Old English poetry — even in works that vividly depict war and warriors, whose cultural center *is* the hall — there lies, in often the most profound kinds of ways, the concept of 'home.' "[26] More specifically, Hrothgar's retainers in *Beowulf* spend the night sleeping on mead-benches in the hall known as Heorot, but they do so only by virtue of belonging to a select group of warriors. King Hrothgar, we are told, withdraws from his hall at night so that he can sleep with his queen, Wealhtheow, in quarters elsewhere. Nor does Beowulf spend a night in Heorot after he has killed the hall-intruder, Grendel.[27] The hall may have functioned as a sort of surrogate home for young, unmarried warriors who shared a homosocial bond, that is, it was the setting for Anglo-Saxon barracks life.[28]

When we compare Old English literary works with those from the related culture of medieval Iceland, the difference in matters of home is immediately evident. As William Ian Miller has demonstrated, Icelandic legal and literary texts are all about home and homelessness as means of defining place, of putting Iceland on the map.[29] These texts give us some idea of what Icelandic homes looked like inside and out, what they were made of, how a dead body should be removed from one, how they formed a farmstead with barns and fields, and why being without a fixed domicile was to be feared. From the sagas, especially, we gain a sense of daily domestic life in all of its aspects, even including the most noble way to die within one's own home when besiegers have broken all honorable rules of combat by setting fire to it. If the Anglo-Saxons did not build houses for the ages, they also did not put home (in the sense of literal dwellings) at the center of their legal culture as did the Icelanders. Numerous Anglo-Saxon law codes survive from throughout the period, but they do not often refer to home in ways that define a sense of place, though some of their clauses cast oblique, if fascinating, light on the subject. Thus, one can ask what it means for shaping a culture's definition of home that some of its law codes specify penalties for strangers that wander off the beaten path: "If a man from a distance or a foreigner goes off the track, and he neither shouts nor blows a horn, he is assumed to be a thief, to be either killed or redeemed."[30] This clause, from a late seventh-century code of Wihtred, king of Kent, is not anomalous and, indeed, appears in virtually the same form in the contemporary laws of Ine, king of Wessex.[31] In a society without organized police to protect neighborhoods and houses against outsiders, it made sense to have strangers announce their presence, especially, one presumes, when they neared residents' houses. If this clause is not directly about home, it certainly is evidence that the Anglo-Saxons distinguished between their immediate neighbors and outsiders from elsewhere. Home, for an Anglo-Saxon, was partially defined as the place where one knew everyone else or, conversely, where one was known and recognized by those who also lived there. It was where you were not an outsider.[32]

The notion of home as the place where one is at ease appears memorably in the so-called *Rune Poem,* a work of twenty-nine sections that follows the sequence of the traditional Scandinavian alphabet but that is written in Old English. In each section, the poet glosses the meaning of the runic character's name by articulating cultural commonplaces. Under the runic character written out in Old English as *eþel,* the poet offers a statement that is meant to articulate the desired order of things in the Anglo-Saxon world:

> (eþel) byþ oferleof   æghwylcum men,
> gif he mot ðær rihtes   and gerysena on
> brucan on bolde   bleadum oftast.

Eþel is much beloved by every man, that he might enjoy there in his house all that is right and proper in continual prosperity. (ll. 71–73)[33]

If the Anglo-Saxons displayed embroidery samplers on their walls, this passage could have been their text for "Home, Sweet Home." It is particularly suggestive for seeming so banal in its statement of how one is to live prosperously in a house ("on bolde"). And yet the passage has more to offer because the word that goes untranslated above — *eþel* — has a range of meanings that is relevant to ways in which place is constructed from various aspects of experience. It can designate everything from an animal's abode to larger and more amorphous categories of place such as "native land," "country," "ancestral region."[34] The *Dictionary of Old English* offers these various senses for *eþel:* "one's own country," "one's true home," "home," "homeland," "land of one's birth," "(hereditary) land," "(ancestral) domain."[35] The most recent editor of *The Rune Poem* translates *eþel* in this passage as "the family land" to suggest home as a place of loyalty defined by the enduring source of wealth and by kinship relations.[36] *Eþel* is home, then, in ways that also speak to complex allegiances, however they might be determined. And, if one might hazard a guess in the instance of *The Rune Poem, eþel* draws on a variety of emotive connections: as the land that has been worked by a family for generations, as the site that links one to the memory of ancestors, perhaps even as the territory of an incipient Englalond.

Yet the force of this passage, and it has force because it does register a necessary cultural conviction, derives from the way *eþel* is given a local habitation in the phrase "on bolde" (in a house). The place of allegiance does not depend entirely on some abstraction but draws as well here on the word *bold,* which customarily designates an actual structure, for example, a dwelling, home, or building of importance such as a palace, hall, or mansion.[37] *The Rune Poem* suggests that home in Anglo-Saxon England is best understood both as the setting of experience and also as a means to interpret that experience: it can be taken in both the most literal and the most figurative sense. Home is the place that shelters one against the elements and vicissitudes of life; it is also the place that gives one a sense of larger identity.

Looking through Old English poetry for moments of the domestic can yield scattered but valuable insights. These moments do not cohere in any obvious way to form a unified vision of home as it was lived day in and day out. In that respect, the poems are consonant with the manifold ways in which the Old English vernacular conveyed ideas of home as place. For all their seeming reticence about evoking home in their poetry, the Anglo-Saxons had a remarkably wide lexicon for designating home in its various senses. As Riedinger observes, "There are at least fourteen synonyms for 'home' in Old English poetry: *eðel, eard, geard, ærn, bold, reced, cnosl, cyþþ, worðig, wic, eodor, hof, hus,* and *ham*." While these words had various connotations — some suggesting home-land, others a physical building or enclosure, and yet others associations with family — "all could and usually did, mean 'home.' "[38] Among these synonyms, the most immediately relevant are *ham* and its numerous compounds. The Old English word *ham* is, self-evidently, the origin for Modern English *home* and carries a similarly wide range of senses: home, house, abode, dwelling, resi-dence, habitation, house with land, estate, property, district, region, neighbor-hood, place where rest, refuge, or satisfaction is found, and, finally, native country.[39] Given the propensity of the Anglo-Saxons to coin words by combin-ing elements, there are also many compounds in which *ham* appears, most im-mediately numerous place-names in which it is joined to a personal name, as in the charter references noted in the previous chapter to Ricinga*haam*, Budin-*haam*, Deccan*haam*, and Angenlabes*haam*. A complete discussion of Old En-glish *ham* compounds would fill this chapter, but some examples will serve to demonstrate its range in the Anglo-Saxon lexicon, though it should be noted that some are very rare: *hambringan*, "to bring a wife home," "marry"; *ham-cuþ*, literally "known at home," or "familiar"; *hamcyme*, "coming home," "return"; *hamfæst*, literally "fast at home," or "dwelling at home"; *hamhæn*, "domestic fowl"; *hamland*, "enclosed pasture land"; *hamleas*, "homeless"; *hamsiþian*, "to return home"; *hamstede*, "homestead"; *hamweard*, "home-ward"; *hamweorud*, "the group of people associated with a home." That *ham* can be combined to form each of the semantically significant parts of speech (noun, verb, adjective, and adverb) may also be taken as a measure of its lexical usefulness.

These compounds suggest that *ham* could be used to ground life in place, as in the adjectives *hamfæst*, evoking that sense of fixity or security that comes with being at home, or in *hamcuþ*, identifying the familiar with that which is known at home. Similarly, when used in compounds describing direction, *ham* provides a sense of home as being where one is rooted in place, as in the verb *hamsiþian* and the adverb *hamweard*. The latter example is especially reso-nant when it appears in a passage such as the following from the *Anglo-Saxon Chronicle* as it relates the journey in 855 of King Æthelwulf:

> And þy ilcan geare ferde to Rome mid mycclum wurðscipe. 7 þær wunade .xii. monað. 7 he feng to Karles dohter Francna cining þa he hamweard wæs. 7 ge sund ham com.

> And in that same year he journeyed to Rome with much pomp and lived there for twelve months. He took in marriage the daughter of King Charles of the Franks as he was traveling homeward and arrived home in good health.[40]

As even this brief, relatively formulaic passage from the *Chronicle* illustrates, home is the place by which one defines much of what can happen in life. Is it familiar like home? Is it safe like home? What is the relation of a given place to home in terms of direction? Am I heading away from it or toward it? In a culture of road maps and numbered streets, of global positioning systems in automobiles, finding home seems simply a matter of following the defined coordinates that mark every site on the planet. But *hamweard* did not always designate a journey plotted out on the map from Rome to England, such as that made by Archbishop Sigeric in the late tenth century.

Nothing in the language bound the word *ham* to an earthly referent. It refers as commonly and perhaps even more memorably to the heavenly as to the earthly home. That the same word could denote both does not evidence poverty in the vernacular word stock but rather a widespread semantic practice in the poetry by which the same terms — such as *ham, rice, epel* — could designate both realms. Old English poets loved these polysemous terms as a means of aligning the two realms, of articulating their similarities while also suggesting their differences.[41] This verbal technique manifests the Christian belief that the conditions of life in the earthly home are but a shadowy version of the life that the saved will know in the heavenly home. To use the same set of words to designate both suggests the mysterious way in which the earthly home is the necessary precondition to the heavenly and thus must be, as such, incomplete in itself. And yet the local sense of home cannot be dispensed with entirely because that is the closest to the eternal sense of home known by mortals. This way of knowing through analogy — and thus the use of polysemous terms — means that the local and earthly must always remain necessary in the imagination and theology of Anglo-Saxon Christianity.

Whether Old English poets used *ham* or *epel* or one of the other synonyms available to them, they did so to evoke the final destination, the place to which life's journey would lead the true Christian after death. In many of these lyric poems, the afterlife is represented as the place of eternal domain that does not perish or decay as do the structures built by humankind on earth. Perhaps the most explicit statement that the local and mortal are preparation for the universal and eternal comes toward the end of *The Dream of the Rood,* where the dreamer-narrator of the poem explains the sacrifice of Christ's earthly life and the gift of the heavenly home:

> Si me dryhten freond,
> se ðe her on eorþan ær þrowode
> on þam gealgtreowe for guman synnum.
> He us onlysde ond us lif forgeaf,
> heofonlicne ham.

> May the Lord be a friend to me, he who earlier suffered here on earth on the
> gallows-tree for the sins of men; he redeemed us, and gave us life, a heavenly
> home. (ll. 144b–48a)[42]

The redemption of human sin through the crucifixion of Christ on earth yields
entry for human beings into heaven, the eternal home. The poem thus turns
after this passage, tellingly, to Christ's harrowing of hell and ends with his
triumphant return to the kingdom of God, "þær his eðel wæs" (where his
home was; l. 156b). In this phrase, *eþel* denotes some larger homeland or
territory of the saved to which those previously exiled in hell can return. The
use of *eþel* connotes a politics of salvation, and thus can be poetically parallel
to, and theologically identical with, the kingdom of God, "on godes rice" (l.
152b), mentioned several lines earlier.

This summoning up of the heavenly home is, at its best in Old English
poetry, preceded by passages of haunting beauty in which the transience of the
earthly home is set in place so that it can be described unflinchingly and thus
lamented all the more evocatively. The Old English poets are far more expressive in these catalogues of all that has gone from the earth than they are in their
descriptions of the heavenly home. The heavenly home may be all the more
mysteriously alluring in their poems for never being described in precise terms;
indeed, that seems its beauty. If an implicit contrast with the lost wonder of
earthly life is didactically sufficient to manifest the immutable glory of the
heavenly home, it also seems at times poetically inadequate. For the poets
achieve great descriptive and emotional power by describing the ruins of the
earthly home, its shattered buildings and lost treasures. All that most compels
them belongs to an immediate and local sense of home.

The concluding statement of *The Seafarer* may, in these terms, seem formulaic in its exhortation that the audience should think of the final blessed home
in the heavens:

> Uton we hycgan   hwær we ham agen,
> ond þonne geþencan   hu we þider cumen,
> ond we þonne eac tilien,   þæt we to moten
> in þa ecan   eadignesse,
> þær is lif gelong   in lufan dryhtnes,
> hyht in heofonum.

> Let us consider where we have a home and then think how we might go there,
> and also struggle so that we may be allowed to enter into that eternal blessed-
> ness where life is dependent on love of the Lord and joyful bliss in the heavens.
> (ll. 117–22a)[43]

The poet links the significant terms *ham,* "home," *hyht,* "joyful bliss," and
heofon, "heaven," through alliteration so that together they form an envelope

pattern to contain the passage as a whole. His technique here is essentially homiletic: he has reached the end of his poem, and he works to emphasize its central Christian truth. In his translation of *The Seafarer,* Ezra Pound cut this passage because he believed it to be the doctrinal interpolation of a later Christian poet.[44] Pound was right to see this passage as distinct from all that precedes it, though before rejecting it he might have considered why the poet made no attempt to speak of the heavenly home in anything other than abstract and seemingly unimaginative terms.

Precise description of the heavenly home would have required a measure of invention on the poet's part that might have opened the way to doctrinal error. Moreover, such invention might well have distracted the audience from the final exhortation to think of how they are to make their journey to heaven. The poet's genius for description is not at issue here, simply his decision to reserve it for telling of life on this earth. For his lines earlier in the poem about the return of spring are arguably the most memorable in Old English for setting an immediate sense of lived place within the natural cycle:

> Bearwas blostmum nimað,   byrig fægriað,
> wongas wlitigiað,   woruld onetteð;
> ealle þa gemoniað   modes fusne
> sefan to siþe,   þam þe swa þenceð
> on flodwegas   feor gewitan.

> The groves take on blossoms, the cities grow fair, the meadows turn beautiful, the world comes alive; all then urges the restless one, the spirit on its journey, the one who thinks to depart far across the sea streams. (ll. 48–52)[45]

Within the figurative logic of the poem the journey to the heavenly home begins with the departure from the earthly home — and does so necessarily when it is at its most flourishing. For there lies the measure of renunciation, whether one chooses to read the poem literally as the account of a wandering spirit eager to explore new places or allegorically as the path of the soul to its final home. Either way, home is the place that must be left behind, and the poet signals as much through his description of its vernal beauty.

For the poet of *The Wanderer,* the earthly home figures as the place of ruin and desolation, the site of loss and regret. In these ways, it drives the exile to seek his true home with God. The speaker of the poem, separated from his home — "eðle bidæled" (l. 20b) — laments the transience of earthly life through a series of questions: "Hwær cwom symbla gesetu? Hwær sindon seledreamas?" (Where have the banquet seats gone? Where are the joys of the hall?; l. 93).[46] All that remains, he tells us, is a fragment of a building, a tragic synecdoche of the earthly home: "Stondeð nu on laste leofre duguþe / weal wundrum heah, wyrmlicum fah" (A wondrously high wall decorated with serpentine patterns / Stands now as a trace of the beloved company; ll. 97–98).[47] All that exists on earth is human-made and thus transient, loaned by God, as the poet says in a series of exclamations using the Old English adjective *læne*, "loaned, temporary, transient," to punctuate his mournful refrain. By contrast, the poem ends by asserting that all in heaven stands fast and immutable, outside the workings of time (l. 115).

The linked tropes of the earthly home as transitory and the heavenly home as eternal run throughout much of the religious poetry in Old English because they express a basic element of the Christianity shared by poets and audience. For them, the true home is not where one makes it in some contingent or improvised fashion but rather where it is found in the life beyond. This may explain a certain measure of *contemptus mundi* among Old English poets, or at least it would seem to do so were they not so devoted to evoking the beauty of all that fades from the earthly home. Modern readers of *The Seafarer* and *The Wanderer* are likely to feel sometimes that their poets were drawn more to what must be renounced on earth than to what will be enjoyed in heaven. This reading, one I have shared at times, seems in the end to be misplaced, for it denies the imaginative conclusion that the poets expected from their readers: the evoked pleasures of a lost world are but a pale shadow of the inexpressible grandeur of the eternal home. And yet, that grandeur can be only distantly apprehended through the force of the immediate and the ephemeral, the known and the local.

To locate the heavenly through the places of the earthly home is a necessary act of approximation, and also a necessary reminder that to live on earth is to be in a fallen state that precludes the direct apprehension of the heavenly. It is also an identification of the ways in which a sense of place has direct value to the salvation of the believer's soul: Christians who do not understand the earthly home is transient cannot comprehend the higher truth of their religion. The Old English poems — *Genesis, Exodus, Daniel, Christ and Satan* — gathered in the Junius Book depict the consequences of the Christian fall as a dislocation into place, as I argue in the final chapter. The expulsion from Eden not only made time and mortality facts of human life, it also made possible the idea that dramatic events in human history are best apprehended by being set in place. There is in the human condition, then, a felt need for figural or metaphoric representation through which the experience of immediately visible exterior places opens the way, at least in part, to a vision of more distant, more ineffable places.

The specificity of place matters in this poetic attempt to evoke what is by definition beyond the human ability to depict. The approximation of the unknown through the known in Old English poetry often makes the lord's hall and the gifts received there by retainers seem more compelling or, at least, more comprehensible than their heavenly counterparts. In poems like *The Wanderer* or *The Seafarer,* there is a disjunction between the tangible and the ineffable, the material, and the spiritual. This disjunction is itself the site of meaning in these poems: their elegiac and didactic force is meant to move their audiences across this divide from the known to the unknown. Their gamble as poems is to risk everything on their evocation of earthly places as a means to make the heavenly seem all the more compelling.

Yet without that evocation of the earthly, the heavenly cannot be glimpsed, without the depiction of the seen there can be no apprehension of the unseen. Such is the familiar paradox necessary to Christian modes of representation. That figures of place can evoke the heavenly home in Old English poems depends largely, as I have argued, on a theological interpretation of the fall. A similar, though not precisely equivalent, use of place can also be found in Old English poetry by which descriptions of setting are used to evoke interiority. When speakers of poems or characters within them are silenced by the heroic code of locking one's word-hoard, depictions of physical surroundings can often provide some understanding of their spiritual or psychological condition. There is, in each type of representation, a reliance on the places of earthly experience. For these places provide the literal or concrete sense that is necessary if these forms of figuration, whether theological or psychological, are to be successful. There is in all of this a saving grace by which the familiar and immediate allows for something more than the familiar and immediate without, however, becoming only the strange and distant. A description of spring blossoming in a town, as offered by the Seafarer, remains commonplace because it evokes an annual event that is as predictable within the natural cycle of seasons as the speaker's desire to leave the safety of home is within the psychological drama of the poem. Its setting of home is not at all dramatic or revelatory; indeed, that it should be so predictable makes the speaker's restlessness seem all the more comprehensible as a human desire.

The psychologically compelling landscapes of Old English poetry are rarely if ever colored with a sense of the exotic or distant. Wherever the Wanderer and Beowulf and the Woman of *The Wife's Lament* might find themselves — and they are often in forbidding or ominous places — they remain within a known landscape of lived experience as comprehended by the English. The fauna and flora are native to Anglo-Saxon England as both a geographical and a poetic place; they are gannets, gulls, wolves, deer, oak trees, and brier hedges rather than rocs, ostriches, tigers, hippopotami, date palms, and other curiosities that astonished the northern imagination. For a sense of place enlivened by such fauna and flora, one turns to the tales of distant Asia in the Old English translations of *Alexander's Letter to Aristotle* or *The Wonders of the East*. These texts, as I will suggest in Chapter 6, may be read as belonging to manuscript compilations that served as "books of elsewhere," that is, as excursions extending beyond the demarcated boundaries of Englalond. Such compilations take their audience to a place other than where they are in their actual lives, one that is as distant to them in its ecosystem as in its geography. They are meant to move their audiences outward to encounters with all that is exotic and virtually unmappable, and yet more often than not return them home.

Poems like *The Wife's Lament, Beowulf*, and *The Wanderer* use moments of landscape description to represent the psychic life of characters and thus move their audiences inward. Even the monsters of *Beowulf* are part of the Anglo-Saxon imaginary; they are the figures that haunt the marches and margins of the homeland. There are, one notes as an initial premise, very few descriptions of interiority in Old English secular poetry that are accomplished through abstract psychological or philosophical terms.[48] Nor does Old English often seem a confessional poetry, one that lingers long over moments of intense inner turmoil. Beowulf's rejoinder to Hrothgar after Grendel's Mother has killed his beloved counselor Æschere is typical: "Selre bið æghwæm, / þæt he his freond wrece, þonne he fela murne" (It is better for each one that he avenge his friend than mourn much; ll. 1384b–85).[49] The role of the hero is to act on an event such as a friend's death and not to interpret its consequences. This is not to say that a character like Beowulf does not mourn — his use of the adverb *fela*, "much," is deeply moving in this line — but rather that he can act without long introspection at this moment in his life. Nor is this to say that the aged Beowulf, his hall burned and kingdom ravaged by the dragon, does not inquire into the meaning of his own life. This does, however, suggest that such moments are rare in the shorter, elegiac lyrics of Old English poetry.

The more characteristic Anglo-Saxon gesture toward self-revelation occurs when speakers — usually a man, but occasionally and compellingly a woman — admit that they cannot express their innermost thoughts to others because they are lone exiles who dare not risk such disclosure of self. This reticence is not at all the same as the laconic style of the classic American hero, "the saint with a gun" in D. H. Lawrence's memorable phrase, because speakers in Old English poems do wish that they could reveal the secrets of their breast-hoard or heart's thought.[50] Their silence seems to follow less from shame at powerful emotions than from fear of possible consequences. *The Wanderer* offers a classic moment of this struggle in which silence triumphs:

> Oft ic sceolde ana   uhtna gehwylce
> mine ceare cwiþan.   Nis nu cwicra nan

þe ic him modsefan   minne durre
sweotule asecgan.   Ic to soþe wat
þæt biþ in eorle   indryhten þeaw,
þæt he his ferðlocan   fæste binde,
healde his hordcofan,   hycge swa he wille.

> Often I alone each dawn must bewail my cares. There is now no living man to whom I dare reveal clearly my mind's thought. I know truly that it is an honorable custom in a nobleman that he bind fast his heart's feelings, guard his thoughts, think what he will. (ll. 8–14)[51]

This statement about what cannot be said openly registers all the more powerfully because it is spoken in something very much like a dramatic monologue, that is, in a highly stylized moment of performance that is meant to be overheard rather than to appear as part of an exchange. And yet it is the monologue of a man who laments that there is no one alive to whom he can speak. The Wanderer is alone, so much so that as he sails the winter sea he laments all those who are gone and imagines himself performing acts of fealty toward his lord. His silence has been imposed on him by the circumstances of exile, of being without lord or home. So stark is this declaration that one might add to the description of Anglo-Saxon ideas of home offered earlier in this chapter a further claim: home is where one can speak one's hidden thoughts. Exile carries with it a self-imposed burden of silence.

There are moments, however, when this code of reticence breaks down. The most famous of these are doubtless in *The Wanderer* and *The Seafarer,* when their speakers do open their breast-hoard. Set as they are on the untrackable sea, where any sense of place must be fleeting and illusory if it can even be said to exist, these poems are perhaps best read after *The Wife's Lament* and *Beowulf.* For these two poems contain moments where descriptions of landscape offer at once both a sense of place for the setting of the poem and a glimpse into the interior condition of a character. *The Wife's Lament* is spoken by a woman separated from her husband by circumstances that admit of various interpretations, none of them happy and none of them accepted by all modern critics. In the midst of this poem appears what may well be the most naked, unfettered admission of personal suffering to be found anywhere in Old English secular poetry. Some critics have suggested that this urgency is a function of the speaker's gender, that as a woman she is not bound by the constraints of heroic honor and shame that fetter the speech of male speakers such as the Wanderer. Given the rarity of poems in Old English with explicitly female speakers, however, it is difficult to propose a reading of *The Wife's Lament* based solely on the gender of its speaker.

Indeed, many of the facts she tells about her condition appear as well in poems spoken by men: she begins by saying that she is offering a *giedd*, "tale, poem, riddle," about "minre sylfre sið" (my own journey; ll. 1–2a), as does the Seafarer; she laments the suffering of her exile ("A ic wite wonn minra wræcsiþa"; l. 5) and calls herself a "wineleas wræcca" (friendless exile; l. 10a), as do he and other male speakers in the poetry. Her monologue diverges markedly from theirs, however, when she describes how she has been forced by men — unnamed but seemingly enemies of her husband — to live in a setting more fitting for wild animals than people. Her speech at the center of the poem is brief and, once heard, impossible to forget:

> Heht mec mon wunian   on wuda bearwe,
> under actreo   in þam eorðscræfe.
> Eald is þes eorðsele,   eal ic eom oflongad,
> sindon dena dimme,   duna uphea,
> bitre burgtunas,   brerum beweaxne,
> wic wynna leas.   Ful oft mec her wraþe begeat
> fromsiþ frean.   Frynd sind on eorþan,
> leofe lifgende,   leger weardiað,
> þonne ic on uhtan   ana gonge
> under actreo   geond þas eorðscrafu.

> Men commanded me to live in a wooded grove, under the oak tree in this earth-cave. This earth-hall is ancient, I am all filled with longing, the dales are dark, the hills are high, the bitter strongholds are overgrown with briers, the joyless place. The departure of my lord often fills me with sorrow. Friends are on the earth, lovers alive who lie in bed while I must go out alone at dawn under the oak tree around the earth-cave. (ll. 27–36)[52]

The power of this lament comes, on repeated readings, not only from what the woman reveals about herself but also from the way she speaks about, and thus through, her landscape.[53] The ominous oak tree, the earth-cave that seems a lonely inversion of the mead-hall, the dark valleys and high hills, the site overgrown with briers — this is where she finds herself in both the most literal and the most psychological senses. It is through this sense of place that she finds a way to speak of her abandonment and confinement. She is outside the bounds of the civilized life of society symbolized by the hall in Old English poetry, both secular and sacred. Her dwelling is at once an *eorðscræf*, "earth-cave, earth-den," and an *eorðsele*, "earth-dwelling," an instance of variation that suggests she must live in the earth as would an animal. The *sele* she evokes in the compound *eorðsele* is not that of the generous lord celebrated elsewhere in the poetry. Her state is thus outside the norm of human experience, and for reasons that seem hardly at all of her doing. No wonder she should say at the start, "Ic þis giedd wrece" (l. 1a) — I recite this *giedd,* meaning "song," "tale," "narrative," and — most to the point, perhaps — "riddle." For the story of her love is an enigma, not merely to us as we read the poem, but also to her as she finds herself in a foreboding, unsheltering landscape.

That she must dwell in this landscape, a fit setting for and expression of her loneliness, is a measure of her despair. She does not say that she feels buried by unhappiness or overshadowed by gloomy thoughts — such artfully meta-phorized descriptions would not be part of her work as the speaker of an Old English poem. Her ability to register the immediate circumstances of her condi-tion by describing the earth-cave and the looming trees provides some sense of her interior condition. For all that the immediate landscape of this poem seems ominous and frightening, its description relies heavily on the precise demarca-tion of natural features, such as one notes in the boundary clauses of Anglo-Saxon charters. She refers twice to the "actreo" (oak tree; ll. 28a and 36a) as well as to cities "brerum beweaxne" (overgrown with briers; l. 31b) and a "wuda bearwe" (grove of trees; l. 27b). Such markers of the landscape appear in boundary clauses, though obviously without the emotional resonance they contain in *The Wife's Lament.* The comparison of clause and poem is apt, however, in that it allows us to credit the poet with a precise means for demar-cating place and thus for using it to reveal what cannot be spoken directly. The poet does not work by sketching a moody atmosphere of loneliness, but rather by giving it a local habitation. There is also, in my reading, a kind of cultural familiarity with boundary clauses underlying the poem's description of place, or at least a shared sense that a landscape with demarcating features is not entirely distinct from the human. Indeed, that is the predicament of the Woman in *The Wife's Lament:* to be somewhere between the legally demarcated land-scape of a charter and the untraceable outlines of a natural world beyond human interpretation. Or, to return to the poet's use of variation, her *eorðsele* must be an *eorðscraef,* her hall must be a cave.

The description of wild landscape as a counter to the world of human com-munity appears very dramatically in *Beowulf,* most especially in the poem's technique of setting the light and warmth of Heorot against the dark, monster-haunted zone where Grendel and his Mother dwell.[54] Using a legal term found in an Anglo-Saxon charter, one might describe this zone as *nanesmonnesland,* "no-man's-land."[55] To place this setting in the narrative: Grendel's Mother has gained her revenge for the wounding of her son at Heorot by seizing Hrothgar's beloved counselor Æschere; Beowulf has delivered his pungent epigram to Hrothgar that it is better to avenge a friend's death than to mourn much; he has then set out to fight the second monster. At this moment, the poet must quite

literally move his hero from the celebratory world of a hall adorned with gold
and woven banners (no matter how damaged by the previous night's fight) to
the battleground of a mere occupied by Grendel and his Mother. The journey is
not merely one of physical distance through the wastelands and marches where
Cain's kin are doomed to live. It is also the journey that the newly proven hero
must take toward the underwater cave where he will be isolated in his combat
with Grendel's Mother:

> Lastas wæron
> after waldswaþum   wide gesyne,
> gang ofer grundas   swa gegnum for
> ofer myrcan mor,   magoþegna bær
> þone selestan   sawolleasne
> þara þe mid Hroðgare   ham eahtode.
> Ofereode þa   æþelinga bearn
> steap stanhliðo   stige nearwe,
> enge anpaþas,   uncuð gelad,
> neowle næssas,   nicorhusa fela;
> he feara sum   beforan gengde
> wisra monna   wong sceawian,
> oþ þæt he færinga   fyrgenbeamas
> ofer harne stan   hleonian funde,
> wynleasne wudu;   wæter under stod
> dreorig ond gedrefed.

The tracks of Grendel's Mother were widely seen along the forest-paths, the
route over land as she went straight over the dark moor, bearing the best of
hall-thegns soulless who had guarded the hall with Hrothgar. Then the man
of noble birth [Beowulf] passed along the rocky cliffs on a narrow, climbing
path, a dangerous footway, an unknown passage to precipitous cliffs where
many water-monsters lived; he went before with some of the wiser men to
survey the place; then suddenly he found mountain trees, a joyless wood, over
which the hoary grey cliffs leaned. The pool lay beneath, bloody and stirred
up. (ll. 1402b–17a)[56]

The landscape in this passage is far more symbolically charged than are the
atmospheric settings we enjoy in horror movies. It is the poet's means for
offering some glimpse of the hero's mind as he moves from hall to mere. Under
the circumstances, Beowulf could reveal his own thoughts only by opening his
word-hoard and thus transgressing his code — a transgression that would be all
the more obvious because he is surrounded at this moment in the poem by his
own companions as well as some Danes.[57] The grimly foreboding nature of this
landscape has its obvious parallels with the landscape of *The Wife's Lament*:

each is a gloomy site with overhanging trees set beneath cliffs. Within the extended narrative of *Beowulf,* this landscape offers a kind of demarcation, as poetically precise as boundary clauses are legally precise, to indicate the difference between the hero's second monster fight, with Grendel's Mother, and his first, with Grendel. No longer will he remain in the known and human-made world of the hall at Heorot, but rather he must venture into the unknown and disordered world of the underwater hall of the Grendelkin. This landscape of the mere is yet more dehumanizing because it isolates Beowulf from his companions; he will soon dive into the mere, swim to the bottom, and there do battle alone with Grendel's Mother. As is so frequently the case in later medieval romances, the increasingly wild and unsettled landscape setting for these two episodes in *Beowulf* signals an increasingly dangerous and uncertain quest.[58]

As the poet describes Beowulf moving through this inhospitable landscape, we notice how many of the adjectives describing the terrain also speak to his inner state. The way is narrow, dangerous, unknown, just as his fate is uncertain and imperiled; the pool is bloody and stirred-up, just as his thoughts are vengeful and agitated. The correspondence between the exterior and the interior is handled so deftly through naturalistic description that it seems pointless to distinguish absolutely between the setting and the hero of this narrative moment. The listing of natural features in this passage from *Beowulf* has some similarities with the lists of natural features in boundary clauses (e.g., paths, trees, pool) as well as some dissimilarities (e.g., the dwelling place of monsters), but the overall effects of these lists are radically dissimilar. Boundary clauses conclude by returning to their starting point, giving a reassuring sense of closure: the parcel of land is bound, limited, and conveyable as a legal grant. In them, place can be known; in *Beowulf,* place remains mysterious. The passage in *Beowulf* moves in a straightforward direction without any sense of closure; it leads characters and audience alike into a no-man's-land where landscape features demonstrate not the presence of the human but rather that of the monstrous. Yet even here the landscape remains recognizable and can be used to evoke the interior condition of those who move through it.

The path to Grendel's mere may be narrow, but it can be followed; Beowulf may be in danger, but he is not lost in the landscape. For all of its wildness, this scene has none of the hallucinatory effect that the sea has on the speaker of *The Wanderer:*

> Þinceð him on mode   þæt he his mondryhten
> clyppe and cysse,   ond on cneo lecge
> honda ond heafod,   swa he hwilum ær

in geardagum   giefstolas breac.
Ðonne onwæcneð eft   wineleas guma,
gesihð him biforan   fealwe wegas,
baþian brimfuglas,   brædan feþra,
hreosan hrim ond snaw,   hagle gemenged.

It seems to him in his mind that he embraces and kisses his lord, and lays his hands and head on his knee, just as he did sometimes before in past years when he approached the gift-throne. Then the friendless man awakes again, sees before him the yellow waves, the birds bathing, spreading their feathers, the driving frost and snow mingled with hail. (ll. 41–48)[59]

As almost every reader of this poem has felt, there is a deep correspondence, to the point of the pathetic, between the speaker's emptiness and the harshness of the scene, between his loneliness and the unpopulated seascape. This correspondence depends on the poem having been set in a seascape rather than in a landscape, in a place where human habitation cannot appear either as reality or even as possibility but only as a fleeting image of the Wanderer's desire.

The setting of these lines expresses all that the Wanderer cannot say for himself in words: the sheer presence of relentless cold and storm stands as the place and thus also as the manifestation of his inner condition. Afraid to speak out his heart's thoughts lest he leave himself vulnerable in his exile, the Wanderer moves across a winter seascape that strips away all of the usual signs of life in a social world: there is no lord, no mead-hall, no gift-throne. There is nothing that can be set in a landscape, fixed on a map, circumscribed with the brevity of a boundary clause. There are only seabirds that the speaker mistakes for comrades, and they drift away, leaving him alone. No place within the landscape of Anglo-Saxon England could be sufficiently apart and alienating and alone for this particular lament. It is a truism but one relevant here: there was no primeval wilderness in the Anglo-Saxon landscape, no place so dramatically and starkly beyond the mark of human habitation and use that it could serve as the setting for *The Wanderer*.[60] If any sense of place in Anglo-Saxon England approaches the horror of vacancy, it is the sea in this poem.

It is that sheer fact of a lone self, battered but still lamenting, that creates this seascape in the imagination. For what Anglo-Saxon ever sailed alone in a ship, especially in winter? As we know from Icelandic sagas, even such accomplished sailors as the Vikings did not willingly venture alone to sea in winter. What kind of a poem is *The Wanderer* in seeming so detached from the simple realities of its society? To which one might answer: the struggle to express interiority in Old English poetry is so acute, and places such great strain on the psychological as well as poetic vocabularies of the culture, that it yielded this seascape beyond the conventions of the merely realistic. In its departure from the customary nautical prudence of the Anglo-Saxons, the poem imagines a seascape by which to evoke an interior condition that cannot otherwise be expressed.

The vacancy of the seascape in *The Wanderer* is the necessary place to set its speaker's final words about the impermanence of life on earth:

> Her bið feoh læne, her bið freond læne,
> her bið mon læne, her bið mæg læne,
> eal þis eorþan gesteal idel weorþeð.

> Here treasure is transitory, here a friend is transitory, here man is transitory, here kinship is transitory, all this foundation of the earth will become worthless. (ll. 108–110)

Quoted out of their setting, these lines can seem utterly platitudinous: that all on earth is loaned by God, and thus transitory, would hardly seem to require so much poetic work to be persuasive. But if one sets these lines in their place, and considers that the literal referent of *her* is the sea, then one can read them as deeply moving in their steadied confrontation with the radical emptiness of the sea. For the sea offers no sense of place to hold one long on earth; there one can see no familiar landmarks that endure reassuringly over the years. No other sense of place can better prepare one, the poet understands, for the final safety of heaven: "Wel bið þam þe him are seceð, / frofre to fæder on heofonum, þær us eal seo fæstnung stondeð " (Well is it for him who searches for mercy, for comfort from the father in heaven, where for us all permanence rests; ll. 114b–15).

The setting of *The Seafarer* is in some sense even more vacant than that of *The Wanderer* because it is a place of nature that cannot yield even descriptions of the old stonework raised on the earth by now-departed peoples. In this poem, the sea is a place characterized by the loud call of birds and disappearing memories of human companionship:

> Þær ic ne gehyrde butan hlimman sæ,
> iscaldne wæg. Hwilum ylfete song
> dyde ic me to gomene, ganetes hleoþor
> ond huilpan sweg fore hleahtor wera,
> mæw singende fore medodrince.

> There I heard nothing but the roar of the sea, the ice-cold wave. Sometimes the song of the wild swan served as my joy, the voice of the gannet and the sound of the curlew for the laughter of men, the singing of the mew for mead-drink. (ll. 18–23)

Or, a few lines later, the sea is described yet more starkly as a site of stormy weather:

> Nap nihtscua,   norþan sniwde,
> hrim hrusan bond,   hægl feol on eorþan,
> corna caldast.

> The shadow of night grew dark, it snowed from the north, frost bound the earth, hail fell to the ground, the coldest of grains. (ll. 31–33a)

That the seascape cannot be demarcated or defined in any of the ways customary to the Anglo-Saxons renders it the necessary setting for the poet's vision of earthly life as ephemeral.

The sea serves as a setting in both *The Wanderer* and *The Seafarer* for the same reason, for there no speaker can evade the limits of human life or linger to make a home for himself or find comfort in the immediate surroundings. It is the place where the Christian teaching to look heavenward cannot be evaded. Other Christian societies used the desert as the place to retreat to and contemplate the transitory nature of human life, and still others used forests for that lonely purpose. The Anglo-Saxons imagined the sea for that purpose because they lived on an island that was not barren or desolate. The sea becomes in their poetry the setting to depict the absence of a sense of lived or immediate place to call home.

The sea thus becomes the setting for explorations into the inner spiritual life. There, all of the features that typically defined or demarcated place for the Anglo-Saxons were stripped away. It becomes the place of a final human loneliness, a setting for those moments of extremity or crisis in which the claims and ties of the local, the immediate, the familiar were renounced.

PART **II**

Geography and History

3

Englalond and the Postcolonial Void

If a sense of place depends at first on some experience of topography, the lay of the land, it may also draw on a knowledge of history, the record of past events on that same land. On a site much used for agriculture or defense, the shape of the land can testify vividly to the transformations worked by human occupation. Landscape is both topography, as it shows traces of water and wind, and history, as it reveals traces of human actions. The human actions may be as local as the daily track of people and animals across a stream between homestead and pasture, or as far ranging as the ancestral migration of tribes and the pilgrimage of believers between home and sacred site. To remember being somewhere for a long time is to develop a sense of place.

There are thus good reasons for beginning with the local and the literal rather than the universal and the figurative. Focusing on the extant material evidence can provide a valuable counterweight, perhaps even a corrective, to sweeping generalizations about patterns of belief. To say, for example, that medieval Christians believed Jerusalem to be the center of the earth may well be true, but if stated as an absolute claim it can lessen one's ability to understand how an Anglo-Saxon Christian in eighth-century Northumbria might have defined a sense of home on the earth. The boundary clause of an Anglo-Saxon charter offers, in this regard, an intimate, ground-level view of the landscape by following the fords and paths of those who have worked the land. It offers a topography of daily use and represents a specific parcel as having a local past during which these fords and paths were gradually marked on the landscape. The boundary testifies to the ways human beings demarcated and shaped the land. The full text of a charter, as it names the parties and witnesses to the legal transfer, has a different value as a historical document because it treats the parcel of land as self-contained and eternal in itself rather than as part of a larger human landscape and thus as subject to change in the future. As they lay out boundaries, charters have no need to embed themselves in a historical past of politics and religion; their intent is more limited and more localized in scope. As they assert the eternal duration of the grant, they remove that particular parcel of land from historical changes, or at least they do so as a necessary legal fiction.

Under different circumstances, a sense of place can ground itself almost entirely in a sense of the past, as when a group defines itself by remembering a common site of origin. By moving beyond the local or the circumscribed to the distant place whence it migrated, a people can acknowledge the claims of the distant world and give a larger scope to its geographical identity. In such cases, more is at stake than local knowledge. For the Anglo-Saxons, one might ask how more distant locations shaped their perceptions of the world and their orientation in it. This enlarging of geographical knowledge often happened in Anglo-Saxon England through an immersion in the historiographic tradition. The books of the Pentateuch, for example, gave the Anglo-Saxons a deeply historical sense of their place on earth within God's creation, and their influence explains in large measure how the Anglo-Saxons fell into place as converted Christians, as I trace in Chapter 7. Likewise, the Anglo-Saxons had a vivid imagination of regions elsewhere, such as the ancestral territories of Germania or the distant reaches of a wondrous Asia. Their poetic and manuscript anthologies were often shaped into what one might call "books of elsewhere": collections of texts that rarely make explicit reference to England and yet are profoundly rooted in England because written entirely or largely in the vernacular of the place. Gathered for an audience of English speakers, a manuscript such as Junius 11, Cotton Tiberius B v, or Cotton Vitellius A xv transcends the limits of the insular horizon by casting a longer view across the Channel. The poetic cartographies of *Beowulf* and *Exodus,* to cite only two instances, owe their composition on the island quite directly to a history and geography that had Rome as a focal point. To oversimplify for the moment: the Germanic tribes migrated to Britain from Germania in the wake of a political void left by the withdrawal in A.D. 410 of Roman legions from the island; these same Germanic peoples were Christianized on the island by a series of missionaries, starting in 597 with Augustine and his fellow monks, who arrived from Rome. That the Anglo-Saxons had a generously expansive view of their place on earth and within Christendom, one capable of celebrating Geats and Danes in Scandinavia and Israelites in the Sinai, can largely be attributed to factors that originated in Rome, first as it was the seat of imperium and subsequently of *sacerdotium*. Shortening the geographical distance of Rome for the Anglo-Saxons was its historical proximity, for it had left its mark on their home terrain. The fact that Rome was far distant for the traveler and yet close at hand for the resident of the island gave a sense of historical complexity to Anglo-Saxon ideas about place.

For the Anglo-Saxons in the postconversion centuries, Rome was the center of western Christendom, the source of missionaries and papal decrees, and the destination for pilgrims and bishops receiving the pallium. Within the present moment of Anglo-Saxon England, that is, from the seventh through the eleventh century, looking at Rome meant most literally taking the long vista from the periphery to the metropole. The actual journeys made there by Anglo-Saxons had set stopping points along a well-known itinerary; the churches they saw and prayed in, once there, were built in stone on a massive scale. So compelling were its claims on their spiritual and political being that Anglo-Saxons journeyed to Rome with surprising regularity despite the straight-line distance of 900 miles. Within that same present moment of Anglo-Saxon England, there was another and more historical Rome — the capital city of an empire that had once had Britannia as one of its distant provinces and that then had left it to survive by itself in a postcolonial void. Knowledge of this historical Rome endured for the Anglo-Saxons on their home ground through Latin texts as well as their own historical works. More spectrally, it also survived on the landscape, with its stone-paved roads or abandoned military camps and walls that were used as quarries for *spolia*. Anglo-Saxon England had its own Mediterranean past on its immediate landscape.

From our distant perspective, a millennium and more later, we can see clearly that these two ideas of Rome coexisted among the Anglo-Saxons and, no doubt, sometimes overlapped in experience and imagination. To understand how these senses of history shaped the Anglo-Saxons' ways of living on their island, though, it is helpful to separate them into the near view of Rome as a past that endured on the island both physically and intellectually, and the distant view of Rome as the current papal seat and pilgrimage site. Doing so reminds us as well of the Anglo-Saxons' practice of historicizing and interpreting their geography so that places belonged to their own particular moment in time rather than to some undifferentiated accumulation of past events.

There is no Anglo-Saxon text, to my knowledge, that explicitly describes human-made features of the landscape that predate the Romano-British period. This absence may well seem unsurprising.[1] For why should the Anglo-Saxons have had such an accurately defined sense of periodization or cultural shifts that they could or would notice such features? As a corollary, this does mean that no Anglo-Saxon text describes in a recognizable manner a stone circle as prominent to the eye from afar as Stonehenge or Avebury; a chalk image as visible as the White Horse of Uffington or the priapic giant above the monastic foundation at Cerne Abbas, where Ælfric wrote his homilies and saints' lives at the turn of the millennium; or a construction as massive as the Iron Age hill forts that still sit atop ridgeways across the southern part of the island. Nor do Anglo-Saxon texts other than charters make much of the earthworks that rise above and define the landscape in many places across the island. Such earthworks belonged very much to the landscape inherited by the Anglo-Saxons, as can be seen by their presence on the rise above the River Deben at a time when the Anglo-Saxons left behind the most famous of all their graves, the funerary ship of Sutton Hoo, loaded with treasures gathered from across the then known world. Reflecting on this site as evidence for an early Anglo-Saxon sense of place can be illuminating, for its contents suggest England at that time functioned as a kind of colonial contact zone: silver spoons from the eastern Mediterranean, a great "Coptic" bowl, coins from thirty-seven different Merovingian mints, gold and garnet fittings for jewelry and weapons. Martin Carver, the most recent archaeologist to excavate the grave site, has written evocatively of how the Anglo-Saxons found the scene: "The farmers [of Roman Britain and before] had gone, but their earthworks were still visible: a network of low banks along the terrace looking out over the ancient tidal breathing of the Deben."[2] The inherited landscape, then, is that which is marked by past creations that make it attractive for a present generation and also for future ones.

Carver speaks as well of "how the people of the early Middle Ages could recognize the 'vocabulary' of the landscape, choosing for a new development an old site that either never lost its meaning, or could be readily invested with the properties of a tradition."[3] The term *vocabulary* seems a more illuminating metaphor for the historical encrustations on the Anglo-Saxon landscape than does the customary *palimpsest* because it admits the simultaneous circulation of many different elements while the other designates what was once present but has since been scraped away. *Palimpsest* refers to a single surface that has been used and reused in a series of moments so that the currently visible image obscures all that came before.[4] *Vocabulary* as a metaphor for landscape acknowledges, by contrast, the simultaneous presence of elements from different periods, such as one finds with Anglo-Saxon churches built in the midst of Iron Age ramparts, as at Hanbury in Worcestershire.[5]

Given that the Anglo-Saxons were not prone to philosophizing about the value of place to organize their experience, it can be illuminating to consider a comparative perspective. Writing of the ways in which the Western Apache view place, the ethnographer Keith Basso provides us with a means to approach the symbolic and historical meanings of landscape in Anglo-Saxon England, that is, to understand the vocabulary of the scene in nonliteral ways: "Landscapes are available in symbolic terms as well, and so, chiefly through the manifold agencies of speech, they can be 'detached' from their fixed spatial moorings and transformed into instruments of thought and vehicles of purposive behavior. Thus transformed, landscapes and the places that fill them become tools for the imagination, expressive means for accomplishing verbal deeds, and also, of course, eminently portable possessions to which individuals can maintain deep and abiding attachments, regardless of where they travel."[6]

The relevant dynamic in Anglo-Saxon England was less spatial travel, as it is for the Apache, than temporal imagination, of casting oneself back into a landscape that survived from earlier generations made up of a people other than one's own. The common feature of Basso's claims for the Apache and mine for the Anglo-Saxon English is that we both depict a people capable of moving out of the "here and now" to shape cultural identity through an understanding of the historically stratified landscape. Such an understanding often depends, in turn, on a geographical orientation.

In insular texts such as Gildas's *Ruin of Britain*, Bede's *Ecclesiastical History*, and Cynewulf's *Fates of the Apostles* and *Elene*, the authorial vantage is set in the north looking south, even if the words *norþ* and *suð* do not always appear. The Anglo-Saxon gaze looked, typically, toward the south and especially toward Rome and the Holy Land.[7] Like other forms of the gaze, the Anglo-Saxon one had a certain element of desire to it: it looked for a purpose, to accommodate a need, to satisfy an absence, to close a distance. It was about more than mere referentiality along the points of the compass. One might call it a telescopic gaze because it elided or overlooked the fact of great distance: as the crow flies, it is many hundreds of miles from Canterbury to Rome, and even more from Canterbury to Jerusalem. The fact of intervening distance is, for Bede or Cynewulf, not immediately relevant because there is a kind of figural correspondence, in Erich Auerbach's sense of that term, between the place of England and the place of Rome.[8] Rome precedes England in Christian time; the conversion of England completes the mission of Rome in later time; both remain very much actual places on the earth. Just as figura, or a figurative imagination, can close great gaps of time in religious history, so narratives can close great distances.

Closing this distance was not, however, simply a matter of figural reading. There were survivals of Roman occupation — roads, walls, temples, baths, and the like that stood on the landscape in their stone-built solidity — that enabled and perhaps even forced Anglo-Saxons to accomplish that act of cultural and historical alignment. When Rome withdrew the last of her legions from Britain in 410, she left the island in something like a postcolonial void in relation to the larger world.[9] Britain was a postcolonial society in the most literal sense of the term in the period after the Roman Empire ceased to function as a political, military, and economic entity on the island and before Englaland emerged later in the Anglo-Saxon period as an incipient nation within the larger sphere of Christendom.[10] At the start of this postcolonial period lies a period of almost two centuries, conveniently defined by the dates for the withdrawal of the Roman legions in 410 and the arrival of Roman missionaries in 597, for which the evidence is very scattered, sometimes contradictory, often tantalizingly incomplete, and usually found in sources written for an explicitly partisan purpose. It is no accident that James Campbell called these years "the lost centuries" and cautioned: "The natural vice of historians is to claim to know about the past. Nowhere is this claim more dangerous than when staked in Britain between A.D. 400 and 600."[11]

The interpretive challenge faced by the modern scholar is to locate the traces left behind in texts and buildings by the inhabitants of this period as well as the traces left behind in the retrospective interpretations of these artifacts by those who wrote or built in the subsequent Anglo-Saxon period. Elleke Boehmer has suggested one method by which to characterize a wide variety of medieval English writing as postcolonial: "Marlow in Conrad's 'Heart of Darkness,' for example, draws attention to the similarities between the British colonization of Africa and the conquering of Britain by imperial Rome many centuries before. According to this view, *Beowulf* and Chaucer's *Canterbury Tales* could be read as postcolonial texts."[12]

To set strict limits on what might be categorized as postcolonial in the context of Old English literature would be self-defeating. Instead, I have been guided by Boehmer's assertion that "*postcolonial* literature is that which critically scrutinizes the colonial relationship."[13] A sense of anteriority is not in itself enough to qualify a work as postcolonial within Anglo-Saxon England; that sense must in some way be a part of the cultural work done by the text. What did it mean to live and compose where the Roman Empire had once had its most northerly outpost? What did it mean to live amid the physical remains of what had been a flourishing province? There are ways of scrutinizing the colonial relationship in Anglo-Saxon texts, even if they do not seem at first to show any concern with explicitly political questions. It would be premature to expect a stable or reasonably coherent understanding of a postcolonial Anglo-Saxon England given the state of our knowledge, though certain lines of inquiry can be followed. The most immediately promising of these lines is to ask how the English looked at the physical survivals of Roman occupation that surrounded them.

Insular writers both Celtic and Saxon rely on a vividly literal trope to memorialize the presence of imperial Romans in Britain and thus to identify their own temporal distance from these predecessors. In his *Ruin of Britain,* composed circa 540, Gildas offers a jeremiad denouncing the corrupt state of Celtic Britain during the period of Germanic attacks. Because he writes as a Christian, and in Latin, Gildas can depict the barbarian invasion in terms that reveal both his own cultural affiliations and his horror at the political chaos of the time:

> Ita et cunctae coloniae crebris arietibus omnesque coloni cum praepositis ecclesiae, cum sacerdotibus ac populo, mucronibus undique micantibus ac flammis crepitantibus, simul solo sternerentur, et miserabili visu in medio platearum ima turrium edito cardine evulsarum murorumque celsorum saxa, sacra altaria, cadaverum frusta, crustis ac si gelantibus purpurei cruoris tecta, velut in quodam horrendo torculari mixta viderentur.

> All the major towns were laid low by the repeated battering of enemy rams; laid low, too, all the inhabitants — church leaders, priests and people alike, as the swords glinted all around and the flames crackled. It was a sad sight. In the middle of the squares the foundation-stones of high walls and towers that had been torn from their lofty base, holy altars, fragments of corpses, covered (as it were) with a purple crust of congealed blood, looked as though they had been mixed up in some dreadful wine-press.[14]

The observer here describes events through the cultural norms and styles of *Romanitas,* or Roman-ness. The established order of urban life has been destroyed and its public spaces filled with the ruins of stone walls and towers; the sacred altars built to ensure prosperity have been shattered; the central squares of cities are littered with mutilated bodies. In Gildas's vision of events, these horrors were attributed to a group of migratory barbarians that spoke Germanic dialects rather than Latin and typically built in timber rather than stone. The destruction of masonry buildings thus serves for Gildas as a sign that his larger cultural world is being vanquished.

Gildas's scene represents a cautionary instance of cultural regression, for within the model known as lithicization, it reverses the progression by which stone replaces wood as a building material because stone is more permanent and fire-resistant as well as more prestigious, being more difficult to work and thus more costly.[15] For Gildas, the Roman civilization that commanded his allegiance was built of stone and meant to last out the centuries. Another marker of Gildas's cultural identity, and one that he turns here to an urgent pathos, is his description of the blood-soaked corpses in urban squares that look as if they had been mangled in a winepress. Gildas's simile is vivid in itself but would also have reminded his audience that wine was another obvious attribute of Romanitas in Britain, as the island's extensive trade with Bordeaux and its environs demonstrates.[16]

Gildas portrays the period of the Germanic invasions as a world turned to chaos: the enduring stone structures of a Romanized society fall, the altars are desecrated, wine denotes bloodshed and dismemberment rather than the pleasures of a civilized life or the rituals of the liturgy. Through such images, he depicts this period in British history as marking an irreparable break with the past: the Roman civilization of towns has been reduced to rubble. Within *The Ruin of Britain*, this passage appears in the historical section and stands as a kind of preface to, or warrant for, the religious polemic that follows. This prefatory section registers Gildas's understanding from reading the Old Testament that history precedes denunciation, that the Pentateuch and Chronicles precede the prophets Isaiah and Jeremiah.[17] That stone structures cannot survive cataclysms, that barbarians topple the enduring achievements of Romanitas, that blood flows in the streets like wine — these are all proof for Gildas of a historical void that seems destined to extend beyond his own lifetime, if not far into the future.

As an avid reader of Gildas, Bede followed his predecessor's lead in evoking Roman Britain as a culture of stone-built structures — and yet he did so from a very different perspective. Writing from what he thought to be the other, or triumphalist, side of the void, Bede could run a line of continuity from the years following the withdrawal of Roman legions to the flourishing of Anglo-Saxon Christianity during his own lifetime early in the eighth century:

> Fracta est autem Roma a Gothis anno millesimo CLXIIII suae conditionis, ex quo tempore Romani in Brittania regnare cesserunt, post annos ferme quadringentos LXX ex quo Gaius Iulius Caesar eandem insulam adiit. Habitabant autem intra uallum, quod Seuerum trans insulam fecisse commemorauimus, ad plagam meridianam, quod ciuitates farus pontes et stratae ibidem factae *usque hodie testantur;* ceterum ulteriores Brittaniae partes, uel eas etiam quae ultra Brittaniam sunt insulas, iure dominandi possidebant.

> Now Rome was taken by the Goths in the eleven hundred and sixty-fourth year after its foundation; after this the Romans ceased to rule in Britain, almost 470 years after Gaius Julius Caesar had come to the island. They had

occupied the whole land south of the rampart already mentioned, set up across the island by Severus, an occupation to which the cities, lighthouses, bridges, and roads which they built there *testify to this day* [emphasis added]. Moreover they possessed the suzerainty over the further parts of Britain as well as over the islands which are beyond it.[18]

For Bede, as for Gildas, the visible signs of Roman occupation were made of stone and masonry: cities, lighthouses, bridges, and — most dramatically across the landscape — roads that cut from point to point with a straight-line directness that spoke of an imperial will to power over the terrain.[19] As Robert Hardison writes, "Roman roads were laid perfectly straight in an outlying place like Britain not because it was easy to do it that way but to show that even this wild did not defeat the Roman mind, which could treat it as if it were a plane."[20] Seen from the British perspective, these Roman roads would also have symbolized, as Richard Muir observes, "the inadequacy of indigenous arrangements" and thus would have set the relation between the colonizer and the colonized in a literally hierarchical material form.[21]

Bede does not add that most of these stone constructions were in a state of disrepair, as they must have been, when he wrote more than three hundred years after the departure of the legions in 410. Eroded by weather, overgrown with vegetation, quarried for building materials, these Roman structures would still have denoted the presence of an imperial power to a later people that built characteristically, though not exclusively, in wood. Nor would the survival of these Roman constructions into the Anglo-Saxon period have posed any great mysteries to a writer like Bede: the textual record provided by Roman historians made clear which colonizing power had raised those lighthouses and roads, bridges and walls. Even if such accounts had not been available to Bede and others, they could have learned who had built many of these structures, and when, from the inscriptions on them. The Romans were adept at using writing in highly visible ways to assert their power and celebrate their accomplishments. What response the surviving inscriptions of Roman Britain might have evoked from Anglo-Saxons has not been much considered by scholars, but one basic point can be made: the language in which they were written was not a dead or lost language in need of reconstruction or decipherment.[22] These stones remained behind and could be read, at least by some members of the community. For a cleric with fluent Latin like Bede, these texts and inscriptions told a story of Roman occupation and then withdrawal. Such traces of Rome were not opaque or mysterious in ways that pre-Roman structures like Stonehenge or Avebury appear to have been to the Anglo-Saxons. Instead, the traces of empire were for Bede evidence of a void that had been filled through a new and more enduring connection with Rome, one that returned Christianity and Latin to the island.

That Roman roads survived as the visible traces of an empire that had once included the island may explain the Anglo-Saxon practice of locating churches near — but not on — them, as with the Church of the Holy Cross at Daglingworth that lies about a mile off the main Roman road between Cirencester and Gloucester and that was built with Roman stone.[23] These roads could not have been ignored in an otherwise agrarian landscape, and they may have remained useful for transport well into the Anglo-Saxon period, but they also endured resonantly as evidence for the fading of all that was human-made within the scope of Christian history.[24] Anglo-Saxons who knew the story of these Roman roads may well have sensed a somewhat melancholy air about them, not unlike that expressed in the *ubi sunt* catalogues of ruined halls and stone walls in the Old English poetic elegies.

The poet of *The Wanderer,* for example, memorably invokes the ruination of walls and wine-halls as a measure of the decay of the earth and of the Christian desire for the heavenly home:

> Ongietan sceal gleaw hæle   hu gæstlic bið,
> þonne ealre þisse worulde wela   weste stondeð,
> swa nu missenlice   geond þisne middangeard
> winde biwaune   weallas stondaþ,
> hrime bihrorene,   hryðge þa ederas.

> The wise man must perceive how ghostly it will be when the riches of all this world stand abandoned, as now in various places throughout this world walls stand windblown, frost covered, buildings swept by snow. (ll. 73–77)[25]

The poet completes his lamentation by stating, in a trope that resonates through Old English lyric poetry, "eald enta geweorc idlu stodon" (the old works of giants stood empty; l. 87). For all its haunted beauty, this passage from *The Wanderer* seems by design not to be located in any specific time or place; within the poem, it occupies a spiritualized rather than historicized landscape. Yet from the perspective of a people that remembered the postcolonial period of their own past, the passage could be read with a more precise historical valence. For its depiction of ruined stonework as proof of earthly temporality, and therefore of transience, rests on a vision of Christian history that came with the conversion of the Anglo-Saxons.

The passages in *Maxims II* and *The Ruin* that describe old stone-built cities and then lament them as the work of giants seem more explicitly historical or worldly, though that may be because neither poem offers the final Christian consolation of *The Wanderer.* The poet of *Maxims II* opens with a statement of the accepted political order in the world of human beings — that a king should rule the kingdom — and then speaks of stone-built cities that are so monumental they can be seen from a long distance:

> Cyning sceal rice healdan.   Ceastra beoð feorran gesyne,
> orðanc enta geweorc,   þa þe on þysse eorðan syndon,
> wrætlic weallstana geweorc.

> A king should hold the kingdom. Cities may be seen from afar, those that are on the earth, the skilled work of giants, the artfully crafted work of wall stones. (ll. 1–3a)[26]

The description of these cities refers primarily to their prominence on the landscape but also opens the possibility for a more temporal vantage: these cities can be seen as having their own distant history. That the "work of giants" refers to baths and walls used by human beings rather than, as might possibly seem the case, stone circles like those that survive at Stonehenge or Avebury is evident: *weallstan* specifically refers to stone that has been cut and dressed for use in building a wall.[27] Moreover, the stone walls of *Maxims II* encircle a stronghold ruled by a *cyning* and protect it as a human city, as the Old English word *ceaster* makes clear. The connection between *cyning* and *ceaster* here is as much political as alliterative.

Moreover, the word *ceaster* — a borrowing of the Latin *castra* — would evoke a more densely historical meaning for any reader alert to the Roman inflections of the word. For an Old English poet, *ceaster* would have been a necessary synonym for the native *burg* to denote a stronghold or fortified location. Given the frequency of *castra* as an element in Old English place-names, though, the Roman origin of the word could have been recognized even by those many Anglo-Saxons without Latin. Such are the ways that traces of empire linger in language, even after the colonizers have departed. Just as *castra* became Old English *ceaster* and an element in later place-names as –*caster*, –*cester*, and–*chester*, so too *burg* entered Latin and then Italian, as in the *Borgo* Santo Spirito of Rome.[28]

The "work of giants" as a trope for the past imperial grandeur of Roman Britain establishes a scale of material history by identifying the use of stone with a past age of superhuman accomplishment. The common historical and poetic trope of a golden age followed in an inevitable process of decline by silver, iron, and even baser metals, has its equivalent in the celebration of a past era as noble because it worked in stone. *The Ruin*, the fullest expression of this trope in an Old English text, speaks with precise and even loving attention about such characteristics of Roman construction as the use of cut and dressed stones, roof tiles, mortar joints, and reinforcing metalwork such as clamps.[29] The familiar reading of *The Ruin* as specifically evoking the city of Bath is possible, though it ignores the fact that the postcolonial landscape of Anglo-Saxon England was filled with the remains of Roman baths, including some far distant from Bath at sites like Chesters near Hadrian's Wall.[30] The Roman practice of building baths at forts and other garrison sites was no doubt meant to ease the rigors of life in a military outpost, but it also had the deliberate effect of marking the spread and maintenance of imperial power. The presence of baths across the British landscape testifies to Peter Wells's claim, in *The Barbarians Speak,* that "the army was the Roman institution that had the most direct and most profound impact on the indigenous peoples of temperate Europe."[31]

The Ruin becomes far more evocative if freed from any specific location and read instead as evoking a type of site that would not have been uncommon on the landscape. This effect can be traced partly to the static nature of *The Ruin;* no one speaks or acts in it, the site molders away across the turn of generations, the scene is haunted with a meaning that can be articulated only through precise description.[32] The opening lines of the poem, as they present an envelope pattern of present tense verbs around past forms, articulate a vision of history as the flow of time between the decaying stonework in the scene and the speaker who describes it:

> Wrætlic is þes wealstan,   wyrde gebræcon;
> burgstede burston,   brosnað enta geweorc.
> Hrofas sind gehrorene,   hreorge torras,
> hrungeat berofen,   hrim on lime,
> scearde scurbeorge   scorene, gedrorene,
> ældo undereotone.

> The building stone is wondrously crafted, broken by fate, the city places ruined, the work of giants decays. The roofs are fallen, the towers toppled, the frost-covered gate destroyed, the rime is in the mortar, built refuges from storms are damaged, torn, collapsed, eaten under by time. (1–6a)[33]

The terminology here of building types, as well as the emphatic rhymes to sound out the inevitability of time's passing, mark this as the most evocative use of the trope of stonework in Old English. These lines survey the range of building types in much the same way as does Bede's sentence about lighthouses, bridges, and roads.

The walls of the buildings outlast, the poet says, kingdom after kingdom — "rice æfter oþrum" (l. 10b) — so that what was once the scene of human pleasure now stands empty and desolate, but not mute. Modern readers have found it hard not to treat the poem allegorically or at least symbolically, so that this one ruined site can be made to speak to the transience of all earthly habitation and thus to the decline of the world. It is difficult to argue against this interpretation and perhaps unnecessary; the poem may well evoke through the force of an implicit contrast a habitation elsewhere that will last out the ages. *The Ruin* urges its audience by implication to think of a home beyond, as does *The Seafarer*: "Uton we hycgan hwær we ham agen, / ond þonne geþencan hu we þider cumen" (Let us consider where we have a home and then think how we might go there; ll. 117–18).[34] Yet if we respond to the imagery of *The Ruin*, to its ruggedly hewn but precisely fitted masonry, we can see that it builds with layers of history that are absent from *The Seafarer* and most other Old English poems.

The single half-line "hrim on lime" (rime on lime, or, more prosaically, the frost on the mortar) becomes in context a law of historical causation about the decline of imperial power in its physical manifestations: once its great structures are abandoned, and nature is free to take its course, even the work of giants decays and crumbles. The speaker of the poem has a keen eye for the literal signs of historical change: the walls, he adds a few lines later, are "ræghar ond readfah," or grey with lichen and stained with red (l. 10a). With these two colors, the poet paints the scene before him: the grey of lichen that has grown unchecked over the abandoned structures and the red of the rusting iron clamps and reinforcing bars used in their construction. Later in the poem, the speaker will describe the collapse of the buildings' arched roofs with their tiles (ll. 30–31a), another marker of Roman construction, and also will praise as "hyðelic" (l. 41a), or convenient, the ways in which the "stanhofu," or stonehouses, enclosed the hot springs of the bath (l. 38a).

If the tone of *The Ruin* is elegiac, it has about it a more plangently historicized note of loss and lament than one usually hears in Old English poetry. Its incomplete, fragmentary state in the Exeter Book makes it impossible to know if *The Ruin* moved, as do *The Wanderer* and *The Seafarer*, from describing the decay of earthly habitations to celebrating the eternal home of heaven. What remains of the poem, though, is enough to show that its poet understood the inescapable historicity of human life on earth, that the present and the past are not a single undifferentiated mass, that the remains still standing in England can demonstrate that those who came before were profoundly different in their ways of life. From the details of that evocation, of mortar and cut stone, of iron rebar and roof tiles, of houses and baths, the poet gives to that idea of the past its own defining architectural features and thus fixes it in a moment far distant from his present. And yet that sense of the Roman past belongs to the same place as does the present of Anglo-Saxon England. Within this vision, a place is not isolated in a single or fixed moment of time but instead contains historical strata. There is something very knowing about this way to identify a place, something that seeks to register in the local and immediate the measure of the distant and long ago.

Stepping back from the text of *The Ruin,* one can see that the monumentality, the historical fact of this scene would be visually all the more striking in an agricultural landscape such as that of Anglo-Saxon England, in which most structures, from animal sheds to aristocratic halls to substantial churches, were built of wood. As the poet of *Maxims II* notes, stone-built structures in such a landscape would be highly conspicuous.[35] That those who built such stone structures are now gone becomes a cautionary tale as one thinks about the future. But that they were here belongs inescapably to one's sense of the present landscape. One can call these builders giants, but that is for the poet an ethnographic term not unlike the names of past or mythic tribes that appear in Bede's *History.* *The Ruin* finds its subject in the need to interpret a visible feature of the landscape that does nothing yet troubles the eye because it cannot be evaded. And from this fact, that the site must be observed, comes an acutely rendered description of the world here and now that makes one all the more reluctant to offer an allegorical reading of the poem.

The ruins of this poem, unlike the setting of *The Seafarer,* are not universal, but rather they are contingent on circumstances of time and place. *The Seafarer* metaphorizes the journey across an oceanscape to lead its audience to the heavenly home elsewhere; *The Ruin* metaphorizes the enduring stonework of a lost people to lead its audience to some richer sense of Christian life in a specific setting. Michael Hunter's literal statement that "Roman remains were used as a quarry for current needs" in Anglo-Saxon England has its poetic truth as well.[36] The poet's vision of these masonry ruins may be likened to spolia, that is, remains of Roman buildings, such as carved friezes, lintels, dressed blocks of stone, that were incorporated into the construction of new buildings during later periods. In both the Old English poem and the builder's use of spolia there is a gesture of appreciation. As Erwin Panofsky remarks of *The Ruin,* the masonry ruins may be "interpreted as a symbol of the destructive forces of destiny, reducing to rubble the proudest efforts of man while yet appealing to the aesthetic perception."[37]

In our postdeconstructive time, it may seem ironic that *The Ruin* is itself something of a ruin in its manuscript condition because eleven of its forty-nine lines are damaged beyond reading; but enough remains for us to know that its use of setting is meant to distance the universal or the elsewhere by depicting the sheer fact of what endures in the here and now. In the most fundamental way, the poem teaches that one aspect of being an Anglo-Saxon, a native of that homeland, or *eðel,* is the need to ponder a landscape with its scene of crumbling masonry and then to deduce its historical as well as its spiritual meanings. In a brilliant discussion of the psychological appeal of ruins, the architectural historian John Summerson observes that a ruined building no longer maintains the usual distinction between exterior and interior but stands instead "as a single combination of planes in recession, full of mystery and surprise, movement beyond movement; and since it retains all the while the character of architecture — a structure designed for use — it suggests its own participation in life: a fantastic participation."[38] The ruined building's "movement beyond movement" becomes the Old English poem's "time behind time" in the landscape.

The true elsewhere of *The Ruin* is the past of its landscape: the time of giants, of stonework, of those who left their mark on the landscape. Its present moment is, by contrast, one of declining value, a time of human beings who build in wood and wonder what it must have been like to enjoy the pleasures of hot springs enclosed within stone buildings. There is always about the inherited landscape a temptation of nostalgia, a hint of some lost golden age. As a corollary, one might wonder if the Anglo-Saxons, who did not see their landscape as primeval, could ever celebrate it as sublime.

The stones that litter the texts of Gildas, Bede, and the Old English poets can be read as the visible traces of a colonial past. The methods of Roman colonization need, especially in our own postcolonial time, to be understood on their own terms as extending citizenship to Britons in the centuries before 410. They were not subjected to the same practices of colonial oppression that characterized European imperialism in Africa and Asia during the modern period. In this regard, 410 must be understood as marking the withdrawal of Roman troops from Britain — not the abandonment of the island by its Roman citizens. The effects of that military action were certainly profound, especially for those who remained on the island and thought of themselves as belonging to Romanitas.[39] Most visible from the archaeological record is the fact that money was no longer coined in Britain and that the large-scale manufacture and marketing of pottery ceased after 410 or so. As Peter Salway has said of those years, "the feature that startles anyone used to Roman sites in Britain is the almost total absence of coins or pottery."[40] Coins and pottery are in their own ways not simply evidence of Roman occupation but also evidence of a larger empire in which the province of Britannia was part of a trade economy that could make a market for local goods in distant places. The absence of coins and pottery after 410 is correspondingly a sign that once-thriving mercantile connections with the outside world had ceased in Britain, or at least had been severely curtailed.

Nonetheless, traces of Roman imperial power remained visible on the landscape of the Anglo-Saxons and continued to haunt their imaginations in later centuries.[41] The texts quoted in this chapter offer a line of memorial transmission and a theory of historiographical interpretation by which to understand these remnants of the Roman imperium. In that respect, these texts bear out the claims made by Bill Ashcroft in his *Post-Colonial Transformation:* "Place is never simply location, nor is it static, a cultural memory which colonization buries. For, like culture itself, place is in a continual and dynamic state of formation, a process intimately bound up with the culture and the identity of its inhabitants. Above all place is a *result* of habitation, a consequence of the ways in which people inhabit space, particularly that conception of space as universal and uncontestable that is constructed for them by imperial discourse."[42]

To locate the terms of Ashcroft's argument in Anglo-Saxon England, a post-colonial zone quite distant in time from the post–World War II societies he examines, one might alter his final clause to read "constructed for them by imperial discourse and architecture." That is, the recognition of being a post-colonial zone or place of habitation registered by the Anglo-Saxons in texts is also visible through their references to the fate of Roman stone-built architecture. To live knowingly in a landscape filled with the material remains of the colonizing power — its ways of building with, most notably, dressed stone and rounded arches, as well as its practice of inscribing texts on buildings and monuments — was to locate oneself in Anglo-Saxon England as a postcolonial place.

These Roman stones were not merely literary tropes for Gildas, Bede, and the poets of *The Wanderer, Maxims II,* and *The Ruin.* They were also present on the landscape, both as they survived in derelict structures and as they were visibly reused in newly built Christian churches. W. G. Hoskins has speculated that the presence of Roman ruins in townscapes may well have altered the routes taken by pedestrians: "It has been suggested, for example, in certain towns of Roman origin where the Saxon or early medieval streets do not lie exactly on the line of the Roman streets, that these must represent the irregular tracks tramped out in Saxon times by people who were forced to walk around the ruins of tumbled Roman buildings."[43] Hoskins does not identify sites where this rerouting may have occurred, but his comment reminds us that ruins are not merely picturesque features on the landscape to be appreciated by those of an antiquarian bent. They can also impinge on the course of daily life in seemingly trivial and yet enduring ways. The stones of Roman ruins would have been part of the familiar scene for those who lived in sites that had once been (or were near to) Roman streets, towns, camps, or forts — a condition that was common in such areas of Anglo-Saxon England as Northumbria, especially in the frontier region near Hadrian's Wall, or in the villa-rich environs around Cirencester in Gloucestershire.[44] We know nothing reliable about the circumstances of when and where Gildas or the poets of *Maxims II* and *The Ruin* lived, and thus cannot localize them within the Anglo-Saxon historical landscape of wood or stone buildings. About Bede, however, we know a good deal more because he tells us the relevant facts of his life and because he spent most of it in a very circumscribed area.

From the age of seven until he died at sixty-two, Bede tells us, he lived in the monastic community of Wearmouth and Jarrow in the north of England, a region that had been heavily built by the Romans. He also tells us that he was born in the territory of that monastery, though he does not specify the location of his birthplace. He adds that he was educated at Jarrow under the guidance of Benedict Biscop and then Ceolfrith.[45] In his *Lives of the Abbots of Wearmouth and Jarrow,* Bede provides a fond description of Benedict's role in building the monastic church at Jarrow:

> Nec plusquam unius anni spatio post fundatum monasterium interiecto, Benedictus oceano transmisso Gallias petens, cementarios qui lapideam sibi aecclesiam iuxta Romanorum quem semper amabat morem facerent, postulauit, accepit, adtulit.

> Only a year after work had begun on the monastery, Benedict crossed the sea to France to look for masons to build him a stone church in the Roman style he had always loved so much. He found them, took them on and brought them back home with him.[46]

Bede goes on to relate that the church was built rapidly so that a year after the foundation was laid, the gables had been raised, and one could imagine mass being said within it. The year was A.D. 674, Bede tells us, a year after his birth. He was thus not an eyewitness to the building of St. Peter's Church at Jarrow, though he certainly could have heard of it from monks who had been present. From one of them he might easily have learned that the church was raised so quickly at least in part because it was built from reused Roman stones that had been taken from the wall that, as he notes in the *Ecclesiastical History* (I.xi–xii), was built by Hadrian to keep the Scots and Picts at bay. Or Bede might well have determined the Roman provenance of these stones from his own observations, for he was born in the region and would have grown up surrounded by them and by the local lore about their origin.

That Bede says nothing in the *Lives of the Abbots* about the source of the stones used at St. Peter's in Jarrow is not in itself proof that he was ignorant of their provenance. Indeed, this kind of technical matter as it relates to everyday life rarely interests him. Nonetheless, it is noteworthy that he should have been familiar with a church that was built knowingly to be, among its more obvious purposes, "an impressive, monumental Roman memorial," in the words of Tim Eaton. In his illuminating study of the use of Roman spolia in Anglo-Saxon England, Eaton argues that the use of stones from Hadrian's Wall was a means for Benedict Biscop "to appropriate some of the authority associated with its construction."[47] Given Benedict's love for churches in the Roman style — a matter that would seem at least as much of material as of design, though the two can hardly be separated in this regard — it is not surprising that St. Peter's at Jarrow was built from Roman stone as a matter of cultural affiliation, even if there were also factors of economy and convenience to consider.

The assimilation of Roman materials and thus Roman history at Jarrow extended to the interior precincts of the church. As Eaton explains, two fragments of a Roman inscription that belonged to a "war memorial or *tropaeum*" from Hadrian's Wall were used to form the horizontal arms of a cross set inside of St. Peter's. The reconstructed Latin inscription speaks directly to the triumph of Roman imperial power over the barbarians:

> Son of all the deified emperors, the Emperor Caesar Trajan Hadrian Augustus, after the necessity of keeping the empire within its limits had been laid upon him by divine precept . . . thrice consul . . . after the barbarians had been dispersed, and the province of Britain had been recovered, he added a frontier-line between either shore of the Ocean for 80 miles. The army of the province built this defence-work under the charge of Aulus Platorius Nepos, emperor's propraetorian legate.[48]

If one can imagine an eighth-century monk reading this inscription, or at least making adequate sense of it as a Roman military trophy, then one can also ask what he might have thought about the shifting fortunes of empire and colony and, more specifically, of the role played by Rome as the capital of Anglo-Saxon England. The highly conscious reuse of this Roman stonework with its inscription at the very heart of Northumbrian Christianity would have been evidence for Bede that the postcolonial void had been bridged. The island of Britannia, once a province of the *imperium*, was now a community of Christians who looked to Rome and the papacy for spiritual direction and political guidance. This process of cultural reassimilation was eased greatly by the fact that Latin was the language of the empire and army that left behind such inscriptions as well as of the clerics who turned them to their own purposes. The use of such spolia at a center of monastic learning such as Jarrow demonstrates that there was no religiously decreed aversion to the imperial past of Britannia.[49] One can argue further that there was even a triumphalist assertion in the Anglo-Saxon use of Roman spolia; it did not merely represent

Figure 9: St. John's Church, Escomb, County Durham, from the south.

an act of homage to the past of imperial Rome but also stood as a statement that the truly enduring empire of Rome within human history was Christian not pagan, was ruled by a pope not an emperor. This revisionist model of historical causation allowed the imperial conquest and Romanization of the island by Claudius in A.D. 43 to be seen as a distant but necessary precondition for the later migration and then conversion of the Anglo-Saxons.

Or, in starker terms, the Anglo-Saxons entered Christendom because the island had once been a colony of Rome. Such a reading of history, by which the postcolonial void is explained, can be seen in the very fabric of the small church of St. John at Escomb in County Durham that dates to the late seventh or early eighth century. This church, perhaps the most beautiful example of ecclesiastical architecture to survive intact from the Anglo-Saxon period, is relatively small and simple in design (Figure 9). The interior of the nave is approximately 43 feet 6 inches by 14 feet 6 inches, and that of the chancel is approximately 10 feet by 10 feet.[50] Many of the exterior stones bear visible evidence of Roman origin, especially in the tooling of their outer surfaces in broached and feather-broached patterns (Figure 10).[51] Other stones used in the exterior walls do not bear any such signs and may perhaps have been quarried locally for the construction of the church. More directly evocative of

Figure 10: St. John's Church, Escomb, reused Roman stone.

Rome as both imperial power and papal seat is the arch that joins nave and chancel (Figure 11). H. M. Taylor and Joan Taylor have described this arch as possessing "outstanding dignity," a quality that is all the more evident because of the "narrow and lofty proportions of the nave." The solemnity of the interior at Escomb is heightened by the fact that the component parts of the arch are highly crafted: "the semicircular arch is itself formed of well-cut voussoirs with radial joints" (Figure 12).[52] The arch fits beautifully into the interior space of the church, yet it was not built for use at Escomb. If anything, the church was more likely to have been built around this arch that was taken entire from a Roman building, most probably from the nearby fort at Vinovia, or Binchester.[53] Whether the builders at Escomb planned the church around this piece of spolia, or set it within their preestablished design, the arch is unquestionably the defining architectural element of the building's interior.

For anyone standing in the nave, the arch directs attention toward the sacred liturgical space within the chancel; it focuses the vision of worshippers as they look toward the altar. It also, in enforcing that line of vision, distinguishes the laity from the clergy. Any arch set between nave and chancel would have had this effect, regardless of whether it was built by Romans or Anglo-Saxons, whether it was elegant or crude in its workmanship. The point re-

Figure 11: St. John's Church, Escomb, interior arch.

Figure 12: St. John's Church, Escomb, detail of interior arch.

mains, however, that the arch at Escomb was Roman built and thus introduced a historical dimension into the interior of the church: it announces that
the faith by which an Anglo-Saxon might gain salvation was introduced into
the island by missionaries from Rome. Within that church building, the human progress toward the holy is demarcated by this Roman arch, and thus the
interior of the church as a whole can be read as recording a form of historical
allegory. At Escomb, as at Jarrow, the historical syncretism of the church
building as being both Roman and English was made plausible, in fact, could
only be interpreted, through the colonial past of the island.

Yet, the skeptic asks, is this reading of the arch at Escomb, our postcolonial
take early in the twenty-first century, a playing with historical materials in an
act of interpretive bricolage? Would any Anglo-Saxon have thought of the
church interior at Escomb in this historical way? Would he or she have done
more than gaze at its beauty and register its solemnity within the church? We
can never know, but certain probabilities might be registered in favor of the
historical reading I have proposed. First, the artistry by which the church and
the arch as a whole were brought together suggests that the builders of Escomb were alive to the beauty and significance of the arch. Having transported
it from a ruined Roman site, they would have known of its provenance. The

skill and style with which the arch has been reconstructed suggests direct familiarity with its privileged status as spolia and some awareness of its historical significance. Second, the textual evidence presented earlier in this chapter suggests that Anglo-Saxons, whether they used Latin or Old English, were interested in the origin of building stones and in the ways they demarcated historical periods. For them, stones found amid derelict or ruined Roman sites were not simply blocks of rock without history, inert masses with no story to tell. Third, and perhaps most telling, there is no reason to assume that those who lived during the period were somehow less alert to the complications of their own history than we privilege ourselves as being some twelve hundred years later.

The material fabric of the church at Escomb is an intact space that invites one to think on the shifting patterns of history from the time of Roman imperialism to the triumph of Anglo-Saxon Christianity. Nor is that invitation reserved simply for inquiries about the distant past. It holds as well for the visitor who travels to Escomb today. Located as it is amid the old coal-mining regions of County Durham, Escomb does not have a setting of rural beauty like that of Odda's Chapel at Deerhurst. Instead, St. John's at Escomb now sits within the walls of a circular churchyard that is in turn surrounded by modern council estates. Guidebooks lament this intrusion of the modern on the Anglo-Saxon, and those who had seen Escomb told me before my visit to expect the worst, as if the church were situated in the middle of some urban wasteland straight out of Gildas's bloodstained pages. Such pastoral responses to the present are all too easy to assume and all too reductive, as one realizes at Escomb after reading that the key to the church can be found hanging on a hook at one of those very same council houses. One understands, that is, that the present and the past are set together in Escomb and in that way preserve each other's claims on our attention. In an analogous way, I suspect, an Anglo-Saxon worshipping at Escomb could not have thought about the present moment in Englalond without considering that the arch inside the church was a remnant of a past that had been artfully assimilated rather than discarded as rubble on the land.

One fact shadows all that can be written about postcolonial Anglo-Saxon England. After the withdrawal of Roman troops in 410, the population of the country declined sharply and did not return to a comparable level until sometime well after the Norman Conquest. Historians argue about the precise numbers for the island's population throughout the period—whether for pre-410, 800, or 1200, to choose regular intervals—but most agree on a general trend of sharp population loss that was not reversed for many centuries.[54] This decline in population, combined with the evident collapse of a money economy and regular trade networks, made for substantial changes in the social and economic lives of those who lived in Britain. In this less populated landscape, some land (especially that which was marginal) may have been left untilled as the need for agricultural produce declined along with the available humanpower.[55] The landscape may have grown quieter as fewer people and domestic animals moved across it, as fewer fields were cultivated, and as fewer trees were chopped down or otherwise harvested for fuel and building materials. The shrinking of cultivated land and the decreased need for timber products meant that woodlands "seem to have advanced during the period of instability and economic decline following the collapse of Roman rule."[56] The psychological effects that came with witnessing the reversion of arable land to woodland after 410 are perhaps beyond our ability to diagnose, but that same phenomenon carried with it a sense of historical regression that is, as I have argued, discernible in texts.

While there is no compelling evidence to characterize the period after 410 in Britain as cataclysmic or apocalyptic, there are reasons to imagine that it was often difficult in terms of material circumstances and sometimes eerily melancholy.[57] A comparable sense of melancholy appears in Old English poetry, even in those works that seem to have no thematic relation to the aftereffects of Roman colonization, such as *Beowulf*.[58] *Melancholy* may be too resonant with the sentiments of a later and perhaps, in this context, anachronistic Old English poetic tradition to be useful for describing the decades immediately after 410. Richard Muir has described the withdrawal of the legions as initiating a "prolonged phase of introspection and localism," a formulation that neatly registers both the psychological and economic consequences of that political act.[59] That phase was brought to closure, in a move that complicates any simplistic application of postcolonial theory to Anglo-Saxon England, by the reconnection of the island to Rome through the agency of Christian missionaries.

What might it have meant to live in this postcolonial world, to occupy a less densely populated landscape that was dotted with buildings and other structures that had lost some or all of their original functions?[60] This question would no doubt require different kinds of answers depending on when one lived in the postcolonial years. Stone spolia would have taken on different uses and resonances for someone like Bede living in a reasonably peaceful and Christianized area of Englalond than they would have for a Briton who had fought at Mount Badon and been momentarily heartened by that short-lived victory over the barbaric Saxons. These kinds of questions are necessary as well for our own postcolonial time, and asking them may help us avoid some of the too-easy binaries of a rigid postcolonial theory.

The case of Anglo-Saxon England establishes, for example, that the relations between metropole and colony, center and periphery, cannot be set in a single unchanging relation of the powerful and the dispossessed. Nor can the metropole itself be seen as fixed and unchanging. If Rome was the capital of Anglo-Saxon England, as I explore in the following chapter, it became so in an ecclesiastical and spiritual fashion that was radically different from its role as imperial capital of the province of Britannia, and yet that also depended on its past status. The fact that the geography between Rome and that island, known variously as Britannia, Albion, and England, remained constant did not mean that the relations of political, economic, and religious power were similarly constant. In that regard, we may say that geography enabled relations between Rome and England, but it alone did not determine their precise nature.

The example of postcolonial Anglo-Saxon England also suggests that politics and the relations of power are not always made visible through ideology, indigenous resistance movements, or widely circulated manifestoes. Sometimes the evidence for politics and the relations of power takes very different forms, such as stones and the narrative purposes to which they can be put by writers. Meditating on the later medieval landscape of the troubadour poets, W. S. Merwin has said: "The moving of stones is the course of history, and of rubble and forgetting."[61] Sometimes the historical void is that rubble and all that lies forgotten amid its stones. At other times, that stonework seems more comprehensible as part of a familiar landscape that people traverse, farm, timber, and live upon. Landscape is, in this case, not simply the work of nature; it is also the product of the human hands that have altered it and the eyes that have looked over it. To speak of the postcolonial landscape of Anglo-Saxon England is thus to turn to historical purposes the assertion of James Corner that "landscape is less a quantifiable object than it is an *idea,* a cultural way of seeing, and as such it remains open to interpretation, design and transformation."[62]

In a society where literacy in either Old English or Latin was an unusual skill, the historical record could not exist entirely in written form: oral accounts both reliable and fabulous survived, as we know from Bede's preface to the *Ecclesiastical History,* and monumental accounts in the form of earthworks, stone structures, and ruins on the landscape also survived. The material past of Roman rule survived and provided an alternative version to the written record that is perhaps sometimes more accessible. In doing so, the historical landscape also had a larger cultural function that transcended mere curiosity or antiquarianism. Writing of the landscape, W. G. Hoskins has said that the Anglo-Saxons had "no eye for scenery, any more than other hardworking farmers of later centuries."[63] One can wonder if farmers, Anglo-Saxon or otherwise, may have appreciated landscape in ways that were not as much scenic as they were experiential: they knew the land and its capacity to produce crops and sustain livestock; they knew what had been built on it; they knew who crossed it. In that regard, the built landscape could be registered, if not appreciated, by those who might have had little interest in the picturesque. To advance this claim, one might consider an observation by D. W. Meinig in *The Interpretation of Ordinary Landscapes:* "Every mature nation has its symbolic landscapes. They are part of the iconography of nationhood, part of the shared set of ideas and memories and feelings which bind a people together."[64] The landscape of Anglo-Saxon England, as it held Roman ruins and also spolia turned to new purposes, was a way of deciphering the postcolonial void. The Romans — and they had indeed been giants — were gone from the island, although their buildings survived to be recycled and their language to be turned to the purposes of Christian learning and salvation. And there remained the fact of Rome herself, the city that did not disappear but rather underwent profound alteration within its old setting of stone-built buildings.

4

Rome as Capital of Anglo-Saxon England

As it shifted from being an imperial to a religious center, Rome emerged for the Anglo-Saxons as more than a political memory or trace on the landscape. As they became adherents of the Roman church, with its liturgical practices and customs for dating Easter, the English took on as well a more contemporaneous relation to the city. No longer the capital of a past empire that had left its roads and walls and language on the topography of Britannia, papal Rome became a source of missionary activity, doctrinal teaching, ecclesiastical authority, manuscripts both sacred and secular, as well as a destination for pilgrims. It had for the Anglo-Saxons the vitality of a major urban center and so became a site on their contemporary map.

That events in Rome could read something like late-breaking news for the Anglo-Saxons can still be felt from the *Chronicle* entry for the year 816:

> Her Stephanus papa forðferde, 7 æfter him wæs Paschalis to papan gehalgod. 7 þy ilcan geare forbarn Angelcynnes scole.

> In this year, Pope Stephen died and after him Paschal was ordained as pope. And in that same year the hostel of the English people burned down.[1]

This passage is the complete entry in the C Text for that year: nothing else that happened anywhere in the known world, including England, compelled this chronicler's attention.[2] As it notes the death of one pope and the ordination of his successor, the opening sentence of this entry reads like many others in the *Chronicle*. Popes died with predictable regularity, and for reasons both religious and political, it was necessary to record the end of one's term and the start of the next's. Every expression of this sequence would remind English readers of the *Chronicle* that Rome was the seat of western Christendom precisely because the spiritual authority of the papacy endured beyond any of its human incumbents. The substance of the second sentence — "ond þy ilcan geare forbarn Angelcynnes scole" — is unusual within the *Chronicle*, however, and reveals something important about the English connection to Rome. *Scolu* can be translated variously as "school" or "quarter" or "hostel"; here it designates the well-known institution for English pilgrims in Rome that was founded originally in the late eighth century.[3]

Members of the *gens Anglorum* resident in Rome had, according to the *Vita Paschalis* in the *Liber pontificalis,* the habit of describing this scolu as a "burh" in their own tongue ("quae in eorum lingua burgus dicitur").[4] Given that *burh* in Old English typically designates a fortified site or stronghold — some form of refuge — the scolu of the 816 entry evidently refers to a hostel where the *Angelcynn* could lodge safely while in Rome, whether there as students, pilgrims, or visiting ecclesiastical dignitaries. Pope Paschal contributed generously to the rebuilding of this scolu or burh after the fire of 816, an additional reason if any were needed for remembering his ordination in the *Chronicle*'s entry for that year. The 816 *Chronicle* entry is, to stress the obvious, entirely about Rome, about popes and a scolu or burh for pilgrims visiting that city. These references to the center of Christendom demonstrate how fully the compilers of this authoritative English record of events established their sense of cultural identity through reference to Rome. To invert the idiom of a later century, they were not "Little Englanders" whose range of vision ended abruptly on the near shore of the Channel.

As is customary in the *Chronicle*, the 816 entry does not announce the necessary connection between its contents and the island, but it would certainly have been apparent to an alert contemporary. The text refers to the burning of the "Angelcynnes scolu," a fact that would have been of significance chiefly to members of that group, and it does so in Old English rather than Latin, a practice that would have limited its currency among Christian readers belonging to other linguistic or ethnic groups. The language of this passage itself emphasizes the significance of the event to the audience of the *Chronicle*. More subtle, but no less telling in this regard, is that the entry opens with *her*. This Old English word is conventionally translated as "in this year" because it refers to the "here" defined by the specific location of an entry on the manuscript page, its site on the vellum leaf, but the word also carries a larger locative inflection that makes the events recorded within a given entry relevant to the here of England.[5] That this particular entry notes the burning of a hostel for English pilgrims articulates a very specific connection between the island and Rome, because such travelers would have been a common type of Anglo-Saxon, perhaps *the* most common type, to find their way to the city.

This detail about the scolu suggests that Rome shaped the Anglo-Saxon imagination as much by ordinary events — fire being no surprise in the early medieval world — as by large symbolic actions or canonical texts. That a site in Rome could be designated with a feature of the Anglo-Saxon homeland — a burh — has had consequences for the Holy City to the current day. As Wilhelm Levison asked some years ago, "How many Englishmen who pass the Borgo Santo Spirito, walking from the Ponte Sant' Angelo to St. Peter's, are aware that they are crossing a district which was originally an English 'borough'?"[6] This instance of unlikelihood — of an Old English word becoming Latinized and then Italianized — suggests that the relations between Anglo-Saxon England and Rome were as much a matter of cultural proximity as of geographical distance: the places may have been far apart, but the people could sometimes be very close. As Levison's enduring book on England and the Continent demonstrates, an émigré German scholar lecturing at Oxford in 1943 was particularly well situated to appreciate the complexities of *burh* becoming *borgo*. His own experience of displacement allowed him to recognize the twists, both linguistic and historic, that have long marked the process of influence between England and the Continent, and that have made it more than a one-way street heading north across the Alps.

The simple linguistic twist of *burh* to *borgo* reminds us that English pilgrims went to Rome in a year such as 816 because of its great sanctity within their own insular history. Their journey covered terrain that had been crossed and recrossed for centuries by those who looked northwest from Rome to the island. The two great Anglo-Saxon works of history — the *Chronicle* and Bede's *Ecclesiastical History of the English People* — are deeply implicated in Roman events but also, and more influentially, in what one can call a Roman vision for reading the map of the world.[7] In the early sections of each, England has little independent history apart from that of Rome, as is seen most obviously in the first entry of the A Version of the *Chronicle*, which opens not with a reference to the island but with one to Rome:

> Ær Cristes geflæscnesse .lx. wintra. Gaius Iulius se Casere ærest Romana Breton lond gesohte. 7 Brettas mid gefeohte cnysede. 7 hie ofer swiþde, swa þeah ne meahte þær rice gewinnan.

> Sixty years before Christ's Incarnation, Gaius Julius, the first emperor of the Romans, visited the land of the Britons. He defeated the British in battle and overcame them, though he could not establish a kingdom there.[8]

In the unfolding teleology of the *Chronicle,* the insular history of the Anglo-Saxons begins centuries before any of their tribal ancestors actually or mythically migrated from Germania; indeed, their history begins when Rome encountered that same island at a time when the ancestors of the Anglo-Saxons were resident in their continental homelands. As this entry in the *Chronicle* suggests, there was never a single Anglo-Saxon sense of place determined entirely by the geography of the island; rather, there were many such senses from the start, and they were fixed on locations that included some far beyond the Channel. The historiographic tradition of the Anglo-Saxons was never limited to the purely insular but instead always looked past the territorial limits of Britannia, or Englalond. The Anglo-Saxons were, in other words, aware of the larger world, both through their own migratory experience as well as through their acquired textual tradition. This sense of a larger geographical scope is immediately apparent in the early sections of the *Anglo-Saxon Chronicle.* Although written retrospectively in the late eighth century, most of them bear the mark of a Roman legacy. For example, the entry for A.D. 1 notes first that the emperor Octavian ruled for fifty-six years and only then adds that Jesus Christ was born in this year; the entry for A.D. 2 records the persecutions practiced by Herod in the eastern regions of the empire; that for A.D. 16 relates that Tiberius became emperor; and so on. This interweaving, throughout the early annals of this Anglo-Saxon record, of events in imperial Rome and the Holy Land sets into place the factors that will come over the centuries to create a sense of historical geography in England. Necessarily, these events reveal a significant line of connection between Britannia and Englalond in the northwest and the Holy Land in the southeast, a line that runs through Rome. This Anglo-Saxon mapping of Christian history is not unique to the *Chronicle* but can also be found, as I argue below, in a very different work such as Cynewulf's *Elene.* Sometimes the best way to find England on the map was to trace the route from there to Rome and points beyond.

This sense of geography was not neutral in its premises or scientific in its methods. It did the necessary work of religious and cultural interpretation by sacralizing and historicizing places. Events in England belonged to a larger patterning of history that in turn allowed for some measure of periodization. Not only could events from the past be set in different places, they could therefore also be set in different moments. This interpretive geography had its origins in a Roman vision of the world, as contained most conveniently for later generations in Pliny's encyclopedic *Natural History;* in time, it was absorbed into Anglo-Saxon culture, most memorably through the opening sentences of Bede's *Ecclesiastical History.* This highly influential historian of the Angelcynn located his people on a map of the world that he had learned from reading Roman writers and thereby gave them a sense of geographical identity that always acknowledged the centrality of Rome. As J. M. Wallace-Hadrill has observed of the work's exemplary force: "The *Historia* is a cry to Northumbrians, and to all Englishmen, to weigh the moral lessons of their past in the light of the works of Rome."[9] Bede's sense of geographical history, of narrative deployed through place, must be read as the inescapable, if belated, legacy of Roman empire-building. His knowledge of the world was tied directly to the sense of living on a distant and isolated island that he derived from his reading of Roman geographers. This intellectual tradition reached Bede partly through Pliny and partly through various Christian writers, most notably Isidore of Seville and Gildas.[10] The influence of Bede's reading appears very explicitly at the start of the *Ecclesiastical History:*

> Brittania Oceani insula, cui quondam Albion nomen fuit, inter septentrionem et occidentem locata est, Germaniae Galliae Hispaniae, maximis Europae partibus, multo interuallo aduersa.

> Britain, once called Albion, is an island of the ocean and lies to the north-west, being opposite Germany, Gaul, and Spain, which form the greater part of Europe, though at a considerable distance from them.[11]

Placing the island of Britain in the northwest — rather than referring to Rome as standing to the southeast — follows from the practice of Roman writers who used the vantage of their capital city to orient themselves in the world.

Bede looks at his homeland not as the center of the world, as is so often the case with nationalist or protonationalist writers, but as the far periphery of a region mapped from Rome.[12] The Rome that he invokes for this purpose is at once the capital of the old empire, as represented by a figure like Pliny, who was both natural historian and admiral of the fleet, and also the center of Christendom, as proclaimed by the presence of the papacy. Bede was native to an island that had been a province of the empire and that was also, in more recent memory, a converted region within Christendom; he thus understood fully that the complex history of his island had been shaped by centuries of decisions made in Rome.

Bede's geography was more than a purely scientific concern relating to the points of the compass.[13] For the tradition that shaped his work by portraying Britain-Albion-England as remote implied consequently that it was less than civilized. For a Roman pagan like Pliny, this remoteness was a political matter because the island was the far northwestern frontier of the *imperium;* for a Christian writer like Isidore of Seville, or more especially Gildas, this remoteness became a measure of spiritual isolation and deprivation. The classic and frequently quoted statement of this sacralized geography appears in Gildas's *Ruin of Britain* as it relates the initial conversion of the British during the reign of Tiberius. Reading his account one must struggle to remember that he was British rather than Roman, so fully had he internalized the political geography and accompanying ideology of a writer like Pliny. His language might almost suggest that he had turned against his British compatriots to identify himself with the Romans were it not that his belief and affiliation rested on a Christianity shared by both Romans and Britons:

> Interea glaciali frigore rigenti insulae et velut longiore terrarum secessu soli visibili non proximae verus ille non de firmamento solum temporali sed de summa etiam caelorum arce tempora cuncta excedente universo orbi praefulgidum sui coruscum ostendens . . . radios suos primum indulget, id est sua praecepta, Christus.

> Meanwhile, to an island numb with chill ice and far removed, as in a remote nook of the world, from the visible sun, Christ made a present of his rays (that is, his precepts), Christ the true sun, which shows its dazzling brilliance to the entire earth, not from the temporal firmament merely, but from the highest citadel of heaven, that goes beyond all time.[14]

In these sentences, Gildas translates the fact of geographical distance into a condition of spiritual frigidity that can only be warmed by Christ's rays.[15] In Gildas's sentences, Christ is by design placed not in any fixed location on earth but rather rules from Heaven. Anglo-Saxon writers who lived in the years after 597 knew that the earthly agent of their renewed conversion and potential salvation — their spiritual warming, to use Gildas's trope — was Pope Gregory the Great. For that reason alone, Rome was a city to be venerated.

That Bede narrates his *History* through the terms of Roman geography might seem yet another instance of the colonized subject accepting the perspective of the imperial center, that is, of the peripheral figure accepting the remote location or status dismissively assigned to him by the agents of a powerful metropole. If there is a certain self-evident logic to this argument, that Bede in remote Northumbria accepted the hegemony of Rome, there is a historical factor that complicates any formulaic use of postcolonial theory to read his condition.[16] As he completed the *Ecclesiastical History of the English People,* Bede knew that he was writing the history of missionary conversions, an action that strikingly reverses our formulaic understanding of center and periphery. Being a missionary in heathen lands, on the political and religious periphery, meant becoming central to the dynamic of the Christian faith and emulating the most honored of human exempla in Christian history, the original apostles who ventured across the world to spread the faith, as in Cynewulf's *Fates of the*

Apostles. By contrast, remaining at the center of Christendom, in Rome, was to risk becoming marginal to the great enterprise of missionary conversion unless, like Gregory the Great, one actively promoted that distant work. A model of capital and periphery was very much the rhetorical paradigm favored by Anglo-Saxons for narrating the missionary conversions of northwestern Europe, even if it may not be entirely adequate today for understanding their historical actualities.

The relation between the periphery and the center in a missionary or apostolic church is realized brilliantly by Bede in his *History* through the figure of Pope Gregory. As the dominant figure of Books I and II of the *History,* Gregory's life story offers a means by which to reconcile within missionary history the seemingly contradictory terms of center and periphery. For he had wished, before becoming pope, to dedicate himself to the active conversion of the Anglo-Saxons. As Bede relates the story, Gregory was prevented from fulfilling his desire by the citizens of Rome, who did not wish him to journey so far from the city: "non tamen ciues Romani [*scil*. concedere uoluerunt], ut tam longe ab urbe secederet."[17] Thus when he became pope, Gregory set about to achieve the conversion of the Anglo-Saxons by sending Augustine of Canterbury and his fellow monks to the island. What Gregory could not do himself, he had others do, and in that way he testifies in Bede's *History* to the institutional authority and centrality of the papacy in Rome.[18] For this episode demonstrates that the power of a capital lies in its ability to reach the far edges of its territory and there work its will—whether political, religious, or some combination of the two—through its chosen agents.[19] The distance of its reach is the measure of the center's power. That measure of power, as it is registered and accepted on the periphery, comes to influence its sense of place: it always acknowledges that the center is elsewhere. And yet in acknowledging that Rome was a powerful center, the Anglo-Saxons did not thereby relegate themselves to some abject sense of the marginal. There was no self-contempt, I think, in their recognition of themselves as peripheral precisely because it gave them a valuable role in writing the missionary map of northern Europe. To be situated there allowed them to discover their destined work in Christendom.

Bede is not interested simply, one must add, in the abstract relations of power between apostolic Rome and converted England. He is also deeply fascinated with the mechanisms of power, with the techniques of accommodation that allowed Gregory to close the 900 miles between the two places. This fascination explains Bede's practice of including in the *History* numerous letters sent by Gregory to Augustine after he left Rome. These letters, the so-called *Libellus responsionum,* fill much of the first book of the *History* and are customarily interpreted as forming a manual for missionary work.[20] So, no doubt, they are because they offer pragmatic advice on all sorts of difficulties faced by Augustine. Some of Augustine's questions for Gregory concerned matters of clerical life, such as the living arrangements of bishop and clergy, or of marriage law as it concerns the permissible degrees of kindred, or of relations between bishops in Britain and Gaul. These kinds of issues reflect, at least in part, the missionary enterprise of Augustine and his companions as they worked in a strange land without established ecclesiastical arrangements and policies.[21]

Augustine framed other questions far more specifically around the gendered bodies of the Anglo-Saxons, particularly of women. These suggest vividly that his anxieties and uncertainties about the place of women in the church had everything to do with his perception of having been dispatched to a peripheral culture. As is evident from Gregory's comments in the longest section of the *Libellus responsionum*, Augustine had asked him for direction about such matters as the baptism of a pregnant woman, or the interval before a new mother might enter a church after giving birth or before her husband might have intercourse with her, or whether a menstruating woman might enter a church.[22] None of these questions, one must note, pertained only to England in the first days of conversion. Women throughout Christendom had babies, menstruated, required baptism, were sexually desired by their husbands. Augustine was, perhaps unsurprisingly, not certain about the approved customs for handling these matters, especially those relating to women's sexuality and bodies, for he had been prior of the monastery of St. Andrew in Rome before setting out on his mission and thus was not accustomed to matters relating to the laity, especially to women. He had been isolated from women while living at the center of Christendom, a condition that was possible because Rome had long been converted and monastic life there was conventionally regulated.

For a missionary on the periphery of Christendom, however, all was different. Augustine could not withdraw to a male world of monks bound together by shared practices. He had instead to face the uncertainty of a life lived without accepted rules and full of challenges to his limited experience of the world. Not the least of these challenges was what to make of women as they converted and practiced the faith and lived very much within their bodies. No doubt Augustine learned much from working among the Anglo-Saxons that he would never have known had he stayed in his monastery in Rome. In the conventional account of conversion work, it is the missionary who is said to bring enlightenment. That such must often have been the case should not, however, prevent one from considering that a missionary like Augustine must also have learned much as he proselytized in a distant and strange land. Whatever questions Augustine may have asked about women while he was isolated on the island of Britain, Gregory could answer from the seat of the papacy. For his letters also stand, when read from his perspective at the center, as clear evidence of Rome's ability to determine practices in England. The issues that troubled Augustine, especially those about women and their seemingly unruly bodies, had been settled in Rome. Thus Gregory tells Augustine that a pregnant woman may be baptized and certainly should be if she or her newly delivered baby is at risk of death; a new mother may enter a church immediately after giving birth if she wishes to give thanks to God; a husband should wait until the child is weaned before resuming sexual relations with his wife; and a woman may enter a church and even receive Holy Communion while menstruating because this "natural overflowing cannot be reckoned a crime."[23] There are no hesitations or equivocations in Gregory's responses: he speaks with all of the power bestowed on him by his papal office. If there are matters of uncertainty along the periphery where Christianity has yet to be fixed in place, there are also definitive answers that emanate from the center.

These letters stand, when read from an insular perspective, as clear evidence of Rome's ability to set the course of events in England.[24] The presence of these letters in the *History* established a model for the future development of the Anglo-Saxon church in its relation to Rome and came to influence the practices of later Anglo-Saxon missionaries, like Boniface, who worked on the continent.[25] For anyone who read Bede's *History* later in the period, perhaps during the reign of King Alfred, these letters would have seemed to look southward to the authority of Rome and eastward to the region of missionary vocation in the Germanic homelands. For such a reader, interpreting Bede's narrative with historical retrospect, Gregory and Boniface would have been joined as exemplary figures in common cause through the conversion history of the Anglo-Saxons. Out of such joinings came a geographical triangulation of Rome, Germania, and England.[26] Through that self-identification a kind of geographical self-location emerged: the region once newly converted by Roman missionaries now became a site from which English missionaries could seek out a further periphery. The center remains Rome, but all else changes to accommodate the progress of ecclesiastical expansionism.

This vision of Rome as driving the missionary dynamic of western Christendom finds a particularly native expression in Cynewulf's *Fates of the Apostles*. The speaker of the poem explains that he has traveled far and wide to gather the stories of the twelve saints and then solicits the prayers of his English audience for his own salvation so that he can make the final journey to his heavenly home. He begins his catalogue of exemplary lives, or more accurately, deaths, with Peter and Paul in Rome:

> Lof wide sprang,
> miht ond mærðo,   ofer middangeard,
> þeodnes þegna,   þrym unlytel.
> Halgan heape   hlyt wisode
> þær hie dryhtnes æ   deman sceoldon,
> reccan fore rincum.   Sume on Romebyrig,
> frame, fyrdhwate,   feorh ofgefon
> þurg Nerones   nearwe searwe,
> Petrus ond Paulus.   Is se apostolhad
> wide geweorðod   ofer werþeoda!

The fame, the might and the glory of the lord's servants spread widely over the earth, as well as their no small fame. Providence directed the holy band to where they had to declare the law of God, explain it before men. Certain brave and warlike men, Peter and Paul, yielded up their lives in Rome through the oppressive treachery of Nero. That apostleship is widely honored among nations. (ll. 6a–15)[27]

Once he has centered the exemplary figures of Peter and Paul in Rome, the speaker can expand his catalogue of apostles outward through Greece and beyond to the Holy Land, Asia, and finally to Africa. After this mapping of the twelve original apostles, he finishes his task by bringing the burden of his poem home to England.[28] He controls the geographical and missionary momentum of the poem by speaking of himself in English and beseeching prayers on his behalf from an English audience that alone in Christendom could decipher his enigmatic runic signature (ll. 88–106).

Through the localizing power of the linguistic vernacular, especially as it includes this signature, Cynewulf adds an English coda to the apostolic geography of the first Christian missionaries: their originary work had long been completed in Rome and other regions named in the Gospels but much remained to be done in the north and northwest of Europe. Through the force of exempla, the poem's speaker imaginatively extends the missionary travels of Christ's companions to England. His catalogue of apostles must end with the linguistic community of the Anglo-Saxons if it is to achieve its desired end of leading the audience to heavenly salvation. But before making that geographical leap homeward it must begin as it does in Rome.

Thinking of Rome as the capital of Anglo-Saxon England is far easier if we use the term in its etymological sense as the head (*caput*) city of a culture rather than as the central political city of a nation-state.[29] Rome is the capital of Anglo-Saxon England, in my argument, by analogy with Walter Benjamin's description of Paris as the capital of the nineteenth century. In the two Exposés (written in 1935 and 1939) that open his *Arcades Project*, Benjamin proposes a set of conditions — linguistic, literary, political, architectural, material — that made Paris the capital of an epoch without regard to the boundaries found on a map.[30] These conditions, as they involved the use of prestige materials such as iron for buildings and new commercial enterprises such as department stores, were Benjamin's markers of modernity in nineteenth-century Europe. As such, they cannot easily be translated back to the eighth or eleventh century in order to describe Rome's relation to England, though that presence of stone buildings would not have lessened its status as a capital for visitors. Benjamin's deft reworking of the fixed binary of capital/nation into the figurative pairing of capital/century offers a precedent for reimagining the binary of capital/nation so that it can refer to places that were hundreds of miles apart and not joined in any explicit political sense. Rome had been the capital of the island while it was still Britannia within the empire and retained, at least in the aura of memory, something of that position even after the last legions were withdrawn. But that political aura, even if it were still possible for us to locate its presence in extant works from the culture, would most likely read as a kind of subtext to Rome's emergent, postimperial status as a religious capital during the period. A text like the *Libellus responsionum* rests upon, to put it simply, the accepted geography of power between Rome and England.

If Jerusalem stood at the center of the earth in Bede's cosmology, as it did for most of his contemporaries, Rome figured in his historical imagination as capital city when he engaged with the history and current state of the English church and people, as he learned of them from living informants. Jerusalem appears but twice in the *Ecclesiastical History,* and in each case it is as the setting for events of the early Church, especially in Book V where Bede subsumes into his text large sections of Adomnan's account of the Holy Land.[31] By contrast, the felt presence of Rome as the great capital registers throughout the *History,* especially in its early books and then again toward its conclusion, as Bede relates pilgrimages made there by the English.[32] The distinction between these two cities needs to be clarified and maintained: Jerusalem may have been the center of the world for Bede within the abstract cosmology of the universal church, but Rome was the capital of England within the political and conversion history of the Anglo-Saxons.

In arguing for Paris as capital of the nineteenth century, Benjamin offers an epigrammatic observation that resonates with this description of Rome as the capital of Anglo-Saxon England: "World exhibitions are places of pilgrimage to the commodity fetish."[33] As department stores and arcades proliferated, as an abundance of consumer goods became available, there arose a further phenomenon: huge international exhibitions displaying — even fetishizing — new goods and products were organized to draw visitors from all over the world. Early in the twenty-first century, one might paraphrase Benjamin's epigram by replacing "international exhibitions" with "shopping malls," but his point remains the same: such places draw people from everywhere as consumers or pilgrims or tourists. If the descriptive term for this kind of visitor changes, the power of a site to attract them from afar indicates that it serves the function of capital. A place takes on the role at least in part because it sets travelers in motion; it may itself be immobile, but it must attract people from elsewhere in its own territories and even beyond. The relation between capital and outlying territories works in two directions, though rarely in a precisely reciprocal balance.

Benjamin's formulation of the city as a locus of cultural capital, as a source of ideas that become transformative and vital, can help us better understand the relation between Rome and Anglo-Saxon England. For what was transformative and vital in the north and northwest of Europe in the eighth or eleventh century was Christianity. It was the idea that most fully engaged the intellectual and spiritual energies of the continent just as an incipient modernity did so with the energies of the nineteenth century. And in each case, that sense of the new and vital was seen as having its source in a very specific place: Rome or Paris. If Rome was the center from which radiated ecclesiastical authority over matters of doctrine and practice, it was also the source for much of the material culture of the English Church, as can been seen most famously from the frequent journeys between Rome and Northumbria made by Benedict Biscop to gather books, liturgical objects, and the like for his monastery in the far north of England.[34]

To speak of the intellectual and spiritual capital of Anglo-Saxon England is largely to identify the legacy of Rome. Even a quick glimpse through a standard reference source such as Helmut Gneuss's *Handlist of Anglo-Saxon Manuscripts* illustrates the range of Latin works known in England.[35] A less systematic but certainly more vivid illustration of Rome's centrality comes from the works listed by King Alfred as most necessary for men to know and thus as most necessary to be translated into the vernacular. Of these Latin books only a few, such as the Psalms and Augustine's *Soliloquies,* had no immediate thematic connection with Rome as the historical center of empire. Others included in Alfred's translation program had explicit authorial connections with Rome as capital city, whether they were written by Boethius, the high-ranking Roman administrator who fell out with the emperor Theodoric (*The Consolation of Philosophy*), or by Gregory, one of the greatest of the city's pontiffs and its loyal son (*Pastoral Care* and *Dialogues*).[36] Other works selected by Alfred for translation took Rome as historical subject, whether by Orosius, to rebut charges that the conversion to Christianity had led to the fall of the city

(*History against the Pagans*), or by Bede, to locate the conversion history of his people (*Ecclesiastical History*). The Latinity of these works would also have underscored the intellectual preeminence of Rome, for Latin was the language of the capital and required translation into the language of the periphery. Alfred would not have spoken of this selected group of works as modern in the way that Benjamin used that term for a writer such as Baudelaire, but we can see that his translation project was in fact a forced program of spiritual modernization that sought to reconnect the poorly educated and peripheral Anglo-Saxons to the center of Christian belief and culture.

The most encompassing historical work produced by the Alfredian program, the Old English version of Orosius's *History against the Pagans,* is at once a translation, an expanded paraphrase, and a remapping of the original Latin text. A work originally written at the behest of St. Augustine of Hippo to counter charges that the abandonment of the old gods in favor of Christianity had led to the sack of Rome becomes, in this large process of cultural adaptation, a celebration of the pax Romana and the spread of the true faith. In this process, as Dorothy Whitelock has shown, the Anglo-Saxon translator "retains the thread of expansion of Rome" and in fact emphasizes the theme of empire as he found it in the original.[37] This theme of imperial Roman expansionism prepares for the spread of Christianity outwards from Rome. The shared capital city at the center of both movements yields the necessary pattern for the historical synthesis of the Old English *Orosius.*

It is thus not at all surprising that the longest passage concerning the island in the Old English version should narrate the empire's northward course to Britannia under Julius Caesar:

> Æfter þæm þe Romeburg getimbred wæs vi hunde wintra 7 lxvii, Romane gesealdon Gaiuse Iuliuse seofon legan, to þon þæt he sceolde fif winter winnan on Gallie. Æfter þæm þe he hie oferwunnen hæfde, he for on Bretanie þæt iglond 7 wið þa Brettas gefeaht 7 gefliemed wearð on þæm londe þe mon hæt Centlond. Raþe þæs he gefeaht wiþ þa Brettas [eft] on Centlonde, 7 hie wurdon gefliemede. Heora þridde gefeoht wæs neah þære ie þe mon hæt Temes, neh þæm forda mon hæt Welengaford. Æfter þæm gefeohte him eode on honde se cyning 7 þa burgware þe wæron on Cirenceastre, 7 siþþan ealle þe on þæm iglonde wæron.

> Six hundred and sixty seven winters after Rome had been built, the Romans gave seven legions to Julius Caesar so that he could campaign in Gaul for five years. After he had overcome them, he went to the island of Britain and fought against the Britons and was put to flight in the land that men call Kent. Soon afterwards he fought [again] against the Britains in Kent and they were put to flight. Their third battle was near the river that men call the Thames, near the ford that men

call Wallingford. After this battle the king and the townfolk who were in Cirencester surrendered to him, as did afterwards all those who were on the island.[38]

The references to "Centlond," or Kent, here are the translator's addition,
presumably included to add a greater geographical specificity to the passage
for an English audience.[39]

Yet even these anglicizing references cannot disturb the flow of the original
text; this passage about Britain is simply one moment in the narrative of
Caesar that then returns to Rome and political struggles there. Britain is one
frontier in the expansion of the Roman Empire, a fact made compellingly
evident by the way in which it is dated: "Æfter þæm þe Romeburg getimbred
wæs vi hunde wintra 7 lxvii," that is, 667 years after Rome was built, or
"timbered." The formula for dating events in the Old English *Orosius* from
the foundation date of Rome has something like the locative force of *her* as it
opens annals in the *Anglo-Saxon Chronicle*. The regular appearance of each
formula establishes in the relevant text the geographical scope of its reference.
The events included in *Orosius* happen in a world that understands why dates
are based on the founding of Rome, that is, in a place that acknowledges that
city as a capital. Or they occur in a world that understands the vernacular *here*
to mean both in this year in the manuscript and in the view of those who live
on the island. An Anglo-Saxon reading through the Old English *Orosius*
would thus be able to interpret it as recording a kind of cultural conversion:
the history of the world mattered as an eschatological preparation for the pax
Romana under Augustus Caesar and the birth of Christ. From that time and
place came, in turn, the religion that was transported to England.

The original intent of Orosius's *History* would not have been of immediately topical relevance in Anglo-Saxon England. From the composition of
the *Historiae adversum paganos* in the years between 410 and 420 to its
translation into English at the end of the ninth century, the course of Christianity had established a new Rome. From that city emanated a spiritual authority greater than any political power that had once been centered there. The
triumphalist vision of history had proved that Orosius was right: Christianity
endured, Rome renewed herself, the pagans who bemoaned the abandonment
of the old gods were long gone. The world had changed.

That change was not simply historical; it was also geographical. For that
same Anglo-Saxon reading the translation of Orosius would have known of a
larger European world than the one that had been colonized by Rome.[40] This
knowledge of a larger world at the north of the continent is registered un-
forgettably in the Old English *Orosius* by the accounts of Ohthere and Wulfstan devoted to Scandinavian regions and beyond. These added passages have

long been favorites of Anglo-Saxonists because they appear to be based on personal experience of sailing through the regions described and also because they are about parts of the world little noticed by Latin geographers. As personal accounts rather than textual compilations, as northern rather than Mediterranean, the voyages of Ohthere and Wulfstan have long been standard items in Anglo-Saxon readers for modern students. In a discipline often suspicious of Latin-derived texts as never quite authentically native, regardless of the fact that they were translated into the vernacular, these accounts seem to offer vivid stories of seafaring adventure. Read in isolation, Ohthere and Wulfstan's voyages are far more exciting and engaging about the map of the world than are more bookish Old English texts.

Set within the context of Orosius's larger history, however, Ohthere and Wulfstan's voyages take on a very different effect. They belong to an Anglo-Saxon map of the world, one that knows more about the distant north than did any Roman geographical treatise with its customary references to Britannia and then, more vaguely, to Ireland and Thule. But even that enlarged Anglo-Saxon map has Rome at its center and dates those events that can be dated — as Ohthere and Wulfstan's voyages cannot be — by the foundation of Rome. The Old English translation has grafted, and far from seamlessly, the matter of Ohthere and Wulfstan into an otherwise quite conventional account of the tripartite world as drawn by Roman geographers, that is, of Europe, Asia, and Africa. Thus to the map of Europe, the Anglo-Saxon translator adds Norway, Sweden, and adjoining regions with their coastlines.

Having done so, the translator returns to the more familiar map of Europe in which Greece and Italy figure prominently. His subsequent reference to the course of the Rhine as it debouches into the North Sea across from Britannia is taken from the Latin original, which, in turn, owes that piece of information to Pliny's *Natural History* or a work derived from it.[41] In this respect, the voyages of Ohthere and Wulfstan as they move northwards from England are set in the Old English *Orosius* in such a way that, once finished, they must be followed in the geographical narrative with a return to the island:

> Brittannia þæt igland, hit is norðeastlang, 7 hit is eahta hund mila lang 7 twa hund mila brad. Þonne is be suðan him on oðre healfe þæs sæs earmes Gallia Bellica, 7 on westhealfe on oþre healfe þæs sæs earmes is Ibærnia þæt igland, 7 on norðhealfe Orcadus þæt igland.

> The island of Britain extends to the northeast and is 800 miles long and 200 miles wide. To the south across the arm of the sea is Belgic Gaul, and on the west on the other side of the arm of the sea is the island of Hibernia, and on the northern part is the island of the Orcades.[42]

The translator's description of Britain's size and location is largely identical with that found in the opening sentences of Bede's *Ecclesiastical History,* though the arrangement of details follows a different order:

> Brittania Oceani insula, cui quondam Albion nomen fuit, inter septentrionem et occidentem locata est, Germaniae Galliae Hispaniae, maximis Europae partibus, multo interuallo aduersa. Quae per milia passuum DCCC in boream longa, latitudinis habet milia CC.

> Britain, once called Albion, is an island of the ocean and lies to the north-west, being opposite Germany, Gaul, and Spain, which form the greater part of Europe, though at a considerable distance from them. It extends 800 miles to the north, and is 200 miles broad.[43]

As Colgrave and Mynors point out in their note to his passage, Bede may well have taken the Latin text of Orosius's *Historiae adversum paganos* as his inspiration for this geographical opening to his *History*.[44] In this relation, Orosius's Latin *Historiae,* the Old English *Orosius,* and Bede's *History* are all followers of Pliny, as noted earlier. Each uses this geographical lore about Britain for its own specific purposes. In the case of the Old English *Orosius,* it is to map a world that has grown larger in the four centuries or so since the composition of the Latin original. It is a world that has a more distant northern periphery, one that has been described by travelers rather than writers. But that region remains peripheral, if no less fascinating, when it is set in a historical work that has Rome at its physical and temporal center. However arid that bookish geography may seem today, it had its own way of absorbing into its interpretive scheme new information about relatively uncharted places.

The historiographic and geographic uses of Rome surveyed thus far demonstrate how deeply the Anglo-Saxons were shaped by Rome's self-presentation as capital. In this way, they closed the distance and eased the isolation they felt — or were led to feel — from reading Roman texts. One might still say, for this reason, that Rome figures more as a textual than an actual city, or perhaps it figures mainly as an intertextual city in works such as the *Chronicle* or Bede's *History*. That process of rejoining England to Rome was not simply a case of transporting and translating books; it was also accomplished through the travels of pilgrims that recognized Rome as a common destination. The *Anglo-Saxon Chronicle* and Bede's *History* contain numerous references to pilgrims who made their way to Rome, ranging from aristocrats, such as the very young Alfred in 853, to ecclesiastics, such as Bishop Sigeric in 990. There were certainly other less-celebrated pilgrims, but they did not earn mention in contemporary sources. To evoke eyewitness accounts of Rome as an imperial and papal capital by Anglo-Saxons one would need texts of a sort that do not survive, if they were ever composed. More specifically, one would need extended pilgrimage accounts like those written by Egeria about the Holy Land in the fourth or fifth century or Master Gregorius about Rome in the thirteenth century (perhaps) and Margery Kempe in the fifteenth, to cite a few for which one dearly wishes there were Anglo-Saxon equivalents. In an ideal world of textual survivals, there would be at least one Anglo-Saxon account of Rome that did for the city in the ninth century what Gregorius claims to do, namely, to narrate "the wonders which once were or still are in Rome, of which the traces or the memory remain alive to this day."[45]

In the absence of Anglo-Saxon pilgrimage accounts, one can offer some sense of what eighth- or tenth-century English visitors could have seen in Rome and how they might have used that experience to think of their homeland.[46] Certain immediate impressions would likely have registered themselves on any such traveler to Rome, starting with the recognition that it was much larger in area and population than any city in England.[47] Many of its buildings, especially those that survived from the glory days of the empire, were built in stone with elegant arches and soaring domes, while most buildings in England were framed in timber and finished with wattle-and-daub.[48] Even those rare structures in England that were made of stone, almost all of which were churches, were built on a far smaller scale than was a basilica such as St. Peter's. Indeed, the difference of scale would have been an eloquent measure of what it meant to be in a capital city with a long and illustrious history of architectural construction in the service of power.

To be more precise, one might envision Anglo-Saxon pilgrims from a small church such as St. Laurence's at Bradford-on-Avon or St. John's at Escomb as they entered the basilica of St. Peter's in Rome. Determining the dimensions of an Anglo-Saxon church involves calculating the area of its various parts as they stand today or can be measured by archaeological research. Thus any calculation must be provisional and is useful in the present context only for broadly comparative purposes. Using the floor plans and figures in H. M. Taylor and Joan Taylor's authoritative *Anglo-Saxon Architecture*, one can compute the area of Bradford-on-Avon as approximately 1,135 square feet with nave walls reaching to 25 feet, and the area of Escomb as approximately 1,050 square feet.[49] These are admittedly quite small structures in their dimensions, though they would have stood more prominently on the Anglo-Saxon landscape for being built in stone. Nonetheless, they would have seemed tiny, even fragile, by comparison with St. Peter's in the Vatican as it could be seen during the period of Anglo-Saxon pilgrimages.

A very rough calculation of its size, based on the floor plans in Richard Krautheimer's *Corpus Basilicarum Christianarum Romae,* yields a figure for

St. Peter's of 663,815 square feet, a vastly larger construction than any parish church in Anglo-Saxon England.[50] Indeed, St. Peter's would have been in its surface area some six hundred times larger than Escomb or Bradford-on-Avon. Its overall size would have seemed yet larger in ways that are difficult to calculate because its walls were considerably higher than those of any English church, thus giving it a much greater interior volume. Even to a twenty-first-century American, old St. Peter's would have seemed vast because, to use our inevitable measure for such things, it would have been too large to fit within a football field. To an Anglo-Saxon visitor, its size alone would have seemed astonishing, and that response would have been, one suspects, compounded by the extraordinary range of materials used in its interior, especially the various types of marble gathered as trophies from various sites in the old Roman Empire. Entering this basilica would have been compelling evidence for Anglo-Saxon pilgrims that they had indeed arrived in a great capital city that had shaped both their political and religious history. And yet, for all that the scale was vastly different, an alert Anglo-Saxon pilgrim could have noticed that its method of stone construction and use of arches was not unfamiliar from sites in England, even if they were in ruins or had been partially quarried for their materials.

The Rome that figures in this chapter is a place of literal buildings that burn down, a site of pilgrimages that establish the route between the English Channel and the city, a seat of visionary popes that send missionaries out to do their work. As a city that Anglo-Saxons traveled to and from, Rome also determined how they looked at their own home place on the map of the world. For these reasons, Rome would likely have had greater actuality for the Anglo-Saxons than did such famous biblical cities as Jerusalem and Babylon. Or perhaps one should say, it had a greater extratextual presence for the Anglo-Saxons than did Jerusalem or, certainly, Babylon because it was a place more frequently visited. Yet there is something of a modern preference for the touristic over the readerly in this last claim, something of our own cultural prejudice that authentic knowledge of a place must be based on personal experience. The danger of applying this prejudice to early medieval Europe is that it obscures the fact that Rome's status as capital for the Anglo-Saxons was also derived in great measure from its status as a source of texts, partly in the sense of physical manuscripts brought to England but more in the sense of a culture that produced and disseminated a textual tradition by which pagan scholarship was absorbed into Christianity. Taken in that way, the notion of Rome as capital may also help us deal with the category confusion created by a too-literal joining of the words *empire* and *Anglo-Saxon England* in a single breath. For Anglo-Saxon England was certainly not an imperial province in the way Britannia had been as late as the very early fifth century. Yet if we consider the ways in which the Anglo-Saxons imagined empire, we can gain a richer sense of their vision of Rome as a capital.

The place of imperial Rome in Anglo-Saxon texts was certainly not restricted to historical prose works such as the *Chronicle* and Bede's *Ecclesiastical History*. Of the Old English poems that consider the matter of Rome, perhaps the most revelatory is Cynewulf's *Elene* because it remaps imperial history to accord with an Anglo-Saxon sense of the world. Cynewulf could, in fact, be characterized as the most notable of those Old English poets who in their work looked south toward Rome and beyond: *The Fates of the Apostles, Elene, Andreas,* and *Juliana* are all written from the vantage point of England because they are all written in the vernacular and three are signed with the poet's idiosyncratic runic signature. This combination of Old English and runic alphabet locates these four poems in Anglo-Saxon England because only there would they have stood any chance at all of finding a significant audience. Ironically and yet suitably, three of these four poems survive uniquely in a manuscript found in the monastic library of Vercelli, a regular stop on the route between Anglo-Saxon England and Rome as traced by the itinerary of Archbishop Sigeric.[51] Whatever readership the poems in this manuscript might once have had, in Vercelli, the readers would surely have been limited to Anglo-Saxons either resident there or passing through on the pilgrimage route.

Nowhere in his poems does Cynewulf's gaze from the north register the complexities of Rome and empire more suggestively than in the geographical rewritings of *Elene*. For there he presents a very Anglicized version of the decisive battle by which Constantine is converted to Christianity after witnessing the sign of the Cross.[52] This conflict that would have profound consequences for the religious life of the Roman Empire and Britain is not set in *Elene* where it was said in the sources to have occurred — at the Milvian Bridge near Rome — but instead on the far frontier along the Danube. In this location, Cynewulf can depict Constantine as the defender of the empire's northern border and victor over a formidable assortment of Germanic tribes that includes the Franks and Hugas (l. 21b) as well as others:

> Cyning wæs afyrhted,
> egsan geaclad,   siððan elþeodige,
> Huna ond Hreða   here sceawede,
> ðæt he on Romwara   rices ende
> ymb þæs wæteres stæð   werod samnode,
> mægen unrime.

The king was frightened and struck with terror when he looked at the invading army of the Huns and Hrethgoths, [and saw] that they had gathered a force by the shore of the water at the end [or edge] of the Roman kingdom, a countless number. (ll. 56b–61a)[53]

In *Elene* the making of history is placed on the northern edge of empire because Cynewulf is writing for an audience in England. A historical episode of internal strife among Romans becomes poetically in *Elene* a conflict between the forces of urban civilization and frontier barbarians.[54] Put another way, writing centuries after its end, Cynewulf sees the conversion of Rome and its empire as determined by events along its frontier in ways that yet again rewrite the conventional relations of center and periphery. Through this significant rewriting of political geography, the poem takes on a specific religious meaning that implicates Constantine's vision of the Cross into the history of northern Europe — of Franks, Hugas, Huns, and Hrethgoths along the Danube — so that it can have a kindred or figural significance for the Anglo-Saxons in England.[55]

The originary history of that vision can, through *Elene,* be located yet further in the north, because the lineage of Constantine and his mother, Elene, could readily be traced to the colonial outpost of Britain. The British origin of Constantine, the emperor who made Christianity the accepted religion of Rome, was known to the Anglo-Saxons from various sources, including Bede's *History* (I.viii). There is, as tourists to York will remember, a modern statue commemorating Constantine as both British legionnaire and Christian emperor outside the minster. Its presence there would not, I suspect, have puzzled Cynewulf, though he might have wondered about the language of the inscription. In another tradition, Elene was also said to have been born in Britain.[56] The geography of political empire and thus of Christendom is portrayed in Cynewulf's poem from the vantage of England: the setting of history is explicitly shifted northwards to connect it more closely to the England of the poem's audience and to their experience on the periphery; and the heroic figures of the poem, Constantine and Elene, can be seen as having insular origins. The decisive event that initiates the acceptance of Christianity within the Roman Empire is placed by Cynewulf very much within the conceptual territory of Anglo-Saxon history. His poem inscribes the geographical gaze of north looking south, indeed, of north relocating history to render it comprehensible within its own part of the world. One can rephrase Cynewulf's use of geographical perspective by drawing on the convention of the imperial outpost writing back to the metropole, that is, of colonies and colonized subjects speaking back to the imperial capital and thereby shifting the relation of center and periphery or, as is so often the case, of north and south.

Earthly history ends in *Elene* in the opposite quadrant of a mapped world, along its southeastern edge — the Holy Land — with the discovery of the True Cross by Elene and with the conversion of the Jews led by Cyriacus, né Judas. The poem asks its audience to trace, as it were, an approximately diagonal line between Britain, at its upper or left end, and Jerusalem, at its lower or right end. On this line, Rome serves as a pivot. It conjoins ideologically and geographically two very distant and disparate parts of the world that are alike, however, in being peripheral. Cynewulf's portrayal or, if one prefers, historical placement of Constantine bears a curious resemblance to the emperor's own presentation of self, as described by Peter Salway: "He certainly made much in later years of the origin of his rule in distant Britain, across the Ocean, and liked to dwell on the notion of a divine mission that had swept his power from the far west of the empire to its extreme east."[57]

As Cynewulf develops the poetic geography of *Elene*, Constantine comes to represent the still center of Rome, from which power emanates and to which allegiance is due. As the emperor ponders the meaning of his vision and desires to convert to Christianity (Cynewulf relates), he develops a fascination with the literal Cross upon which Christ was crucified and makes its rediscovery a primary matter of his religio-political policy. Significantly, however, he enacts this policy by remaining at the center and sending his mother, Elene, to discover the Cross and convert the Jews who have for centuries kept it hidden. If his defeat of the northern invaders fulfilled the heroically imperial role of the Roman frontier general, his decision to send Elene on this mission to the Holy Land casts him in a role analogous to that of popes sending missionaries far afield from Rome, as Gregory did with Augustine.[58]

By conscious design, Cynewulf endows Elene with a heroic presence that befits and also embodies her imperial authority. The remainder of the poem demonstrates graphically that Elene is more than capable of exercising that authority — sometimes with a ruthless intensity that tolerates no opposition and shows no mercy. She reveals in this poem a kinship with her son Constantine, at least as he was described by Gregory the Great in his letter to King Æthelberht of Kent as an exemplum of the imperial conqueror in the service of the faith.[59] Elene demands, for instance, that the Jews deliver the Cross to her, she harangues their leaders, she throws Judas into a cell without food for a week until he reveals what she wants to know about the location of the Cross — and she thereby succeeds in the mission that the emperor Constantine has entrusted to her. For not only does she uncover the True Cross, as well as the crosses of the two thieves crucified with Christ, she also locates the nails with which Christ was fastened to it. The consequent conversion of Judas to Christianity and his elevation as Cyriacus the bishop brings the Jews to the true faith and their lands into the realm of Roman Christendom. It is a triumphalist

narrative that shows no concern for the oppressive consequences of its religious imperialism. Elene fulfills her mission even more spectacularly than
Augustine in England or Boniface in Germania would succeed in theirs; but
she becomes in Cynewulf's vision as much the representative of secular Rome
as of Christianity. She is not simply a figure in religious history, a saintly
woman and mother of the emperor; she is also implicated in policies of rulership and empire building.

For the decisive moment in the poem comes when Elene, surrounded by the
newly converted Jews, speaks back to the imperial center through an act of
instruction that becomes a paradigm for aligning the spiritual truths of Christianity with the worldly concerns of political empire. After Cyriacus brings the
nails of the True Cross to Elene, she puzzles about what should be done with
them or, more precisely, how their literal form could be given a spiritual
meaning in the world. She therefore calls on an unnamed wise man to give her
advice, and he tells her:

> Þu ðas næglas hat
> þam æðelestan   eorðcyninga
> burgagendra   on his bridels don,
> meare to midlum.   Þæt manigum sceall
> geond middangeard   mære weorðan,
> þonne æt sæcce mid þy   oferswiðan mæge
> feonda gehwylcne.

Command that the noblest of earthly kings, of princes to put these nails on his
bridle as a bit for his horse. That will come to be honored among many across
the earth, since with it he will be able to conquer in battle every enemy. (ll.
1172a–78a)

To make clear that the literal will be made figurative through this process, he
adds: "Bið þæt beacen gode / halig nemned" (That sign will be called "Holy to
God"; ll. 1193b–94a). The object made of nails is at once a *midl* and a *beacen*,
a bit and a sign, that will ensure the triumph of the Christian emperor. Cynewulf narrates that Elene immediately did as she was advised and sent the sign
across the sea to her son, Constantine. Within the powerful narrative flow of
the poem, Elene's act seems the culmination of her mission: she has found the
Cross as well as the nails, she has converted the Jews, and, most astonishingly,
she has transformed a literal object into a figurative sign. Yet the terms of this
sign are carefully calibrated to matters of religion and politics, to show how
the one is to guide the other. That a bridle made from the nails of the Cross
should control the horse of the true emperor and also render him invincible
speaks to the larger meaning of the poem: the act of conversion forever alters a

people and their realm, whether it be Constantine and his fellow heathens in Rome or Judas-Cyriacus and his fellow Jews in Jerusalem. And by figural implication, the Anglo-Saxons in England. It is Elene, the woman born on the northwestern periphery and sent to the southeastern periphery, who finds the literal Cross and reveals its meaning to the center. There is in that triumph the basis for her sanctification but also a vision of a woman who is distant from the center of empire in Rome and for that very reason far from abject.

The conversion of the Jews in *Elene* is significant not simply within Christian history, for it relates to the eventual end of human time, but also within Anglo-Saxon history because of the ways in which Old English poets, especially that of *Exodus,* appropriated the Old Testament history of the Jews for their own historicist purposes. The conversion of the Jews through the efforts of *Elene* brings them into Christendom, just as the preconversion past of the migrating Germanic tribes was envisioned in the Anglo-Saxon north as having brought them into Old Testament history. Yet *Elene* is also remarkable for having its work of conversion enforced by the figure of Elene, mother of an emperor and herself a saint. That nexus of political, saintly, and maternal power resonates with the conventional gendering of Rome as female, as in Horace's lines about Rome as the "queen of cities": "Romae principis urbium / dignatur suboles inter amabiles / vatum ponere me choros."[60] There is thus a certain historical accuracy in Cynewulf's characteristic and frequently employed epithet for Elene, "cwen," as when toward the end of the poem she gathers the recently converted Jews together and urges them to maintain their faith and accept the authority of Cyriacus as their bishop (l. 1204b) who would in that office be ultimately answerable to the pontiff in Rome.[61]

Anglo-Saxon England did not become thoroughly Romanized in the centuries after its initial conversions; much remained of the native Germanic tradition even after centuries of Roman influence, despite its enormous prestige. Not least, Old English remained the vernacular of the land and was not replaced by a Romance language derived from Latin as happened in many of the old provinces of the empire. Stephanie Hollis observes acutely that "in a post-colonial age it is perhaps easier to accept that Roman-Christian culture did not succeed in permanently eradicating other cultures from the moment it came into contact with them."[62] To assert the presence of Rome as the capital of Anglo-Saxon England is not to deny that culture's enduring relation to the ancestral homelands in Germania. Rather, it is to suggest that the formal ideologies of religion and politics by which the Anglo-Saxons interpreted that same continental history — as well as their continuing relations with Germania through the work of missionaries and with the Holy Land through the work of hagiographers — derived in large measure from Rome. The Anglo-Saxons retained their ancestral connections of language and history, perhaps even of some religious beliefs, but they came more and more to interpret them through categories that were in origin Latin and Mediterranean.

Nine hundred years or so fell between Pliny's description of Britain as a distant province of Rome and Sigeric's return from Rome with his pallium. In that interval, Christian writers in England learned to make a place for themselves on the map. Casting themselves on the north, along the periphery, gave both dramatic and spiritual coherence to their history. But looking south toward Rome set them in a necessary relation to the sources of their Christian faith, history, and learning. That perspective was sufficiently familiar by the 990s to make the road from Rome to England seem a familiar series of predictable overnight stops on a well-traveled route. In ways that would have stunned Gildas, England ceased being "an island numb with chill ice and far removed, as in a remote nook of the world" that was "virtually at the end of the world." This transformation happened, in no small measure, because the Anglo-Saxons found their spiritual empire in Christendom and their capital city in Rome.

From Bede's World to "Bede's World"

This chapter turns on a site in Northumbria that has been known since at least the eighth century A.D. as On Gyrwum in Old English and Ingyruum in Latin.[1] There, in Jarrow, Bede lived in a monastery from his childhood until he died in 735. There, too, in the late nineteenth century, Palmer's Shipyard prospered as an engine of British industrialism, and during the depression years of the 1930s, unemployment was endemic after the shipyard was driven into insolvency by a man named McGowan. In 1936, 207 unemployed men and women set out from Jarrow on a march to London to protest against the miserable economic conditions on the Tyneside. Carrying banners reading "Jarrow Crusade," they were led by their local M.P., Ellen Wilkinson, known among the Geordies as "Wee Ellen" or "Red Ellen" for the color of her hair as well as her politics. She would later write an account of the place under the title *The Town That Was Murdered: The Life-Story of Jarrow.*[2] Years later, in 1976, a journalist named Guy Waller who accompanied the marchers remembered tersely: "There was a saying in Jarrow, probably still is to this day, St. Bede founded it, Sir Charles Mark Palmer built it and McGowan buggered it."[3] And there in Jarrow, in the 1990s, a historical re-creation of various Anglo-Saxon buildings was opened not far from St. Paul's Church and called "Bede's World."[4]

Throughout Bede's writing there runs an abiding concern with ideas of place, whether conceived of as the geography of the known world or the topography of the Holy Land or England. This claim may seem to counter the usual veneration of Bede as the writer who, through his work on the *computus* and his use of anno Domini dating for the *Ecclesiastical History,* shaped time to meet the demands of religious practice and historical narrative.[5] His sense that time matters, that it must be shaped to a coherent and eschatologically meaningful order, that it must emplot the same events it records — all this has made him seem like our contemporary as a historian. For unlike his immediate predecessors in the narrating of Christian history, such as Jordanes or Gregory of Tours, Bede writes with a chronology that is recognizably our own: his years 449, 597, and 731 belong to the same continuum as does our 1936, 1976, and 2006.[6] While we may evade or disguise this recognition by labeling our years C.E. rather than A.D., we also know that our choice of tag is finally less significant than is our use of the same ongoing count of years. Indeed, C.E. is a convenient designation: it may refer to *Common Era,* as standard usage has it, but it retains a figurative trace of *Christian Era.*

The work of the Christian computus, and specifically the setting of a canonical date for the annual celebration of Easter, is most immediately a matter of calculating time so that the liturgical calendar for the remainder of the year can be fixed, promulgated, and then consistently observed.[7] Yet the reason for setting this date has everything to do with Christendom as a place occupied by believers who maintain themselves as a community through the simultaneous observance of the same set of liturgical practices across great distances of space. If from the Holy Land where Christ lived and died, to Rome where Peter and Paul were martyred, to distant Britain at the edge of the known world, believers were to worship according to the same calendar, then there would be a unified community of Christendom. Following the same liturgical calendar, as it was calibrated from the date of Easter, meant as well that all those who lived as Christians across this vast region would be guided and inspired by the same body of religious history. The past, especially as it was commemorated through the days of saints and martyrs, would be known equally to all those who lived at the present moment in Christendom. Just as the liturgical calendar provided a historical record of the faith, so its shared observance across geography established the community of believers. Setting the date for Easter was more than a matter of scheduling.

That the major religious controversy recorded in the *Ecclesiastical History* should center on methods for calculating the Easter date is thus richly emblematic of Bede's sense of place, for it demonstrates that questions of time acquire their significance — and also their answers — within the literal and cognitive realms of place. Put more simply, the Synod of Whitby, a meeting held in 663 or 664 chiefly to debate which custom should be accepted for dating Easter, becomes significant in Bede's telling because it raises a question that must be settled with reference to the newly converted region that would be known as Englalond.[8] Whether the practice to be followed should be of Irish or Roman provenance became a matter of dispute because the region in question did not have a continuous history of being Christianized. A theological argument about the computus was thus also a political matter. Or, to use the terms of the previous chapter, the decision as to which would be the established method for calculating Easter meant accepting or rejecting the central authority of Rome. The missionary conversions along the distant frontier should be understood as attempts to impose the spiritual authority of Rome on collective groups rather than on individuals. The controversy at Whitby arose in no small measure because conversion in the early Middle Ages was usually understood in relation to place: it was the inhabitants of a city or tribal kingdom or geographical region that had accepted the faith and entered Christendom.

Bede's account of the debate at Whitby establishes that the most compelling argument for the Roman practice — as advanced by that party's spokesman, the priest Wilfrid — was based on geography. Fundamental to his authority in this debate was the fact that he was said, unlike his adversaries in the Irish faction, to have been to Rome, where he studied religious doctrine: "nam et Romam prius propter doctrinam ecclesiasticam adierat."[9] As Wilfrid argued against the Irish position defended by Colman, he cited the use of the Roman practice not just in Rome or even in Italy or Gaul but everywhere else in Christendom:

> Tum Uilfrid, iubente rege ut diceret, ita exorsus est: "Pascha quod facimus" inquit "uidimus Romae, ubi beati apostoli Petrus et Paulus uixere, docuere, passi sunt et sepulti, ab omnibus celebrari, hoc in Italia, hoc in Gallia, quas discendi uel orandi studio pertransiuimus, ab omnibus agi conspeximus; hoc Africam, Asiam, Aegyptum, Greciam et omnem orbem, quacumque Christi ecclesia diffusa est, per diuersas nationes et linguas uno ac non diuerso temporis ordine geri conperimus.

> Then Wilfrid, receiving instructions from the king to speak, began thus: "The Easter we keep is the same as we have seen universally celebrated in Rome, where the apostles St. Peter and St. Paul lived, taught, suffered, and were buried. We also found it in use everywhere in Italy and Gaul when we travelled through those countries for the purpose of study and prayer. We learned that it was observed at one and the same time in Africa, Asia, Egypt, Greece, and throughout the whole world, wherever the Church of Christ is scattered, amid various nations and languages."[10]

Wilfrid anchors his argument rhetorically in Rome through the memory of the martyred Saints Peter and Paul. He offers them as historical precedents to support his position on the Easter controversy and also to remind his audience of its duty to extend their apostolic work into regions where the two saints had never ventured. His argument set the terms of the debate at Whitby by appropriating to itself both the warrant of the past in Rome and the dynamic of the future in Englalond.

Against this uniformity of practice, Wilfrid can cite as exceptions only the Picts and Britons, who alone in all the world follow an unorthodox custom because, as he says, they live in the two remotest islands in the ocean or, more exactly, not even everywhere in them: "cum quibus de duabus ultimis Oceani insulis, et his non totis." And from there, he adds scornfully and decisively for his argument, they resist the practice of the rest of the world: "contra totum orbem stulto labore pugnant." Wilfrid functions, in this debate, as the spokesman for Roman orthodoxy and thus as the mouthpiece for Bede's ecclesiastical politics and geography. His is the voice charged with rejoining those distant islands and their people to the center of the Christian world by enforcing the proper practice for dating Easter. In response to Wilfrid's argument, Colman can only assert the customary practices of the Irish church, a position anchored in local allegiances rather than universal practices.

The terms by which Wilfrid counters Colman in the Whitby debate are directly related to the most explicitly moralizing statement about place in the *Ecclesiastical History*. Just as Bede advances his own position on Easter through the words of Wilfrid, so he offers a maxim about the love of place by quoting from Pope Gregory the Great's letter of advice to Augustine of Canterbury: "Non enim pro locis res, sed pro bonis rebus loca amanda sunt" (For things are not to be loved for the sake of a place, but places are to be loved for the sake of their good things).[11] Bede uses Gregory's letter on strategies for converting the English and also developing a native church in a manner that is fully consistent with his use of Wilfrid's speech at Whitby; each contains the words of a central figure from the ecclesiastical history of the Anglo-Saxons as it unfolded on the island, and each is meant to convey Bede's own point of view. Understanding Gregory's injunction requires, however, reading it in context. For Augustine's question to Gregory, as it provokes this maxim, conveys his uneasy dislocation from the center of Rome as well as his newfound knowledge of church practices in Gaul:

> II. Interrogatio Augustini: Cum una sit fides, sunt ecclesiarum diuersae consuetudines, et altera consuetudo missarum in sancta Romana ecclesia atque altera in Galliarum tenetur?

Augustine's second question. Even though the faith is one are there varying customs in the churches? And is there one form of mass in the Holy Roman Church and another in the Gaulish churches?[12]

There is an element of surprise in Augustine's question which suggests that the possibility of different practices coexisting within the one Church had probably not occurred to him while he was resident in Rome.

Gregory responds to Augustine's question with great tact because he must accommodate the presence of diverse practices without in any way calling into question the existence of the universal Roman Church:

> Respondit Gregorius papa: Nouit fraternitas tua Romanae ecclesiae consue-
> tudinem, in qua se meminit nutritam. Sed mihi placet ut, siue in Romana siue
> in Galliarum seu in qualibet ecclesia aliquid inuenisti, quod plus omnipotenti
> Deo possit placere, sollicite eligas, et in Anglorum ecclesia, quae adhuc ad
> fidem noua est, institutione praecipua, quae de multis ecclesiis colligere pot-
> uisti, infundas. Non enim pro locis res, sed pro bonis rebus loca amanda sunt.

> Pope Gregory answered: My brother, you know the customs of the Roman
> Church in which, of course, you were brought up. But it is my wish that if you
> have found any customs in the Roman or the Gaulish church or any other
> church which may be more pleasing to Almighty God, you should make a
> careful selection of them and sedulously teach the Church of the English,
> which is still new in the faith, what you have been able to gather from other
> churches. For things are not to be loved for the sake of a place, but places are
> to be loved for the sake of their good things.[13]

As Paul Meyvaert has noted, Gregory's words here are consistent with his belief in the notion of "diversity within unity," that is, of variation within ecclesiastical practice.[14] For Bede, of course, this toleration of diversity could not extend to a controversial matter such as the date of Easter. Variation in that matter would mean fragmenting Christendom into regions of disparate and contradictory observance. Bede, as J. M. Wallace-Hadrill has put it, understood "the western Church for what it was: a confederation of Churches, often fissile, divergent, ignorant, and passionately local."[15]

Within the *Ecclesiastical History,* Gregory's injunction that places are to be loved for the sake of their good things (*res*) or practices is a powerful counter to localist claims, such as Colman offered in defense of the Irish church. For if places are to be loved because of their good things, then it follows that there must be larger principles to determine what is good and therefore to be loved. In this determination, places have no special authority in themselves because, as the history of missionary conversion proved over and over again, the customs and practices of a place can and do change over time. As proof for this claim,

Bede could have referred to his own history of the *gens Anglorum:* as a migratory, pagan people they conquered a Christian island many years before their own conversion was initiated by the work of Augustine and his fellow monks.

Gregory's imperative that a place is to be loved for the goodness of its things or attributes must have struck Bede with a particular force because he had lived his life at a single site. As a place, Jarrow certainly could be loved because of its good things — its tradition of monastic observance, its brilliance as a center of learning, and its setting near the northern frontier of Christendom. As if remembering Gregory's use of *res* in his maxim about places, R. W. Southern has offered this personal testimony: "Few men can have spent more years or worked more hours on the same spot than Bede did; and to me at least the site of the monastery at Jarrow, where he lived and died, is one of the most moving things in England."[16] In its piety of place, this sentence puts one in mind of Bede's own *Lives of the Abbots of Wearmouth and Jarrow,* though paradoxically much of that work relates the frequent journeys between Northumbria and Rome made by the great founding abbots. Yet the paradox is more apparent than real: some abbots may have traveled by necessity, but in doing so they allowed many other monks to stay in place and observe their devotional duties.

Remaining in place enabled a monk to practice the contemplative life, and if he was a scholarly monk, like Bede, it also enabled him to explore the meanings of place in Christian history and belief. In that regard, demarcating the world as he knew it, designating it as Christian or pagan terrain, as converted or yet-to-be converted, was fundamental to Bede's sense of his work as a historian and as a biblical commentator in the cause of religious orthodoxy.[17] Bede offers us the necessary facts by which to appreciate his concern with place in a brief autobiographical statement that concludes his *Ecclesiastical History.* There he demonstrates that a developed sense of place need not depend on wide travel, as is often thought necessary in our own time, but rather can follow from a contemplative regimen in which the observer detaches himself from the immediate circumstances of physical reality:

> Qui natus in territorio eiusdem monasterii, cum essem annorum VII, cura propinquorum datus sum educandus reuerentissimo abbati Benedicto, ac deinde Ceolfrido, cunctumque ex eo tempus uitae in eiusdem monasterii habitatione peragens, omnem meditandis scripturis operam dedi, atque inter obseruantiam disciplinae regularis, et cotidianam cantandi in ecclesia curam, semper aut discere aut docere aut scribere dulce habui.

> I was born in the territory of this monastery. When I was seven years of age I was, by the care of my kinsmen, put into the charge of the reverend Abbot Benedict and then of Ceolfrith, to be educated. From then on I have spent all my life

in this monastery, applying myself entirely to the study of the Scriptures; and, amid the observance of the discipline of the Rule and the daily task of singing in the church, it has always been my delight to learn or to teach or to write.[18]

This passage has customarily been taken as evidence for Bede's devotion to the Benedictine ideal of *stabilitas loci,* and so, undoubtedly, he intended it to be read. But he did so in the fullest sense, for that ideal of stability meant staying in a place so that one could better contemplate the mysteries of God's creation as revealed in scripture and providential history and then write about them in commentaries and histories and lives of abbots and saints. For Bede, *stabilitas loci* meant focusing on the essential matter of place by abjuring the distractions of travel or aimless wandering in the mapped world.[19] As proof that he had honored this ideal throughout his life, Bede added a list of his own writings to this personal sketch. Indeed, that bibliography is his autobiography, the record of a lifetime spent in monastic scholarship. Many of these works, especially his numerous biblical commentaries, would have transported readers far beyond his home ground of Northumbria.

Bede says that he lived "in eiusdem monasterii habitatione" (in this monastery) since he was a young boy, and he offers a general sense of its location when he speaks, in the previous sentence, of being a member of "monasterii beatorum apostolorum Petri et Pauli, quod est ad Uiuraemuda et Ingyruum." That he does not further locate Wearmouth and Jarrow for an audience that might be unfamiliar with Northumbrian geography is not deliberate obfuscation but simply the economy of a writer who expects his readers to remember a passage that appeared a few chapters earlier in Book V. In his account of the Pictish king Nechtan's desire to convert to Christianity, Bede embeds the site of his home monastery into the political and ecclesiastical geography of his narrative:

> Siquidem misit legatarios ad uirum uenerabilem Ceolfridum, abbatem monasterii beatorum apostolorum Petri et Pauli quod est ad ostium Uiuri amnis, et iuxta amnem Tina in loco qui uocatur Ingyruum.

> So he sent messengers to the venerable Ceolfrith, abbot of the monastery of the apostles St. Peter and St. Paul, one part of which stands at the mouth of the river Wear and the other part near the river Tyne in a place called Jarrow.[20]

Bede's message here could hardly be clearer. His monastery was the recipient of Nechtan's request because it was named for two great apostles martyred in Rome, because it observed Roman practices, because it was the seat of a famous missionary abbot, and because it was located on the near frontier between Christian England and pagan Pictland. Or, more implicitly, because Jarrow and Wearmouth, as centers of apostolic missions, were becoming a type of Rome set at the end of the road that led from the papal city to Northumbria.

We know that Bede did travel in Northumbria on occasion to gather material for his *Ecclesiastical History;* he went as far afield as a day or two's journey to such religious centers as Lindisfarne and York to examine documents and interview those who had known, or known reliably about, the heroic pioneers of the Northumbrian conversions. But he otherwise showed none of the desire or willingness for travel that marked his predecessors at Jarrow and Wearmouth. Most notably, Bede was utterly unlike Benedict Biscop, who journeyed ceaselessly between Rome and the Continent so that he could bring back books and other necessary materials to set a monastic culture firmly in place in Northumbria.[21] Bede, by contrast, reminds one of nothing so much as the Sinologist mentioned in passing in one of John le Carré's novels: the man who knew everything there was to know about China but who had never crossed the English Channel and who was, in the world of espionage, considered all the more expert for maintaining that distance.

This portrait of Bede as the man who understood the importance of place in history and exegesis but who knew only one place in his adult life owes much to Robert Hanning's *The Vision of History in Early Britain.* Writing of Benedictine monasticism in the time of Bede as "the great paradox of Christian Europe," Hanning ponders further how it was that "Britain, an island far from the traditional center of European civilization, should witness a vigorous rebirth of Christian social ideals and their artistic expression."[22] For Hanning, the answer lies largely in the wide-ranging work of conversion effected first by Roman missionaries on the island of Britain and then later by missionaries from that same island who ventured back to the Continent.[23] Missionary work in the centuries following the Age of Migration across northern Europe was of necessity defined as movement through space, as turning specific places from pagan error to Christian truth. It was concerned less with the saving of individual souls than with the winning of regions and their populations. If, by a more skeptical reading, missionary Christendom was a kind of belated or even deformed version of Roman empire-building in which pope superseded emperor and politics morphed into religion, the means for measuring the success of both remained geographical: how many people and how much territory does one control?

Bede's sense of geographical history, of narrative deployed through place, must also be read as a legacy of Roman empire-building. That sense of the world was tied directly to the fact that Bede lived on a distant and isolated island. Ultimately, Bede's knowledge of geography derived from Pliny the Elder's *Natural History,* though it was mediated and complicated by having reached him through a series of Christian texts, including Orosius's *History against the Pagans.* Hanning's phrase — "an island far from the traditional center of European civilization" — encapsulates the vision of Britain within that long tradition of geographical study. Bede offers a particularly memorable expression of that tradition in the opening sentences of the first book of his *Ecclesiastical History:*

> Brittania Oceani insula, cui quondam Albion nomen fuit, inter septentrionem et occidentem locata est, Germaniae Galliae Hispaniae, maximis Europae partibus, multo interuallo aduersa. Quae per milia passuum DCCC in boream longa, latitudinis habet milia CC, exceptis dumtaxat prolixioribus diuersorum promontoriorum tractibus, quibus efficitur ut circuitus eius quadragies octies LXXV milia conpleat.

> Britain, once called Albion, is an island of the ocean and lies to the north-west, being opposite Germany, Gaul, and Spain, which form the greater part of Europe, though at a considerable distance from them. It extends 800 miles to the north, and is 200 miles broad, save only where several promontories stretch out further and, counting these, the whole circuit of the coast line covers 4,875 miles.[24]

By beginning in this way, by writing in Latin to place the island in relation to the Continent, Bede pays homage to his predecessor who was at once natural historian, civil servant, and admiral of the Roman fleet. Indeed, Bede's key phrase here "inter septentrionem et occidentem" derives directly from the *Natural History* and is the orientation of someone looking, like Pliny or Isidore of Seville, from the Mediterranean toward Britain. Bede opens his *History* with this vantage point to identify where Britain/Albion/England appears on the mental map of Christendom because that is the great theme of his work. Within a few chapters of Book I, Bede shifts his vantage point and writes as one looking from the island south towards Rome and the remains of the old empire. Had he opened with this other perspective, his first sentence would have located Britain in terms of what lies to its southeast. Bede's world is thus, at least at the start of his *History,* shaped by a consciousness of Rome, seat of empire and papacy, as the center of the world inhabited by human beings.

From reading Pliny and accepting the orientation of a Latin geography that took Rome as its vantage point, Bede knew that he lived in the far north. That knowledge was not simply a neutral matter relating to the points of the compass. For it came to Bede not as a bundle of facts and names but as an implicit theory of geographical representation in which his home island appeared as the back of beyond. After describing the Rhine Delta, Pliny writes:

> Ex adverso huius situs Britannia insula clara Graecis nostrisque monimentis inter septentrionem et occidentem iacet, Germaniae, Galliae, Hispaniae, multo maximis Europae partibus magno intervallo adversa. Albion ipsi nomen fuit, cum Britanniae vocarentur omnes de quibus mox paulo dicemus.

> Opposite to this region lies the island of Britain, famous in the Greek records and in our own; it lies to the north-west, facing, across a wide channel,

Germany, Gaul and Spain, countries which constitute by far the greater part of Europe. It was itself named Albion, while all the islands about which we shall soon speak were called the Britains.[25]

Pliny's reference to Britain lying to the northwest follows, quite strictly, from his narrative cartography in Books III and IV of the *Natural History;* in them, he organizes geography as a coherent and decipherable body of knowledge by constructing a sequential catalogue that begins with the Straits of Gibraltar and then moves place by contiguous place in a predictable direction through the remainder of the known world until it reaches, as here, Britain.[26] Beyond lies only the remoter region of Thule, which is for Pliny less a part of the northern world than it is beyond the northern world. Pliny's cartographic sequence with Britain at its virtual end does suggest a remoteness that comes with being located on the far frontier of empire.

The setting of Britain in the far northwest that we find in Pliny is echoed in Isidore of Seville's *Etymologies* where he explains that Britain is an island in the ocean and lies across the water from Gaul and Spain:

> Brittania Oceani insula interfuso mari toto orbe divisa, a vocabulo suae gentis cognominata. Haec adversa Galliarum parte ad prospectum Hispaniae sita est.

> Britain, an island in the ocean, cut off from all the rest of the world by the intervening sea, has taken its name from that of its people. It is situated opposite the territory of the Gauls and faces Spain.[27]

That Isidore follows Pliny's placement of Britain is noteworthy in this context because his *Etymologies* served as the necessary cultural encyclopedia of the early medieval West, especially in England.[28] Put another way, reading Pliny's geography through Isidore was another form of religious conversion; the map of the pagan empire as written by Pliny could, through the intervention of Isidore, be made to serve the purposes of a Christian exegete and historian like Bede.

The crucial next stage in the worldview that Bede inherited from his predecessors may be located in Gildas's *Ruin of Britain.* Writing in a sixth-century Britain marked by warfare between the Christian Celts resident on the island and the pagan Anglo-Saxons invading it, Gildas endows this element of northern remoteness with a theological and moral resonance that will be registered throughout Bede's *History.* From the north looking south, Gildas says that "Brittannia insula in extremo ferme orbis limite circium occidentemque versus" (The island of Britain lies virtually at the end of the world, towards the west and the north-west).[29] The geography in this passage takes a more explicitly sacralized form as Gildas tells of the first conversion of the British during the reign of Tiberius:

Interea glaciali frigore rigenti insulae et velut longiore terrarum secessu soli visibili non proximae verus ille non de firmamento solum temporali sed de summa etiam caelorum arce tempora cuncta excedente universo orbi praefulgidum sui coruscum ostendens, tempore, ut scimus, summo Tiberii Caesaris, quo absque ullo impedimento eius propagabatur religio, comminata senatu nolente a principe morte delatoribus militum eiusdem, radios suos primum indulget, id est sua praecepta, Christus.

Meanwhile, to an island numb with chill ice and far removed, as in a remote nook of the world, from the visible sun, Christ made a present of his rays (that is, his precepts), Christ the true sun, which shows its dazzling brilliance to the entire earth, not from the temporal firmament merely, but from the highest citadel of heaven, that goes beyond all time. This happened first, as we know, in the last years of the emperor Tiberius, at a time when Christ's religion was being propagated without hindrance: for, against the wishes of the senate, the emperor threatened the death penalty for informers against soldiers of God.[30]

With these passages Gildas changed radically the way in which those on the island, whether Britons or Anglo-Saxons, looked south, for he established that looking south toward Rome and the Holy Land was the way to divine illumination. More historically, looking in that direction was to locate in Rome and its empire the source for the conversion of the Britons.[31]

Gildas knew he was in the north because he had read Roman authorities; he knew he belonged to their north, a position he exploited with great force to animate his jeremiad. Indeed, he recognized that it was entirely to his rhetorical advantage to occupy the northern edge of Latin, Mediterranean Christianity because it was a place of peril, just as he also had his own sense of north as the place whence came the barbarian invaders. In his historicized and sacralized geography, the north functions as a shifting signifier: it is at once Britain, the place of benighted belief; and also Germania, the source of danger for those who live to the south. Even the north, it would seem, needs to demonize its own form of the north.

More generally, as these passages in Gildas reveal, the creation of a British and then (through Bede) of an Anglo-Saxon geographical identity was calibrated on accepting Rome's vantage point. The Britons and later the English learned to see themselves as the Romans saw them: on the northwest, far off, in the regions of cold and spiritual darkness. That Gildas was a Briton, and very much neither Angle nor Saxon, reminds us that ethnicity was not a determining factor for those who saw their native island as being on the northern edge of the world. Instead, it was religion and its attendant geographical culture that gave these writers (whether by origin Celtic or Germanic) this sense of northern isolation. The perspective of north looking south belonged to those who were Christian in their faith and Latin in their learning. The continuity of that identity from the sixth to the eleventh century, across enormous political and linguistic changes, explains how it is that Wulfstan in his *Sermon to the English* of 1014 could invoke Gildas in a manner that reads as all but inevitable for addressing the circumstances of his own moment.[32] Both Gildas and Wulfstan occupied the same Christian north because, and there is no paradox here, they both feared the incursions of outsiders from a north that lay beyond. If north was the compass point from which Anglo-Saxons learned to expect danger, it was also the region in which they would experience the peril of falling into sin and thus of violating their covenant with God, as was proven in another narrative context by Isaiah (14:12ff.) on the fall of Satan. In this world, north was not simply a compass point.

Bede's *History* begins with the perspective of Roman geography that sets Britain in the northwest, but it then shifts to assume the perspective of the Anglo-Saxon gaze looking back at Rome. Where this shift of vantage from Rome to Britain is first registered in the *History* can be debated, though it has certainly been accomplished by the concluding sentence of the sixth chapter of Book I, where after relating the persecutions of Christians led by Diocletian and Maximianus Herculius, Bede writes: "Denique etiam Brittaniam tum plurima confessionis Deo deuotae gloria sublimauit" (In fact Britain also attained to the great glory of bearing faithful witness to God).[33] Bede can claim Britain as a site of martyrdom by looking south toward the source of the persecutions in Rome and Constantinople. Or, put another way, Bede manifests his vantage as a writer not merely by describing events in Britain but also by tracing them to their origins. To understand why things happen in the world of Britain one must sometimes look south.

Bede's technique for opening the *History* — his choice to look at the island from Rome — may be compared anachronistically but usefully to a filmmaker's establishing shot that begins from afar and then moves in to the actual location of the film. In each case, the opening establishes the relation of the work's setting to the world elsewhere, and in each, once that relation has been established, the director can shift point of view so that what had been the object of the gaze becomes in turn the vantage of sight. Using a different theoretical idiom, Uppinder Mehan, in dialogue with David Townsend, raises a similar issue: "What intrigues me is how Bede is able to represent himself, while adopting the perspective of the metropolitan center, so as not to be entirely abject."[34]

Bede could adopt this perspective without rendering himself abject because he understood, first, that Christian history was continuing to spread outwards from the Roman metropole to the far reaches of Britain, and further, that it was his life's work to contribute to that missionary work, as biblical exegete and expert in computus and, later, historian. Being on the periphery was proof for Bede of his lifework's importance. If in a moment of doubt he ever thought of himself as abject, he had only to think of the great exemplary figure of his *History*. For Gregory the Great had wished, before he became pope, to dedicate himself to converting the far frontier of Britain and was persuaded to remain in Rome only by the intervention of the city's inhabitants, who would not allow him to leave. As Bede notes, therefore, one of Gregory's first acts as pope was to send Augustine of Canterbury and his missionary companions to further the work he himself could not accomplish.[35] Being in the metropole was, by the logic of the missionary's calling, to be peripheral rather than central because no work remained to be done there.

This vision of the world as demarcated by the places of conversion has its origins in the New Testament, especially the Gospels, and the narratives of Christ's life and the deeds of the apostles. In Bede's corpus, that vision finds its most explicit expression, predictably enough, in what is arguably his least original work and one of his earliest (probably A.D. 702–3). His *On the Holy Places* is not a traveler's account or itinerary but a handbook for the reader of holy scripture. Derived from such earlier authorities as Adomnan, Bede's Latin work surveys the Holy Land to give a sense of the hagiographical as well as topographical reality of the region. Taken in the abstract, as a disembodied text, it could serve any reader of Latin anywhere in Christendom because it has no vantage point of its own; it does not tell one how to get to the Holy Land from England or anywhere else, but instead it presumes one is already there, as a traveler, whether actual or readerly, pilgrim or exegete. In that respect, it bears a striking resemblance to tourist guidebooks of our time that have no concern with how their readers get to Bangkok or London or Buenos Aires: all that matters is that they are in Bangkok or London or Buenos Aires. In another respect, however, *On the Holy Places* is utterly unlike a tourist guidebook of our time because its assumption that its readers are on site, gazing at the places and buildings it describes, is a kind of exegetical fiction. That is, readers of Bede's work are far more likely to be in the Holy Land imaginatively because they are studying scripture rather than literally because they are physically making a pilgrimage.

Much of what gives *On the Holy Places* its interest today, despite its derivative nature, is that it should work so hard to evoke the physical setting of the Holy Land. Bede is at pains, if only as a redactor of inherited material, to make the Holy Land seem the world where Christ and his followers walked, to evoke it as a landscape of rock and vegetation rather than simply as a fixed circuit of memorable religious sites. Bede's work is particularly noteworthy for its description of Holy Land topography; it summons up the physical actuality of the place for those who will never make the journey there in person. Thus it says, for instance, of the territory surrounding Jerusalem:

> Circa Hierusalem aspera ac montuosa cernuntur loca. Hinc quoque sep-temtrionem uersus usque ad Arimathiam terra petrosa et aspera per interualla monstratur, ualles quoque spinosae usque ad Thamnicam regionem patentes. Ad Caesaream uero Palestinae ab Aelia quamuis aliqua repperiantur angusta et breuia aspera loca, praecipue tamen planities camporum interpositis oliue-tis. Distant autem LXXV milibus passuum. Longitudo uero terrae repromis-sionis a Dan usque Bersabee tenditur spatio CLXV milium, ab Ioppe usque Bethlehem XLVI milibus.

> Around Jerusalem one can see rough and mountainous places. North of here, as far as Arimathea, one can also see rocky and rough land in places. The valleys which extend up to the region of Thamna are also full of thorns. But between Aelia and Caesarea of Palestine, there are mostly level plains with olive groves here and there, although one may occasionally see short stretches of rough terrain. Now Aelia and Caesarea are 75 miles apart. In fact, the length of the promised land from Dan to Beersheba is 165 miles; 46 miles from Joppa to Bethlehem.[36]

The governing verb of this passage — *cernuntur* — belongs to the genre of the work: it is meant to endow readers with the power of vision that would enable them to transcend the distance between where they read and where they read about. In that same way, Bede includes simple ground plans for various sites in the Holy Land such as the Lord's Tomb, the Church of Golgotha, the Church of Constantine, and the church atop Mt. Zion where the Last Supper was held and where Mary died.[37] In this way, readers can follow his descriptions of architecture and visualize the spatial relationships that are so difficult to regis-ter in prose. Some historians of English cartography count these ground plans as the earliest surviving maps from that nation; ironically if appropriately, given Bede's standing as the founder of English historiography, these are im-ages of locations far distant from that island.[38]

The purpose of this passage and many others like it in *On the Holy Places* is not so much to aid in the exegesis of a specific scriptural quotation as it is to make the distant and, for northern readers, exotic terrain around Jerusalem part of their spiritual landscape. To read the Bible in a devout and thoughtful manner requires this grounding in landscape, this specifying of olive trees and thorns, mountains and valleys, as well as the designation of distances in terms that would allow an English reader to measure the sacred landscape mentally. That the Roman mile could serve as an accurate and comprehensible unit of measure for the distance between Dan and Beersheba as well as it could for the distance between Jarrow and Lindisfarne is another legacy of the Roman Empire.

Bede's *On the Holy Places* opens at the center with Jerusalem and then proceeds in an orderly fashion outwards to surrounding regions such as Bethlehem and Jericho, then Mount Tabor and Damascus, and finally Alexandria and Constantinople. The inclusion of these last two cities may be surprising, but they belong in the work because, as Bede explains, they were among the sites visited by the Gallic bishop Arculf, who later, through the agency of a contrary wind, found himself beached on the island of Britain. There he dictated his account of the holy places to Adomnan and in doing so became the source for Bede's little book.[39] That Arculf found himself stranded in Britain would not have seemed the result of a malevolent nature to Bede but rather the workings of a divine providence intent on enlarging the knowledge of the world among those who inhabited that cold and northern island.

In this way, Bede's *On the Holy Places* stands as the textual equivalent of a pilgrimage object such as the "Reliquary Box with Stones from the Holy Sites of Palestine," one of the treasures of the Vatican Museum. This sixth- or seventh-century wooden box, measuring $9\frac{1}{2}$ by $7\frac{1}{4}$ by $1\frac{5}{8}$ inches, is decorated with a cycle of pictures showing scenes from Christ's life and contains actual stones from the holy sites where these same scenes took place. It is, quite literally, an object of memory designed to bring the terrain and history of the Holy Land back to wherever its pilgrim-owner returned home from his journey. No wonder that Diane De Grazia should say: "This painted box, though modest in scale, is one of the most evocative and compelling objects to have survived from early Palestine, indeed from the whole of the early Christian world."[40] Bede's *On the Holy Places* is, in this analogy, a textual reliquary that closes the distance between the originary center of Christian belief and the distant north. His text is a guide for diminishing the remoteness of the island, and thus its distance from the warming rays of Christ the sun. When read knowingly as the work of Bede, and in the company of his *Ecclesiastical History, On the Holy Places* acquires a precise place of origin because its authority resides in its being the work of that English scholar.

A work like *On the Holy Places* may not be a masterpiece or even particularly original, but it nonetheless has its place in the world of Bede's writing because it supplies the information that every reader of the Bible would need but that only a traveler could be expected to know from first-hand experience. Although it emphasizes the physical terrain of Jerusalem and its environs, *On the Holy Places* organizes its materials in a manner that reflects Bede's handling of geography elsewhere in his corpus. Regardless of which part of the world he surveys, he relies on a cartography that is essentially narrative rather than visual in technique. He locates places not by setting them on an illustrative map but by citing them in an ordered sequence beginning with a well-defined site and then moving outward. This technique is not original to Bede; he inherited it, as I have suggested, from a tradition exemplified by Pliny's *Natural History*. Places for Bede have no absolute location as fixed by longitude and latitude; they exist instead in relation to each other. The relation between this way of ordering places and the ritual of pilgrimage is implicit in his *On the Holy Places* because it was meant to inspire its readers to a kind of mental tourism that would take them from their native place to Jerusalem and its environs. That Bede himself had never made such a journey, and instead relied on the writings of others to compile his treatise, perhaps made him more alert to the need to present his geographical and topographical lore lucidly: he had to imagine it for himself in order to reconstruct it for his audience. Being a library traveler can have its benefits.

Bede's letter to Bishop Acca, discussed in the Introduction, lays down a fundamental principle for reading narrative cartography: the sequence of places is itself a form of knowledge and thus can contain the literal and figural meanings of a narrative. That Bede should assert this principle in the course of interpreting the exodus story as found in the book of Numbers is itself additional evidence of its validity. For the exodus was the great biblical narrative of movement, of journeying through places, and thus exemplified the ways in which an event is to be mapped through its sequence of places. That the exodus story became the necessary paradigm for the Anglo-Saxons to articulate their own ancestral history was largely the work of Bede in his *History*. His use of the same technique in *On the Holy Places* translated into a different form of journey, not an *utgang* from the land of captivity but a pilgrimage to be made mentally in the footsteps of Jesus.

Place matters in Bede's writing as the setting for history, though not simply in the obvious sense of being the location where events happen over the generations. More crucially, place becomes setting in Bede's work because it allows him to contain the layers of the past that he must register if he is to achieve his ends as historian and exegete. Put most reductively, a sense of place allows the historian to manage the vagaries of chronology within the framework of a fixed, identifiable location. That sense of place can be demarcated in various forms, depending on the work that must be done. For exegetical geography, Bede follows the path that Jesus and his apostles walked. For the history of the gens Anglorum, Bede works within an island territory circumscribed by the sea. He thus describes his most famous work as "Historia ecclesiastica nostrae insulae ac gentis in libris V," and is careful to specify in its second sentence the measure of that island's circumference.[41] The region surveyed in the *Ecclesiastical History* would not have been at all exotic or distant to his Anglo-Saxon readers. To them, it would have been home ground, native soil, the site of their own religious history and identity. It was a place of elm and hawthorn, not olive and thorn. Placing *On the Holy Places* beside the *Ecclesiastical History* demonstrates that Bede's sense of place was not invariant but instead responded to the demands of genre. The history of his own island requires less topographical information than does his account of the Holy Land; the account of the Holy Land requires less global positioning than does the history of his own island.

With all of these issues in mind, one can return to the opening chapter of the *Ecclesiastical History* and its catalogue of the island's natural resources. After he has set its position in relation to northwestern Europe and enumerated its dimensions in miles, Bede turns to the landscape of Britain in ways that make believable his later statement that the Angles and Saxons chose to invade the island because of its fertility ("insulae fertilitas").[42] Indeed this explanation of the invaders' motives has been set into the narrative of the *History* from the very start, for Bede describes the island as all but paradisal in its abundance:

> Opima frugibus atque arboribus insula, et alendis apta pecoribus ac iumentis, uineas etiam quibusdam in locis germinans, sed et auium ferax terra marique generis diuersi, fluuiis quoque multum piscosis ac fontibus praeclara copiosis; et quidem praecipue issicio abundat et anguilla.

> The island is rich in crops and in trees, and has good pasturage for cattle and beasts of burden. It also produces vines in certain districts, and has plenty of both land- and waterfowl of various kinds. It is remarkable too for its rivers, which abound in fish, particularly salmon and eels, and for copious springs.[43]

The island is also notable for mussels and the pearls they contain as well as whelks and the dye they yield. Bede also notes that the island contains various precious metals as well as high-quality jet, such as can still be purchased by tourists to Whitby. Not just desirable for its crops and mineral resources, the island is also well watered with rivers and springs, both hot and salt, that make for excellent bathing. This mention of springs is undoubtedly a reminder of the Roman custom for bathing, but Bede is quick to preclude any suggestion of pagan licentiousness by noting that in his own time men and women bathe separately. If Britain is paradisal, it is only so metaphorically: the separation of the sexes to maintain decorum is a sign of their postlapsarian state. This kind of descriptive information about Britain is quite different from that offered in *On the Holy Places,* but it fulfills the same function of providing a deep geographical setting for historical exposition.[44]

Bede's description of the island certainly does make it seem a worthy destination for migratory peoples — a fact that he amplifies by noting that at the moment of his writing there are five languages spoken on the island because five different peoples have made the journey there from parts elsewhere:

> Haec in praesenti iuxta numerum librorum quibus lex diuina scripta est, quinque gentium linguis unam eandemque summae ueritatis et uerae sublimitatis scientiam scrutatur et confitetur, Anglorum uidelict Brettonum Scottorum Pictorum et Latinorum, quae meditatione scripturarum ceteris omnibus est facta communis.

> At the present time, there are five languages in Britain, just as the divine law is written in five books, all devoted to seeking out and setting forth one and the same kind of wisdom, namely the knowledge of sublime truth and of true sublimity. These are the English, British, Irish, Pictish, as well as the Latin languages; through the study of the scriptures, Latin is in general use among them all.[45]

In Bede's account, the originary migration was that of the Britons who provided the island with its name:

> In primis autem insula Brettones solum, a quibus nomen accepit, incolas habuit; qui de tractu Armoricano, ut fertur, Brittaniam aduecti australes sibi partes illius uindicarunt.

> To begin with, the inhabitants of the island were all Britons, from whom it receives its name; they sailed to Britain, so it is said, from the land of Armorica, and appropriated to themselves the southern part of it.[46]

Bede then goes on to relate, in the remainder of the opening chapter and the chapters that follow in Book I, the continuous unfolding of this migration history. For understanding Bede's sense of place, though, it is this first migration of the Britons that seems most significant precisely because it elides certain necessary questions. Bede relates that the Britons were the first of these five peoples to arrive in Britain, and thus he establishes that they were not indigenous to the island from the beginning of remembered time. But he does not explicitly state whether they found the island uninhabited when they arrived or whether they displaced those they found settled there. From his prose, it seems impossible to determine which was the case, though it is noteworthy that he works hard to imply that the island was always inhabited by the ancestors of its present occupants. The point then would be that the history of the island is there to be read — perhaps better, there to be heard — in the voices of those who occupy it as he writes. There are, in his interpretation of the place, no lost tribes or exterminated aborigines, no primal tragedy of displacement.

There is another way to articulate what Bede does not do in his geographical description of the island: he never states explicitly or dramatically that it was once uninhabited and then settled through divine agency. Knowing that the Germanic tribes had come to Britain as pagan mercenaries and then as conquerors of the native Celts in the fifth century A.D., Bede could hardly indulge in Edenic fantasies about the island as having been an unspoiled paradise where the Anglo-Saxons could redeem their fallen nature. Perhaps the most remarkable aspect of the island's history as shaped first by Bede in his *History* and then as echoed and retold by the compilers of the *Anglo-Saxon Chronicle* (from the early 790s onward) is that these migratory ancestors did not find an empty island, as did those who settled Iceland, or a virgin land, as did those who imagined America to be without Native Americans. The Anglo-Saxon accounts of place in Bede or the *Chronicle* have none of the innocence that marks Geoffrey of Monmouth's relation of the island's history. Consider, for example, the dream that Brutus has early in his *History of the Kings of Britain*, in which the goddess Diana addresses him: "Brutus, beyond the setting of the sun, past the realms of Gaul, there lies an island in the sea, once occupied by giants. Now it is empty and ready for your folk. Down the years this will prove an abode suited to you and to your people; and for your descendants it will be a second Troy."[47] Bede can offer no such liberating stories about the Anglo-Saxons arriving in Britain; he tells us only that they saw the island was more fertile and clement than were their homelands in northwestern Europe, and thus they stole it away from the Celtic Christians who had hired them as mercenaries.[48] The landscape there was more alluring because it promised greater abundance.

Generations later, after their conversion to Christianity beginning with the mission of Augustine of Canterbury in 597, the Anglo-Saxons would come to think of their ancestors as having made an exodus across the North Sea to a promised land.[49] Imagining Britain as Canaan is to place its landscape in Old Testament history, and that means to acknowledge the occupation of the island was also an act of dispossession.[50] For the promised land can only be defined as "promised" if those who once lived in it have been unworthy and thus must be driven out. Anglo-Saxons who had read Bede's map of the Germanic migration knew that their migrating ancestors had not known the luxury of an island without prior inhabitants; their story of place had always to deal with the intertwined acts of possession and dispossession, both as historical fact and future possibility that began with the Britons.

For Bede place serves as the necessary setting for history — whether it be in the Holy Land or on the island — because it gives a precision to his writing that cannot be acquired through chronology alone. The opening chapter of the

History is in that sense his set piece of geographical history, for there he weaves together seamlessly a sense of place and the dynamic of time. He teaches his readers that things change over time in this place yet also insists on the possibility of historical exposition and comprehension. But the opening chapter of the *History* goes deeper because the place it portrays is in its fertility and abundance itself an agent of historical change: it has drawn various peoples from the earliest Britons to the invading Saxons. Bede's observation that Latin is the language common among some, though certainly not all, members of the other four groups asserts the unifying presence of Christianity and its intellectual tradition. This language is the source of unity among these diverse peoples, if not always in political fact then certainly in Bede's historical awareness of place. This assertion of Latin's currency carries with it the obvious weight of the Christian faith, including such elements as the liturgical calendar and also the writings of Roman geographers that enabled Bede to locate the place of the island in the known world. Through this mingled sense of place, at once spiritual and geographical, Bede related the local to the universal. It also allowed how to love the island for its good things, such as he celebrated in his opening chapter. The crops, vines, pearls, hot springs, and precious metals were alike good things in being present on the island where he set the history of these five peoples.

By a certain reckoning, Bede's world now survives as eleven acres dotted with re-created Anglo-Saxon structures in Jarrow on the south bank of the Tyne. The site is a short walk from St. Paul's Church, once part of the monastery where Bede lived his adult life. For those versed in the history of several different eras, this is hallowed ground. The site of Bede's World is entered through a visitor center which has, to quote the official brochure, "paved courtyard, central atrium and pool, reflecting the Continental style of architecture."[51] With its light-colored stucco finish and design reminiscent of Rome, this building is meant to suggest the Mediterranean world that was home to the missionaries who ventured north to convert the Angles and Saxons.[52] The modern visitor thus enters a site of re-created Anglo-Saxon structures through the portal of Roman culture, a telling allusion to the importance of Bede as local hero, but also an acknowledgment that the Anglo-Saxons were themselves practiced in looking south toward Rome. Or, to put it in different terms, the Mediterranean style of this building is meant to establish the seriousness of the historical project: Bede's World will not be a fantasy theme park of the Dark Ages with blue-faced warriors and wizards chanting spells. In this vision of Bede's world, there is nothing pagan.

The re-created site is surrounded by a high earthen wall planted with trees that will in time provide a wooded barrier to separate it from its immediate surroundings. The buildings inside the wall are re-creations based on serious archaeological research and include a timber hall, a monastic cell, a bake house, and several animal shelters and barns.[53] The grounds are planted with various crops that would have been cultivated in eighth-century England: grains such as spelt, emmer, and barley; vegetables such as onions, radishes, garlic, parsnips, cabbages, and turnips; as well as useful plants such as woad and medicinal herbs. As the information sheet distributed at the site explains, "On the farm we keep the following primitive breeds of animals: Greylag geese; Bantams; Dexter cattle; Pigs; Goats; Sheep including Soay, Hebridean, North Ronaldsay, Shetland, Herdwick, Portland and Manx Loghtan breeds. Apart from the goats these are all close in size and colouration to the animals that would have been kept by the Anglo-Saxons for wool, eggs, meat and leather."[54] Another telling measure of authenticity is the aroma of manure, for the site is not sanitized as are most re-created farm villages in the United States.

On the earthen wall at its northern point, that is, where it is closest to the Tyne, stands a monumental cross made in 1996–97 by Keith Ashford. Not an exact copy of any surviving Anglo-Saxon monumental cross, it is a pastiche of their typical elements: biblical images, vine scrolls, beasts, an archer. Ashford's cross also contains an image that would have been as puzzling to the Anglo-Saxons as are some of those on the Ruthwell Cross to us today: "the figure of a welder at work on a boat keel." This image is a quiet acknowledgment that the setting of Bede's World is not eighth-century Northumbria but a parcel of twentieth-century "derelict industrial land." For as you stand today on that earthen wall near Ashford's cross, you look out at one of the most industrialized landscapes ever created by human beings. In one direction, there is a large tank-farm holding petrochemicals, in another there are large yellow construction cranes looming over the replica cross (Figure 13). Rows of electrical pylons with their high-tension lines tower overhead. Across the River Don, along the eastern edge of Bede's World, is a vast parking lot packed with new Nissan automobiles from a nearby factory that are waiting to be loaded onto cargo ships for export. Beyond, on the horizon, you can see the outlines of huge shipyards and collieries along the River Tyne. This is an industrial landscape of coal and iron, of forging metal into ships that made nineteenth-century Britain the greatest empire Europe had known since the fall of Rome. It was in its time, through World War I, one of the most prosperous areas of industrial England, with skilled and good-paying jobs. Most of those who lived in Jarrow worked in Palmer's Shipyard, or depended on it indirectly for their livelihoods.

Looking at the landscape today from atop the embankment at Bede's World can seem at first utterly disconcerting. For what is this bucolic site doing amid

Figure 13: Bede's World, Jarrow, Tyne and Wear, with surrounding industrial sites.

a landscape of industrial decline and human suffering? Modern gestures, such as adding a welder making a boat to the replica cross, or displaying a mural of the Jarrow Crusade in the museum at Bede's World, seem only to exaggerate the disjunction. If the site of Bede's World is geographically correct, its surroundings seem so utterly alien as to destroy any possibility of authenticity. How can the history of twelve hundred years ago be understood on this site? A monument to the passing of British industrialism, to the loss of a working-class culture of skilled craft unions would seem far more appropriate for this setting. By contrast, Bede's World would seem better sited anywhere in the Northumbrian countryside, perhaps within walking distance of Lindisfarne or Hexham.

Or so the site seemed to me as I wandered around it on an overcast day in May 2000. There were very few visitors there, so I could photograph the village without people obscuring the scene. After a while, it became something of a challenge to photograph the various parts of the village in ways that would visually echo the surrounding industrial landscape. Thus, a round hut of wattle and daub could be seen as having the same outline as the petrochemical tank behind it, and Ashford's cross looked stunning in profile as it soared upward amid a forest of yellow cranes and electrical pylons (Figure 14). These

Figure 14: Bede's World, with surrounding industrial sites.

visual jokes were my way of deconstructing whatever claims Bede's World might have had to historical authenticity.

Sometimes, though, the scholar's purism misses the point. As I talked with a man tending the grounds, another way of thinking about Bede's World emerged. After telling me about the work that remained to be done on the site, he added that he had grown up nearby as the son of a shipyard worker on the Tyne. He spoke about a pedestrian tunnel beneath the river that came out a short distance away in Jarrow; it was built so workers could cross over to the shipyards from Newcastle. It had, he said, the longest wooden escalators in the world, and workers were practiced at shooting their bicycles off them as they reached the top. In the middle of that replica Anglo-Saxon site, the history which seemed most intensely alive to me at the moment belonged to the earlier twentieth century. Even though I could walk in five or ten minutes to St. Paul's Church with its eighth-century chancel, the Age of Bede seemed far distant. But the site released in my mind another play of time. That a place could hold in suspension two radically different moments in British history separated by twelve hundred years — agricultural village and industrial landscape — taught a way to think about Bede's world of the eighth century. For he traced in his *Ecclesiastical History* a cultural shift as profound as that from village to shipyard, though it took only a century or so. As he recorded the transition in Britain from pagan to Christian, Bede set his history in place.

To argue that Northumbria has some essentialist claim on history as its defining quality in both the eighth and the twentieth centuries would push the point of this study too far. Yet as one reads writers trying to define the character of contemporary northern England, such a claim or one very like it appears regularly and acquires a certain plausibility. The scriptwriter Alan Plater remarks in a searching essay entitled "The Drama of the North-East": "Memory becomes history becomes legend, and writers are the stewards in charge of the process. In the North-East, we have long memories and a massive burden of history."[55] His frame of reference is meant to include writers of the last seventy years or so, but to speak in this geographical setting of "long memories and a massive burden of history" is also to invoke Bede. We can find similar ideas in the opening paragraph of a more theorized essay by Stuart Rawnsley, "Constructing 'The North': Space and a Sense of Place": "It [the north of England] is a reified landscape which encapsulates various rhetorical interpretations of the past and the present, of classes and cultures, and of geographical and topological features of a large area of England. No other region has such an intensified 'sense of place.' "[56] With a few minor adjustments, such as specifying "Northumbria" and replacing "classes and cultures" with "religions and tribal regions," this passage would certainly not have puzzled Bede. He might even have enjoyed its heavily Latinate diction.

If there is an abiding sense of the north as a historically distinct place, as Plater and Rawnsley suggest in very different ways, it owes more than a little to the example set by Bede. For he is always known there, and rarely anywhere else, as St. Bede. That honorific, bestowed by his native region and not by distant Rome, suggests that if he is to be considered the patron saint of anything, it should be of the ways human beings locate their history through a sense of place.

PART III

Books of Elsewhere

6

Books of Elsewhere: Cotton Tiberius B v and Cotton Vitellius A xv

That we have no evidence for an Anglo-Saxon encyclopedia that might compare with Pliny's *Natural History* or Isidore of Seville's *Etymologies* does not mean that knowledge as a delineated circle or fixed body was alien to the culture. By a certain reading, Bede's lifework is encyclopedic in range, especially as it relates to matters of geography. His writings on place are directly purposive: to locate and describe the setting of his people's history; to retrace the territory traversed by Jesus and his apostles; to strengthen the unity of Christendom by establishing a means for dating Easter wherever it must be celebrated; to interpret the topography of the Exodus so as to understand the narrative form of the Bible. Bede's sense of place follows not from abstract definition or sentimental association but from his appreciation of the ways in which place determines the topic at hand. He understood that various genres and subjects have their geographical aspects or affinities. His encyclopedism seems remarkable today for crossing genres and for being the product of a single authority. More fruitfully, the search for Anglo-Saxon encyclopedism leads us to manuscripts containing works by multiple hands on a single subject or closely related set of subjects. Such manuscripts can be interpreted as encyclopedic in intent even if they lack the explicit structure that, for example, Isidore provided by breaking his *Etymologies* into twenty books. Anglo-Saxon readers of an encyclopedic manuscript would have had to organize its contents for themselves, though they would certainly have been guided by its thematic emphases.[1]

That an Anglo-Saxon manuscript could be a compendium of works related by topic or genre brought together by one or more individuals in one or more stages is a familiar claim, though few scholars will agree on the exact generic or thematic principle that guided the creation of any specific example. At times, the order of a manuscript seems self-evident: *Genesis, Exodus, Daniel,* and *Christ and Satan* follow this sequence in Junius 11 because it is biblically canonical and any other would suggest a misunderstanding or, more dangerously, a recasting of biblical history. The reading of Junius 11 as a narration of the human fall into a knowledge of places, such as I offer in the next chapter, may be unorthodox, but it depends on a widely known ordering of biblical history. Other Anglo-Saxon manuscripts can seem coherent in their contents without being fixed or inevitable in their order, even if we assume, as is not always the case, that the order we have is the same that an original reader would have known. The poems of the Vercelli Book seem, for instance, consistent in their sense of hagiographical didacticism, so that they emphasize such New Testament events and figures as the Crucifixion (*The Dream of the Rood*), the first apostles (*The Fates of the Apostles*), and their continuation in later time through the discovery of the True Cross (*Elene*). This thematic emphasis aside, however, the poems in the Vercelli Book could appear in different sequences without diminishing its value as a compendium, for, as Donald Scragg has observed, "It is difficult to discern any principle of arrangement in the items of the collection."[2]

Other Anglo-Saxon manuscripts seem to verge seductively on thematic unity, especially if one suppresses a text or argues that an original design was altered when an unrelated work was tacked on later. Thus four of the five texts in British Library, Cotton Vitellius A xv — the so-called *Beowulf* manuscript — display a deep interest in and expert knowledge of monsters, so much so that readers have sometimes defended the manuscript's unity by extending this principle to its fifth text, *Judith,* by representing its villain, Holofernes, as a metaphoric monster of drunkenness and sexual debauchery.[3] Monsters obviously interested the compiler of Vitellius A xv because they often belong to the ecosystem of places elsewhere, but he was not interested simply in compiling a monsterology comparable to such established generic collections as bestiaries and martyrologies. To anticipate the second half of this chapter: other interests and needs having to do with stories of place more likely guided the compiler of Vitellius A xv in the choice of these five texts. Finally, beyond those manuscripts that tantalize us with their apparent or almost unity, there are others that seem to have been gathered by no evident principle of selection.

These manuscripts are often known by blandly descriptive titles, such as that given by the editors of the Early English Manuscripts in Facsimile volume to British Library, Cotton Tiberius B v: *An Eleventh-Century Anglo-Saxon Illuminated Miscellany.*[4] A more neutral description of a manuscript as hodgepodge would be hard to imagine.

Yet one may wonder if the apparent absence of coherence in Anglo-Saxon manuscripts — or at least in certain manuscripts — has more to do with the limits of our own ways of thinking than with the manuscripts themselves. A useful premise for shaping our approaches to these manuscripts would be to remember that compiling a collection of more than fifty or one hundred leaves was no small undertaking; it required a good number of prepared animal skins, inks and pigments that were not always found easily to hand, exemplar texts that may have had to be borrowed from other monasteries, and enough competent scribes to complete the work. Compiling Vitellius A xv or Tiberius B v was most emphatically not like adding another photocopied or downloaded article to a file folder, such as I have, labeled "A-S MSS, Misc." A further premise for such study is that manuscript compilations, or at least some of them, may reflect material circumstances or intellectual needs or literary tastes that are more idiosyncratic than normative, more the expression of personal desire than the dictates of a set discipline. If pressed to the extreme, this claim might seem to preclude any persuasive account of a manuscript's contents. Who, for example, would want to specify the common subject or genre or style that led someone to include *Alms-Giving* and *Homiletic Fragment II* alongside *The Wanderer* and *The Ruin* in the Exeter Book?[5] A less rigorous reading of the Exeter Book would speak of its compiler's desire to collect a range of Old English poems into something more like a generic survey than a personal gathering, that is, more like a college-level anthology of British literature than either of the two highly idiosyncratic Oxford books of modern British poetry edited by W. B. Yeats and Philip Larkin.[6]

That the contents of an Anglo-Saxon manuscript might reflect a compiler's interests more deeply than a culturally determined schema is not in itself reason to renounce all hope of understanding its principles of inclusion. With such a manuscript there are matters of probability to be noted, recurrent topics to be registered, internal affinities to be suggested. A means to think about how manuscripts were put together in Anglo-Saxon England appears in this trenchant remark by Caroline Walker Bynum: "Texts are studied — indeed sought — because something about what they confront seems relevant."[7] To seek out texts because they confront what seems relevant suggests an active intellectual curiosity, not merely the workings of a received authority in which all that is necessary can be found in already available texts. To seek texts for their relevance is an act of exploration; to gather them into a manuscript for one's future use or that of other readers is to participate in an encyclopedic culture.

Some of the most famous manuscripts to survive from Anglo-Saxon England were evidently designed as compendia of learned materials. In turn, some of these may be read as "books of elsewhere," or gatherings about place that reveal a sustained engagement with the larger cultural implications of geography. Two of the most revelatory books of elsewhere are British Library, Cotton Tiberius B v and Vitellius A xv.[8] Compared with Junius 11, for example, these two manuscripts are neither fixed in order nor continuous in their narrative content. They may well have demanded more attention of their readers, that is, a deeper curiosity about the subject of place, if they were to be understood as books of elsewhere. More an archive of place materials than a treatise on geography, a manuscript of this type has no theory or narrative or myth to govern its contents, but rather it reflects its compiler's preoccupation with a subject. Such a manuscript was not necessarily designed for continuous reading from start to finish but could be consulted sporadically or nonsequentially. It would no more lose its reason for being when read in that way than would an encyclopedia by Pliny or Isidore.[9]

Tiberius B v and Vitellius A xv are books of elsewhere in the immediate sense that one pays very limited attention to the island of Britain or Englalond and the other pays none at all. Tiberius B v contains some lists of English rulers and bishops as well as a spot on its *mappamundi* labeled "Brittannia" [*sic*], but the vast bulk of its material refers to places far distant from the island. And Vitellius A xv is, as has often been remarked, utterly oblivious of places and stories of Englalond, though it roams widely through India, the regions of a mythical East, central Scandinavia, and the Holy Land. This fascination with places elsewhere is one of the signal features of Old English poetic manuscripts, though it has seldom been explored or even noted. Of the four great poetic codices from Anglo-Saxon England, only the Exeter Book registers the presence of England in poems like *Guthlac A* and *B* and more distantly *The Ruin.* From reading the poems in Junius 11, the Vercelli Book, and Vitellius A xv, one would have no idea that, at the level of literal geography, there was any such place as Englalond. Only the vernacular language of the poems would suggest that such a place existed because there had to be somewhere populated by people who used this language. The vantage point of these books of elsewhere is England, where they would they have found their audience. To comprehend the vernacular of these manuscripts meant that one was likely to have been born in England or to have lived there for a long while. For Old English poems that are self-consciously about the island and its history — *The Battle of*

Brunanburh, The Battle of Maldon, Durham, The Menologium — one turns to the nonpoetic codices, in fact, often to the collective manuscripts of the *Anglo-Saxon Chronicle*. Indeed, manuscripts such as British Library, Cotton Tiberius B i, with *The Menologium, Maxims II,* and the *Chronicle* poems, might be described as making up the book of *her,* that is, the book of here, of Englalond, of the space on the vellum leaf, of the year to be registered in the annal.[10]

On the face of it, Tiberius B v and Vitellius A xv are an unlikely pair. The first offers a mix of didactic and scientific texts that would seem to reward consultation far more than continuous reading, even if its vivid illustrations would likely have engaged those viewers who could read neither Latin nor Old English. The second contains various works that require no knowledge of *computus,* cartography, or the like but instead satisfy the desire for poetic and prose narratives. It is not hard to imagine an audience listening to the works in Vitellius A xv with pleasure and fascination (even the prose works that modern scholars tend to pass over in favor of *Beowulf*) because they contain extended descriptions of unfamiliar places and beings, vivid passages of violence and conflict, and some lively instruction in religious history. By contrast, the works in Tiberius B v seem largely of archival interest: dynastic lists of rulers are far less entertaining than the adventures of Alexander the Great; the itinerary of Archbishop Sigeric as he headed home from Rome is far less memorable than the account of Beowulf's journey to Denmark and his slaying of Grendel and his Mother. The manuscripts also differ in physical appearance: Tiberius B v is, or was meant to be, a luxury manuscript with extensive illustrations on the large scale, while Vitellius A xv is at best unprepossessing in appearance. And if it is hard to imagine why so much of any monastic Anglo-Saxon manuscript was given over to the deeds of a pagan Scandinavian monster slayer, no such question arises about the computistical tables and lists of bishops in Tiberius B v.

All of this being acknowledged, there is one obvious matter in common between these two manuscripts that argues for their association, if not their affinity: both contain the Old English text and illustrations of a work commonly known as *The Wonders of the East.*[11] This shared text encourages one to envision the two manuscripts as forming a discursive continuum that has the factual lore of Tiberius B v at one end and the narrative forms of Vitellius A xv at the other — in which *The Wonders of the East* occupies a midpoint that allows it to be read in differing ways depending on its manuscript context. *The Wonders of the East* can be read as a catalogue or anatomy of monsters in the context of Tiberius and as an incipient or progressive narrative through regions occupied by monsters in the context of Vitellius. Reading these two manuscripts as being in significant measure about matters of place and geographical knowledge supports the underlying argument of this book that the Anglo-Saxons did not have a single idea about place but rather knew it in many different ways, from a brief boundary clause in a charter to an expansive narrative that runs from the fall in Eden through the final homecoming in heaven.

That descriptions of place can appear in many genres is another way to say that geography is a subject that runs across the culture of Anglo-Saxon England. A partial listing of genres in Tiberius B v would include computistical tables, lists, calendars, itineraries, treatises, drawings, and maps, and in Vitellius A xv such a list would include prose hagiography, journey narratives, and heroic verse. Neither manuscript establishes a definitive or authoritative genre for representing places; instead, each contains an array of genres for doing different kinds of cultural work with place. For this same reason, a book of elsewhere need not display a fixed or standard order for its contents. Indeed, Tiberius B v was reordered during the seventeenth century in a way that obscured its original sequence but that also reveals an early modern sense that maps should preface geographical treatises as a form of illustration.[12] There is also some evidence that Vitellius was reordered during the Anglo-Saxon period, when *Judith* was shifted to its now final position after *Beowulf*.[13] While determining the exact codicological structure of Anglo-Saxon manuscripts has its value, it should not obscure the probability that such manuscripts were not always read as we typically read our books, in sequence from start to finish. My argument about the encyclopedic geographies of Tiberius B v and Vitellius A xv does not depend on any specific sequence for each manuscript, either the one it might have had originally or has now.

We have no extant testimony from Anglo-Saxon England about how manuscripts were read or even how they were consulted. Perhaps our best way into that question therefore follows from a consideration of how a genre creates horizons of meaning or expectations of reading, that is, how a list of popes or a table of Easter dates would be read differently from the life of a saint or the tale of a monster slayer. Anglo-Saxon compilations of factual knowledge, or what was believed to be factual knowledge, typically have their own internal order: papal or regnal lists are chronologically organized usually from earliest to latest, while geographical treatises typically begin with a specific point of origin and then move sequentially forward. An experienced reader who knows a genre's relevant principle of internal order can move selectively through the mass of material in a list or treatise to find the desired information: who was the fourth pope, or where is the major city of a specific region? A reader unfamiliar with the list or treatise will need to work through it from the start to find the desired information but in doing so may also learn to deduce its internal principle of order and thus the means by which the facts of names or places are organized. By contrast, the reader of an extended narrative such as a saint's life or a heroic poem gains much less from moving in and out of the text because doing so vitiates or even destroys its reasons for being. A manuscript that gathered diverse narratives that were not composed from the start as companion pieces, it seems plausible to assume, would not impose a mandatory order for its contents. By contrast, a designed collection of narratives, like Ælfric's *Lives of the Saints*, follows an established sequence derived from the liturgical calendar. In other words, even if we could be certain of the original order of texts in Tiberius B v or Vitellius A xv, we should not therefore conclude that it could have been read only in that same order.

Cotton Tiberius B v was most likely written in the second half of the eleventh century by a single scribe responsible for both the Old English and the Latin texts, with a few additions done by a second hand. Its place of origin is uncertain, though some paleographical as well as internal evidence suggests Canterbury. N. R. Ker has argued that folios 19v–24r likely date "to the time when Sigeric was archbishop of Canterbury (989–95)" because they contain a list of archbishops of Canterbury ending with his name as well as his itineraries both within and from Rome.[14] Other sections of the manuscript may well have been, as it were, preexisting gatherings of material that the compiler of Tiberius B v brought together for his own purposes. That is, the compilation of this manuscript should most likely be understood as the collecting of available booklets of materials on various subjects rather than wholesale compiling in which every text was found standing alone.[15] The size of the manuscript—about 10 by 8½ inches—as well as its complex and elegant program of illustrations suggest that it was the product of a major scriptorium with access to a wide range of materials that could be copied to create a book of place. While the manuscript contains some later additions that most likely indicate it was at Battle Abbey in the twelfth century, its original contents (if not their exact order) were gathered at the same time in the eleventh century and thus may be attributed to a consistent set of interests on the part of its compiler.

The contents of Cotton Tiberius B v have been described by its editor, P. McGurk, as falling into four large divisions:

> The following categories embrace the contents of the Tiberius miscellany though clear dividing lines between them are not easy to draw: *geographical,* the *Marvels,* Sigeric's journey to [sic] Rome, the stations at Rome, the zonal map, Priscian's translation of *Periegesis* and the *mappa mundi; scientific,* the computistical matter, Ælfric's *De Temporibus Anni,* and the *Aratea; historical,* the lists, episcopal, regnal and other, and the genealogies; and *ecclesiastical,* the calendar which was closely associated with the computistical items

and the lost Raban Maur's *De laude crucis*. The three surviving cycles of illustrations reinforce the strongly secular content and make Tiberius one of the most lavishly illustrated secular manuscripts of the early Middle Ages.[16]

As a brief description of a complex manuscript according to conventional categories, McGurk's sentences can hardly be bettered, especially because they acknowledge that the dividing lines between the four categories are sometimes blurred rather than distinct. One might suggest, however, that these lines are in fact insufficiently blurred or, perhaps more accurately, that they correspond to *our* sense of how texts are to be classified rather than to that of an Anglo-Saxon manuscript compiler.

McGurk's four categories — geographical, scientific, historical, and ecclesiastical — all relate directly to the matter of place, though the latter three certainly need not be read exclusively in that manner. With reference to Tiberius B v, the categories of scientific and ecclesiastical might be more usefully termed computistical, because the relevant works in each category have largely to do with determining the date for Easter and the remainder of the liturgical calendar. The theory of the computus, and its attendant methodology, may be heavily mathematical, but its reason for being and its consequences are directly geographical in nature.[17] As I argued in the previous chapter about Bede's exemplary account of the Synod of Whitby in the *Ecclesiastical History,* the need to calculate an authoritative date for Easter derives from the larger need to preserve orthodoxy of belief and practice among all Christians and thereby to demarcate the territorial range of Christendom. By worshipping in calendric harmony with Rome, Whitby or any other equally remote point on the Christian map would thus belong within the same territory of belief. And here we need to remember, if only by noting the absence of boundaries on the mappamundi in Tiberius B v, that visual cartography was a very vague matter in early medieval Europe and utterly lacked the specificity of textual cartography as it wrote nations and regions onto its map. Christendom would likely be understood by an Anglo-Saxon less as a region of fixed borders than as a territory of common beliefs and practices, among which the religious calendar was central.

The most opaque texts in Tiberius B v to a modern reader are probably its computistical and calendric tables, and the errors in them suggest that they were hardly transparent to an Anglo-Saxon reader.[18] As forms for calculating the date of Easter and the sequence of the liturgical feasts that depend on it, they are hardly susceptible to the explication that one can apply to more literary texts in the manuscript. Similarly, the tables in the manuscript for determining the age of the moon (f. 9r) or for calculating on what day of the week the first day of each month in a twenty-eight year cycle will fall (f. 11r) or for creating a concordance of the decennoval cycle, lunar cycle, and age of the moon on January 1 and March 22 (f. 17v) provide chronological information necessary for maintaining religious orthodoxy and community.[19] As such, each table remains valuable as an archive, even when it contains errors or records Easter cycles for past years, as do the tables on folio 16r for the period A.D. 969–1006, which predate the presumptive date for Tiberius B v by at least two generations.[20] In addition to these various types of tables, the manuscript contains texts that can be read either as explaining its calendric and computistical materials, such as a largely complete text of Ælfric's *De temporibus anni,* or else as translating them into more accessible forms, such as a metrical calendar of the twelve months with illustrations showing each month's labor and sign of the zodiac. Viewed on a large scale, the contents of Tiberius B v can be taken as being at least partially self-glossing, so that the opacities of computistical tables, for example, are clarified by the prose explanations of handbook texts.

The *De temporibus* is not credited to Ælfric in Tiberius B v but instead bears the heading "Incipiunt pauca de temporibus Bedæ Presbiteri" in red capital letters.[21] Acknowledging Bede as the chief source for the work no doubt gave it added authority but also identified it as the product of an English writer, indeed, of the most famous English writer. The user who went directly to the *De temporibus* would have found this form of identification especially useful. A user who did read the manuscript sequentially would encounter this reference to Bede on folio 24r immediately after the end of the itinerary for Archbishop Sigeric's voyage from Rome to the English Channel and might well have taken it as an answer to the question that that list of places posed implicitly: namely, what lies across the Channel from the Norman coast where it leaves off?[22] One answer would be the land where Bede had lived, which he had, in some arguable way, helped to create as an entity through his *Ecclesiastical History.*

At a more local level, the opening sentence of the *De temporibus* testifies to the encyclopedic richness of Bede's writing and also to Ælfric's way of presenting that richness in his brief treatise: "Ic wolde eac gyf ic dorste pluccian su(m) gehwæde andgyt of ðære bec þe beda se snotera lareow gesette" (I wanted also if I dared to pluck some slight learning from the book which the wise teacher Bede wrote).[23] The claim that the text at hand is the work of someone who has "plucked" from the works of the wise scholar Bede is literally true, but it also describes how an encyclopedic work can be created. The verb *pluccian* in the Tiberius B v text of this sentence is more revealing than the verb *gadrian* found in other manuscripts of the *De temporibus* because it suggests an active intelligence at work that selects the best pieces from Bede's works rather than one that simply gathers texts together.[24] One might apply, at least metaphorically, the verb *pluccian* to Tiberius B v as a whole to describe it as a selection of materials chosen by an informed and engaged compiler.

This compiler understood that a work about time and its modes of calcula-tion must also be a work about place, as is clear from the very start of the *De temporibus* and its account of God's creation of the heavens and earth over seven days. The content of this section is quite familiar as it summarizes the opening chapters of Genesis, though Ælfric makes some effort to explain the spiritual significance of the creation.[25] The creation is, of course, the founda-tional Christian story of place, from which flow all other such stories, which are not limited simply to those concerning earthly places. Ælfric's teaching in the *De temporibus* that the heavens are part of the creation and thus part of any encompassing Christian sense of place helps one understand why the compiler of Tiberius B v should have included so much material about the heavens, including three zonal maps as well as Cicero's translation of the *Aratea*.[26] More specifically, Ælfric's section *De anno* (ff. 25r–25v) lists the twelve signs of the zodiac with a translation of each sign's Latin name into Old English (for example, "An þæra tacna is gehaten aries þ(æt) is ramm" [One of those signs is called Aries, that is the Ram]),[27] but this section can also be read as a prose summary of what has earlier been represented visually in the manu-script by folios 3r–8v, devoted to the labors of the month, each of which contains an image of its appropriate zodiacal sign. Within this same section about the year in the *De temporibus*, Ælfric acknowledges the different prac-tices that various peoples have for beginning the year, an explicit acknowl-edgement that cultural practices may be inventoried by place:

> Romanisce leodan ongynnað heora gear æfter hæðenum gewunan on winter-licere tide. Ebrei healdað heora geares anginn on lenctenlicre emnihte. Ða greciscan onginnað hyra gear æt þæm sunnstede . ⁊ ða egiptiscan on hærfest.

> The Roman people begin their year according to the heathen practice in the wintertime. The Hebrews observe the onset of their year at the vernal equi-nox. The Greeks begin their year at the solstice. And the Egyptians do so at harvest time.[28]

Similarly, when Ælfric explains that days are not of uniform length throughout the creation, he illustrates his teaching with a geographical survey that touches on India, Alexandria, the island of Meroe, followed by unspecified northern regions and the island of Thule.[29] The text of *De temporibus* in Tiberius B v omits from this survey about summer nights what other versions contain, namely a paragraph on Italy, glossed to mean Rome more specifically, and another on England; but it does include an authorial claim to having often seen in northern lands summer nights when it remained light. Ælfric's claim "we sylfe foroft gesawon" (we ourselves saw it very often) could also have been taken by readers of Tiberius B v as a specific act of authorial self-location.[30]

If Ælfric introduces these various measures of geographical difference in the *De temporibus*, he is careful to do so within a larger framework of Christian uniformity, as is manifested most evidently in its section, *De æquinoctiis*. The problem of the equinox relates directly to the setting of the Easter date and thus to the territorial unity of Christendom. Ælfric begins by noting that those most expert in *gerimcræft*, or computus, are from the East or Egypt ("ac ealle þa easternan ⁊ egiptiscan þe selost cunnon on gerimcræfte"), an arresting counterpoint to the portrayal of such regions as monster lands elsewhere in the manuscript.[31] After acknowledging these authorities, Ælfric offers what may seem to be a very simplistic rule: "Us is neod þ(æt) we þa halgan easter tide be ðæm soðan regole healdon næfre ær emnihte ⁊ oferswiðum ðeostrum" (It is necessary that we hold Holy Easter according to the true rule, never before the equinox and the longer nights).[32] For anyone who could read and use the sort of computistical tables that occupy numerous folios of Tiberius B v, this "true rule" is next to useless. From another point of view, however, this reference to the rule for calculating the date of Easter is more important doctrinally than scientifically, more a reminder that there is such a rule for Christians to follow than a formula for calculating that date. Knowing that Easter must never be held before the equinox when the hours of darkness are greater than those of light will not fix its precise date in any year, but it will help one to avoid the most egregious errors or heresies. Ælfric offers a true rule for laypeople rather than experts in computus because it has the great advantage of being tied to a natural and observable phenomenon that occurs across the created world and thus can help to insure the uniformity of sacred practice within Christendom.

If Christendom could be demarcated as a territory of orthodox practices, it could also be identified as having a center or capital, Rome, that held authority over practices in marginal or peripheral areas. Any region that acknowledged the spiritual authority of Rome and its pope, especially by sending its bishops there to receive the pallium, was locating itself within Christendom. To assist in that end of geographical definition, Tiberius B v contains a long list of popes, beginning with Peter and ending with Adrian, as well as archbishop Sigeric's itinerary home from Rome after receiving his pallium. It is through the conjunction of such seemingly nongeographical texts that a manuscript such as Tiberius B v establishes itself as a book of place. If a list of rulers creates a territory, one defined by all those who accept their authority, that technique of historical recording can be used for all sorts of territories, both ecclesiastical and secular. The various lists of bishops in Tiberius B v have the effect of defining episcopal sees, that is, of dividing Christendom into more local and more comprehensible regions. That the manuscript contains, as we shall see, lists of bishops in England as well as in such remote sees as Jerusalem and Antioch demonstrates that this technique of geographical demarcation could provide a format for accommodating local and foreign knowledge alike.[33]

Tiberius B v contains, in parallel with these papal and episcopal lists, regnal lists for the rulers of various kingdoms in England. David Dumville has usefully cautioned against assuming that these regnal lists are genealogies in the strict sense, even when announced as such in the manuscript, because they do not always contain rulers related by blood.[34] Instead, they offer a sequence of rulers for a region over time, though on occasion the sequence is massaged to avoid political embarrassments or to cover gaps in knowledge. The regions demarcated by these regnal lists — such as Mercia, Wessex, or Northumbria — are notoriously vague in their borders. Even Northumbria, which would seem clearly demarcated as the region north of the Humber, had shifting borders over time, even to the point sometimes of extending south of that river.[35] Defining and enforcing the territory of an Anglo-Saxon kingdom in a historical text, whether list or narrative, could be accomplished by recording all of its rulers back to a moment of origin. Doing so would establish that it was an identifiable entity because it acknowledged a specific sequence of rulers.[36]

Computistical tables and lists of popes, bishops, and kings have immediate chronological functions, but these are apparent and efficacious only within geographically acknowledged areas. Such forms can significantly augment the ways in which a sense of place is created by religious belief or political affiliation. Moreover they can do so even when they appear straightforwardly as tables or lists without any explanatory text. In a culture accomplished in the use of such tables and lists, these forms would not have required extended explanation, any more than does a telephone directory or set of football scores to us today. The evident transparency of such forms, at least to those practiced in their use, is suggested by the likelihood that certain of the regnal lists in Tiberius B v were created by someone who took names — and only names — out of the narrative passages in Bede's *Ecclesiastical History,* that is, by someone who could dispense with the very same context that we as twenty-first century readers struggle to recreate.[37]

The list as it offers a sequence of rulers, either ecclesiastical or secular, for a given region is the most elemental form in Tiberius B v, other than the mathematical tables for the computus. Lists of this sort forgo context for specific information, and in doing so they indicate that the matter more in need of mnemonic framing, because harder to remember, is the series of names and thus the matter less in need of mnemonic framing, because easier to remember, is the place or location. Or, as seems likely from the practice of the scribe of Tiberius B v, a title can provide sufficient context for the subsequent list of names, as one finds with the first such list in the manuscript (f. 19v): "Incipiunt nomina pontificum Romane urbis per ordinem" (Here begin the names of the pontiffs of the city of Rome in order) in red capital letters across the top of the leaf.[38] There follows a list of popes beginning at I with Peter and running through to CXI with Adrian, after whom appear eleven numbered but vacant spaces reserved for the names of future popes. The open-ended nature of this list, signaled by numbers CXII through CXXII, acknowledges both the ongoing existence of the papacy through time and also its centrality to the English, who would add names as necessary to document its continuing ecclesiastical authority.

The list of popes begins a long series of lists, stretching from folio 19v, column 1, through folio 24r, that includes emperors, bishops, kings, and abbots. Appearing as it does at the start of this series, the papal list clearly establishes the religious geography for all those that follow: each name is to be understood and located with reference to Rome as the center of Christendom. Thus, immediately following, we find a list headed "Incipiunt per ordinem nomina episcoporum Hierosolime civitatis" (Here begin the names of the bishops of the city of Jerusalem in order) that names seventy-seven incumbents with no space reserved for additions.[39] The order of these two lists is itself significant geographically because it acknowledges an organizational hierarchy in which Rome as the seat of the papacy occupies the primary position followed immediately afterwards by Jerusalem as the central city of the Holy Land. The third list in this section reverts to Rome but in this case with the sequence of emperors—"Incipiunt nomina imperatorum Romane urbis" (Here begin the names of the emperors of the city of Rome)—beginning with Julius Caesar and numbering fifty-four in total, ending with Eraclius, though adding without number Odda and leaving twelve blank lines after him.[40] Starting this list with Julius Caesar has at least as much to do with English as Roman history, for he was the first Roman leader to invade or otherwise visit Britain, a fact that occupies the first dated entry (sixty years before Christ was born) in both the A and E versions of the *Anglo-Saxon Chronicle*.[41] After the list of emperors, the next five lists in this section of Tiberius B v are headed:

1. Incipiunt nomina episcoporum Hierosolime urbis (an additional roster of twenty-six bishops of Jerusalem)
2. Deinde surrexerunt post Christi ascensionem pontifices novi testamenti (fifty-six figures from "Iacobus" to "Cyrillus martyr")

3. Nomina episcoporum Alexandrie urbis (twenty-eight names from "Petrus apostolus" to "Philippus")
4. Nomina pontificum Antiocene urbis (twenty-seven names from "Petrus apostolus" to "Ysidorus martyr")
5. Nomina archiepiscoporum Dorobornensis ecclesiae (twenty-four names from "Augustinus" to "Sygeric")[42]

The clustering of lists for Rome, Jerusalem, Alexandria, and Antioch at the start of this section has the geographical imperative of locating these central sites within the Christian world ruled from Rome, as well as the historical warrant of bringing together the important figures in the early (that is, the pre-English) history of Christianity.

The movement in these lists from the pontiffs of Antioch to the archbishops of Canterbury crosses a far distance of geography and in doing so knowingly connects the island to Christian history. That it does so through the figure of Augustine is a reminder of this missionary's role in the conversion of the English as well as the fact that he departed from Rome under the direction of Gregory the Great. Each of these lists may have its own immediate internal purpose of recording a necessary sequence of figures, but taken as a group they map out the place of England within Christendom by providing the crucial connection, via Augustine, back to Rome.[43] After introducing the archbishops of Canterbury, the compiler of Tiberius B v then moves into a series of twenty-eight additional lists having to do with England. The first eighteen are given over to episcopal sees arranged in a roughly south to north order from nearby Rochester (Hrofhensis) through to Northumbria, York, Lindisfarne and beyond to Whithorn in Galloway (Casa Candida).[44] This sequence of episcopal lists offers a mapping of the pertinent divisions of Christian England, all of which are understood to be dependent on Canterbury. Each may preserve a necessary list of names, but together they form a map of English bishoprics that was more complete and precise than any visual map from the period seems likely to have been. This sequence of bishoprics moving from Canterbury northwards also suggests schematically the geographical sequence by which the English were converted. After the episcopal lists in this section of Tiberius B v comes a series of nine secular lists, including regnal lists for the West Saxons, the Northumbrians, the Mercians, as well as genealogies for Mercia, Lindsey, Kent, East Anglia, and Wessex.[45] These secular lists are not as geographically ordered as are the episcopal lists that precede them, but they do nonetheless cover most of Englalond.

The compiler of Tiberius B v was interested, I would argue, in presenting these lists in such a manner that together they would form a map of Anglo-Saxon political geography. This intent is most evident from folio 22v, which has as its heading in red capital letters across the top of the leaf: "Haec sunt genealogie per partes Brittannie regum regnantium per diversa loca. Norð-hymbrorum" (These are the genealogies of kings ruling in various places in different parts of Britain. Of the Northumbrians).[46] The fascinating aspect of this heading is its identification of a geographical whole — "Brittannie" — and its division into constituent parts — "per diversa loca" — and then its explication of that distinction through a listing of relevant parts into four columns containing what the manuscript calls the "genealogies" of Deira and Bernicia.

Each of the episcopal lists in Tiberius B v is an implicit reminder of the presence of Rome at the head of the ecclesiastical hierarchy. The relations of power encoded by this hierarchy — that English bishops stand below the archbishop of Canterbury, and he in turn stands below the pope — are carried by the sequential layout of these folios. In their regular use of three or four vertical columns, these folios impose a strict manner of reading on anyone consulting the manuscript: the sequence within each list matters because it records the progression through time, which is the declared subject of each list; but the sequence through many lists and their place-name headings provides a more geographical orientation. The reader coming to the last leaf in the section of the manuscript devoted to lists, folio 23v, will encounter there a chiefly horizontal layout of lists rather than the more typical vertical layout of earlier leaves. That is, the horizontal format is used for three large blocks of script that run from ruled margin to ruled margin, each beginning with a prominent capital letter to mark its status as a new item. In the upper right section of the leaf, between its right edge and the ruled margin, is a list of the nineteen abbots of Glastonbury, seemingly a continuation of the list technique employed on preceding leaves. For the most part, however, folio 23v is occupied by three large blocks of prose lists: the first is a list of tenth-century popes beginning with Leo in 903, thus picking up where the earlier papal list on folio 19v ended after a hiatus of eighteen years; the second is a list of the sites visited by Sigeric when he went to Rome to receive the pallium in 989; and the third is his itinerary from Rome to the English Channel as he headed home to assume his duties as archbishop of Canterbury.[47] The material on folios 23v and 24r was added to the preexisting bundle of episcopal lists that survives, with some differences, in other Anglo-Saxon manuscripts. That the compiler of Tiberius B v added this leaf of material about Rome, listing its tenth-century popes, its holy sites, and the route from there to the Channel, may simply reflect his sense that these three new lists should be used to update the lists he had inherited. The attraction of form might well have come into play here: the new lists belong with the old lists. Such may well have been the case, but I suspect that something more was at stake.

First of all, the compiler of Tiberius B v added these three lists in horizontal, margin-to-margin format rather than the vertical columns of his source material. He might well have recorded all of this added material in vertical format, but I would argue he chose not to do so in order to underscore visually his use of these three new lists to complete the section or booklet of lists. Working in a geographically pointed manner, he began by adding his first horizontal list to update the list of popes that had fallen behind in the interval since the opening list on folio 19v was compiled. He then added a list of important sites in Rome to illustrate its significance as a holy city, a place elsewhere from England, but still one that could be known by the English. As a case in point, he cited the travels (*adventus*) of Sigeric while he was in Rome.[48] That Sigeric was archbishop of Canterbury where these folios were prepared may explain the immediate choice of his travels in Rome, and much the same could be said for the decision to include his continental itinerary as he returned from Rome to Canterbury. By the time all of this material—that is, the contents of folios 19v–24r—came to be copied into Tiberius B v, the argument for local celebrity may well have faded; there had been other archbishops in Canterbury after Sigeric's death in 994/5.[49] Sigeric's association with Canterbury would not have been forgotten; indeed, it was there for anyone to read at the end of the list of archbishops on folio 21r. With that in mind, the horizontal Rome–Canterbury lists on folios 23v–24r would have provided a strikingly appropriate form of closure to the list section of the manuscript: a section beginning with the popes of Rome would end with the return of an English archbishop from Rome after being raised to his office there. The explicitly geographical lists of Sigeric's pilgrimage in Rome and his voyage home would highlight the geographical substrate of the numerous chronological lists that precede them. A reader finishing this section of the manuscript would thus have been encouraged to think about the ways in which the categories of geography can contain the complexities of chronology.

Such a reader would also have been brought back to England, or at least to a port on the other side of the Channel. By including Sigeric's itinerary in this section of the manuscript, the compiler underscored the relation of England to Rome and the remainder of the world. Indeed, the lists of English bishops and rulers on folios 19v–24r are—along with the image of Britannia on the mappamundi—the most explicit references to Englalond in Tiberius B v. Though the sum of English materials in the manuscript is relatively low, they serve the useful function of providing a geographical orientation or vantage for its user. That the English lists sit among those about Rome and Jerusalem establishes a model of similarity and difference that also holds for reading the other works in Tiberius B v as a whole. The fact of similarity relates to forms of human organization, both sacred and secular, while that of difference relates to those individuals who have occupied positions within those forms of human organization. The point may be elementary, but it has the effect of suggesting that other places far afield share fundamental elements with those in England and therefore are not unknowable or absolutely alien. Elsewhere is, in this formulation, a place of similarity and difference, though the ratio between these two must be recalculated depending on where one locates that place elsewhere. This claim about the need to negotiate similarity and difference applies as well to the names on the visual mappamundi of the manuscript: the familiar place-names of *Brittannia, Cantia,* and *Lundona* occupy the same visual field as do the more remote ones of *Armenia, India,* and *Ethiopica deserta.*[50] Just as the presence of the Roman papacy covers all of the episcopal lists on folios 19v–24r of Cotton Tiberius B v, so the Latin nomenclature of its mappamundi uses language to inscribe a measure of cultural similarity over the differences and distances of geography.

That the English lists appear among those about Rome and Jerusalem also signals that a place or region can be defined by a sequence of authorities regardless of its earthly location: indeed, the list offers a typology for writing places by acknowledging the central fact of human life, namely, that popes, emperors, bishops, and kings succeed each other because they are mortal and live in a fallen world of many places rather than a prelapsarian Eden. As I argue in the following chapter about the book of elsewhere known as Junius 11, the human fall into sin was also the fall into place or, more exactly, into a knowledge of places distinguished by language and customs. Every list that follows the turn of generations in this or any other manuscript is a tacit acknowledgment of mortality and thus, by extension, of the dispersion of human beings after the fall.

The most vivid portrayal of postlapsarian geography in Tiberius B v appears in the so-called metrical calendar that occupies folios 3r–8v. These leaves are some of the most frequently reproduced from the manuscript because they contain vivid illustrations showing the labors of the month. Each of these leaves falls into three major sections: the labor of the month illustrated in a panel that occupies the top fifth or so of the page; then immediately below it a vertical list of days for the month giving the feasts or saints to be celebrated, with some errors; and then the relevant sign of the zodiac illustrated in a circle in the lower right corner. Time is everywhere present on these pages, and thus so is place: for the dominant visual element of each leaf shows human beings at work within the agricultural world, and the dominant textual element follows month by month the sequence of earthly time. Each month illustrates what it means that human beings live in a post-Edenic world in which men must earn their bread by their own sweat. As God says to Adam in the Old English *Genesis:*

> Hwæt, þu laðlice
> wrohte onstealdest;   forþon þu winnan scealt
> and on eorðan þe   þine andlifne
> selfa geræcan,   wegan swatig hleor,
> þinne hlaf etan,   þenden þu her leofast.

Yes, you hatefully have given rise to sin; therefore you must labor and must earn for yourself your food in the earth, display a sweaty brow, and eat your own bread for as long as you live here. (ll. 931b–35)[51]

That working the soil is the fundamental condition for fallen men explains the somewhat anomalous depiction of men plowing with oxen and sowing as the labor for January in the calendars of Tiberius and related manuscripts.[52] That such work would not have been undertaken in England until a later month in the springtime has been remarked, but that may confuse practices of agriculture with matters of spiritual chronology as they relate to a sense of earthly place. The calendar begins in winter according to the Roman practice, as Ælfric observes in his *De temporibus* (as noted earlier), and the work that fallen men must do in that calendar begins with plowing and sowing. The sequence of the year within this calendar is more spiritually than agriculturally determined, for the year that begins with plowing and sowing in January ends with threshing in December. The year that begins with planting seed ends with separating the wheat from the chaff, a reminder of the judgment that awaits all human beings at the end of time and their earthly lives.

The metrical calendar thus inscribes a richly nuanced sense of place, one that begins with the saving labor of those who live on earth. It might also be noted that these twelve illustrations would likely have been the most recognizable part of Tiberius B v to a nonliterate Anglo-Saxon who viewed the manuscript, for not only do they not require an ability to read, but they also depict familiar activities such as trimming vegetation (February), tending sheep (May), harvesting (June), and cutting wood (July). These illustrations are in that sense comparable to the vernacular boundary clauses found in Anglo-Saxon land charters that are otherwise written in Latin. For both these illustrations and the boundary clauses work at the level of an immediate landscape by depicting it through its familiar features. The Tiberius illustrations do not, at least to my eye, depict any features of flora or fauna that would have perplexed the English viewer, as do some of the illustrations earlier in the manuscript that accompany *The Wonders of the East.*

This is not to say that the artist of these calendar illustrations set out to depict an English landscape, let alone an identifiable location, but rather that he represented the activities of the agricultural year that would have been performed within such a landscape. The landscape may be more specifically English in its labors than its topography, but that representation captured another sense of place to complement those that appear elsewhere in Tiberius B v. And, indeed, those other senses appear on the same leaves of the manuscript as do the illustrations of the labors. For there one finds other temporally inflected markers of place, including the signs of the zodiac as they belong to the demarcation of the celestial realm, and an indication on the leaves for January through June of "the number of hours in the days and in the nights," as they would help the reader track the spring equinox and thus the period, if not the exact date, for Easter.[53] The other standard measure for Christendom in the manuscript, the calendar necessary for worship, is registered in the entries for each day giving feast and saints' days. These entries do not show an unusual preponderance of saints native to or important in England, though some such are present; instead, the calendar records a more typical sequence of the church's holy feasts and registers an inclusive sense of Christendom.

The calendar gives Tiberius B v a vision of place as familiar and its labors as predictable: the sense of time they illustrate belongs to the agricultural year, even if they do not always seem entirely appropriate to the month in which they appear. An English user of the manuscript would not feel any sense of puzzlement at what the illustrations depict, certainly not in the way she or he might have felt when looking at those that accompany the Latin and Old English texts of *The Wonders of the East*. For these depict, among other scenes, gold-digging ants as big as dogs; human cannibals on a gigantic scale, at least twice as large as their normal-sized victims; a 150-foot-long dragon; headless men whose faces appear on their chests; Ethiopians; and such hybrid beings as the griffon and phoenix.[54] Such illustrations, as well as the accompanying descriptive texts, have encouraged some modern scholars to read the *Wonders* as a work that depicts the "East" as a region of the cultural Other that displaces European fears about the potential chaos of nature and the savagery of human beings onto a conveniently remote region.[55] Such readings suggest that the *Wonders* is in various ways a work of the orientalizing imagination. Without denying the value of such readings and the late antique, early medieval tradition *Wonders* embodies, I would suggest that the work is more knowing in its use of place as geographical, ecological, and cultural concept.[56] When read in the manuscript context of Tiberius B v, *Wonders* appears as a work that deftly mediates between various significant categories: between here and elsewhere; between textual and visual; between vernacular language and learned language; and, most subtly, between familiar and exotic. To the extent

that *Wonders* is about the East as a cultural location, it works through categories of likeness and difference — the same categories that are deployed in many
other works in the manuscript as they present facts necessary for constructing
a sense of place.

The text we call *Wonders* is not titled in the manuscript, though its opening
words are written in large capitals that might well have served a comparable
function of announcing a new work: "Colonia est initiu(m)."[57] The Latin text
has priority over the Old English in the manuscript, both by size and position,
so that the eye is drawn more immediately to *colonia* than to its vernacular
equivalent lower on the same page, *landbunes*. The Latin word is better at-
tested than the Old English one and designates either a territory or country or
a community of settlers.[58] In either sense, *colonia* as a Latin term belongs to a
geography of empire that must by its very structure have a center, that is, a
capital place that bestows the category label of *colonia* on a distant and subordinate region. A text that opens by referring to a colonia suggests about itself
that it occupies a more central vantage, perhaps even a capital, where one can
read about that other place.[59] An Anglo-Saxon reader of Tiberius B v, especially one familiar with its lists of Roman emperors and various Latin texts,
could have localized the geography of center and remote periphery by remembering that Britannia had itself once been a colonia.

The opening section of *Wonders* does much to normalize the colonia it
describes, even if the proper name it uses would have had no obvious resonance for an English audience:

> Seo landbuend on fruman from antimolima þam landum . ðæs landes is on
> rime þæs læssan milgetæles ðe stadia hatte fif hund 7 þæs micclan milgetæles
> þe leuua hatte ðreohund 7 eahta 7 syxtig . On ðam ealande byð micel menigeo
> sceapa 7 þanon is to babilonia þæs læssan milgetæles stadia hundteontig 7
> eahta 7 syxtig and ðæs micclan þe leuua hatte fiftyne 7 hundteonig.

> The colony is at the beginning of the land Antimolima; that land is in count
> 500 of the lesser measure known as stades, and 368 in the greater measure
> known as leagues. On that island are a great many sheep. From there to
> Babylon it is 168 in the lesser measure of stades and 115 in the greater
> measure known as leagues.[60]

That the colony is at the beginning or the edge of an island measurable by two
different scales of human measurement, *stadia* and *leuuae;* that its most notable fauna is the familiar *sceap;* and that its distance to the famous biblical city
of Babylon can be measured — all this demarcates a place more knowable than
unknowable. This sense of familiarity is reinforced by the first illustration on
the leaf that shows seven sheep being sheep, that is to say, grazing on a hilly

landscape — much as they might on the English downs. The next section in the text notes that the colony is settled mainly by merchants, a group that must by definition negotiate between a here and an elsewhere in order to secure its living. The text then introduces its first note of the wondrous by noting that next to the city of Archemedon, where the merchants live, can be found rams as big as oxen.[61] This statement is in some measure undercut by the accompanying illustration that shows four rams on a landscape but with no scale of comparison to establish their exceptional size. Within the prose section, moreover, this detail about enormous rams is buried by other statements of fact:

> Seo landbunes is swiðost cypemonnum geseted . þær beoð weðeras acennede on oxna micelnesse . þa buað oð meda burh þære burhge noma is archemedon . seo is mæst to babilonia byrig . þanon is to babiloniam in þæs læssan milgetæles stadia .CCC. 7 þæs maran þe leuua hatte .CC. from archemedon . þær syndon þa mycclan mærða þ(æt) syndan ða geweorc þe se miccla macedonisca alexander het gewyrcean. Ðæt lond is on lenge 7 on bræde ðæs læssan milgetæles ðe stadia hatte .CC. 7 þæs micclan ða leuua hatte .CXXXIII. 7 an half mil.

> The colony is heavily settled with merchants. There are rams born there the size of oxen; they live up to the city of the Medes. It [Archemedon] is the biggest city after Babylon. From there to Babylon it is 300 in the lesser measure of stades and 200 in the greater which is called leagues. There are great monuments there that the great Macedonian Alexander ordered made. That land is in length and breadth 200 of the lesser measure called stades and of the greater measure called leagues 133 and a half.[62]

That Archemedon is second only to the great Babylon in size; that its distance from that city can be determined by the two systems of measurement; that it contains buildings raised by Alexander of Macedon; that its dimensions are also measurable in stadia and leuuae — all this also designates a place that is more knowable than unknowable. Later sections of *Wonders* that follow, one after another with at most minimal links or transitions between them, will introduce more unfamiliar beings and practices. The crucial point to recognize about the opening leaf of *Wonders* in Tiberius B v, though, is how unexotic or unfrightening it seems for all its distance, how much a part of the knowable world it represents, how its categories are grounded in the customary geographical terms of Latin writers. Even the one oddity — rams as big as oxen — entails the distortion of a being's size not of its nature.

The third section of *Wonders* signals a movement into the extraordinary, but it does so in a manner that seems characteristic of the work as a whole, that is, it begins with the familiar in order to illuminate the ways in which it can turn unfamiliar and sometimes terrifying:

Sum stow is mon færð to ðare readan sæ seo is gehaten lentibelsinea . on ðan
beoð henna akende gelice ða þe mid us beoð reades hiwes. ⁊ gyf hi hlyc mon
niman wile oððe hyra æthrineð ðonne forbærnað hi sona eall his lic . þ(æt)
syndon ungefregelicu lyblac.

There is a place as one goes toward the Red Sea which is called Lentibelsinea.
In it hens are born red in color much like those among us, and if any one tries
to take or touch them then they will immediately burn up all his body. That is
amazing magic.[63]

This technique of writing similarity in order then to articulate difference is the
oldest trick of travel writing, one that seems essential whether the announced
genre is scientific, ethnographic, impressionistic, or poetic. Another version of
this trick appears in the next section of *Wonders* in order to lend an affect to
the translation from Latin (ultimately Greek) to Old English. In Lentibelsinea
there is, along with the inflammatory red hens, another kind of beast with
eight legs and terrifying eyes called, in the Latin, "oculos . . . gorgoneos" and,
in the Old English, "wælkyrian eagan."[64] That replacement of *gorgon* by
valkyrie is worth a study in itself, but for now it will do simply to observe that
it is an act of translation from one language and place to another language and
place. Or, in the terms offered earlier, it is a translation from elsewhere to here.

The sense of place in *Wonders* as encompassing, even juxtaposing, the familiarity of home and the unfamiliarity of the foreign gets written into one of
its most haunting sections, that concerning the "Donestre":

Ðonne is sum ealand on ðære readan sæ þær is moncynn þ(æt) is mid us
donestre genemned . þa syndon geweaxene swa frihteras fram ðan heafde oð
ðone nafelan . ⁊ se oðer dæl byð manneslice gelic ⁊ hi cunnon eall mennisc
gereord . þonne hi fremdes kynnes mann geseoð ðonne næmnað hi hine ⁊ his
magas cuðra manna naman ⁊ mid leaslicum wordu(m) hine beswicað ⁊ hi
onfoð ⁊ þæn(ne) æfter þan hi hine fretað ealne butan his heafde ⁊ þon(ne)
sittað ⁊ wepað ofer ðam heafde.

Next there is an island in the Red Sea where is a race of men called among us
the Donester, which are shaped like soothsayers from head to navel, and the
other part is most like a human body. And they know all human tongues.
When they see a person from a foreign group, then they name him and his kin
with the names of familiar people, and with lying words they betray him and
seize him, and afterwards they eat all of him except his head and they sit then
and weep over the head.[65]

The need to incorporate the outsider by eating its body and leaving the head to
be mourned over suggests an extreme version of the ambivalence that characterizes many works that depict places elsewhere: the foreign must be assimi-

lated in an almost physical way so that it can be made part of the traveler's body, and yet that act of incorporation can never be complete — the head remains — and becomes the object of regret to the traveler and so, by extension, to the reader as surrogate traveler.[66] Elsewhere is, in this vision, dangerous because it can never be fully consumed and leaves one disconsolate at the attempt. At the very least, some residue remains that cannot be normalized or naturalized into a complete narrative. The reader of *Wonders* in Tiberius B v cannot fully consume its foreign element: some of its facts or lore remains incompletely assimilated because lacking in narrative context.[67]

This incomplete assimilation might be described more exactly as an encounter with scattered facts that are evidently related but that have not been brought to a synthesized depiction or coherent narrative. The reader is left with pieces that relate to each other and yet is given no way to reconcile their differences or resolve them into a whole or otherwise live with them. This experience occurs most acutely in *Wonders* when the reader must register two very distinct races of people encountered by Alexander the Great. The first is made up of women with boars' tusks, hair to their heels, oxtails, bodies as white as marble, extreme height, and camels' feet: "Þa he hi lifiende gefon ne mihte þa acwealde he hi for ða(m) hi syndon æwisce on lichamon 7 unweorðe" (When he could not seize them alive, he killed them because they were disgusting in body and unworthy).[68] Three sections later, *Wonders* turns to a neighboring region and introduces another race:

> Ðis mannkynn lifað fela geara 7 hi syndan fremfulre menn. 7 gyf hwylc mann to him cymeð þonne gyfað hi him wif ær hi hine onweg lætan . se macedonisca alexander þa ða he him to com þa wæs he wundriende hyra menniscnysse ne wolde he hi cwellan ne him nawiht laðes don.

> This group of people lives for many years, and they are generous people. If any man comes to them they give him a woman before they allow him to leave. When the Macedonian Alexander came to them, he was amazed at their humanity. He would not kill them or do them any harm.[69]

Within a traveler's account the experience of meeting one race that is disgusting and then another that is humane can offer an occasion to moralize on the extraordinary diversity of God's creation. Or, in another sort of travel account, it can afford a moment of reassurance to the stay-at-home reader: even among those who fill one with horror there are others who move one with their generosity. Or, it's not all bad out there. *Wonders* does not offer any such explicit moments because of its generic limitations, as they are immediately evident in Tiberius B v; instead it provides a sequence of factual statements and illustrations about those regions that lie beyond the familiar colonia mentioned at its start. If *Wonders* edges toward some incipient narrative in ways that most other works in Tiberius B v cannot because they are lists or tables, it certainly does not reveal the same possibilities of interpretation it does when read in Vitellius A xv in company with, most richly, *Alexander's Letter to Aristotle*. There, as I shall suggest, the narrative of *Alexander's Letter* provides a metacontext for interpreting *Wonders* as a narrative of place.

When read within the larger frame of Tiberius B v, however, *Wonders* offers a catalogue of beings and practices related to each other chiefly because they are set in lands distant though not utterly alien. There are some momentary connections of setting or behavior to link sections, but the text cannot be read as a sequentially organized itinerary that follows a mappable or repeatable order like that of Sigeric's itinerary homeward from Rome. Nor does any other work in the manuscript encourage one to read *Wonders* as a narrative, even one as loosely plotted through similar territory as Mandeville's *Travels*. Instead, the text offers passages and illustrations that seem like a series of loose pages that have fallen out of an album and been put back in an imperfect order. That these passages and images seem to be related depends on the opening statement about the colonia and lands yet further afield because that allows one to understand them from a distant and more central vantage point. As *Wonders* ends with a long and quite surprising paragraph about Mambres and his brother Iamnes, the idolatrous magician, one can either argue a narrative is about to open that will contain all that has come before in the work or else one can conclude that the work's miscellaneous character has been yet again confirmed.[70]

This manuscript's version of *Wonders* also contains illustrations of the text, so it would have been accessible to (at least) three kinds of audience: those who could follow the text in Latin, presumably by reading it themselves as a learned language; those who could follow the text in Old English, either by reading it themselves or by hearing it read to them as a native language; and those who could follow the text through the illustrations as a nonverbal language. These audiences might well overlap, especially to the extent that an Anglo-Saxon reader of the Latin version would almost certainly have been able to read the Old English and illustrated versions as well. The point to be stressed is that the compiler of Cotton Tiberius B v sought to make the eastern ethnography of *Wonders* as accessible as possible to as many Anglo-Saxons as possible. Running throughout this text is an obvious fascination with the monstrous, the deformed, the alarming. Yet what these images almost always modify or deform is the natural order of things as found in the immediate, familiar site of England as well as in the distant, imagined sites of the East. The category of the monstrous in *Wonders* does not yield beings utterly different or unimaginable for an English reader or viewer. If these beings sometimes seem freakish, they are not freaks that can be mentally quarantined in a distant elsewhere. Instead, their appearance in *Wonders* might well have led an Anglo-Saxon reader or viewer to ponder the ways in which the distant regions of this text are populated by beings at once like and unlike those to be found on the island.

That ability to contain both here and elsewhere, the familiar and the strange, as necessary places characterizes the written map of Anglo-Saxon England. Its geographical contours may sometimes be difficult, if not impossible, to discern, but its ethnographic and cultural descriptions are immediately comprehensible. For that reason, it is not enough to represent *where* on this map; one must also depict *who*. The great strength of a written map, such as those found in Tiberius B v, becomes evident when one turns to the sole surviving Anglo-Saxon mappamundi, also found in Tiberius B v.[71] This map has Jerusalem roughly at its center and England in the lower left-hand corner, strangely configured, with a scattering of islands to its north representing the Orkneys, a small island immediately to its northwest (the Isle of Man), a somewhat larger island running east–west (that should run north–south) that is labeled "Hibernia," and then almost at the corner edge of the map itself another island that looks a bit like Iceland that is labeled "Tyleni," or Thule.[72] England, Wales, and Scotland look rather strange on this map because Cornwall and Wessex extend too far west in relation to the north–south axis of the island. This island looks far more like a boomerang than its image in a modern atlas. It looks, in fact, like nothing so much as an angle, as if the mapmaker was familiar with the etymology of the tribal name *Angle* that was associated with the island of England as an angle or corner on the earth (as in Thietmar of Merseburg, for example) rather than with the ancestral region in Germania known as *Angulus*.[73] The spiritual geography of the map enforces this reading: if Jerusalem is the center of its world, then England is at its far end, set at an angle to continental Europe and the rest of the world, both known and imagined.[74] To understand this map's placement of England, we must look at it not as it is usually reproduced, as a freestanding sheet with no manuscript context, but instead as part of a large manuscript containing an extraordinary range of information about the geography of this world and beyond. Fred C. Robinson has taught us that Old English texts must be read in manuscript context, and the lesson holds equally when, as here, that text is drawn rather than written.[75]

In its current state, Tiberius B v ends with the world map as, one might think, a visual cartographic summa for the widely diverse contents of its ethnographic and geographic texts. The evidence suggests, however, that the map originally appeared before the text of Priscian's *Periegesis*, a tour of Rome, but it did not illustrate that text because the two bear little if any relation to one another.[76] Once one gets over the visual appeal of the mappamundi in Tiberius B v, that is, its value as an Anglo-Saxon rarity and, more alluringly, as a link with our cartographic practice, one can see how relatively little information it offers beyond a rough outline of Europe and parts of Asia and a plethora of place-names. But about those place-names it has little if anything to say. Writing of Dionysius Periegetes and his didactic versifying of an Alexandrian map, Christian Jacob makes a larger claim that can be applied to the Cotton map as it sits among a textual repertory in the manuscript: "The supremacy of the *logos* over the map it describes, of the literary frame of geography over its visual and mathematical construction, is explained through cultural practices — a written text, a recited poem could reach a far wider audience than any map on a papyrus roll or on a large wooden or stone panel."[77] If we place the Cotton mappamundi in its immediate manuscript context, we can see how limited a form of representation this visual map appears beside written and illustrated maps like *Wonders*. These works shaped a rich and detailed sense of place in Anglo-Saxon England by negotiating similarity and difference. The use of both Latin and Old English, even on occasion for the same text, was more than a strategy for reaching various audiences: these forms accomplish the work of cultural transfer by which elsewhere or the exotic, such as the Latin book of monsters not resident on the island, can be transplanted to familiar ground through the vernacular and the visual. What can be written about in the native language, this transfer insists, cannot remain entirely foreign or incomprehensible.

Cotton Tiberius B v has been described by its editor, Patrick McGurk, as a "visual secular collection."[78] It is visual in offering illustrations, a map, diagrams, drawings, and the like; it is secular in addressing a lay audience, though much of its material is religious in origin and nature; and it is a collection in being an encyclopedia of the world and its celestial regions that makes use in varying proportions of Latin and Old English. The manuscript as a whole teaches a great deal of information about popes, monsters, kings, cannibals, mythological figures memorialized by constellations, routes from Rome, and the like. As is true of Latin encyclopedias, the works in this manuscript are valuable for their raw information and also for their ways of knowing, specifically, for forms of calculating and representing the earth and its inhabitants. Modern scholars tend to ransack rather than read these Latin encyclopedias because they help us interpret the texts that interest us, which are rarely if ever the encyclopedias themselves. To rephrase this claim in terms specific to Cotton Tiberius B v, we should not pull out the mappamundi and treat it as distinct from the manuscript, as somehow more congruent with our ways of working and thus as more valuable than the written maps found elsewhere in the collection. To the contrary, if we use the mappamundi in its immediate manuscript context, we can see how impoverished a form of representation the visual map can seem when set beside written and illustrated maps like *The Wonders of the East.*

The Anglo-Saxons learned about the world by writing about it; in Tiberius B v, they found a variety of forms adequate to that purpose, such as monster lore, regnal and episcopal lists, pilgrimage accounts, a text of the so-called *Aratea,* Cicero's translation of Aratus's poetic astronomy,[79] excerpts from the Latin encyclopedias of Pliny and Isidore about times and places, and the account of Rome traditionally ascribed to the grammarian Priscian. These materials can accurately be described as learned in origin, if not always in presentation or audience. A sense of place as it becomes formalized as a written map of the world must in some measure depend on learned sources because the subject is one of large distances and wide perspectives. As a corollary, most of these materials cast light on England obliquely, that is, as the place where one learns about elsewhere, and thus about home.

Even computistical texts for setting the Easter date and thus in consequence the other moveable feasts of the calendar are a way of mapping the world of Roman Christendom because through that commonality of observance an orthodox religious realm is demarcated. In a practice that had important consequences for Anglo-Saxon ideas of place, the tables used for calculating paschal dates, prepared in Rome and then sent to England, served as the original format for compiling the annalistic materials that would become in the 890s the *Anglo-Saxon Chronicle.* In that account of history, each year's entry opens with the Old English *her.*[80] That word itself signals a rich and complex sense of place: in the *Chronicle, her* means conventionally "in this year" because it marks the place in the manuscript where the year's record is to be written; "here in this manuscript" means "here in the record of history." But in this context *her* also marks the larger location of England, as in this entry: "Her forðferde Eaduuard king. ⁊ Harold eorl feng to ðam rice" (Here King Edward died. And Earl Harold succeeded to the kingdom).[81] The difficulty we have in translating the *Chronicle*'s use of *her* — that *here* in Modern English is locative rather than temporal in reference — can be eased if we take the Old English usage to mean "here and now" or "in this time and place." Yet again, a text that seems indisputably dedicated to time and the writing of history reveals its inclusion as well of place and the writing of geography.

The technical complexity and relative unfamiliarity of most texts in Tiberius B v help to justify my lengthy discussion of the manuscript, though much remains to be explored in this most undervalued of Anglo-Saxon compilations.

The five works in British Library, Cotton Vitellius A xv, are, by contrast, much better known either as major poems in themselves — *Beowulf* and *Judith* — or as the immediate companions to these poems — *The Passion of St. Christopher, The Wonders of the East,* and *Alexander's Letter to Aristotle.* Any critical study about this manuscript has the advantage, as is not the case with Tiberius B v, of drawing on the modern reader's memory of these five texts, so much so that such a study becomes a return to a familiar and much-admired group of texts and places. Indeed, that sense of return or rereading is central to the human experience of being in place: the encounter with a site, particularly for those who live in societies with limited opportunities for personal travel, is most likely to be a reencounter with a site, a return on a frequent, perhaps daily basis to the known territory of experienced life. The narrative device at stake in each of the five texts of Vitellius A xv is, I would argue, a moment of return, whether by a character in the tale or by its teller. Central to this argument that the texts of Vitellius A xv together constitute a book of elsewhere are those moments in each text when return to a place becomes foregrounded so markedly that it deepens or enlarges the meaning of the text. Such moments establish place as more than mere setting for narrative.

The Passion of St. Christopher as it survives in Vitellius A xv is very incomplete, though its broad outlines are reasonably clear, and its details can be filled in by consulting related texts from Anglo-Saxon England.[82] In its fragmentary state, the version in Vitellius A xv, however, makes no explicit reference to forms of the monstrous and, more specifically, to Christopher's membership in the race of dog-headed people. From passing references in the extant text, a very alert reader might deduce that Christopher deviates from human norms: the device on which he is tortured is said to be twelve feet long, the same as his height, and the king who persecutes him calls him "wyrresta wilddeor," the worst of wild beasts.[83] This phrase, though, could easily be intended as a metaphoric rather than a literal insult, one especially revealing when uttered by a pagan ruler as he persecutes a Christian saint. Nor does the text make explicit in its current state that this persecution takes place in a previously unconverted region, presumably India, that will subsequently experience conversion as a direct result of Christopher's martyrdom. The text can be treated in many ways as a familiar narrative of top-down conversion as dictated by a ruler, such as appears frequently in Bede's *Ecclesiastical History.*

Yet the conversion story in *Christopher* relies heavily on the matter of place conceived in the most literal way possible, as the soil of the earth on which the narrative takes place. The conversion story here unfolds as an unnamed king (evidently the same Dagnus who appears in parallel texts) challenges Christopher to demonstrate the divine power of his God by curing the blindness inflicted on him inadvertently during his persecution of the saint. For the king was blinded, with ironically divine justice, when the very same arrows he had commanded his minions to aim at Christopher were shot into his royal eyes. Christopher responds by telling the king to return to the site of the martyrdom:

> Cum þonne to minum lichaman 7 nym þære eorðan lam þe ic on gemartyrod wæs 7 meng wið min blod 7 sete on þine eagan þonne gif þu gelyfst on god of ealre heortan þære sylfan tide þu bist gehæled fram þinra eagena blindnesse.

> Go then to my body and take there the clay of the earth on which I was martyred and mix it with my blood and put it on your eyes and if you believe in God with all your heart at the same time you will be healed of the blindness of your eyes.[84]

The king returns to the site, follows Christopher's instructions, and is promptly healed.[85] As a direct consequence, he then accepts the divinity of the Christian God and proclaims his dominion throughout the kingdom.

The outline of the story — the martyrdom of a saint leads to the conversion of a people through the miraculous healing of its leader — is hardly unique to this *Passion of St. Christopher*. As a text within a manuscript about representations of elsewhere, however, *Christopher* establishes some crucial concepts for understanding the sanctity and salvific power of place. In the large historical sense, the text represents missionary martyrdom as a paradigm for conversion as it is practiced across the dimension of space: for what is converted is a region and its people rather than individual souls that have come separately to God. Through missionary work, Christendom as a territory of belief is enlarged and also unified through a regularized liturgical calendar and centralized papal control, both discussed earlier with reference to Tiberius B v. But *Christopher* engages with place in another and potentially far more localizable manner, that is to say, it speaks of a place of martyrdom in distant India in ways that would have been familiar to an Anglo-Saxon audience from accounts of martyred saints on their own island.

The narrative of this Christopher story contains two elements fundamental to a hagiographical sense of place: first, the conversion consequent on the healing of blindness brings spiritual illumination to the people of a political region and second, this healing is worked in significant measure through the soil on which the saint was martyred. These two elements serve as the common features shared by a site of martyrdom in India and one in Englalond, and thus can serve to identify certain necessary principles of belief and power across Christendom. Of these two, the most conventionally obvious concerns the healing of an individual's blindness as a means to enable the spiritual illumination of the larger group to which he or she belongs. Thus, for example, Bede relates early in the *Ecclesiastical History* that the decisive miracle worked by Bishop Germanus in his campaign against Pelagianism in Britain was to cure the blindness of a young girl. And she is not simply any young girl; she is said to be the daughter of a certain tribune, that is, of a figure central to the power structure of Britain at the time.[86] As Bede relates the story, Germanus acts with decisive force:

> Nec mora, adherentem lateri suo capsulam cum sanctorum reliquiis collo auulsam manibus conprehendit, eamque in conspectu omnium puellae oculis adplicauit, quos statim euacuatos tenebris lumen ueritatis impleuit. Exultant parentes, miraculum populos contremescit; post quam diem ita ex animis omnium suasio iniqua deleta est, ut sacerdotum doctrinam sitientibus desideriis sectarentur.

> He tore from his neck the little bag which hung down close to his side, containing relics of the saints. Grasping it firmly, he pressed it in the sight of all on the girl's eyelids; her eyes were immediately delivered from darkness and filled with the light of truth. The parents rejoiced while the people were overawed by the miracle. From that day the evil doctrine was so utterly banished from the minds of them all that they thirsted eagerly after the teaching of the bishops.[87]

Bede hastens to add that the damnable heresy of Pelagianism was suppressed with this miracle and orthodoxy was restored to the land. As a measure for the conversion of place, the miraculous healing of the blind figure — especially if related in one way or another to political power or its representatives — is as powerfully compelling in Bede's *History* as in *Christopher,* that is, as efficacious in the immediate here of England as in the distant there of India.

The other characteristic motif in the Vitellius A xv account of Christopher is that soil from the site of martyrdom ("þære eorðan lam") possesses healing powers. The sense of place associated with martyrdom is thus localizable as the earth beneath one's feet. This remarkably literal sense of place is as closely tied to lived experience as is the boundary clause of a land charter. That soil can possess miraculous powers because of the presence of a saint on it appears not simply in accounts of distant martyrdoms, such as Christopher's, but also in accounts of the most recognizably famous of English saints, and one crucially important to the creation of a political sense of England as an *ecclesia*. I refer to Cuthbert and the stories told about him by Bede, especially that concerning the healing of a demonically possessed young boy who lived on an estate belonging to the monastery of Lindisfarne. When the howling boy is brought to Lindisfarne — that most dramatic of holy spaces in England because demarcated as an island (Figure 15) — he is cured by a priest who thought to draw on the power of Cuthbert:

Figure 15: Lindisfarne, Northumberland, the causeway leading to Holy Island.

Tunc ecce quidam de presbiteris edoctus in spiritu per opitulationem beati
patris Cuthberti illum posse sanari, uenit clanculo ad locum ubi nouerat
effusam fuisse aquam, qua corpus eius defunctum fuerat lotum, tollensque
inde modicam humi particulam immisit in aquam. Quam deferens ad patien-
tem infudit in ore eius. Quo horribiliter hiante, uoces diras ac flebiles emit-
tebat. Statim autem ut attigit aquam, continuit clamorem, clausit os, clausit et
oculos qui sanguinei et furibundi patebant, caput et corpus totum reclinauit in
requiem.

Then one of the priests, being instructed in spirit that he could be healed by
the help of the blessed father Cuthbert, came secretly to the place in which
he knew that the water had been poured wherein his dead body had been
washed. Taking a small particle of the earth, he put it in water and brought it
to the patient, pouring it into his mouth, which was gaping wide in a horrible
manner, and uttering fearful and lamentable cries. But as soon as he touched
the water, he restrained his cries, shut his mouth and his eyes which before
were wide open, bloodshot and furious, while his head and his whole body
sank into repose.[88]

As this episode suggests, the healing power of place is specific and local: it
depends on soil that was mixed with the water once used to bathe Cuthbert's
body, and it is soil found on the holy site of Lindisfarne.

Quoting these passages from Bede's writing beside *The Passion of St. Christopher* suggests a set of tropes that constitute the grammar by which hagiography locates itself on a site and associates its work with the power of place. These passages, as a whole, suggest that place can have agency in the working of Christian history and thus must be registered as scrupulously as is time, that other narrative marker. That a holy place acquires an aura of reverence because of its history and its attendant healing powers is not exclusive to any one site on the map of Christendom; indeed, such places can be said to constitute landmarks on the mappamundi of Christendom as it charts both the familiar and the distant, the native and the foreign. When these sites become enfolded into narrative, as occurs in these various works of hagiography, they become the objects of pilgrimages, either literal or imaginative. Even mental pilgrimages, such as an Anglo-Saxon might make after hearing *The Passion of St. Christopher,* would entail a journey or return to a literal place and its soil, the same soil that can be mixed with the martyred blood of a Christopher to cure blindness, or with the bath water of a Cuthbert to cure possession. In that way, the tale told about Christopher presents a miracle that could occur anywhere in God's creation and thus deexoticizes its setting in India by suggesting the setting's fundamental correspondence to sites in England, such as Lindisfarne.

The third work in Vitellius A xv, *Alexander's Letter to Aristotle,* is also set explicitly in India and reads as a kind of incipient quest-romance, a sequence of adventures in parts far distant among monsters and other wondrous creatures. What India might mean as a geographical designation is never specified in this work, nor is its location set relative to other places. The work does not, as do so many Roman treatises, structure its geography through a sequence of locations such as a traveler would follow to reach, as happens in the prenarrative, or backstory, of this work, India from Greece. Instead *Alexander's Letter* simply specifies its location in India, though Alexander (its announced author) does refer to earlier letters he has sent to Aristotle and thus allows for the possibility of such a geographical sequence. Still, as the work stands in Vitellius A xv, it is very much about India and all the wondrous and surprising beings both human and bestial to be found there:

> Ond for þon þe ic þe wiste wel getydne in wisdome, þa geþohte ic for þon to þe to writanne be þæm þeodlonde Indie ⁊ be heofenes gesetenissum ⁊ be þæm unarimdum cynnum nædrena ⁊ monna ⁊ wildeora, to þon þæt hwæthwygo to þære ongietenisse þissa niura þinga þin gelis ⁊ gleawnis to geþeode.

> And since I know that you are well set in wisdom, I thought to write to you about the great nation of India, and the disposition of the heavens, and the countless varieties of serpents, and men, and wild beasts, so that your learning

and knowledge might contribute to a certain extent to the understanding of these novelties.[89]

This India cannot be read as quite the same as that in *The Passion of St. Christopher* because it is, by self-definition, before the time of Christian conversions. Its precise historical moment is not specified, but it is sufficient that it is the India conquered by a pagan Greek emperor writing to his old teacher, the philosopher Aristotle.[90]

If *Alexander's Letter* is indeed a romance, as I have suggested, what then is the quest of its central figure?[91] A partial answer appears in the third section of the work, one that serves as well to suggest why Aristotle is indeed the ideal audience for this letter:

> Seo eorðe is to wundrienne hwæt heo ærest oþþe godra þinga cenne, oððe eft þara yfelra, þe heo þæm sceawigendum is æteowed.

> The earth is a source of wonder first for the good things she brings forth, and then for the evil, through which she is revealed to observers.[92]

Reading *Alexander's Letter* as a text about the earth as setting for both good and evil suggests that its representation of India may have less to do with versions of the wondrous and strange than with its potential for locating a decisive moment through which to explore these categories. Its process of inquiry or quest has less to do with monsters than with place. For of all the beings Alexander encounters on his adventures, none is more striking than the three-hundred-year-old bishop or holy man he meets in India late in his traveling life:

> Wæs he se bisceop .X. fota upheah, ⁊ eall him wæs se lichoma sweart buton þæm toþum ða wæron hwite. ⁊ þa earan him þurh þyrelode, ⁊ earhringas onhongedon of mænigfealdan gimcynne geworhte, ⁊ he wæs mid wildeora fellum gegerwed.

> The bishop was ten feet tall and his entire body was black, except his teeth were white. And his ears were pierced through, and ear-rings hung down made of many kinds of jewels, and he was dressed in the skins of wild-animals.[93]

His title *bisceop* seems meant to convey a measure of religious eminence rather than ecclesiastical office because he tends the sacred trees of the Sun and Moon, which are most decidedly non-Christian. He greets Alexander with courtesy and asks why he has come to the region, to which Alexander responds that he wishes to see the sacred trees of the Sun and Moon. This request is granted by the bishop on condition that Alexander and his men are free of the touch of women, a standard of purity that seems unaccompanied by any explicit doctrinal content. After various ritual moments among these trees, Alexander and his men are told by the bishop that each of them should think secretly of what he most wants to know and not tell anyone else:

> Ða cwæð se sacerd: "lociað nu ealle up 7 be swa hwylcum þingum swa ge willon frinan, þence on his heortan deagollice, 7 nænig mon his geþoht ope-num wordum ut ne cyðe."

> Then the priest said: "Look up, all of you, and think secretly in your heart what you want to know, and let no one openly reveal his thought in words."[94]

True to his sense of high destiny, Alexander asks whether he will hold sway over the entire world and then be able to return home to his mother and sisters in Macedonia.[95] The episode here is quite remarkable: the decisive moment in Alexander's quest concerns no external foe, either human or monstrous, but an encounter with self-knowledge and heroic destiny. If there is a compelling echo of this moment elsewhere in Vitellius A xv it can be only in the self-reflections of the aged Beowulf after the dragon has come. The trees of the Sun and Moon, we have learned earlier, speak both Greek and Indian, but the tree answers Alexander in the Indian language, that is to say, in the language of the place.[96] In an explicitly signaled moment of negotiation between unfamiliar and familiar, the bishop must translate the words of the oracular tree from Indian into Greek for Alexander. And those words are chilling:

> "Ða unoferswyðda Alexander in gefeohtum þu weorðest cyning 7 hlaford ealles middangeardes, ac hwæþre ne cymst þu on þinne eþel ðonan þu ferdest ær, for þon ðin wyrd hit swa be þinum heafde 7 fore hafað aræded."

> "Alexander, unconquered in battle, you shall become king and lord of all the world, but you shall never return to your homeland whence you came, since your fate has so decided it on your head, and so decreed it."[97]

Alexander is not the only traveler to learn that he has gone too far and will not return home alive, but this moment which demarcates the limits of his own life turns *Alexander's Letter* from an inventory of wondrous events and beings into a narrative about the impossibility of return.[98] For the sacred grove of the Sun and Moon is the place where the figure of worldly pride acquires a mea-sure of self-knowledge by learning the limits of his power and life. He also learns that in the following year, sometime in May, he shall be betrayed in an unexpected way while in Babylon and there die of poison.[99] That he will die in Babylon suggests a westerly return on his part toward Greece and thus that India has been the far point of his journey both geographically and narratively, for there his quest achieves something more profound than a knowledge of wondrous beasts and practices. *Alexander's Letter* ends with Alexander re-minding his old teacher Aristotle that his impending death must be kept secret lest it dispirit his army and encourage his enemies.[100] At this moment, as one remembers forcefully that Alexander in India is writing back to Aristotle in (presumably) Athens, the reason for including *Alexander's Letter* in Vitellius A xv becomes evident: it inscribes in its very structure the negotiation of here and elsewhere, and it can even be said to make the terms of that dialectic interchangeable or reversible so that one can take the here in question to be Alexander's location as narrator in India rather than Aristotle's location in Greece or, more textually, the reader's location in England.

That *Alexander's Letter* articulates a narrative with a sense of movement both geographical and chronological, through both place and time, explains its presence in Vitellius A xv. Its sense of place is widely encompassing in scope, but that sense of place is most powerfully registered through the work's para-digmatic representation of elsewhere — in the setting of the trees of the Moon and Sun — as the setting for the heroic encounter with the limits of earthly life. The work establishes that narrative as the movement through places can relate directly to the trajectory of a human life. In that regard, it belongs very much within the same interpretive conventions as do *Beowulf* and *Judith*. Yet unlike the title characters of these two poems, Alexander is thwarted in his attempt to return home. Having gone too far, he can only gesture at return by journeying back toward Babylon. And yet, one must also observe that Alexander does return home to Greece — not as triumphant war-king but as the author of his own experiences in distant regions. *Alexander's Letter* acquires its exemplary value because it sets forth the relation between journey and narrative in ways that go beyond the obvious parallel that each can be one damn place after another. More radically, its suggests that narrative can complete or fulfill the limitations of journeys taken to places elsewhere because it can figure as an act of return even when its author must remain stranded somewhere between home and the far point of his travels. In its sense that elsewhere is a place to be written about *for those back home* — which is, in turn, another kind of else-where — *Alexander's Letter* stands in Vitellius A xv as a striking counterpart to *Beowulf*.

In moving from the *Passion of St. Christopher* to *Alexander's Letter*, I passed over *The Wonders of the East* in order to create a narrative context that can reveal how reading the work in Vitellius A xv differs from reading it in Tiberius B v. With that context established, we can see that many of the seemingly unlocalized or underexplained statements in *Wonders* take on a quite different cast when encountered in Vitellius A xv, that is, they become features on a recognizable map rather than seemingly disconnected items of lore. This difference is apparent from the very start of *Wonders,* with its statement that the *landbunes,* or colony, is at the edge of the island of Antimolima, and that this island is in turn 168 stades, or 115 leagues, from Babylon: "⁊ þanon is to Babilonia þæs læssan milgetæles stadia hundteontig ⁊ eahta ⁊ syxtig, ⁊ ðæs micclan þe leuua hatte fiftyne ⁊ hundteontig" (and from there to Babylon it is 168 of the lesser measurement called *stadia,* and 115 in the greater measurement called *leuuae*).[101] For the reader of *Wonders* who also knows *Alexander's Letter,* this statement helps to place Antimolima within a certain range of Babylon, a city by now familiar as the setting for Alexander's death, and more important, known to be located between India to the east and Macedonia to the west. Admittedly, this placement of Antimolima and Babylon is by our GPS standards unacceptably vague; but by the standards of Anglo-Saxon textual geography, it is a remarkable improvement over the same information when presented in Tiberius B v.

The greater specificity about Antimolima and Babylon in Vitellius A xv becomes yet more pronounced as one moves into the second section of *Wonders,* which relates that the name of the landbunes is Archemedon:

> Seo is mæst to Babilonia byrig. Þanon is to Babiloniam þæs læssan milgetæles stadia .CCC. ⁊ þæs maran þe leuua hatte .CC. from Archemedon. Þær syndan þa mycclan mærða þæt syndan ða geweorc þe se miccla macedonisca Alexander het gewyrcean.

> It is the biggest city after Babylon. To there from Archemedon is 300 of the lesser measurement, *stadia,* and 200 of the greater, called *leuuae.* There are great monuments there, which are the works which the mighty Alexander of Macedon had made.[102]

The locating of each place, whether Antimolima or Archemedon, with reference to Babylon follows from its role as the great city of the region, that hinterland between Macedonia and India.[103] One would love to know what the text means by those "mycclan mærða" constructed by Alexander, especially because the claim resonates with the Old English trope *enta geweorc* for designating the mysteriously grand constructions of those who long ago occupied the land. Whatever these great monuments might have been for the author of *Wonders,* his reference to them establishes that the territory of the work is in some measure coterminous with that of *Alexander's Letter,* a fact that begins with geography and moves into intertextuality. The greatness of these monuments is at the very least more comprehensible and believable for the reader of *Wonders* who encounters them in the same manuscript that also relates Alexander's expedition across Asia and into India.

Reading *Wonders* within the textual geography of *Alexander's Letter* yields its most illuminating results when we reencounter the two sections in which Alexander is said to meet with two very different peoples in his journey. The first is made up of extremely tall women with camels' feet and boars' teeth whom Alexander kills because of their uncleanness:

> Þa he hi lifiende gefon ne mihte, þa acwealde he hi for ðam hi syndon æwisce on lichoman ⁊ unweorðe.

> He [Alexander] killed them because he could not capture them alive, because they have offensive and disgusting bodies.[104]

The other people encountered by Alexander are notable for their generosity, particularly in sharing their women with visitors:

> Se macedonisca Alexander þa ða he him to com, þa wæs he wundriende hyra menniscnysse, ne wolde he hi cwellan ne him nawiht laðes don.

> When Alexander of Macedon visited them, he was amazed at their humanity, and would not kill them or cause them any harm.[105]

When read in the Tiberius version of *Wonders,* these passages create some general sense that describing these two peoples is a kind of travel writer's trope, a conventional acknowledgment that anyone wandering the earth will find the loathsome and admirable in close proximity to each other, as they are here located in the text. Even that reading may be something of a stretch for the text in Tiberius B v because the work's atomistic quality discourages any form of synthesizing interpretation. When encountered in the context of Vitellius A xv with some memory of *Alexander's Letter,* however, these two passages come to read as exempla for illustrating that work's great statement about the created earth:

> Seo eorðe is to wundrienne hwær heo ærest oþþe godra þinga cenne, oððe eft þara yfelra, þe heo þæm sceawigendum is æteowed.

> The earth is a source of wonder first for the good things she brings forth, and then for the evil, through which she is revealed to observers.[106]

The good and evil beings revealed by *Wonders* turn out to be not so much monsters as varieties of human beings.

If Alexander in the Tiberius version of *Wonders* seems no more than a shadowy reputation, he becomes in the Vitellius version a more realized figure with greater historical and geographical specificity. As it reflects the generic contents of each manuscript, *Wonders* becomes more complexly historical and less sensationalistic in Vitellius than in Tiberius, more about human beings and the use of places to demarcate a life than about the exotic elsewhere.

Wonders certainly does not read as a full narrative in Vitellius A xv, but placing it in the immediate manuscript context of *The Passion of St. Christopher* and *Alexander's Letter* allows one to sketch out some of its possibilities in that direction. Reading *Wonders* in company with these other works makes us in some way like the Donestre, figures who have consumed enough to lament over that which remains. In that process, the monsters in the text figure as necessary features of a culturally variegated landscape rather than the immediate subject of the text.

As it is set in the ancestral homeland of the premigratory Anglo-Saxons and depicts elsewhere as the territory of the past, *Beowulf* is profoundly a work about place. The relation of the continental elsewhere to the audience of the poem in England is articulated through the record of ancestral history, that is, through the movement across the North Sea.[107] This larger historicist reading of *Beowulf* is enabled by the text and certainly does not depend on its context in Cotton Vitellius A xv, though that may have led the compiler to include it in the manuscript. There are other senses of place in the poem, however, that do emerge more vividly when it is read in the context of Vitellius A xv. These senses of place are focused most powerfully in a passage that, in a seeming paradox, is usually treated as the segue between the two great episodes of the hero's life: the breakneck chronology at ll. 2200–2214a that takes Beowulf from young retainer to king and then through fifty years of his rule until the dragon comes. For self-evident reasons, this passage is almost always discussed for its temporal daring, its willed collapsing of the years within a narrative deeply concerned with the workings of time and history. No one, to my knowledge, has thought much about the relation of this passage to senses of place in the poem.[108] Yet any passage that is intensely about time is, as I have argued throughout this book, likely to be intensely about place as well.

These lines from *Beowulf* begin by relating the deaths of the two prior Geatish kings, Hygelac and his son, Heardred; they thus offer a political genealogy that establishes a sense of place much as do the regnal lists in Tiberius B v:

> Eft þæt geiode   ufaran dogrum
> hildehlæmmum,   syððan Hygelac læg,
> ond Heardrede   hildemeceas
> under bordhreoðan   to bonan wurdon,
> ða hyne gesohtan   on sigeþeode
> hearde hildfrecan,   Heaðo-Scilfingas,
> niða genægdan   nefan Hererices . . .

Afterwards it happened that in later days, in the crash of battle, after Hygelac lay dead and swords killed Heardred beneath the shield guard, when the

Heatho-Scylfings, the hardened warriors, had sought him among the victorious people, violently attacked the nephew of Hereric . . . " (ll. 2200–2206)[109]

The dynastic progression from Hygelac to Heardred (with passing reference to Hereric) to Beowulf (in the following line) is the history of the Geats. As a narrative, it is the progression as well from the young Beowulf who leaves Hygelac's court to kill monsters in Heorot, to the somewhat older Beowulf who serves as regent for the young Heardred, and then, finally, to the mature Beowulf who becomes, after Heardred's death, king of the Geatish people. The regnal lists in Cotton Tiberius B v establish very clearly through their headings, as they designate Northumbria or some other such region, that the sequence is meant to mark out territory; it has authority as a political record within the area occupied by subjects who acknowledge the power of the kings it lists. In that respect, these lines from *Beowulf* clearly demarcate a kingdom by offering its line of dynastic succession.

The next name in *Beowulf*'s regnal list is, of course, the commanding figure in the narrative:

> syððan Beowulfe   brade rice
> on hand gehwearf;   he geheold tela
> fiftig wintra   — wæs ða frod cyning,
> eald eþelweard —,   oð ðæt an ongan . . .

> when the broad kingdom came into the hands of Beowulf; he held it well for fifty years — he was then a wise king, an old guardian of the homeland — until a certain one began . . . (ll. 2207–10)

A passage that goes in four lines from *syððan* to *oð ðæt*, from "when" to "until," is a narrative in miniature that concerns how Beowulf ruled: the broad kingdom came into his hands and thus he did not usurp it or take it unlawfully; he held it for fifty winters, a very long time within human reckoning; he was wise because he was aged; he was the long-time guardian of the homeland, the *eþel*, because he was old. If *Beowulf* is, at least partly, a political poem that asks what it means to be an *eþelweard* — and answers in disparate ways through the figures of Scyld Scefing, Hrothgar, Heremod, Hygelac, Heardred, Beowulf, and Wiglaf — then it must also be a poem about place, about the meaning of *eþel*. The idea of home and homeland runs throughout Anglo-Saxon literature and society, as I have suggested in Chapter 2, but it seems strangely suspended in the first two-thirds of *Beowulf*. If this concern enters the poem at all in those lines, it relates to the sanctity of home and hall elsewhere, of life in Denmark rather than Geatland. Read that way, elsewhere is a foreign region for youthful feats of self-exploration and heroic definition, a place where the young can be daring and find riches and glory. At line 2210, however, we must ask what is Geatland because we as audience have spent most of our time abroad, in Denmark and other parts of Germania, either in the narrative present of Beowulf's deeds or in the heroic past of the legendary stories that they prompt. Only after Beowulf becomes king of Geatland do we as audience return there to face the grimly endangered eþel. We must ask, like Beowulf, what it means to occupy and defend the homeland — and the remaining lines of the poem give an answer, at once distant and elegiac, from the perspective of Englalond. Or, if one prefers a simpler narrative explanation for these lines, the poem needs a passage to connect its two great places, Denmark and Geatland, in ways that give meaning to its hero and his encounters with monsters. Either way, one's reading of *Beowulf* must change with this, the poem's final mention of *eþelweard*.

Indeed, that word *eþelweard* receives a fascinating gloss in the immediately following lines as the poem describes the dragon's power:

> oð ðæt an ongan
> deorcum nihtum   draca ricsian,
> se ðe on heaum hæþe   hord beweotode,
> stanbeorh steapne;   stig under læg
> eldum uncuð.

> until a certain one, a dragon, began to hold sway in the dark nights, that one who watched over a hoard on the high heath, a towering stone-barrow; the entry beneath it lay unknown to men. (ll. 2210b–14a)

The immediately engaging word in this passage is *ricsian*, a verb formed from the noun *rice*, meaning "kingdom," "territory," which thus means "to rule." In this passage, it signals that the dragon — not Beowulf — holds power over this homeland, this eþel. That the dragon should rule in the dark nights is appropriate for the unfolding of the narrative, but it also signals that this is a monstrous perversion of proper rulership because it is nocturnal. The verb *ricsian* would seem appropriate for many passages in *Beowulf*, a poem filled with statements about who rules where, but in fact it appears on only one other occasion in the poem:

> Swa rixode   ond wið rihte wan,
> ana wið eallum,   oð þæt idel stod
> husa selest.

> So [Grendel] held power and fought against right, one against all, until the best of halls stood empty. (ll. 144–46a)

Heorot remains in Grendel's control until the young Beowulf appears from Geatland to perform his act of heroism. Reading this passage about Grendel as well as the earlier passage about the dragon, one sees quite evidently that the poet reserves the verb *ricsian* for monsters who by their actions pervert all forms of proper governance, who disrupt the eþel.

The collocation in these two passages of certain elements — that a monster rules or misrules (*ricsian*) at night over a human-built hall — is central to the narrative geography of *Beowulf*. From the perspective of Geatland, when these elements appear together in Denmark, that place becomes an alluring elsewhere and the appropriate territory for the youthful hero's acts of self-definition. All of that changes utterly when these elements appear together in Beowulf's own eþel, where they cannot be safely distanced in a heroic narrative of elsewhere but rather become the terms for the king's final struggle in the most immediately possible sense of here. That the poem should so carefully bring together these elements first in a setting abroad and then in a setting at home suggests that any absolute distinction between elsewhere and here is at best facile and at worst dangerous because it ignores the commonality of events as they occur in human life. Places elsewhere may have their exotic attributes, their foreign color to seduce the eye and attract the best energies of the young, but when understood through the course of a life, they are no different from the places known as home because the same events are likely to occur in both if one lives long enough.

Interpreting the sense of here and elsewhere in *Beowulf* from the vantage of its original audience in Englalond makes the interchange of the two places — here can become elsewhere just as easily as elsewhere can become here — all the more intriguing. What is to be puzzled out about Geatland and Denmark within the narrative becomes all the more evident when *Beowulf* is read from afar in England and in the larger context of Cotton Vitellius A xv. If that is done, then the geographical imagination that underlies the works in this manuscript reveals how a people as a cultural group bound by history and religion and stories locates its place in the world. Or, more accurately, how it understands place as being polyvalent, encompassing multivocal places and forms of orientation. Look elsewhere, the works in Cotton Vitellius A xv seem to say, and what you will see in the end is not the exotic but the here that one calls home, eþel, Englalond. Elsewhere exists and can be visited, either literally or textually, but its ultimate effect is to return you to a more complex understanding of home.

This sense of movement is modeled within the narrative of *Beowulf* when the anonymous messenger journeys from the site of combat with the dragon to report the death of the king to his people (ll. 2892–3027). This moment of return belongs within a series of increasingly anonymous speeches, spoken first by Wiglaf, then by the anonymous messenger, and finally by the unnamed female mourner at Beowulf's pyre, that predict the Geats will fall out of history.[110] This prediction about the future of the Geats is the final consequence of the poem's return to Geatland beginning at line 2200: after spending hundreds of lines elsewhere, the poet must confront the meaning of Geatland as eþel, bound by its circumstances of time and place.

A return to the eþel also signals a narrative climax in *Judith,* the other poem in Cotton Vitellius A xv. The successful defense of the homeland is so much a part of this poem that some readers have treated it as a political allegory for the plight of the English as they tried to rally themselves against the attacking Danes in the late tenth and early eleventh centuries.[111] Perhaps the threat of outside invasion, of attack from elsewhere, gave the Apocryphal story of Judith some added resonance among the English in the years around 1000. If we read *Judith* within its manuscript context, however, the poem takes on a rather different valence. More specifically, its climactic moment depicts the literal return of Judith to her city of Bethulia after slaying Holofernes, a return that confirms her heroic status and also provides a compelling counterpoint to the ending of *Beowulf.* In dramatic contrast to the longer poem, *Judith* portrays the return of the hero to her people as a moment of triumph, of cultural survival, because Judith herself — and not an anonymous messenger — provides the welcome news that she has defeated their enemy, Holofernes:

> Wiggend sæton,
> weras wæccende   wearde heoldon
> in ðam fæstenne,   swa ðam folce ær
> geomormodum   Iudith bebead,
> searoðoncol mægð,   þa heo on sið gewat,
> ides ellenrof.   Wæs ða eft cumen
> leof to leodum,   ond ða lungre het
> gleawhydig wif   gumena sumne
> of ðære ginnan byrig   hyre togeanes gan,
> ond hi ofostlice   in forlæton
> þurh ðæs wealles geat,   ond þæt word acwæð
> to ðam sigefolce . . .

The warriors sat, the watching soldiers held guard in the fortress, as the prudent Judith had ordered the sorrowful people earlier, the shrewd virgin, when she set out on her mission, the daring woman. The beloved one had come back to her people, and the clever woman commanded quickly one of the warriors to come out of the broad city toward her and speedily let them in through the wall-gate, and she spoke these words to the victorious people . . . (ll. 141b–52a)[112]

Her words announce memorably that God will grant her people victory over the Assyrians in the battle that will soon occur.

Read as an intertextual commentary on *Beowulf*, these lines offer a salutary reminder to an Anglo-Saxon audience that the story of the homeland preserved, of the ruler who slays the dangerous enemy and lives, comes not from the ancestral Germanic tradition of their premigratory homelands but from the biblical tradition they gained after their conversion once they had settled in England. Judith may be made into a Germanic warrior, one rewarded with the armor of her vanquished adversary (ll. 334b–41), but she is not transplanted from her home city of Bethulia to regions closer to the English audience. She stands as the figure of heroic victory precisely because she is set in an elsewhere that is accessible to the English through the exegetical tradition of figural interpretation. To the complex geography of Vitellius A xv, *Judith* adds the homeland of the Israelites, a people identified by the Anglo-Saxons as their spiritual ancestors in Christendom.[113] Narrating Judith's return to her home city is thus a means of locating her place in Christendom for later generations. The poem need not announce the relevance of Judith and her defense of the eþel to the English audience because, as a biblical figure, she brought with her an inherent relevance or scriptural warrant that established that she belonged within a religious tradition that spoke directly to the English around the year 1000, even if she was a distant figure chronologically and geographically. Judith may live in a region as distant from England as any in Cotton Vitellius A xv, but unlike Alexander or Beowulf she belongs within an exegetical tradition by which her place and time can be comprehended and located rather than puzzled over as alien or distant or past. The elsewhere of *Judith* presents none of the difficulties of *Alexander's Letter* or *Beowulf*. This interpretive context for *Judith* may explain why a compiler of Vitellius A xv decided that a manuscript filled with exotica, monsters, pagan heroes, and the like should end with this poem, because there the Anglo-Saxon audience would understand the way in which narrative makes its territory: Bethulia may be distant in geography but not in meaning.

However we choose to order the five works of Cotton Vitellius A xv, or, more usefully, whatever order we use to read the manuscript as a compendium of place, we can see that it displays a deep engagement with depicting the past across space, with having Christopher, the Donestre, Alexander, Beowulf, and Judith coexist in the topography of human memory. A topos, we remember, is something more than a literary device: it is also a site, a place, where the past can be held in its complexities, even in its contradictions. None of the works in Vitellius A xv can be read as English in the same way as can Bede's *Ecclesiastical History* or the *Guthlac* poems, that is, as directly about England and as drawn directly from earlier English accounts and materials. To the contrary, these five works are about elsewhere and were taken largely if not exclusively from elsewhere. And four of them certainly existed in some previous form in a language or languages other than English. But there in the manuscript they become English through their use of the vernacular and through the demands that they placed on the only audience that could read them, the Anglo-Saxons. No matter how exotic their flora and fauna, no matter how mysterious their place-names and social customs, these books of elsewhere ended up being read at home, in the eþel known as Englalond.

The narrative mappaemundi created by manuscripts such as Tiberius B v and Vitellius A xv were valuable because, in many different ways and in many different texts, they wrote of both here and elsewhere. For an attentive reader, they provided a remarkably wide range of information about the world and its celestial regions, about its spiritual and political rulers, about the ways in which missionary saints and heroic figures moved across the earth in fulfillment of their destinies. They taught as well that ideas of place can be contained within many different genres, from the seemingly minimalist form of regnal list or computistical table to the more extended treatise or sophisticated narrative. Rhythms of here and elsewhere appear in many of these works, and some such understanding of place as dialectic allows the user of these manuscripts to move toward larger generalizations about the workings of place in human life and divine history. Yet except for the implicitly figural reading that comes with the biblically derived story of *Judith*, the works in Tiberius B v and Vitellius A xv do not provide a master narrative or key to all mythologies by which to understand their contents. Users of the manuscripts must arrive at such larger, more synthesizing readings for themselves, though they would certainly be guided by the principles of Christian interpretation they had learned through formal education or had absorbed through listening to homilies and sermons as part of their religious practice. For an Anglo-Saxon book of elsewhere that offers the Christian master narrative about place — from the fall from Eden to the final arrival in the heavenly home — one turns from these two manuscripts to the great biblical manuscript of Anglo-Saxon England, Bodleian, Junius 11.

7

Falling into Place: Dislocation in Junius 11

Perhaps the most haunting lament in the Hebrew Bible is Psalm 136 in the Vulgate: "Super flumina Babylonis." Its fearful burden is that an exiled people displaced from its home will lose its collective memory and fail to honor its covenant with God. The psalm ends with the bitter truth that the exile of a people must lead to the violent destruction of those who earlier had forced it from its homeland. Under such conditions of historical and spiritual extremity, the psalmist must ask the question that threatens the very existence of an exiled people: "quomodo cantabimus canticum Domini in terra aliena" (How can we sing the Lord's song in a strange land?). The loss of Jerusalem and the banishment to Babylon, the displacement from *terra cognita* to *terra aliena,* imperils the poetic voice by which a people praises God and, by so doing, locates its place in his creation. A people as well as its poet must have some native ground of language and terrain from which to shape a collective identity and fulfill their obligations to God. Exile, as the literal loss of that native ground, puts identity in danger.[1]

"Ofer Babilone bradum streame," the Old English version of Psalm 136, acquires a yet more culturally specific resonance when read within a vernacular lyric tradition that typically portrays exile as the experience of a solitary speaker, or *anhaga.*[2] Such representative figures as the Wanderer and the Seafarer, the speakers of *The Wife's Lament* and *Wulf and Eadwacer,* even the figures known as Deor and Widsith open themselves to psychological and spiritual interpretation because of their self-presentation as individuals. Each suggests a version of how one person is to fare through this world, and some go on to speak of where the soul will find a heavenly home. However we allegorize or psychologize these figures, we must remember that each envisions exile as the condition of an individual rather than a collective.[3] Or, more exactly, each depicts exile as the fate of an individual sundered from the communal group: the retainer without lord and retinue, the woman without husband and kin. In marked contrast, "Ofer Babilone bradum streame" laments the enforced exile of a religiously defined people; its first-person pronoun throughout is the Old English plural *we,* not the singular *ic* of the lyrics. In "Ofer Babilone bradum streame," one hears the voice of the *folc* as it also appears at far greater length in such narrative Old English poems as *Genesis, Exodus, Daniel,* and *Christ and Satan.* From this distinction between anhaga and folc emerges a further question about the conventions of biblical representation as they function in Old English poetry, namely, is there a significant relation between the historical condition of a people and the spiritual condition of its individual members? And then, how do these two forms of exile coexist within the historical memory as it is evoked by the psalmist?

The representation of exile as a collective condition is not restricted to Old English biblical poems; it appears as well in the illustrations of two famous Anglo-Saxon psalters. The illustrator of Psalm 136 in the Utrecht Psalter portrays, on the far right side of the panel, the Israelites as a group sitting beside the river of Babylon with their musical instruments hanging in the trees above them.[4] They are balanced by a group of Babylonians in such a manner as to establish that the terms of experience in this psalm and, by extension, throughout history are collective: the Israelites and Babylonians are alike in that each is figured as a people. In a more delineated illustration for this psalm, the artist of the Harley Psalter fills the frame with a walled city (evidently the Sion of the psalm's first verse) at the far left and the river of Babylon at the far right.[5] Set between city and river are seven figures seated beneath flamelike trees from which hang musical instruments, most notably the large harp of David. From the upper right-hand corner of the frame emerges the hand of God extended in a gesture of blessing. The Babylonians as a people are not represented in this image, an artistic decision that has the effect of emphasizing the Israelites as a chosen people within the Old Testament as well as emphasizing their solitude in exile. The Harley illustrator portrays the narrative of the Israelites, set between the Sion of their home and the river of their captivity, as a condition blessed by God and thus as comprehended within providential history. At the center of this illustration is the hanging harp, untouched by human hand, that poses without need of words the psalm's urgent question: "Quomodo cantabimus canticum Domini in terra aliena?" Beneath that harp, the Israelites appear as a group that knows Sion and Babylon, native ground and territory of exile.

As text and image, Psalm 136 sets religious history within the terms of a group's wandering, captivity, and suffering. In lamenting the condition of displacement, it inspires the Israelites to remember their covenant with God. The Old English version renders this force of displacement both through the imperative of the Babylonians — "Singað us ymnum ealdra sanga / þe ge on Sione sungan geneahhige" (Sing us a hymn from the old songs that you often sang in Sion) — and also through the unanswerable question by which the psalmist responds — "Hu magon we singan sangas drihtne / on þære foldan þe us fremde is?" (How can we sing songs to the Lord in a land that is alien to us?).[6] To sing the song of Sion in Babylon is to utter the lament of an exiled people. This Old English poem, for "Ofer Babilone bradum streame" is more than a simple translation, must be read within the larger history of human exile that runs throughout the Hebrew Bible and beyond.[7] The Babylonian captivity lamented in Psalm 136 followed in time the settlement of the Israelites in Canaan; and that, in turn, followed their exodus as a people across the Red Sea and through the desert where they wandered for forty years. This search for the new home promised by God's covenant with Abraham follows inevitably, if belatedly, from the expulsion of Adam and Eve out of Eden.

Within the Christian interpretive tradition, this sequence of events from Israelite history had a later figurative life, another form of fulfillment or homecoming in the story of Christ in the Wilderness and in his Harrowing of Hell. Christ's forty days reenacts and validates the Israelites' forty years in the desert; his spiritual triumph over Satan's temptation reenacts and validates the Israelites' triumph over the Egyptians. Christ's Harrowing of Hell releases his followers from another state of exilic captivity, one enforced by Satan rather than Nebuchadnezzar. With its patterns of human displacement, literal movement, and promise of freedom through exodus, this sequence of places might well be described as the geography of Christian redemption. It is a way of making sense of earthly history and experience within the narrative of the Bible. This redemptive geography offers a scripturally inflected sense of place that can also be used to read texts.

As a sequence of movements, the expulsion from Eden, the exodus of the Israelites to Canaan, the forced deportation to Babylon, the journey of Christ into hell and his victorious emergence, all belong to history as it unfolds along a geographical dimension.[8] The passing of time also orders the events in this sequence, but it is geography rather than chronology that contains the inherent pattern and thus the meaning of movement across place. Each of these events occurs, unavoidably, within place; more pointedly, each is about place in deep and haunting ways that register loss, exile, displacement, return. Psalm 136 articulates this vision of history as the lament of a displaced folc and thus offers a way to read the Old English poems known as *Genesis, Exodus, Daniel,* and *Christ and Satan;* together they constitute Oxford University, Bodleian Library, Junius 11, that great manuscript collection of poetry about events set elsewhere.[9] Elsewhere means, in this context, places beyond the borders of Englalond or, more specifically, places across the channel that separates it from the continent and all that lies far beyond, such as the lands that Abraham, Moses, Daniel, and Christ knew, or hoped to know, as their home.

Even the most superficial reading of the book of Genesis establishes that the fall of Adam and Eve was a fall into time and its inexorable workings: human aging, mortality in nature, seasonal change, and all the other markers of revealed time that were so ruefully evoked by Old English poets.[10] This expulsion was also, though perhaps less immediately apparent or doctrinally central, an act of falling into place or, more exactly, of falling into a knowledge of places. After the loss of Eden there would be no fixed home on earth but only the restless shuttling of lone exiles and transplanted peoples from place to place. Place, which had in Eden been singular, becomes plural in a postlapsarian world of many places scattered across the earth. Put another way, the price paid by humans for the sins of their ancestors, as we learn from the Bible, is the burden of place and displacement. Wandering, exodus, enforced captivity, spiritual struggle in a figuratively bounded place: these are the settings of Christian experience and history. The names of these settings are familiar: Egypt, Canaan, Jerusalem, Babylon, hell, and then, triumphantly, heaven.

Central to this reading of Junius 11 as a book of elsewhere is the Old English *Exodus* because it most obviously highlights the dynamic of place within the narrative of the Old Testament.[11] Writing in England as a refugee from Nazism, Elias Canetti offered this terse formulation for the history of the Jews: "The story of their wanderings is the story of their belief."[12] The story of the Israelites' migration and diaspora had an exemplary value among later Christian peoples for understanding their own earthly history. The reading of the Old English *Exodus* in my *Migration and Mythmaking in Anglo-Saxon England* falls within this historicized and historicizing sense of place, that is, of place as a history-making argument.[13] Here I want to consider how this logic of place was used not simply to inscribe the transformative migration of the Germanic tribes to Britain but also to denote a larger pattern of human history within the fallen world: that of movement, of the restless search for a place to call home.[14] In the sweep of Junius 11, the exodus matters because it's about a

chosen people being led to its new home through a divinely ordained movement. Exile in Babylon matters to the Israelites because there they remember
Jerusalem and their true faith with heartbreaking poignancy. The desert matters because there the experience of moving from place to place yields its full
significance in the promise of a heavenly home. Adam, Moses, Daniel, Christ,
Satan, Pharaoh, Nebuchadnezzar: such are the names that attach themselves
to the stories of place in Junius 11.

The four poems in this manuscript come to some 5,019 lines, more than half
again as the 3,182 that make up *Beowulf*.[15] The extended length of this collection offers, I would suggest, an ongoing narrative or flow of biblical history
that can be recognized most immediately by locating a few crucial moments in
each poem. J. R. Hall has made the necessary claim that Junius 11 is an "epic
of redemption," thereby arguing for the need to read through — not just simply
in — the manuscript.[16] Writing of its highly articulated illustrations and text,
Catherine Karkov puts the matter succinctly: "While Junius 11 is not a chronicle *per se*, it does both record and construct an historical picture."[17] To describe Junius 11 as a book of elsewhere is to go one step beyond Hall and
Karkov and argue that an Anglo-Saxon reader would have found meaning in
the ways its poems located their historical and theological themes.[18] I do not
address the vexed, and probably unanswerable, question of how or when
some compiler brought these four poems together in a single manuscript,
though I believe firmly that it was done with the expectation that readers
would treat it as a continuous flow of text. In that regard, Katherine O'Brien
O'Keeffe's conclusion is salutary: "The book which Junius 11 presents was
produced less by design than by accretion."[19] By reading these poems for their
references to place as a subject and also for their use of place to structure
narrative, we can gain an immediate appreciation of their literal meaning. The
reading I trace in the following pages is not meant to displace others that are
based on the manuscript's theological or liturgical unity or on its complex
program of illustrations.[20] My concern is less to identify the compiler's inten-
tions than to explore the ways in which an alert and informed reader might
interpret (whether by eye or ear) these poems as four books of religious history, that is, as parts of an improvised but necessary quadrateuch.[21]

By introducing the figure of Christ into the manuscript, *Christ and Satan*
makes possible a figurative reading of *Genesis, Exodus,* and *Daniel* in Erich
Auerbach's sense of the term: "Figural interpretation establishes a connection
between two events or persons, the first of which signifies not only itself but
also the second, while the second encompasses or fulfills the first. The two
poles of the figure are separate in time, but both, being real events or figures,
are within time, within the stream of historical life."[22] After learning that the

worthy souls exiled in hell have been saved, the reader of Junius 11 can resolve the patterns of exile, exodus, captivity, and return in *Genesis, Exodus,* and *Daniel* into a final journey of the soul to salvation. As Phyllis Portnoy has observed of typology in Junius 11: "This interaction of memory and hope is the essence of typology and of ritual; its emotional power lies in its promise of deliverance, not only from Egypts and Babylons, but from the bondage of sin and time and mortality."[23] There is in this resolution a move toward abstraction, a sense that the historicized geography of the Hebrew Bible will give way to an allegorized vision of human experience. Or, to speak more critically, the gripping narrative of the Old English *Exodus* will end with the more predictable homilies of *Christ and Satan.*

The figural structure of Junius 11 depends on a variety of concurrences and identifications that will be traced throughout this chapter, such as the typological relations between Adam, Noah, Moses, and Christ in the poems and more especially their repeated evocation of God's covenant with Abraham as it defines the meaning of place.[24] The immediate and local reference of this typology would have been registered by an Anglo-Saxon audience through the force of the vernacular, as I shall develop later in this chapter, and also through the manuscript's illustrations. As Karkov observes in her study of Junius 11: "Figures from biblical history appear in the drawings accompanied by attributes of Anglo-Saxon life, ensuring that they too become as if alive, and reminding us that the same figures we see here were very much a part of Anglo-Saxon 'historical' texts such as genealogies and chronicles."[25] One can read features that seem anachronistic from our historical perspective as instead deeply implicated in the history-making argument of Junius 11: that elements from everyday life figure in biblical illustrations asserts the connection between the two periods within Christian historiography.

The kinds of associative reading that figura enables for the four poems in Junius 11 are hardly unique to them or even especially esoteric within the Christian hermeneutics of Anglo-Saxon England. No contortions of interpretive skill or patristic learning are necessary to offer such a figural reading. Indeed, Junius 11 as a physical object points to such a reading in ways that were sufficiently rare in an Old English poetic manuscript for an attentive user to have registered them. First, the manuscript numbers the sections of *Genesis, Exodus,* and *Daniel* in a consecutive sequence that runs, with some gaps and confusions, from I through LV. The significance of this numbering is that, atypically for an Anglo-Saxon manuscript, it crosses the boundaries of a single poem and encourages the reader to move seamlessly through the three. Given that the titles we attach to these poems are not found in the manuscript, this kind of continuous reading would have been all the more likely to occur. The manuscript then restarts its numbering system with *Christ and Satan,* running from I through XII.[26] The distinction between the two enumerations is drawn pointedly from biblical history: the first three poems belong to the Old Testament history of the Jews, while the fourth belongs to the New Testament account of Christ's life. This twofold division of Junius 11 is also reflected, or so it would seem, in the statement that appears at the conclusion of *Christ and Satan:* "Finit Liber II. Amen." The presence of a second book presupposes a first, though the manuscript offers no equivalent statement for it.[27] Given that the place where such a statement for Liber I would most likely have occurred — the end of *Daniel* — may well correspond to a gap in the manuscript as we have it, this absence is not surprising.[28] These explicit features of Junius 11 make evident that its four poems belong within the same larger narrative that employs a two-stage sequence as it moves the reader or listener from the primal scene of dispossession in *Genesis* to the heavenly home in *Christ and Satan.*

Reading Junius 11 after surveying the diverse ways in which the Anglo-Saxons mapped their world allows one to consider some of the complex and nuanced forms of mental cartography that come into play in the culture as a whole and, more obliquely, in the manuscript. If the poems are, as I shall suggest, deeply concerned with bounding and delimiting territory, albeit on a scale grander than any Anglo-Saxon charter, they are not radically different in their means of achieving these same ends. They speak of boundaries, of territorial demarcations as they trace their narratives. They are also, and perhaps most powerfully so of any works in the canon, centered on the facts of home and homelessness as they determine the communal identity. Like the inheritance clauses of Anglo-Saxon wills, for example, the poems locate the earthly *ham* or *eðel* or *eard* on the land itself rather than in any human-built structure. So, too, the poems have their own idea of what might be a capital city, whether in a homeland (Jerusalem) or a land of exile (Babylon), because they are not naive about the force of political power in an imperial or colonized world. To argue for the value of place in reading Junius 11 does not, however, depend on any schematic connection between boundary clause and, for instance, *Exodus.* But reading the poem with an appreciation for the rhetorical and locative power of such clauses can also make one more alert to its thematics. That alertness can in turn make one hesitant to interpret the poems of Junius 11 solely in terms of a learned Christian exegetical tradition. Some familiarity with the various ways in which the Anglo-Saxons tracked their world on a daily basis can make us better readers of their poems about places that were at once far distant on the literal map but also immediately present in their spiritual and historical imagination.

The sense of place registered in Junius 11 might most succinctly be described as itinerant, that is, as shaped by the movement—usually coerced and usually sad—between places until the final entry into the heavenly home. The vision that place is not so much where one is rooted over the generations but where one must depart is taught most resonantly in Junius 11 by God's speech in *Genesis* after the disobedience of Adam and Eve. The events that lead to this speech in the Old English *Genesis* follow the familiar biblical sequence, and their outcome is equally familiar:

> Abead eac Adame   ece drihten,
> lifes leohtfruma,   lað ærende:
> "Þu scealt oðerne   eðel secean,
> wynleasran wic,   and on wræc hweorfan
> nacod niedwædla,   neorxnawanges
> dugeðum bedæled;   þe is gedal witod
> lices and sawle."

> The eternal lord, the light of life, likewise passed on Adam a hateful sentence: "You must seek another homeland, a more joyless place, and wander in exile as a naked wretch, deprived of the benefits of paradise; for you there is certain separation of body and soul." (*Genesis*, ll. 925–31a)[29]

These lines contain the irrevocable sentence passed by God. The first experiential suffering human beings must know in the world, and the first atonement they must perform, is to seek another homeland: "Þu scealt oðerne eðel secean." This speech announces the only form of exile from which there can be no literal return; Eden is gone forever and cannot be redeemed experientially but only spiritually, through the sacrifice of Christ and the attainment of heavenly redemption. The dislocation of Adam and Eve from Eden, the sundering of human beings from the first place of human occupation, is accompanied inescapably in this speech by the separation of body from soul.[30] Other Old English poets will at times use the separation of body from soul to represent a form of spiritual exile; here, the poet of *Genesis* is at pains to establish that the inescapable duality created by the separation of body and soul is a consequence of the separation of Adam and Eve from the physical setting of Eden. This consequence is historical because it takes place within time and so must be understood by later readers as extending through time to their own lives. That moment of readerly understanding will by necessity, however, take place somewhere other than Eden: somewhere in the world of fallen human beings that is known by the name of a people, tribe, or ruler. For the audience of Junius 11, that elsewhere would have been Englalond. The parallel put forward in these lines from *Genesis* exists within both historical and spiritual experience; the fact of having been driven from paradise into the confusions of place coexists with the tearing apart of the ineffable soul and the physical body. What holds the two aspects of this parallel together is the knowledge of mortality. To know a variety of places is to live in a fallen world; to have a sense of place, within the terms of God's pronouncement in these lines from *Genesis*, is also to live within the workings of time and thus of death.

The punishment inflicted on Adam (ll. 925–938) follows sequentially from that of Eve, who is made subordinate to her husband and allotted pain in childbirth (ll. 919–924), and also from that of the snake (ll. 903–917). The snake is, one remembers, punished with the promise that a woman will tread on its head. But the Old English poet also prepares for the punishment Adam will know by having God speak thus to the snake:

> Þa nædran sceop   nergend usser,
> frea ælmihtig   fagum wyrme
> wide siðas   and þa worde cwæð:
> "Þu scealt wideferhð   werig þinum
> breostum bearm tredan   bradre eorðan,
> faran feðeleas,   þenden þe feorh wunað,
> gast on innan."

> Then our Savior, Lord Almighty ordered for the snake, the guilty serpent, a long journey and said these words: "You must, weary in your heart, tread forever the bosom of the wide earth, journey footless, for as long as life and spirit remain in you." (*Genesis*, ll. 903–9a)

The serpent's banishment into the wide tracks of the broad earth is not as precisely demarcated by reference to an eðel as is Adam's punishment, presumably because it has a less elevated consciousness of a home place than does he. But even the snake, in its low-to-the-ground way, must know dislocation on the earth for the duration of its life.

The terms of punishment for both Adam and the snake are not arbitrary but follow directly from Eve's earlier encounter with Satan in the poem. As she tells Adam, the fruit she received from God's angel allowed her knowledge across the span of God's creation:

> "Ic mæg heonon geseon
> hwær he sylf siteð,   (þæt is suð and east),
> welan bewunden   se ðas woruld gesceop;
> geseo ic him his englas   ymbe hweorfan

mid feðerhaman,   ealra folca mæst,
wereda wynsumast.   Hwa meahte me swelc gewit gifan,
gif hit gegnunga   god ne onsende,
heofones waldend?   Gehyran mæg ic rume
and swa wide geseon   on woruld ealle
ofer þas sidan gesceaft,   ic mæg swegles gamen
gehyran on heofnum."

"I can see from here where he himself sits — that is to the south and east —
encircled with riches, he who shaped this world. I see his angels move about
him with wings, the greatest of all peoples, the most joyful of bands. Who
could give me such perception if God, the guardian of heaven, had not sent it
straight to me? I can hear broadly and see so widely over all the earth across
the wide creation, I can hear the joyful songs in heaven." (*Genesis*, ll. 666b–
76a)

Eve's pride before the fall is to imagine that she can possess an omniscient
knowledge of place, that she too can have a God's-eye view of creation that is
not impeded by boundaries or other human interventions on the landscape.
Her claim that this gift of sight must be divine in origin is her denial that she
has broken the injunction not to eat of the forbidden fruit. For if she had done
so, how could she have been blessed with the power to see across the wide
creation? Tellingly if inadvertently, her claim reveals the particular value of
geographical omniscience in the poem: it is an attribute of God and thus lies
beyond the scope of human beings. If presuming to some such geographical
omniscience is a measure of her sin, then she is punished appropriately and
inevitably by the displacement she encounters as she lives in the world under
the dominion of Adam. She will wander as an exile on earth because, in terms
inverting her claim to a newfound knowledge of the creation in these lines, she
will have no vision of place or geography, no ability to trace a divinely drawn
map that coherently relates place and time to God's design. As Eve's banishment suggests, the experience of exile has a secondary consequence, that those
who suffer it will be unable to see the coherence of creation. Exile traps human
beings within the particularities of their fallen sense of place; they cannot see
with the sweep and wholeness of God's vision. All they can know is that the
location where they find themselves as exiles is the absence or, at least, the
radical diminishment of home or some other cherished place such as the hall.

For Adam and Eve, the direct experience of the fall into place, their dispossession from Eden, marks their sin. For the generations that follow them
within the Old English *Genesis,* this sense of place becomes fixed as a topos of
dislocation that manifests itself in, and thus explains, the recurring human fate
of exile. A few instances of this topos, all of which follow God's speech of

banishment to Adam, will illustrate this claim. After leaving Eden, Adam and Eve live in a more sorrowful land: "Gesæton þa æfter synne sorgfulre land, / eard and eðyl unspedigran" (They settled after their sin in a more sorrowful land, a poorer region and homeland; ll. 961b–62). The comparative form of the adjectives *sorgful* and *unspedig* designate precisely the nature of their experience: before the fall there was only Eden and thus no possibility or need for the comparative degree when speaking of place. Introducing the comparative in these lines serves to mark the fall by setting it within two distinctly different places: there is nothing vague or unlocalized about the postlapsarian experience of place. In later years, after he has murdered his brother Abel, Cain will suffer exile at God's order: "forþon þu flema scealt / widlast wrecan, winemagum lað " (Thus you, hateful to your people, must wander widespread paths; ll. 1020b–21). Cain himself knows that his fate will be to wander on foot from place to place as the dispossessed of God: "forþon ic lastas sceal / wean on wenum wide lecgan" (ll. 1026b–27). Through that fate, he establishes a genealogy for all those who likewise will in future time wander the borderlands, the marches, the waste places of Cain's kin, such as the Grendelkin of *Beowulf* (ll. 99–114).

As these and other passages suggest, the knowledge that living in the earthly world means dislocation runs as a topos throughout the Old English *Genesis*, and gives the poem its persistent sadness. Yet this same sense of human dislocation will also become the means for achieving new possibilities of life. That the fall was not entirely unfortunate, that the movement from place to place can yield a new homeland, is articulated through the experience of the Hebrews. As the sons of Eber (*Genesis*, l. 1645), the Hebrews set out from the east to find a new homeland:

> Folc wæs anmod;
> rofe rincas   sohton rumre land,
> oðþæt hie becomon   corðrum miclum,
> folc ferende,   þær hie fæstlice
> æðelinga bearn,   eard genamon.

> The people was resolute; the brave warriors sought a roomier land, a journeying people in great multitudes, until they came to where they, offspring of nobles, could steadfastly occupy a homeland. (*Genesis*, ll. 1650b–54.)

The poet's use here of such terms as *rumre land* and *eard* suggests a specific sense of homeland or, more exactly, of the familiar expansionist desire of a people for a larger homeland. The search for more living space has been, from the beginnings of the human record through recent history, a primary motive for mass migration; but in the Old English *Genesis* it is seen more theologically as an aftereffect of the fall. The new land where the Hebrews settle is a green and pleasant land called Sennar (or Shinar). As the setting in a later generation for the Tower of Babel, it becomes the site for a further act of dislocation, as the tribes of humankind are sundered into mutual incomprehensibility: "siððan metod tobræd / þurh his mihta sped monna spræce" (when the Lord scattered through the power of his might the speech of men; ll. 1695b–96). The fact of linguistic difference, in the old sense of the term, becomes another consequence of displacement or exile.

In these various ways, the Old English *Genesis* surveys the meanings that place acquires in a postlapsarian world in order to teach that no place is immutable across the turn of generations. If the green and pleasant homeland of Sennar can become the site of the linguistic dislocation of Babel, then no human-made sense of place can be easily or safely read as inherently stable across time. The only sense of place within Junius 11 that endures beyond the changing rhythm of human history, and in fact makes that rhythm tolerable, rests on the covenant that God makes with Abraham. Read within the flowing narrative of Junius 11, the passages in *Genesis* about this covenant establish a promise about place in a post-Edenic world that will figure centrally in the three subsequent poems. These other poems can, each in its own way, redeem place so that it may serve as something more than the site of loss and suffering. The *Genesis* poet's description of this episode is therefore as central to my reading of Junius 11 as is the earlier passage in which God pronounces exile on Adam and Eve (ll. 925–31a). The *Genesis* poet prepares carefully for this moment by first telling his audience that Abraham travels to Canaan from Egypt or, more exactly, from the territorial boundaries of Egypt: "Him þa Abraham gewat æhte lædan / of Egipta eðelmearce" (ll. 1767–68). The reference here to *eðelmearc* imposes a measure of cartographic precision on the account of Abraham's travels that reflects the Anglo-Saxon habit of demarcating property by writing boundary clauses. *The poet* underscores the nature of Abraham's travels by specifying that he must cross the boundary of one land before entering another, thereby reminding the audience of his travel's significance as it is directed by God. Put simply, it is meant to be a transformative journey for Abraham and his people.

Once he has crossed into Canaan, Abraham travels through the country and there hears the promise of God:

> Him þa feran gewat   fæder ælmihtiges
> lare gemyndig   land sceawian
> geond þa folcsceare   be frean hæse
> Abraham wide,   oðþæt ellenrof

to Sicem com   siðe spedig,
cynne Cananeis.   Þa hine cyning engla
Abrahame   iewde selfa,
domfæst wereda   and drihten cwæð:
"Þis is seo eorðe   þe ic ælgrene
tudre þinum   torhte wille
wæstmum gewlo   on geweald don,
rume rice."

Then Abraham was mindful of the Almighty Father's urging to him that he go survey the land widely throughout the people's nation, by the lord's command, until he, the courageous one, came to Sichem, and the people of Canaan, on the fortunate journey. Then the king of angels, the just ruler, showed himself to Abraham and the lord said: "This is the glorious green earth, the roomy kingdom adorned with fruitfulness, that I will give into the possession of your offspring." (*Genesis*, ll. 1779–90a)

The poet is meticulous here in presenting Abraham as he examines the land of the people, the *folcscearu,* in Canaan. His attention to land in the most literal, tangible sense is a necessary prelude to the words that God will speak to him as he promises the all-verdant earth to Abraham's descendants. The use of *tudor,* "offspring," here designates a promise that will be fulfilled in the future or, by a more local measure of time's passing, in a subsequent poem in Junius 11. However fulfilled, whether in a chronological or codicological future, the promise made to Abraham announces the redemption of place as a folcscearu, or land. Similarly, this vision of a verdant and abundant homeland influences later episodes in Abraham's life. It underlies, for example, his refusal of Abimelech's offer of a home in his realm: "Wuna mid usic and þe wic geceos / on þissum lande þær þe leofost sie, / eðelstowe, þe ic agan sceal" (Live with us and choose a place in this land which is most lovely to you, a dwelling place, which I by right possess; ll. 2723–25). Abraham cannot accept a place in Abimelech's *eðelstow* without imperiling the covenant that he has received from God. He and his descendants must persevere until they can occupy Canaan.

As the Old English *Genesis* turns to the next generation, the sense of the homeland takes on more ominous connotations, for the poet returns to the earlier theme of place as a source of dislocation. He does so most immediately by recording that Ishmael must be sent forth into exile, but he also returns to this theme more obliquely by narrating that Isaac must be led forth to the sacrifice. God's covenant with Abraham promises a future homeland, but it seems to hold no immediate benefit for his sons. While a people can maintain itself over time by cultivating a sense of its own place, such knowledge can never, finally, be separated from the pain of displacement. Thus we are to understand Abraham's grief at driving Ishmael into exile: "Þa wæs Abrahame / weorce on mode þæt he on wræc drife / his selfes sunu" (Then was Abraham afflicted in spirit because he had driven his own son into exile; ll. 2791b–93a). Moreover, God's vision of a green and pleasant homeland defines by harsh contrast the desolate place where Abraham must go to sacrifice his other son, Isaac:

"Siððan þu gestigest   steape dune,
hrincg þæs hean landes,   þe ic heonon getæce,
up þinum agnum fotum,   þær þu scealt ad gegærwan,
bælfyr bearne þinum,   and blotan sylf
sunu mid sweordes ecge,   and þonne sweartan lige
leofes lic forbærnan   and me lac bebeodan."

"When you have climbed up the steep hill on your own feet, the border of the highland, which I will show you hence, then you shall prepare a pyre, a sacrificial fire for your child, and yourself slay your son with a sword's edge, and then burn up the body of the beloved one with the dark fire, and offer it to me as a sacrifice." (*Genesis*, ll. 2854–59)

Here again we can see the poet of *Genesis* cultivating a technique of demarcation, as when he speaks of the "hrincg þæs hean landes," the border of the highlands, that must be crossed to fulfill God's order to Abraham. He must lead Isaac along steep slopes into the highlands because the injunction of sacrifice can be fulfilled only in the wastelands, the marches, territories no human group calls home. *Genesis* ends with the sacrifice of the ram instead of Isaac, and with Abraham's prayer of thanksgiving that reestablishes the bond between God and the Israelites — but these acts must take place beyond the margins of settlement. The scene of Abraham and Isaac in the highlands questions what it might mean that there could be a homeland as sanctuary. That such a question must arise again and again across the turn of generations is itself proof of the fall into place and of the need for the following three poems in the narrative flow of Junius 11.

The story of Exodus follows ineluctably from that of Genesis: they are as conjoined in Junius 11 as in the Hebrew Bible. That the Old English poet of *Exodus* should very early in his poem offer a reminder of the creation story of Genesis, in the form of a summary of God's lesson to Moses, establishes an explicit thematic link between these two narratives, whether as biblical books or vernacular poems. As a telling of the Genesis story, however, these lines from *Exodus* are at best a brief sketch or aid to memory so that the audience can locate the Exodus story within the unfolding of biblical history:

Ða wæs forma sið
þæt hine weroda god   wordum nægde,
þær he him gesægde   soðwundra fela,
hu þas woruld worhte   witig drihten,
eorðan ymbhwyrft   and uprodor,
gesette sigerice,   and his sylfes naman,
ðone yldo bearn   ær ne cuðon,
frod fædera cyn,   þeah hie fela wiston.

That was the first time that the God of the company spoke words to him, where he told him many true wonders, how the wise Lord created this world, the earth's circle and the heavens above, fixed the victorious kingdom, and his own name which before the children of men did not know, the wise race of the fathers, though they knew much. (*Exodus*, ll. 22b–29)

When read as an allusion to the full story of the creation, one meant to be registered by an audience that had just heard or read the 2,936 lines of *Genesis,* however, this passage on the creation (as well as the preceding lines that relate Moses to Abraham) deftly evokes the necessary prehistory of the Israelites' exodus.

Yet more persuasive as a means of linking the first two poems in Junius 11, I would argue, is the opening of *Exodus:*

Hwæt! We feor and neah   gefrigen habað
ofer middangeard   Moyses domas,
wræclico wordriht,   wera cneorissum, —
in uprodor   eadigra gehwam
æfter bealusiðe   bote lifes,
lifigendra gehwam   langsumne ræd, —
hæleðum secgan.   Gehyre se ðe wille!

Listen. We have heard far and near over the earth of Moses' ordinances, the extraordinary laws, for the generations of men — of the reward of life in heaven for each of the blessed after terrible journey, the long-enduring counsel for each of the living — pronounced by men. Let him harken, he who will. (*Exodus*, ll. 1–7).

That "we" far and near over the earth know of Moses' laws is itself stark testimony to the nature of post-Edenic history, for the pronoun *we* and its verb *gefrignan* designate those human beings alive at the moment of the poem's performance. Not only are laws necessary after the fall, they must be observed in a world demarcated by the conventional measures of earthly territory as found in Old English poetry. *Feor and neah* and *ofer middangeard* are poetic formulas, but they are, arguably, all the more evocative in these lines for denoting the accepted and easily comprehensible ways in which the Anglo-Saxons located themselves within God's creation.[31] From the start, the poem emphasizes the spatial dimension, especially as it goes on to speak of the reward of life promised to those who have made the hazardous journey, or *bealusið*. Within the poem's literal narrative, one may read this reward as entry into the promised land of Canaan for the Israelites or, more universally, as entry into heaven for devout Christians. The immediate audience of the poem may also have interpreted this journey as a historical allusion to the Anglo-Saxons' ancestral migration that brought them to the promised island and, once there, to Christendom, through conversion. However one chooses to interpret the opening of *Exodus,* one must at least implicitly offer a situated reading that traces the course of a journey.

The initial route of the exodus, its *forðweg* (l. 32a), is described by the poet as a crossing of land and boundaries led by Moses: "Oferfor he mid þy folce fæstena worn, / land and leodweard laðra manna, / enge anpaðas, uncuð gelad" (He passed through many natural strongholds with the folk, the lands and territory of hostile men, the narrow solitary tracks, the unknown paths; ll 56–58). The journey of the Israelites is fearsome as it takes them through unknown and hostile territory similar to the one Beowulf encounters on the journey to Grendel's mere. That the same line — *enge anpaðas, uncuð gelad* — appears here in *Exodus* and also in *Beowulf* (l. 1410) reveals that a formulaic phrase can be appropriate in apparently very different contexts. If the larger passage in *Beowulf,* as I argued in Chapter 2, reveals the otherwise inexpressible nature of Beowulf's psychological state as he approaches the mere in pursuit of his adversary, so the phrase carries with it a similar resonance for describing the dangers faced on the journey by the people in *Exodus.* Whether it evokes the way of the lone hero or of the historical folc, this description of topography offers a sense of an otherwise inaccessible state of mind. In this part of *Exodus,* the perilous journey of the Israelites is figured heavily as the crossing of a marginal zone or liminal topography: they pass border dwellings in the marshes ("mearchofu morheald"; l. 61a) and encamp near the city of Etham ("Æthanes byrig"; l. 66b) in the border regions ("mearclandum on"; l. 67b). The language here of border regions and neighboring territories accords with the language used in *Genesis,* most notably the word *eðelmearc* in l. 1768, to describe Abraham's journey out of Egypt that leads to God's promise to Abraham and his people of a homeland. The *Exodus* poet stresses this itinerant quality in Abraham's experience, as when he offers a series of meaningful variations to describe him later in the poem:

Þæt is se Abraham   se him engla god
naman niwan asceop;   eac þon neah and feor

halige heapas   in gehyld bebead,
werþeoda geweald;   he on wraece lifde.

That is the Abraham for whom the god of angels created a new name; and to whom also ordered into his keeping near and far the holy bands, control over the people; he lived in exile. (*Exodus,* ll. 380–84)

As a series of variants, the references to Abraham's leadership of his people far and wide and to his life in exile offer a kind of summary exemplum, for from that life can be understood God's covenant about a homeland, and thus the redeeming significance of place on earth.[32]

Reading *Exodus* within the flow of Junius 11 has the effect of placing great emphasis on a passage late in the poem that evokes — at a time of terrible crisis in the migration — the historically earlier moment (as described in the Old English *Genesis*) when God stays Abraham's hand and spares Isaac's life in the steep hills and highlands: "Ne sleh þu, Abraham, þin agen bearn" (Do not slay, Abraham, your own child; *Exodus,* l. 419). Through that moment in the poem, God affirms his covenant with the Israelites and explicitly demarcates the literal territory of the homeland:

"Ac hie gesittað   be sæm tweonum
oð Egipte   incaðeode
land Cananea,   leode þine,
freobearn fæder,   folca selost."

"But they, your kinsmen, free-born of their fathers, the best of peoples, shall settle, between two seas as far as the nation of Egypt, the land of Canaan." (*Exodus,* ll. 443–46)

These lines introduce another familiar trope (*be sæm tweonum*) for demarcating the expanse of earthly habitation. I have argued that this trope is part of the poet's means to accommodate a distinctively Anglo-Saxon rereading of the exodus story, by which the ancestral Germanic tribes who crossed the North Sea become analogous to the Israelites who crossed the Red Sea.[33] Similarly, if we read that phrase as functioning in a manner comparable to the boundary clauses of Anglo-Saxon legal charters, the reference here to the two seas within the larger context of Junius 11 establishes the fundamental geographical range of its four poems. For all four poems are set within the space between the two biblical seas. That is, the two seas designate the outer limits of a region without providing any specific description of the area that falls amid these bounds. God's speech here is dense with geographical specificity, including not just the reference to the two seas but also the mapping of Egypt and Canaan as somehow contiguous or neighboring (through the use of *oð,* "as far as") as well as the use of the terms *land* and *incaðeod* (more commonly, *ingeþeod*) to designate regions of settlement. The references here to a land that lies between the two seas and the two nations may be said to function as features in a boundary clause for the poeticized land charter through which God grants the Israelites a homeland. In that regard, anyone who reads or hears of this gift to Abraham —whether in the Bible or in a vernacular poem such as *Exodus*—may be described as a witness to the transaction or, perhaps, as a party to it as well.

This passage concerning Abraham occurs significantly as a flashback—or embedded narrative moment—within the ongoing account of the Israelites' exodus. As a flashback, this episode with Abraham is meant of course to drive the exodus story into the narrative future, into the time when Moses and his followers cross the Red Sea and then, after another generation, enter Canaan with Aaron as leader. The opportunity for commentary at this moment of the narrative would seem self-evident, but we cannot be certain if any was offered because immediately following the episode of God and Abraham there appears a manuscript break of uncertain length in the text of *Exodus*.[34] When the text resumes, it depicts the Egyptians struck with terror by the onrushing waters that will drown them. At that moment they will suffer the displacement of death, the poet tells us, and the loss of their homes:

> Wæron Egypte   eft oncyrde,
> flugon forhtigende,   fær ongeton,
> woldon herebleaðe   hamas findan,
> gylp wearð gnornra.   Him ongen genap
> atol yða gewealc,   ne ðær ænig becwom
> herges to hame,   ac behindan beleac
> wyrd mid wæge.

> The Egyptians turned back, they fled in fear, they perceived their danger; they wanted coward-like to find their homes, their boasts turned sadder. The frightening rolling of the waves darkened toward them, none of the army there made it back home, but fate trapped them from behind with a flood. (*Exodus,* ll. 452–58a)

The forceful juxtaposition in the manuscript between the offering of a homeland to the Israelites and the destruction of the Egyptians is, as we have it, perhaps more abrupt than the poet intended. Nonetheless, the juxtaposed elements were certainly his work: one people must, by the logic of displacement, lose its homeland as another gains one. This extended passage in *Exodus* (ll. 419–58a) glosses the closing verses of Psalm 136, with their almost apocalyptic sense that the liberation of one people can be accomplished only through the horrifying destruction of those that enslaved it. The Israelites remember their promised homeland and thus are emboldened to continue their exodus at the same moment when the Egyptians are about to perish and lose their homes.

On two occasions in the poem, the Israelites are said to be *eðelleas*, "without a homeland" (ll. 139, 534), because they have been displaced from Egypt and have yet to reach Canaan. In the Old English version of the exodus, a version truncated sharply for political reasons according to my reading, the narrative ends once the Israelites have safely crossed the Red Sea. There they give thanks for their deliverance and recover their treasures from the drowned Egyptians: "Heo on riht sceodon / gold and godweb, Iosepes gestreon, / wera wuldorgesteald" (Rightfully, they shared out the gold and fine cloth, the treasure of Joseph, the glorious possessions of men; ll. 587b–89a). The Israelites have yet to reach their home and complete their escape from the Egyptian exile. That part of the psalmist's prophetic knowledge lies in the future of the next generation. The other part, however, has been fulfilled. In the last line and a half of *Exodus*, the poet assigns the Egyptians to their final place: "Werigend lagon / on deaðstede, drihtfolca mæst" (The guardians, the greatest of troops, lay in the place of death; ll. 589b–90). A certain closure is achieved by that use of *deaðstede*, one that is as grim for the Egyptians as it is hopeful for the Israelites.

The *Exodus* poet traces the lines of sacred history through a sense of place that closes off the past (or parts of it) at the same moment that it opens up the past (or parts of it). There can be no wandering in the desert for forty years if the drained bed of the Red Sea is not the killing ground of the Egyptians; there can be no forward movement or continuation of figurative history without the division of drowned Egyptians and saved Israelites, without the fatal power of the water and the saving ground of the shore. To our mind, there may be something brutal about an evocation of place that serves not as the sustaining ground of human existence but rather as the site where one people meets its end so that another can survive. Yet for that very reason, the Old English poet would probably not have been mystified by the idea that Judaism begins with Exodus because it is a religion sustained by the idea of covenant as it was fulfilled within collective experience.[35] For the Old English poet saw that the continuing spiritual history of the Israelites and thus the figural history of Christians followed from the exodus as that event appeared in its turn within a continuing story that began with the original displacement from Eden.

Within Junius 11, the fullest descriptions of the Israelites in Canaan as well as of the city of Jerusalem appear in the opening passages of *Daniel*.[36] In a poem about the exilic captivity of the Israelites in Babylon as punishment for their sins of pride, these descriptions read more as an evocation of an absent capital than as the celebration of a promised city. Like the poet of *Exodus*, the poet of *Daniel* opens with the conventional verb *gefrignan* to signal that he will relate events from the past that are well known in the narrative present:

> Gefrægn ic Hebreos   eadge lifgean
> in Hierusalem,   goldhord dælan,
> cyningdom habban,   swa him gecynde wæs,
> siððan þurh metodes mægen   on Moyses hand
> wearð wig gifen,   wigena mænieo,
> and hie of Egyptum   ut aforon,
> mægene micle.   Þæt was modig cyn!

> I have heard that the Hebrews lived blessedly in Jerusalem, sharing the gold-hoard, holding the kingdom, as was proper, when through the might of God an army was given into Moses' hand, many warriors, and they departed out of Egypt by a great miracle. That was a bold race. (*Daniel*, ll. 1–7)

The reference at the end of this passage to the going out from Egypt returns one to the Old English *Exodus* in so striking a manner that some readers have concluded that these lines were written specifically to join the two poems in the manuscript.[37] While very tempting, this kind of reading risks valuing a moment of manuscript collocation above the demands of narrative continuity. That is, it does not quite appreciate how a poem about the Babylonian captivity could avoid evoking the lost city of Jerusalem and the exodus from Egypt that had earlier led the Israelites there — especially in a manuscript that encourages crossing the lines between its poems.

Read in this larger context, the story that will unfold around Daniel and Nebuchadnezzar in Babylon has its beginnings in the stories of Abraham and Isaac and of Moses and the flight of his people out of Egypt. The poet of *Daniel* recognized this genealogy for his story, as is evident from the next lines in his opening section:

> Þenden hie þy rice   rædan moston,
> burgum wealdan,   wæs him beorht wela.
> Þenden þæt folc mid him   hiera fæder wære
> healdan woldon,   wæs him hyrde god,
> heofonrices weard,   halig drihten,
> wuldres waldend.

> For as long as they were able to govern the realm, hold the city, there was bright wealth among them. For as long as that people was willing to hold the covenant of their father with him, God, the guardian of heaven, the holy lord, the ruler of wonders, was a good shepherd to them. (*Daniel*, ll. 8–13a)

In this passage of dense variation that uses four epithets to praise God, the poet emphasizes the keeping of the covenant by the Israelites in Jerusalem as the source of their prosperity. Yet the past era when the covenant between God and Abraham was honored is evoked in these lines so that the poet might all the more powerfully move to his subject within the present moment of the poem's narrative.[38]

The experience of exodus and wandering provides the poet of *Daniel* with the resonant image by which he will describe the Israelites' turn into pride and error in Jerusalem: "Þa geseah ic þa gedriht in gedwolan hweorfan, / Israhela cyn unriht don / wommas wyrcean" (Then I saw that nation, the people of Israel turn to error, work unrighteous judgment and commit sins; ll. 22–24a). Using a related language of movement, the poet evokes the Israelites as a people who had been led by God out of exile and into the *eðelland*:

> Wisde him æt frymðe,   ða ðe on fruman ær ðon
> wæron mancynnes   metode dyrust,
> dugoða dyrust,   drihtne leofost;
> herepað tæhte   to þære hean byrig,
> eorlum elðeodigum,   on eðelland
> þær Salem stod   searwum afæstnod,
> weallum geweorðod.

> He had led them at the beginning, those who before were the dearest of mankind to the lord at the start, dearest of peoples, most beloved of God; he showed to these foreign nobles the military road to the high city in the homeland where Salem stood, fortified skillfully and adorned with walls. (*Daniel*, ll. 35–41a)

Having identified the holy citadel, or *ceastre* (l. 42b), of Jerusalem, the Old English poet can affect a brilliant transition into the present time of his narrative by immediately introducing the enmity of the Chaldeans and the plan of Nebuchadnezzar to lay waste to that same city:

> Þa ic eðan gefrægn   ealdfeonda cyn
> winburh wera.   Þa wigan ne gelyfdon,
> bereafodon þa receda wuldor   readan golde,
> since and seolfre,   Salomones templ.
> Gestrudan gestreona   under stanhliðum,
> swilc eall swa þa eorlas   agan sceoldon,
> oþðæt hie burga gehwone   abrocen hæfdon,
> þara þe þam folce   to friðe stodon.

> Then I heard that the race of ancient foes laid waste to the capital city of men. The warriors did not believe; they stole red gold, treasure and silver from that glory of buildings, Solomon's temple. They plundered treasures under the rocky slopes, all such as the nobles possessed, until they had smashed each of the strongholds which had stood as protection to that people. (*Daniel*, ll. 57–64)

The destruction of Jerusalem as a human-built place is the burden of this passage. Its gold- and silver-adorned buildings, including the Temple of Solomon, and its stone walls or structures that tower like a cliff would for an Anglo-Saxon audience suggest a scale and style of building unknown on their own island. What has been destroyed here is the capital or center of a people: its great house of worship, its riches, its protective walls.[39]

In this passage of some thirty lines or so, the poet moves forward through time from remembering the road that led the Israelites to Jerusalem to describing the destruction of that city by the Babylonian king. Such is, in miniature, the knowledge of human places in Junius 11: the entry into a place and the triumph of possession followed by the loss of that same place and the tragedy of exile. This bitter knowledge comes from living in a fallen world of many places and no enduring habitation on earth. It suffuses as well the brief passage in which the *Daniel* poet describes the march of the Israelites east into Babylon: "and gelæddon eac on langne sið / Israela cyn, on eastwegas / to Babilonia" (And also led the people of Israel on a long journey, over the eastward roads, to Babylon; ll. 68–70a). The sense of human place in these poems is always conditioned by the experience of dislocation, as the poet acknowledges here with the phrase *on langne sið*. Only heaven can counter, as we shall see with *Christ and Satan,* this sense of place as loss or change.

The great bulk of *Daniel* concerns the fate of the Israelites once they are in Babylon or, more precisely, the fate of the Israelites as they are exemplified by the prophetic figure of Daniel as well as the three young men, Annanias, Azarias, and Misael, who are put through the ordeal of the fiery furnace by Nebuchadnezzar. In introducing these three, the poet is careful to stress their devoutness and their lineage as the children of Abraham:

> Ða wæron æðelum   Abrahames bearn,
> wæron wærfæste,   wiston drihten
> ecne uppe,   ælmightigne.

> They were in origin the children of Abraham, they were keepers of the covenant; they knew the eternal lord above, the almighty. (*Daniel,* ll. 193–95)[40]

To speak of the three as "Abrahames bearn" is necessarily to evoke the covenant, though with a heartrending irony because the passage is set in Babylon, far from the ruined city of Jerusalem.

Yet the irony proves temporary or false, because as Annanias, Azarias, and Misael survive torture, they demonstrate that the faith of the Israelites can endure in Babylon, even as earlier it had not been honored in Jerusalem. Such is the corollary to the logic of place: the faith neglected by the many in Jerusalem must be redeemed by the chosen few in Babylon. The return to the covenant can only be signaled through a geography of displacement, as Azarias himself says:

> "Siendon we towrecene   geond widne grund,
> heapum tohworfene,   hyldelease;
> is user lif   geond landa fela
> fracoð and gefræge   folca manegum,
> þa usic bewræcon   to þæs wyrrestan
> eorðcyninga   æhta gewealde,
> on hæft heorugrimra,   and we nu hæðenra
> þeowned þoliað."

> "We are scattered across the wide earth, dispersed in groups, without protection; our life is thought in many lands to be vile and infamous by many people, who have banished us as slaves into the power of the worst of earthly kings, into bondage under savage men, and we now suffer the oppression of heathens." (*Daniel,* ll. 300–307a)

As Azarias beseeches God not to abandon the Israelites, he refers explicitly to the covenants, or *treowum,* God made earlier with Abraham, Isaac, and Jacob (*Daniel,* ll. 309–14). The audience of *Daniel* can draw on its deep knowledge of God's covenant with the Israelites from the two preceding poems in Junius 11, most especially from that great scene of recognition which concludes the Old English *Genesis* and the story of Abraham and Isaac. (The reader of *Daniel* can also look forward to a related passage about Abraham in *Christ and Satan,* ll. 455–59, as we shall see.) Almost halfway through *Daniel,* the audience of Junius 11 must pause to remember that passage some one thousand lines earlier, in which a father takes his son into the desolate highlands. To suggest that Junius 11 has at such moments its own intertextuality seems almost beside the point, for the connections that the poems weave among themselves by virtue of being in this one manuscript are the same as those inscribed in the larger historical record found within the Bible. The poems no more create these moments of readerly connection than they could evade them, but they most certainly can highlight the presence of such connections and also explore them for their historical complexities. Thus *Genesis, Exodus,* and *Daniel* teach, each in its own way, that such moments of connection come quite literally with the territory of exile and homecoming. Or, if one prefers to emphasize the readerly reception of the manuscript, it is the audience's ability to range knowingly across the poems that yields such connective moments.

Within this historical territory of homecoming and displacement, the exile of Nebuchadnezzar is one of the most remarkable, even surprising aspects of *Daniel.*[41] For like the Israelites, Nebuchadnezzar is punished, though his form of pride belongs to a powerful ruler rather than a people. In that way—by embodying the individual outcast rather than a captive people—he can serve as a countertype to the Israelites. The poet's description of this episode is thus notably different from his description of the Israelites' exile:

> Swa wod wera   on gewindagum
> geocrostne sið   in godes wite,
> ðara þe eft lifigende   leode begete,
> Nabochodonossor,   siððan him nið godes,
> hreð of heofonum,   hete gesceode.
> Seofon winter samod   susl þrowode,
> wildeora westen,   winburge cyning.

> So he traveled in days of strife the harshest journey of men under God's punishment, of those who while living find their people once more; so it was with Nebuchadnezzar, after God's sudden attack on him from the heavens violently oppressed him. For seven years together the king of the joyous city endured torment in the wilderness of wild beasts. (*Daniel*, ll. 615–21)

In these seven years, Nebuchadnezzar inhabits a different wilderness, filled with beasts, rather than the historically determined landscape of the exodus. He knows a spiritual exile, a period of despair, from which he can return to God and his own people after having been a "nacod nydgenga" (naked and wretched wanderer; l. 632a) and a "wundorlic wrædcca" (wondrous outcast; l. 633a). This depiction of exile in Junius 11 most nearly approximates those found in the lyrics of the Exeter Book in the sense that Nebuchadnezzar is an *anhaga,* though one reduced to that state by spiritual pride rather than by falling out of favor with a worldly lord. Yet Nebuchadnezzar is hardly to be confounded with any of those solitary exiles in Old English poetry, for he does enjoy a happy end to his state. Unlike these others, he lives to know the promise of *Deor*'s refrain "þæs ofereode, þisses swa mæg" (That passed away. So may this.).[42] He returns to Babylon and his throne (ll. 640–74); there, he tells his people of his experience as an exile. Above all, he fulfills through his life the prophecy Daniel made about him in his time of pride: he would be humbled.

In its current state, *Daniel* ends with an episode in which the prophet Daniel interprets at a later time for Belshazzar and his court the meaning of the words that the angel of God writes in crimson letters on the wall of the hall (ll. 712–23). Within the larger reading of Junius 11, this episode is significant because it is precipitated by the Medes' sacrilegious use of the Jewish holy vessels seized in earlier generations during the conquest of Jerusalem. That which is taken from a people when they are driven into exilic captivity and then turned to base uses by unbelievers remains holy. So it may be with the exiled people themselves. Read in this way, the narrative of *Daniel* teaches that a people can keep the faith of its homeland even in a strange land, that exile is not permanent, that there is an answer to the fearsome question of Psalm 136: "quomodo cantabimus canticum Domini in terra aliena?" Or, to acknowledge the significant typology that runs through Junius 11, a people is preserved because there its members—or at least three of them—remember and honor their lineage as "Abrahames bearn."

Within the large narrative of Junius 11, the final answer to the psalmist's question comes with *Christ and Satan*. If it is in many ways the least achieved poem in the manuscript, more a juxtaposed gathering of episodes than a coherent vision of moments from biblical history, *Christ and Satan* significantly enlarges the territory of Junius 11 by moving beyond the narrowly confined sense of sacred space that is conventionally designated in narrative maps as the Holy Land. The poem extends the thematics of place and displacement beyond earthly to cosmic realms by narrating at length the fall of the angels from heaven into the exile of hell.[43] More specifically, it leaves the confines of the earth to translate this thematics of place and displacement onto a larger cosmography so that it can, in turn, be brought back to bear directly on human experience. With *Christ and Satan*, the teachings of Christ and the promise of redemption explicitly enter Junius 11. Christ's sacrifice and victory over Satan give closure to the thematics of earthly or historical place and displacement so that these four poems can be read as a quadrateuch: the fallen angels will be bound eternally in exilic captivity just as the worthy souls rescued by Christ's intervention will enter their true home in heaven. As noted at the outset of this chapter, the appearance of *Christ and Satan* in this manuscript makes possible, even necessary, figurative readings of *Genesis, Exodus,* and *Daniel.*

Yet for *Christ and Satan* to play its concluding part in Junius 11, it must have its own sense of geographical specificity. The poet begins with the story of the creation in ways that enable the reader to recall the text of the Old English *Genesis* as well as its recapitulation in the opening lines of the Old English *Exodus:* "Þæt wearð underne eorðbuendum, / þæt meotod hæfde miht and strengðo / ða he gefestnade foldan sceatas" (It was known to earthdwellers that God had might and strength when he fixed the regions of the earth; ll. 1–3). *Christ and Satan* goes on to emphasize a different consequence of the creation than the first three poems in the manuscript. For it turns its gaze away from the earthbound stories of Adam and Eve, Abraham and Isaac, Moses and the Israelites, Daniel and Nebuchadnezzar to tell about the rebellion of the heav-

enly angels and their subsequent fall into hell. The memory of this displacement may have cast its shadow over the first three poems of Junius 11, but it
becomes the explicit, unavoidable subject in *Christ and Satan*.[44] The poet's
sense of place invokes the infernal regions directly and vividly as the terrain of
spiritual combat. With his very first words, Satan bewails his loss of a heavenly
home precisely because it registers so profoundly in his home of darkness:

> "Hwær com engla ðrym,
> þe we on heofnum   habban sceoldan?
> Þis is ðeostræ ham,   ðearle gebunden
> fæstum fyrclommum."

"Where has the glory of the angels gone, which we should have had in
heaven? This is a dark home, bound painfully with fiery fetters." (*Christ and
Satan*, ll. 36b–39a)

True understanding of his spiritual condition comes to Satan through the
recognition of his physical displacement: he is in another place and thus has
fallen. His hell is quite straightforwardly a demonic parody of heaven, a *ham*
marked by darkness rather than the radiance of God's illumination. As Satan
says to his fellow fallen angels, "Nu ic eow hebbe to hæftum ham gefærde / alle
of earde" (Now I have led all of you from your native place into a home of
bondage; ll. 91–92a). He stands here as an antitype of Moses as the leader of a
people: "Nu ic feran com / deofla menego to ðissum dimman ham" (Now I
have come to lead a company of devils to this dark home; ll. 109b–10). Satan
also tells his followers that this fall will be eternal and will never end with a
return to their homeland (ll. 114–17a). Instead he must wander as an exile:
"Forðon ic sceal hean and earm hweorfan ðy widor / wadan wræclastas"
(Thus I sad and wretched must wander the more widely, travel the paths of
exile; ll. 119–20a).

   These laments of exile run like a threnody through Satan's speeches in
Christ and Satan.[45] Thus, for example, in his memorable speech listing all of
his regrets in a series of expressions using *eala* (ll. 163–67), he concludes,
"Now I sorrowfully must travel the paths of exile, the wide journeys" (sceal nu
wreclastas / settan sorhgcearig, siðas wide; ll. 187b–88). As this and other
passages demonstrate, Satan is the figure of exile in extremis because he and
his band are collectively removed forever from the saving grace of God. They
become the only figures in Junius 11 to fall into a place with no chance of
earthly liberation or heavenly salvation. Their hellish home thus becomes the
ground of struggle between Christ and Satan in the Harrowing of Hell. That
episode can be read in ways that parallel the Exodus story; in each instance,
the worthy exiles are redeemed and brought to safety while the evil oppressors

are, through death or eternal damnation, forever denied entry into the heavenly home. The significant difference between the Israelites of *Exodus* and the rescued souls of *Christ and Satan* lies in the latter's irrevocable entry into the heavenly home. For that *eðel* alone is eternal, unlike the Jerusalem of the Israelites which is bound to the vicissitudes of earthly life.

Christ's mission in *Christ and Satan* is very much that of the guide to the homeland, the figure who fulfills Moses because he is allowed to complete his journey and that of his followers: "wolde manna rim, / fela þusenda, forð gelædan / up to eðle" (he wished to lead forth countless men, many thousands, upwards to their homeland; ll. 399b–401a). The poet celebrates the arrival of the rescued angels in terms explicitly designed to evoke the exile of the Israelites and the covenant made with Abraham:

> Þæt, la, wæs fæger,   þæt se feða com
> up to earde,   and se eca mid him,
> meotod mancynnes   in þa mæran burh!
> Hofon hine mid him   handum halige
> witigan up to eðle,   Abrahames cynn.

> There was joy that the band came up to the homeland, and the eternal one with them, the lord of mankind into the glorious city. The holy prophets, the race of Abraham raised him with their hands up to the homeland. (*Christ and Satan*, ll. 455–59)

As the poet then explains, the Lord had conquered death in ways that the prophets foretold in past days: "Hæfde þa drihten seolf deað oferwunnen, / feond geflemed; þæt in fyrndagum / witegan sædon þæt he swa wolde" (ll. 460–62). Within the poem, this statement can be read as an entirely self-contained expression of a conventional sense of religious history; within the context of Junius 11, the statement can also stand as an injunction to the reader or listener to think back on the poems that precede *Christ and Satan* in the manuscript because there one will learn more fully the history of Abraham and his people.

In its explicitly didactic style, *Christ and Satan* brings a powerful clarity to the thematics of place and displacement in the manuscript. Nowhere in Junius 11 is the distinction between the eternal home of salvation and the eternal site of punitive exile set forth as starkly as it is toward the end of *Christ and Satan*. In the space of eleven lines, God delivers two brief speeches that signal the final resolution of place into two extremes. The first is addressed to those who shall be saved: "Ge sind wilcuman! Gað in wuldres leoht / to heofona rice, þær ge habbað / a to aldre ece reste" (You are welcome! Come into the light of wonder, the kingdom of heaven, where you will always have forever eternal rest; ll. 616–18); the second to those who will be damned: "Astigað nu, awyrgde, in þæt witehus / ofostum miclum. Nu ic eow ne con" (Fall now with great haste, you damned ones, into the house of torture. I do not know you now; ll. 626–27).[46] From each of these judgments, there can be no recourse, no further motion. Place is fixed within the eternal scheme of God's will, exile and displacement are no longer, and the legacy of Adam and Eve's sin is canceled. In his telling of Eve's redemption, the poet of *Christ and Satan* offers a brief passage that sends one back in memory to the passage in *Genesis* where she claims geographical omniscience after eating the fruit. In it, the poet tells us that Christ allows all the falsely imprisoned souls in hell to ascend directly to heaven — all except Eve:

> Let þa up faran   eadige sawle,
> Adames cyn,   ac ne moste Efe þa gyt
> wlitan in wuldre   ær heo wordum cwæð.

> Then he allowed the blessed souls, Adam's race, to ascend, but Eve might not then yet gaze upon glory until she spoke words. (*Christ and Satan*, ll. 405–7)

What Eve must do, revealingly, is to speak with words and thus beseech God for permission to enter the "haligne ham" (l. 413a) of heaven after Satan has returned "ham to helle" (l. 425a) so that she can cease being a dweller in hell ("helwarum"; l. 429a). In her prayer to God for forgiveness of her sins — in which she also makes the necessary typological claim that Christ is the son of her daughter Mary — Eve states the geography that she has learned in an act of penitence, a geography bounded by the necessary contraries of heaven and hell. There is no claim here to a vision of the wide creation, such as she makes in *Genesis*, but rather simply a map for the soul in search of redemption and the eternal home.

Once the affects of the fall are abolished in *Christ and Satan* through Christ's redemption of humankind, an earthbound sense of place fades away because there is no longer any need for movement, only the stasis of *ece reste*, or eternal peace. Until that time, however, human beings are bound to live on earth and thus possess a sense of place. Or so the poems of Junius 11 teach, each in its own way. Within a sense of the past that is determined more by genealogical than chronological specificity, and that reveals greater concern for the turn of generations than for the exact demarcations of years, the crucial framework for recording and interpreting events becomes place and the movement between places. In the Hebrew Bible, that sense of place has its dramatic geography. The expulsion from Eden comes before the flight from Egypt and prepares for it. These two events come before the Babylonian captivity, and both prepare for that as well. Where events happened is a measure of when they happened sequentially within the human time that was brought to earth with the fall. The scope of Junius 11, from the creation to the Last Judgment, is enormous even for a manuscript of over five thousand lines. Much between these two events is elided or omitted by the poems of the manuscript, but much remains and is held in its narrative moment through its thematics of place and displacement.[47]

At the center of this thematics is the idea of covenant because it offers a saving promise about the future homeland to an exiled or migratory people. If such a promise may in turn be read as preparatory to the promise of salvation and the heavenly home ensured through the intervention of Christ, the covenant is nonetheless itself necessary to those in search of a promised land, whether it be the Canaan of the Israelites or the home island of the Anglo-Saxons. Read in this context, Junius 11 is the most wide ranging of the manuscript books of elsewhere that survive from Anglo-Saxon England. If Cotton Tiberius B v and Vitellius A xv seem at first more encompassing, in that they include India and other regions of a suggestively mapped East, they are firmly earthbound in ways that Junius 11 proves not to be. In that regard, a typological reading of the Junius manuscript as an epic of redemption that moves from the fall into place through the triumphal entry into the heavenly home can be taken as offering the most cosmically and historically inclusive sense of place available in Anglo-Saxon England. That the manuscript unfolds through its four poems a master narrative for understanding place on the most extensive scale possible does not mean, however, that it must be taken as an interpretive paradigm for reading all other instantiations of place in Anglo-Saxon texts. That is to say, one need not reverse the order of chapters in this book and use the covenant of place found in Junius 11 to read boundary clauses in charters or telling allusions to Rome in the Anglo-Saxon *Chronicle*. If anything, the reverse seems more likely: these immediately local and precise means of demarcating the map of the lived world can help us read the poems of Junius 11 in ways that reveal their evident usefulness to an audience far remote in distance from the Holy Land.

Junius 11 makes yet one more geographical reckoning as a quadrateuch because it demands that its audience respond to its use of the vernacular. In its geographical and cultural specificity, English was not a universal language in the late tenth century, the putative date of the manuscript; it possessed none of the universalist pretensions of Latin.[48] Nor was it a scriptural language. Even the great vernacular prose stylist of that time, Ælfric, had deep anxieties about translating the Bible into English, especially the books of the Old Testament that were historical in nature and thus told of practices forbidden to good Christians.[49] The poems in Junius 11 are quite free of controversial topics,

such as polygamy, that posed interpretive difficulties for Ælfric and his contemporaries; nonetheless, they remain deeply historical in nature. The use of
the vernacular presented a problem of figural — that is, historicist — interpretation to the early readers of this manuscript, for they had to close the geographical distance between themselves and the inhabitants of the Holy Land.
Through this act of readerly identification, Israelites, Egyptians, Chaldeans,
and the like are made as much a part of the native history of Englalond as the
fallen angels damned in hell and the rescued angels liberated into heaven. The
terrain of belief for Anglo-Saxons begins with the fall into place. In this story,
the use of the vernacular allows elsewhere to become part of one's home
ground.

Conclusion: *By Way of* Durham

As the poems of Junius 11 make evident, the theological fall into place resonated powerfully for the Anglo-Saxons. During the years after 1066, this conjunction of place and the fall could also take on a more immediate political sense, though one must be careful not to overstate the similarity. In such instances, as with the poems of Junius 11, the vernacular language marked out the territory of cultural history and identity. Nowhere in Old English poetry is that sense of politics more completely entwined with a local landscape than in *Durham*, a poem composed so late in the Anglo-Saxon period that one almost hesitates to use this term to date it. In Old English meter and alliteration, it celebrates the city of Durham as a site that holds the landscape and the history of the Anglo-Saxons against the forces of temporal loss and change.[1] The poem alludes to the translation in 1104 of St. Cuthbert to the city, where his remains endure to this day in the cathedral, and the poem is noted in a work by Simeon of Durham completed in 1109. We can conclude that it was most probably written towards the middle of the first decade of the twelfth century, a generation or so after the Norman Conquest. The poem belongs to the medieval genre of the *encomium urbis*, though it has a more complex sense of place as embodying historical predicament than do most such poems.

The poem offers a vivid description of the physical site of Durham as it rests high on the cliffs above the River Wear:

Weor ymbeornad,
ea yðum stronge,   ond ðer inne wunað
feola fisca kyn   on floda gemonge.
And ðær gewexen is   wudafæstern micel;
wuniad in ðem wycum   wilda deor monige,
in deope dalum   deora ungerim.

The weir encloses the strong flow of the water, and among its currents live many kinds of fish. And a great wooded thicket has grown there; many wild animals, countless beasts, live in that place of deep dales. (ll. 3b–8)[2]

This sense of place as constituted by natural setting, as home to fish and animals, is said in the poem's opening line to be known throughout Britain ("geond Breotenrice"; l. 1) — a name for the island that also evokes the historical period when the British held the island between the departure of the Romans and the arrival of the Angles, Saxons, and Jutes. These references to the natural world and the time before the Anglo-Saxons hint at a kind of bygone pastoral era.

When, in the middle section of the poem (ll. 9–17), the eminent Anglo-Saxons buried at Durham are catalogued, there comes as well a shift in the naming of the place.[3] Amid the roll call of the dead interred at Durham appears a reference to the innocent King Oswald as "Engle leo," or lion of the English (l. 12a), that establishes this section of the poem as distinctly English. The names that fill these nine lines, including Cuthbert (d. 687), Oswald (d. 642), Aidan (d. 651), Eadbert (d. 698), Eadfrith (d. 721), Æthilwald (d. ca. 740), Bede (d. 735), and Boisil (d. ca. 660/61), appear within an envelope or ring pattern that begins and ends with Cuthbert, the most famous figure in the city and larger region:

Is in ðere byri eac   bearnum gecyðed
ðe arfesta   eadig Cudberch
and ðes clene   cyninges heafud,
Osuualdes, Engle leo,   and Aidan biscop,
Eadberch and Eadfrið,   æðele geferes.
Is ðer inne midd heom   Æðelwold biscop
and breoma bocera Beda,   and Boisil abbot,
ðe clene Cudberte   on gecheðe
lerde lustum,   and he his lara wel genom.

In that city also as is known to men is the blessed, virtuous Cuthbert, and the head of the pure king, Oswald, the English lion, and bishop Aidan, and Eadbert and Eadfrith, noble companions. Bishop Æthilwald is there with them and the glorious scholar Bede, and abbot Boisil, who taught the inno-

cent Cuthbert with pleasure in his youth, and he absorbed his teaching well.
(ll. 9–17)

To speak of the interred bodies of these famous men at the moment in which he writes, the poet uses the present tense verb *is:* each of them is in Durham. The reader of the poem may well extend that sense of the present to allow for a kind of figural history so that not just the body but the spirit of each is present. Such might be said of any cult site: the bones as well as the spirit of the saint remain present. But here there is a richer reading to consider, namely, that each remains as a kind of governing spirit for the Anglo-Saxons during this time of political change in which most of the leading figures of the Anglo-Saxon church have been removed from office.

In this list, the poet re-creates the circle of Cuthbert by citing within the bounds formed by his name both his significant predecessors and famous followers. In this manner, the poet of *Durham* portrays the saint not as iso-lated but rather as belonging within a flourishing historical moment in the past and at the center of an enduring cult in the present. That the early twelfth-century poet can look back more than 450 years to commemorate great En-glishmen of the seventh and early eighth centuries is possible because of the persistence of place.[4] After the initial reference to Cuthbert, the other names in this catalogue follow sequentially in the order of their death dates until we reach Boisil, who follows alliteratively in line 15 from Bede but who pre-deceases him by seventy-five years or so. The move from Bede to Boisil is explained by the fact that Boisil was Cuthbert's teacher and Bede was Cuth-bert's biographer. To prepare for the final mention of Cuthbert, the poet moves from Bede to Boisil and thus closes the circle. What governs these lines is not an absolute chronology, though the sequence is remarkably good if one con-siders that it is being set in alliterative verse rather than simple prose. (And unlike genealogies of dynastic families, there is no convenient patterning of initial sounds here because these men bore no familial relation to each other.) The chronology in these lines is designed to set Cuthbert's circle in a significant order that relates to the church history of pre-Norman, that is, Anglo-Saxon, England. This genealogy is not one of blood or dynastic succession but rather of men bound by remarkable accomplishments and an enduring relation to Cuthbert. Buried in Durham because of historical events beginning in the late eighth century, each of them bears a significant relation as well to the site of Lindisfarne.

Another way to reflect on this sequence is to read it as a form of hagiograph-ical lineage or transmission: what is known of Cuthbert comes largely from the various lives of him written by Bede, the "breoma bocera," or great scholar

(l. 15). As the chronology in these lines moves forward, it also suggests that the route back to Cuthbert is provided by these same lives of him written by Bede, who is the "latest" member of his circle. When the site of Durham is memorialized through the famous dead who lie there awaiting the final judgment, then the place is identified not with any British ruler or individual but rather with Oswald, the English lion, and the roll call of English church worthies.

With these lines, the golden age of Englalond is localized very specifically among a group of men who all figured prominently at Lindisfarne. The names tell the story. Oswald gave the island to Aidan in 638 for the foundation of a monastery, and in time Aidan became its first bishop. Later bishops of Lindisfarne included Boisil's great pupil Cuthbert (685–87), Eadbert (688–98), Eadfrith (698–721), and Æthilwald (c. 731–37/40). This catalogue of names identifies those who, each in his way, as secular patron, bishop, teacher, or biographer, made Lindisfarne into a great center of the Northumbrian church. That they were all, by the early 1100s, buried at Durham rather than on the Holy Island is an enduring reminder of the sack of Lindisfarne by Vikings in 793. With that attack by outsiders from the north came the end of Lindisfarne as a major center of learning. By cataloguing each of these figures, the poet of *Durham* meant his audience to recollect this fact and thus to ponder a historical parallel between events at the end of the eighth and the beginning of the twelfth century when outsiders, first the Vikings and then their direct descendants the Normans, placed Englalond at peril. Along with this historical parallel is the topographical similarity between Lindisfarne and Durham. Janet Backhouse has observed of the city situated on a loop of the Wear, "It is, like Holy Island, a natural stronghold."[5] The larger historical parallel between the two places seems to come almost of necessity with a nostalgic or pessimistic note.[6] Yet if the parallel is thought through fully it might be seen to offer a more sustaining sense of history: just as the English church and people recovered from the depredations that began at Lindisfarne, so they might yet again recover their native identity and culture from the domination of the Normans. This note is barely sounded in the poem and, finally, may have meant little more to its audience than a reminder that the uses of the past are not merely commemorative.

With the roll call of Anglo-Saxon luminaries, the poet transforms the site of Durham from British (as in ll. 1–8) to English (as in ll. 9–17). Once the poet sets Durham within the recorded history of the Anglo-Saxons, he can make the final move from the city as a place within the physical terrain of Englalond to the city as site from which one may depart for the spiritual home of heaven:

> Eardiæð æt ðem eadige   in in ðem minstre
> unarimeda   reliquia,

ðær monia wundra gewurðað,   ðes ðe writ seggeð,
midd ðene drihnes wer   domes bideð.

Countless relics remain at that place in the minster, where many miracles
happened, as the writings say. Amid them the man of God awaits judgment.
(ll. 18–21)

The modern reader familiar with the river and cliffs of Durham will surely miss
in this poem a description of the great cathedral that sits atop them like a
massive lion (Figure 16). The building in an early stage was there when the poet
wrote, as the references to Cuthbert and then to the minster show.[7] Coming as
they do in a catalogue of eminent Anglo-Saxons, these references remind us that
this poem is a legacy of place that sets a long historical-ecclesiastical tradition in
a precisely realized location. As a consequence, it is also a place where many
miracles have occurred, as the man of God awaits the day of judgment. This last
statement that the city has been the setting for miracles is supported, according
to the poet, by what the writings have said ("ðes ðe writ seggeð"; l. 20b).

Here, in what appears to be the latest of the extant Old English poems, we
find a phrase that in its mingling of writing and saying articulates the ways in
which the postmigration map of Anglo-Saxon England was created and then
spread: as the writing says. In sequence, the poem first maps Durham as a site
of physical beauty and natural life, then as the city of the commemorated dead
who remain in the cathedral to embody the historical and religious continuity
of the English, and finally as a place of relics and miracles that can prepare the
faithful for the final judgment and thus the heavenly home. The poem effects
that movement from the landscape of a known and loved natural place of
animals and flowing water (under the old law) to the unnamable and fearsome
place of judgment (under the new law) through its references to the bishops,
kings, and scholars who made Northumbria a great center of Christendom in
the centuries after their ancestors came to Britain from Angulus. Borrowing
from Wilhelm Busse, I would speak of this roll call of Anglo-Saxon scholars as
a "genealogy of teachers" who must "be ranked above anyone but the king in
Anglo-Saxon society."[8] Busse writes of this genealogy with reference to Ælfric,
to a time when there was still an Anglo-Saxon king. A hundred years or so
later, the poet of *Durham* can no longer connect himself and his place to a
continuous royal genealogy of Anglo-Saxons running back (at least in myth)
to Hengest and Horsa and then further to continental kings and gods. Yet in
serving to delineate a territory in which these ecclesiastical figures were re-
vered, the list in the center of *Durham* functions very much like the lists of
popes, bishops, and kings that appear throughout British Library, Cotton
Tiberius B v, as they also delineate a sense of place. In the absence of political
continuity, however, the poet of *Durham* must evoke a line of scholarly and

Figure 16: Durham Cathedral, above the River Wear.

spiritual continuity and thereby attempt to create a community of belief to outlast dynastic and political change.[9]

Durham celebrates the complex senses of place by which a people must live — from the most local and physical to the most unknowable and distant. That it comes very late in the period, that it has hovering over it one of the great Norman monuments of England, suggests that so nuanced a sense of place may itself be an act of retrospection, a struggle with the betrayals of history. This poem about Durham articulates various senses of the past—of the British era when the place was largely a natural setting, of the Anglo-Saxon era memorialized by the dead—as well as a sense of the future in heaven. But it has little sense of the present except through the workings of figuration, that is, through its claim for the enduring presence of Cuthbert and his circle. It is because place stands as a counterweight to the workings of time that we can speak of how a new people, the Anglo-Saxons, made the enduring geographical site, the island of Britain, into something new and strange. Over time and in turn that same place would be remade by yet another people that came to the island. The lines of history become tangled and broken, but memory survives in place, as the writings say.

Notes

Introduction: Book and Land

1. C. Plummer, ed., *Venerabilis Baedae Opera historica*, 2 vols. (Oxford: Clarendon Press, 1896), I:380, for text; J. F. Webb and D. H. Farmer, ed., *The Age of Bede* (Harmondsworth: Penguin, 1983), 201, for translation.

2. *Dictionary of Medieval Latin from British Sources, s. v. friscus*, meaning "not salty, fresh (with reference to water)," offers a twelfth-century use of the word as its earliest example. R. E. Latham, *Revised Medieval Latin Word-List from British and Irish Sources* (London: Oxford University Press for the British Academy, 1965), *s. v. friscus*, offers a thirteenth-century example of *fresca*, meaning "fresh water."

3. *Dictionary of Medieval Latin from British Sources, s. v. cosmographia*, defines it as "cosmography, description of the world"; and notes *s. v. cosmus*, "world, universe. b. this (transitory) world," that *chosmos* is glossed by the Old English *middangeard*. Latham, *Revised Medieval Latin Word-List, s.v. cosmus*, offers a ninth-century example of *cosmographus*, meaning "geographer." That Bede meant the word to denote those who describe the earth, or geographers, is suggested by his use of the phrase "in libris cosmographorum" in the section of his *De temporum ratione* (XXXV.41–45) devoted to "De quattuor temporibus, elementis, humoribus." This phrase about the book of cosmographers is followed in the next sentence with a citation by name of Pliny's *Natural History*, perhaps the most complete geographical text available to Bede. See C. W. Jones, ed., *Bedae Opera de temporibus* (Cambridge, MA: Medieval Academy of America, 1943), 247, for text, and 370 for n. 41, in which Jones notes that the "libris cosmographorum" is surrounded by mystery but may possibly be the one traded for by Aldfrith.

234 Notes to Pages 2–6

4. Frank M. Stenton, *Anglo-Saxon England,* 3rd ed. (Oxford: Clarendon Press, 1971), 88–90.

5. No charter for this transaction is listed in P. H. Sawyer, *Anglo-Saxon Charters: An Annotated List and Bibliography* (London: Royal Historical Society, 1968); or in the electronic Sawyer, http://www.trin.cam.ac.uk/sdk13/chartwww/eSawyer.99/eSawyer2 .html. For examples of charters contemporary with the Aldfrith-Ceolfrith transaction, see Dorothy Whitelock, ed., *English Historical Documents,* Vol. I (c. 500–1042), 2nd ed. (London: Eyre Methuen, 1979), Items 56, 58, and 59.

6. For contemporary charters making use of rivers as boundary designations, see Whitelock, *English Historical Documents,* Items 54, 55, and 60.

7. For introductory discussion of maps in early medieval England, see Catherine Delano-Smith and Roger J. P. Kain, *English Maps: A History* (Toronto: University of Toronto Press, 1999), 7–48; and Evelyn Edson, *Mapping Time and Space: How Medieval Mapmakers Viewed Their World* (London: British Library, 1997), 1–17, 72–80.

8. F. J. Monkhouse and H. R. Wilkinson, *Maps and Diagrams: Their Compilation and Construction* (London: Methuen, 1971), xii; for a more technical definition of *map,* see 13.

9. See further Margaret Bridges, "Of Myths and Maps: the Anglo-Saxon Cosmographer's Europe," in Balz Engler, ed., *Writing and Culture* (Tübingen: Gunter Narr Verlag, 1992), 69–84; and J. B. Harley and David Woodward, *The History of Cartography,* Vol. I: *Cartography in Prehistoric, Ancient, and Medieval Europe and the Mediterranean* (Chicago: University of Chicago Press, 1987), 326–33, on marvels and legends.

10. For general background, see the recent study by Natalia Lozovsky, *"The Earth is our Book": Geographical Knowledge in the Latin West ca. 400–1000* (Ann Arbor: University of Michigan Press, 2000).

11. Denis Cosgrove, "Introduction," in Cosgrove, ed., *Mappings* (London: Reaktion, 2002), 1–2.

12. Brian Stock, *The Implications of Literacy: Written Language and Models of Interpretation in the Eleventh and Twelfth Centuries* (Princeton: Princeton University Press, 1983) and *Listening for the Text: On the Uses of the Past* (Baltimore: Johns Hopkins University Press, 1990), esp. Ch. 2; Katherine O'Brien O'Keeffe, *Visible Song: Transitional Literacy in Old English Verse* (Cambridge: Cambridge University Press, 1990).

13. For a survey of the subject, see Sealy Gilles, "Territorial Interpolations in the Old English Orosius," in Sylvia Tomasch and Sealy Gilles, ed., *Text and Territory: Geographical Imagination in the European Middle Ages* (Philadelphia: University of Pennsylvania Press, 1998), 79–96.

14. P. D. A. Harvey, *Medieval Maps* (Toronto: University of Toronto Press, 1991), 8. As Woodward acknowledges in *The History of Cartography,* 325: "*Mappaemundi* were thus quite as much written as drawn."

15. On oral maps, see Wystan Curnow, "Mapping and the Expanded Field of Contemporary Art," in Cosgrove, ed., *Mappings,* 252–68, esp. 254.

16. For the concept of narrative cartography, see Nicholas Howe, "An Angle on this Earth: Sense of Place in Anglo-Saxon England," in *Bulletin of the John Rylands University Library of Manchester* 82 (2000), 1–25.

17. For Pliny's use of the Pillars of Hercules as a starting point, see *Natural History*

III.i.3: "origo ab occasu solis et Gaditano freto, qua inrumpens oceanus Atlanticus in maria interiora diffunditur" (The starting point is in the west, at the Straits of Gibraltar, where the Atlantic Ocean bursts in and spreads out into the inland seas); H. Rackham, ed., *Pliny: Natural History,* 10 vols. (Cambridge, MA: Harvard University Press, 1989), II:4–5. See further Trevor Murphy, *Pliny the Elder's Natural History: The Empire in the Encyclopedia* (Oxford: Oxford University Press, 2004), 128–64, on "triumphal geography."

18. See Delano-Smith and Kain, *English Maps,* 3 for a print of this diagram and the comment that it is "the most outstandingly successful practical map of all times."

19. J. P.Migne, ed., *Patrologia Latina* 94:710, for the text (quoted from online version, accessed at http://pld.chadwyck.com); and W. Trent Foley and Arthur G. Holder, trans., *Bede: A Biblical Miscellany* (Liverpool: Liverpool University Press, 1999), 33.

20. Nicholas Howe, *Migration and Mythmaking in Anglo-Saxon England* (Notre Dame: University of Notre Dame Press, 2001), 49–71; and Patrick Wormald, "The Venerable Bede and the 'Church of the English,'" in Geoffrey Rowell, ed., *The English Religious Tradition and the Genius of Anglicanism* (Nashville, TN: Abingdon, 1992), 13–32.

21. As quoted from the F Version of the *Chronicle;* see Peter S. Baker, ed., *The Anglo-Saxon Chronicle,* Vol. 8: *Ms. F* (Cambridge: D. S. Brewer, 2000), 86.

22. Francis P. Magoun, Jr., "An English Pilgrim-Diary of the Year 990," *Mediaeval Studies* 2 (1940), 231–52; Bertram Colgrave, "Pilgrimages to Rome in the Seventh and Eighth Centuries," in E. Bagby Atwood and Archibald A. Hill, ed., *Studies in Language, Literature, and Culture of the Middle Ages and Later* (Austin: University of Texas, 1969), 156–72; Veronica Ortenberg, "Archbishop Sigeric's Journey to Rome in 990," *Anglo-Saxon England* 19 (1990), 197–246. See, for a more general discussion, Blake Leyerle, "Landscape as Cartography in Early Christian Pilgrimage Narratives," *Journal of the American Academy of Religion* 64 (1996), 119–43; and Benet Salway, "Travel, *Itineraria* and *Tabellaria,*" in Colin Adams and Ray Laurence, ed., *Travel and Geography in the Roman Empire* (London: Routledge, 2001), 22–66.

23. Ortenberg, "Archbishop Sigeric's Journey to Rome in 990," 199–200.

24. For a comparative study of Sigeric's itinerary, see Joyce Hill, "Pilgrim Routes in Medieval Italy," *Bollettino del C.I.R.V.I.* 9 (1984), 3–22.

25. Paolo Squatriti, "Digging Ditches in Early Medieval Europe," *Past and Present* 176 (2002), 11–65, esp. 58–61; and "Offa's Dyke Between Nature and Culture," *Environmental History* 9 (2004), 37–56.

26. Harold M. Taylor and Joan Taylor, *Anglo-Saxon Architecture,* 3 vols. (Cambridge: Cambridge University Press, 1965), I:32–34.

27. Richard Muir, *The New Reading the Landscape* (Exeter: University of Exeter Press, 2000), 149–55, for a survey of this phenomenon.

28. W. H. Stevenson, ed., *Asser's Life of King Alfred* (Oxford: Clarendon Press, 1959, rprt. 1998), 41, for text; Simon Keynes and Michael Lapidge, trans., *Alfred the Great* (Harmondsworth: Penguin, 1983), 83, for translation.

29. Stevenson, *Asser's Life,* 79–80; Keynes and Lapidge, *Alfred the Great,* 102–3.

30. Stevenson, *Asser's Life,* 7; Keynes and Lapidge, *Alfred the Great,* 69.

31. For such a suggestion, see Keynes and Lapidge, *Alfred the Great,* 232. Even the skeptical Alfred P. Smyth, who believes the annointing story to be a fabrication for

political purposes, can offer no evidence disproving Asser's claim that Alfred went to Rome as a boy; see his *King Alfred the Great* (Oxford: Oxford University Press, 1995), 12–17.

32. Janet Bately, "Those Books That Are Most Necessary for All Men to Know: The Classics and Late Ninth-Century England, A Reappraisal," in Aldo S. Bernardo and Saul Levin, ed., *The Classics in the Middle Ages* (Binghamton, NY: Center for Medieval and Early Renaissance Studies, 1990), 45–78.

33. Iain Sinclair, *London Orbital: A Walk around the M25* (London: Granta, 2002), 226.

34. On reading during this period, see Nicholas Howe, "The Cultural Construction of Reading in Anglo-Saxon England," in Jonathan Boyarin, ed., *The Ethnography of Reading* (Berkeley: University of California Press, 1993), 58–79.

35. I explore these questions further in "Two Stories, Two Landscapes: Anglo-Saxon England and Contemporary America," in P. Squatriti, ed., *Natures Past: The Environment and Human History,* Comparative Studies in Society and History (Ann Arbor: University of Michigan Press, 2007).

36. Valuable studies of the subject include W. G. Hoskins, *The Making of the English Landscape* (New York: Penguin, 1985); Oliver Rackham, "The Forest: Woodland and Wood-Pasture in Medieval England," in Kathleen Biddick, ed., *Archaeological Approaches to Medieval Europe* (Kalamazoo, MI: Medieval Institute Publications, 1984), 69–105; Oliver Rackham, *Trees and Woodland in the British Landscape: The Complete History of Britain's Trees, Woods, and Hedgerows* (London: Phoenix, 1996) and *The History of the Countryside* (London: Phoenix, 1997); and Della Hooke, *The Landscape of Anglo-Saxon England* (Leicester: Leicester University Press, 1998).

37. Oliver Rackham, *Trees and Woodland in the British Landscape* (London: Weidenfeld and Nicholson, 2001), 39–40.

38. E. V. K. Dobbie, ed., *The Anglo-Saxon Poetic Records,* Vol. VI: *The Anglo-Saxon Minor Poems* (New York: Columbia University Press, 1942), 55.

39. See M. W. Beresford and J. K. S. St. Joseph, *Medieval England: An Aerial Survey* (Cambridge: Cambridge University Press, 1979).

40. Taylor and Taylor, *Anglo-Saxon Architecture,* I:209.

41. Such a conclusion is strikingly evident to anyone who reads through the various essays collected in Catherine E. Karkov and George Hardon Brown, ed., *Anglo-Saxon Styles* (Albany: SUNY Press, 2003).

42. Tim Eaton, *Plundering the Past: Roman Stonework in Medieval Britain* (Stroud, UK: Tempus, 2000).

43. Tayor and Taylor, *Anglo-Saxon Architecture,* I:189.

44. See, among many studies, Martin Carver, *Sutton Hoo: Burial Ground of Kings?* (London: British Museum, 1998), esp. 100–103; and Howard Williams, "Ancient Landscapes and the Dead: The Reuse of Prehistoric and Roman Monuments as Early Anglo-Saxon Burial," *Medieval Archaeology* 41 (1997), 1–32.

45. Tony Wilmot, *Birdoswald: Roman Fort* (Carlisle: Cumbria County Council, 1995), 44–47 for illustrations.

46. For a description and site plan of Knowlton, see Richard Morris, *Churches in the Landscape* (London: Phoenix, 1997), 72–74.

47. See Morris, *Churches in the Landscape,* 72; and O. S. Anderson, "The English

Hundred-Names: The South-western Counties," in *Lunds Universitets Årsskrift ny följd,* 35/5 (1939), 132–33. More generally, see Aliki Pantos, "'On the Edge of Things': The Boundary Location of Anglo-Saxon Assembly Sites," in *Anglo-Saxon Studies in Archaeology and History* 12 (2003), 38–49.

48. The classic statement of this position is Roberta Frank, "The *Beowulf* Poet's Sense of History," in Larry D. Benson and Siegfried Wenzel, ed., *The Wisdom of Poetry: Essays in Early English Literature in Honor of Morton W. Bloomfield* (Kalamazoo, MI: Medieval Institute Publications, 1982), 53–65, 271–77.

49. Sinclair, *London Orbital*, 90.

50. In this respect, I should acknowledge the influence of David Lowenthal, "Past Time, Present Place: Landscape and Memory," in *The Geographical Review* 65 (1975), 1–36; and Keith Basso, "'Speaking with Names': Language and Landscape among the Western Apache," in George E. Marcus, ed., *Rereading Cultural Anthropology* (Durham, NC: Duke University Press, 1992), 220–51.

51. Walter A. Goffart, *Historical Atlases: The First Three Hundred Years, 1570–1870* (Chicago: University of Chicago Press, 2003), 13.

52. Constance Bouchard, "Monastic Cartularies: Organizing Eternity," in Adam J. Kosto and Anders Winroth, ed., *Charters, Cartularies, and Archives: The Preservation and Transmission of Documents in the Medieval West* (Toronto: Pontifical Institute of Mediaeval Studies, 2002), 22–32, at 22.

Chapter 1: Writing the Boundaries

1. My model for this type of reading is Natalie Zemon Davis, *Fiction in the Archives: Pardon Tales and Their Tellers in Sixteenth-Century France* (Palo Alto, CA: Stanford University Press, 1987).

2. See further Ch. 5, "From Bede's World to 'Bede's World.'"

3. The best source for studying a variety of charters and scribal hands is Simon Keynes, ed., *Facsimiles of Anglo-Saxon Charters* (Oxford: Oxford University Press for the British Academy, 1991), Anglo-Saxon Charters, Supplementary Volume I. Relevant examples where one can immediately discern the scribal differences between the Latin text and the Old English boundary clause include: Plate 4, Sawyer 602, a charter of King Eadwig to his thegn Æthelnoth (956); Plate 21a, Sawyer 1028, a charter of King Edward to the Monastery of St.-Denis (1059); and esp. Plate 25a, Sawyer 794, a charter of King Edgar to his thegn Ælfhelm (974). Keynes observes of this final example: "Latin text written in Anglo-Caroline minuscule, probably imitating an example in Bishop's Style I: bounds written in Anglo-Saxon minuscule, of crude appearance" (p. 8).

4. I acknowledge here my debt to Nicholas Brooks, "Anglo-Saxon Charters: The Work of the Last Twenty Years," in *Anglo-Saxon England* 3 (1974), 211–31; Simon Keynes, *The Diplomas of King Æthelred "The Unready," 978–1016: A Study in Their Use as Historical Evidence* (Cambridge: Cambridge University Press, 1980); and Patrick Wormald, "Bede and the Conversion of England: The Charter Evidence," The Jarrow Lecture (Jarrow, 1984). For comparative studies of post-Anglo-Saxon English and continental charters, see Karl Heidecker, ed., *Charters and the Use of the Written Word in Medieval Society* (Turnhout: Brepols, 2000).

5. W. G. Hoskins, *The Making of the English Landscape* (New York: Penguin, 1985);

Oliver Rackham, "The Forest: Woodland and Wood-Pasture in Medieval England," in Kathleen Biddick, ed., *Archaeological Approaches to Medieval Europe* (Kalamazoo, MI: Medieval Institute Publications, 1984), 69–105; Oliver Rackham, *Trees and Woodland in the British Landscape: The Complete History of Britain's Trees, Woods, and Hedgerows* (London: Phoenix, 1996) and *The History of the Countryside* (London: Phoenix, 1997); Della Hooke, *The Landscape of Anglo-Saxon England* (Leicester: Leicester University Press, 1998) and *Anglo-Saxon Landscapes of the West Midlands: The Charter Evidence,* British Archaeological Reports Series 95 (1991); and Peter Robinson, "Mapping the Anglo-Saxon Landscape: A Land Systems Approach to the Study of the Bounds of the Estate of Plaish," in David A. E. Pelteret, ed., *Anglo-Saxon History: Basic Readings* (New York: Garland, 2000), 343–63.

6. Jacques LeGoff, *The Medieval Imagination* (Chicago: University of Chicago Press, 1988), 2.

7. P. H. Sawyer, *Anglo-Saxon Charters: An Annotated List and Bibliography* (London: Royal Historical Society, 1968). For the updated "Electronic Sawyer," see the next note.

8. I quote the text of Anglo-Saxon charters throughout from the online edition *Regesta regum Anglorum* (www.trin.cam.ac.uk/sdk13/chartwww/NewRegReg.html), which may be searched easily by Sawyer number and which is also far more accessible than the increasingly rare print edition of Walter de Gray Birch, *Cartularium Saxonicum: A Collection of Charters Relating to Anglo-Saxon History* (London: Whiting and Co., 1887), 4 vols. This charter is Sawyer 1257. Translation from Dorothy Whitelock, ed., *English Historical Documents,* Vol. I (c. 500–1042), 2nd ed. (London: Eyre Methuen, 1979), 506. On this kind of statement in charters, see Simon Keynes, "Royal Government and the Written Word in Late Anglo-Saxon England," in Rosamond McKitterick, ed., *The Uses of Literacy in Early Mediaeval Europe* (Cambridge: Cambridge University Press, 1990), 226–57.

9. Whitelock, *English Historical Documents,* 376.

10. Hoskins, *Making of the English Landscape,* 301.

11. See further Joy Jenkyns, "Charter Bounds," and Simon Keynes, "Charters and Writs," in Michael Lapidge, John Blair, Simon Keynes, and Donald Scragg, ed., *The Blackwell Encyclopedia of Anglo-Saxon England* (Oxford: Blackwell, 1999), 97–100.

12. Whitelock, *English Historical Documents,* 370: "Detailed boundaries in the vernacular first occur in a possible text in 814; they become normal in the tenth century; but they are frequently added in cartularies to charters too early for this feature."

13. The companion piece to the charter just discussed, the grant by Athelstan to Uhtred of lands at Hope and Ashford in 926, is entirely in Latin and has no boundary clause; see *Regesta regum Anglorum* for Sawyer 397.

14. Della Hooke, *The Anglo-Saxon Landscape: The Kingdom of the Hwicce* (Manchester: Manchester University Press, 1985), 52 and 227.

15. See Christopher Dyer, *Making a Living in the Middle Ages: The People of Britain 850–1250* (New Haven: Yale University Press, 2002), 13–42.

16. *Regesta regum Anglorum* for Sawyer 8; Whitelock, *English Historical Documents,* 482–83.

17. *Regesta regum Anglorum* for Sawyer 1171; Whitelock, *English Historical Documents,* 487.

18. *Regesta regum Anglorum* for Sawyer 1171; Whitelock, *English Historical Documents,* 487.

19. On dating, see *Regesta regum Anglorum* for Sawyer 1171; and Whitelock, *English Historical Documents,* 486.

20. *Regesta regum Anglorum* for Sawyer 262; Whitelock, *English Historical Documents,* 497.

21. Whitelock, *English Historical Documents,* 497, notes that "lengthy boundaries seem, as far as our evidence goes, to have begun with this king [Cynewulf]."

22. *Regesta regum Anglorum* for Sawyer 298; Whitelock, *English Historical Documents,* 523.

23. Whitelock, *English Historical Documents,* 373.

24. *Regesta regum Anglorum* for Sawyer 677; Whitelock, *English Historical Documents,* 558.

25. Nicholas Howe, "An Angle on this Earth: Senses of Place in Anglo-Saxon England," in *Bulletin of the John Rylands University Library of Manchester* 82 (2000), 3–27. For a study of literacy and charters, see Susan Kelly, "Anglo-Saxon Lay Society and the Written Word," in McKitterick, *The Uses of Literacy in Early Mediaeval Europe,* 36–62.

26. For a comparative study of the languages used in charters, see Patrick J. Geary, "Land, Language and Memory in Europe 700–1100," in *Transactions of the Royal Historical Society,* 6th ser., 9 (1999), 169–84. See also his *Phantoms of Remembrance: Memory and Oblivion at the End of the First Millennium* (Princeton: Princeton University Press, 1995), Ch. 3, on "Archival Memory and the Destruction of the Past," where he usefully notes that writing charters is also a way of leaving one's impress on the future: charters protected property rights and also the memories of those involved in legal transactions.

27. Brian Stock, *The Implications of Literacy: Written Language and Models of Interpretation in the Eleventh and Twelfth Centuries* (Princeton: Princeton University Press, 1983) and *Listening for the Text: On the Uses of the Past* (Baltimore: Johns Hopkins University Press, 1990), esp. Ch. 2.

28. Charles Dickens, *Our Mutual Friend,* Part XIII, Ch. 8: "The End of a Long Journey."

29. Hooke, *The Anglo-Saxon Landscape,* 62–63. For the text, see *Regesta regum Anglorum* for Sawyer 80.

30. See further Michael Reed, "Anglo-Saxon Charter Boundaries," in Reed, ed., *Discovering Past Landscapes* (London: Croom Helm, 1984), 261–306.

31. Bosworth and Toller, *An Anglo-Saxon Dictionary and Supplement* (1921), *s. v. snæd.* The word may also mean "a clearing in the trees," which has an analogous sense. It seems not to have survived into later periods of the language.

32. Hooke, *The Landscape of Anglo-Saxon England,* 91, observes: "These records show that the perambulation of an estate to identify boundary landmarks was a very real activity and this practice was of course continued throughout historical times by the tradition of 'beating the bounds' in Rogation week."

33. Catherine Delano-Smith and Roger J. P. Kain, *English Maps: A History* (Toronto: University of Toronto Press, 1999), 32, 114–17.

34. A cross-cultural account of the ways in which properties are demarcated or bounded has yet to be written. The possible means for doing so include the planting of fast-growing

cuttings that take root and sprout along boundary lines in northeast Madagascar. For this information as well as much illuminating conversation on the general topic, I am indebted to Genese Sodikoff of the Department of Anthropology at the University of Michigan. See also Gillian Feely-Harnik, *A Green Estate: Restoring Independence in Madagascar* (Washington: Smithsonian Institution Press, 1991), 464–67.

35. Whitelock, *English Historical Documents,* 546. See further Eric John, *Reassessing Anglo-Saxon England* (Manchester: University of Manchester Press, 1996), Ch. 5, "The West Saxon Conquest of England."

36. *Regesta regum Anglorum* for Sawyer 396; the translation, ignoring mispunctuation in the Latin edition, departs from Whitelock, *English Historical Documents,* 546–47.

37. See further Reed, "Anglo-Saxon Charter Boundaries." On surveying and mapping in the later medieval period, see J. B. Harley and David Woodward, *The History of Cartography,* Vol. I: *Cartography in Prehistoric, Ancient, and Medieval Europe and the Mediterranean* (Chicago: University of Chicago Press, 1987), 493–96.

38. For Athelstan's taste in Latin, see Eric John, *Orbis Britanniae and Other Studies* (Leicester: Leicester University Press, 1966), 48–54; and Frank M. Stenton, *Anglo-Saxon England,* 3rd ed. (Oxford: Clarendon Press, 1971), 352–54.

39. Clifford Geertz, "Local Knowledge: Fact and Law in Comparative Perspective," in his *Local Knowledge: Further Essays in Interpretive Anthropology* (New York: Basic Books, 1983), 167–234. For charters and "local knowledge," see also H. P. R. Finberg, *The Early Charters of the West Midlands* (Leicester: Leicester University Press, 1961), 10.

40. For roads and pathways as markers in charters, see Hooke, *The Anglo-Saxon Landscape,* 58, 145–49.

41. E. V. K. Dobbie, ed., *The Anglo-Saxon Poetic Records,* Vol. VI: *The Anglo-Saxon Minor Poems* (New York: Columbia University Press, 1942), 16–20.

42. Constance Bouchard, "Monastic Cartularies: Organizing Eternity," in Adam J. Kosto and Anders Winroth, ed., *Charters, Cartularies, and Archives: The Preservation and Transmission of Documents in the Medieval West* (Toronto: Pontifical Institute of Mediaeval Studies, 2002), 22–32, at 22.

43. Text and translation from Dorothy Whitelock, ed., *Anglo-Saxon Wills* (Cambridge: Cambridge University Press, 1930), 94–95.

44. Ibid., xx.

45. Ibid., 68.

46. Ibid., 40–41.

47. Eric Ferne, *The Architecture of the Anglo-Saxons* (London: Batsford, 1983), 21. See also T. M. Charles-Edwards, "The Distinction between Land and Moveable Wealth in Anglo-Saxon England," in P. H. Sawyer, ed., *Medieval Settlement: Continuity and Change* (London: Edward Arnold, 1976), 180–87. It should be noted that some translators of Anglo-Saxon boundary clauses, including Whitelock, sometimes use a modern place-name for the Old English place designated in a charter or will, thus misleadingly suggesting that some of these texts do refer to houses or other standing properties (e.g., in the charter just quoted in the text, Whitelock translates "Giddincgforda" as "Giffords Hall" rather than the literal "Gidding's Ford").

48. See further Dyer, *Making a Living in the Middle Ages,* 13–42, esp. 19–21.

Chapter 2: Home and Landscape

1. Harold M. Taylor and JoanTaylor, *Anglo-Saxon Architecture,* 3 vols. (Cambridge: Cambridge University Press, 1965–1978).

2. My focus here is on domestic or familial dwellings, and thus I do not consider the evidence for monastic communities as offering another kind of home. Such evidence, especially as it relates to gender, is well surveyed in Carol Neuman de Vegvar, "The Architecture of Women's Monasticism in Archaeology and in Early Insular Texts," *Visual Resources* 16 (2000), 207–220.

3. C. J. Arnold, *An Archaeology of the Early Anglo-Saxon Kingdoms* (London: Routledge, 1997), 73. For an illuminating discussion, see Sam Lucy, "From Pots to People: Two Hundred Years of Anglo-Saxon Archaeology," in Carole Hough and Kathryn A. Lowe, ed., *"Lastworda Betst": Essays in Memory of Christine E. Fell* (Donington: Shaun Tyas, 2002), 144–69.

4. Charles Plummer, ed., *Two of the Saxon Chronicles Parallel* (Oxford: Clarendon Press, 1892), 25; Version E of the *Chronicle, s. a.* 626.

5. Plummer, *Two of the Saxon Chronicles Parallel,* 11; Version E of the *Chronicle, s. a.* 409/410. An additional example of *getimbran/getimbrian* being used in this more general way occurs in the Old English translation of Matthew 7:24: "Eornustlice ælc ðæra ðe ðas mine word gehyrð and ða wyrcð byð gelic ðam wisan were se hys hus ofer stan getimbrode" (Therefore anyone who hears my word, and does it, is like the wise man who builds his house on stone). For the Old English text, see R. M. Liuzza, ed., *The Old English Version of the Gospels,* Early English Text Society, o.s. 304 (Oxford: Oxford University Press, 1994), I:15.

6. For a virtual tour of Bede's World, go to www.bedesworld.co.uk.

7. See Nicholas Howe, *Migration and Mythmaking in Anglo-Saxon England* (Notre Dame, IN: University of Notre Dame Press, 2001), esp. Ch. 3, "*Exodus* and the Ancestral History of the Anglo-Saxons."

8. For *The Ruin,* ll. 1–2, see G. P. Krapp and E. V. K. Dobbie, ed., *The Anglo-Saxon Poetic Records,* Vol. III: *The Exeter Book* (New York: Columbia University Press, 1936), 227; and for *Maxims II,* ll. 1–3, see E. V. K. Dobbie, ed., *The Anglo-Saxon Poetic Records,* Vol. VI: *The Anglo-Saxon Minor Poems* (New York: Columbia University Press, 1942), 55.

9. Useful general discussions of Anglo-Saxon architecture include: P. V. Addyman, "The Anglo-Saxon House: A New Review," *Anglo-Saxon England* 1 (1972), 273–308; Richard Gem, "Toward an Iconography of Anglo-Saxon Architecture," *Journal of the Warburg and Courtauld Institutes* 46 (1983), 1–18; Simon James, Anne Marshall, and Martin Millett, "An Early Medieval Building Tradition," *Archaeological Journal* 141 (1984), 182–215; and Anne Marshall and Garry Marshall, "Differentiation, Change and Continuity in Anglo-Saxon Buildings," *Archaeological Journal* 150 (1993), 366–402.

10. For ground plans of Yeavering and other royal sites in Anglo-Saxon England, see Alastair Service, *The Buildings of Britain: Anglo-Saxon and Norman* (London: Barrie and Jenkins, 1982), 29.

11. For "grub huts" see Eric Ferne, *The Architecture of the Anglo-Saxons* (London: Batsford, 1983), 15; for "sunken featured buildings" see Martin Welch, *Discovering Anglo-Saxon England* (University Park: Pennsylvania State University Press, 1992), 21.

12. Ferne, *The Architecture of the Anglo-Saxons,* 15–16.

13. Welch, *Discovering Anglo-Saxon England,* 25.

14. Ibid., 26–27.

15. Ibid., 28: "A damp atmosphere makes weaving easier, particularly when producing linen from flax, and a covered man-made hollow would certainly fulfill this requirement."

16. Service, *The Buildings of Britain: Anglo-Saxon and Norman,* 29. For an illustration of a reconstructed noble household in tenth-century Lincolnshire, with hall, weaving shed, kitchen, and sleeping quarters, see Christopher Dyer, *Making a Living in the Middle Ages: The People of Britain, 850–1520* (New Haven: Yale University Press, 2002), Figure 3.

17. Welch, *Discovering Anglo-Saxon England,* 18.

18. Oliver Rackham, *Trees and Woodland in the British Landscape* (London: Weidenfeld and Nicholson, 2001), 43.

19. Leslie Webster, "Anglo-Saxon England, AD 400–1100," in Ian Longworth and John Cherry, ed., *Archaeology in Britain since 1945* (London: British Museum, 1986), 136–38; see also Welch, *Discovering Anglo-Saxon England,* 19.

20. Welch, *Discovering Anglo-Saxon England,* 36.

21. See further the discussion in Brian K. Roberts, *The Making of the English Village: A Study in Historical Geography* (Harlow, Essex: Longman, 1987), esp. 100–102.

22. Krapp and Dobbie, *ASPR* III:138.

23. Krapp and Dobbie, *ASPR* III:139.

24. Krapp and Dobbie, *ASPR* III:160.

25. For discussions of the hall in Old English literature, see Kathryn Hume, "The Concept of the Hall in Old English Poetry," *Anglo-Saxon England* 3 (1974), 63–74; Edward B. Irving, Jr., *Rereading Beowulf* (Philadelphia: University of Pennsylvania Press, 1989), Ch. 4, "The Hall as Image and Character"; and Alvin A. Lee, *Gold-Hall and Earth Dragon: Beowulf as Metaphor* (Toronto: University of Toronto Press, 1998).

26. Anita R. Riedinger, " 'Home' in Old English Poetry," *Neuphilologische Mitteilungen* 96 (1995), 51–59, at 51.

27. For these passages in *Beowulf,* see Fr. Klaeber, ed., *Beowulf and the Fight at Finnsburg,* 3rd ed. (Boston: Heath, 1950), respectively, ll. 728–30a (warriors sleeping in the hall); ll. 661–65a (Hrothgar); and ll. 1299b–1301 (Beowulf).

28. Only when we understand the hall of Anglo-Saxon poetry in these terms can we see how little resemblance it bears to the other forms of home found in medieval and Renaissance societies. See further the various essays in Nicholas Howe, ed., *Home and Homelessness in the Medieval and Renaissance World* (Notre Dame, IN: University of Notre Dame Press, 2004).

29. William Ian Miller, "Home and Homelessness in the Middle of Nowhere," in Howe, *Home and Homelessness in the Medieval and Renaissance World,* 125–42.

30. Dorothy Whitelock, ed., *English Historical Documents,* Vol. I (c. 500–1042), 2nd ed. (London: Eyre Methuen, 1979), 398.

31. Ibid., 401.

32. For a wide-ranging survey of the various ways in which home can be considered, see the special issue "Home: A Place in the World," *Social Research* 58.1 (1991), esp. John Hollander, "It All Depends," 31–49.

33. Maureen Halsall, ed., *The Old English Rune Poem: A Critical Edition* (Toronto: University of Toronto Press, 1981), 90; see also her discussion of this passage, 148–50.

34. "An animal's abode": as in the Old English riddle about the badger, where home is evoked all the more memorably for being threatened. See Riddle 15 in Krapp and Dobbie, *ASPR* III:188.

35. See the *Dictionary of Old English,* Fascicle E (Toronto: Pontifical Institute of Mediaeval Studies, 1996), *s. v. eðel.*

36. Halsall, *The Old English Rune Poem,* 91.

37. See the *Dictionary of Old English,* Fascicle B (Toronto: Pontifical Institute of Mediaeval Studies, 1991), *s. v. botl.*

38. Riedinger, " 'Home' in Old English Poetry," 51.

39. This list contains all of the possible definitions offered in the Bosworth and Toller *An Anglo-Saxon Dictionary and Supplement* (1921). When the *Dictionary of Old English* publishes its entry for *ham* in the near future, there will no doubt be changes and corrections to this list. For a discussion of the development of Modern English *home* in its various senses, see Hollander, "It All Depends," 44–46.

40. Plummer, *Two of the Saxon Chronicles Parallel,* 67; Version E of the *Chronicle, s. a.* 855.

41. For more on the use of polysemy in Old English poetry, esp. *Beowulf,* see Fred C. Robinson, *Beowulf and the Appositive Style* (Knoxville: University of Tennessee Press, 1985), esp. Ch. 2, "Apposed Word Meanings and Religious Perspectives."

42. G. P. Krapp, ed., *The Anglo-Saxon Poetic Records,* Vol. II: *The Vercelli Book* (New York: Columbia University Press, 1932), 65.

43. Krapp and Dobbie, *ASPR* III:146–47.

44. Ezra Pound, *Translations* , intro. by Hugh Kenner (Norfolk, CT: New Directions, 1963), 207–9.

45. Krapp and Dobbie, *ASPR* III:144.

46. As the main entry for *eðel* in the *Dictionary of Old English* notes, the word is often "contrasted with 'exile' variously expressed."

47. Krapp and Dobbie, *ASPR* III:136.

48. See further Malcolm Godden, "Anglo-Saxons on the Mind," in M. Lapidge and H. Gneuss, ed., *Learning and Literature in Anglo-Saxon England: Studies Presented to Peter Clemoes* (Cambridge: Cambridge University Press, 1985), 271–98.

49. Klaeber, *Beowulf and the Fight at Finnsburg,* 52.

50. D. H. Lawrence, *Studies in Classic American Literature* (New York: Viking, 1964), 50.

51. Krapp and Dobbie, *ASPR* III:134.

52. Krapp and Dobbie, *ASPR* III:211.

53. For a similar reading of landscape in the poem and a comparison of Beowulf with Tennyson's Mariana, see Michael Lapidge, "The Comparative Approach," in Katherine O'Brien O'Keeffe, ed., *Reading Old English Texts* (Cambridge: Cambridge University Press, 1997), 20–38, esp. 33–35.

54. For a discussion of landscape terms in the poem, see Margaret Gelling, "The Landscape of *Beowulf," Anglo-Saxon England* 31 (2002), 7–11.

55. Della Hooke, *The Landscape of Anglo-Saxon England* (Leicester: Leicester Univer-

sity Press, 1998), 79. For the text, Sawyer 80, see *Regesta regum Anglorum* [www.trin
.cam.ac.uk/sdk13/chartwww/NewRegReg.html].

56. Klaeber, *Beowulf and the Fight at Finnsburg*, 53.

57. Kenneth Clark, *Landscape into Art* (London: John Murray, 1976), 30, speaks of
"the description of Grendel's Mere in *Beowulf* where the poet sets out to make us share
his terror."

58. See Jacques LeGoff, *The Medieval Imagination* (Chicago: University of Chicago
Press, 1988), 51–58.

59. Krapp and Dobbie, *ASPR* III:135.

60. Hooke, *The Landscape of Anglo-Saxon England*, 139.

Chapter 3: Englalond and the Postcolonial Void

1. For the relevant place-name evidence, see Della Hooke, *The Landscape of Anglo-
Saxon England* (Leicester: Leicester University Press, 1998), 19.

2. Martin Carver, *Sutton Hoo: The Burial Ground of Kings?* (London: British Museum Press, 1998), 100. See further the various studies in Carver, ed., *The Age of Sutton
Hoo* (Woodbridge, UK: Boydell, 1992).

3. Carver, *Sutton Hoo*, 55. To speak of the " 'vocabulary' of the landscape" is to signal
the textual turn that archaeology has recently taken, somewhat to the amusement of
literary scholars who have in the past been scolded by archaeologists for paying insuffi-
cient attention to the material culture of the people whose texts we study. For an extended
exploration of this trope, see Anne Whiston Spirn, *The Language of Landscape* (New
Haven: Yale University Press, 1998).

4. For a characteristic instance of this metaphor, see Jay Appleton, *The Experience of
Landscape* (New York: Wiley, 1975), 12, caption to figure 2. A far more sophisticated use
of linguistic theory as it relates to landscape appears in Spirn, *The Language of Landscape*. Nonetheless, the least successful section of Spirn's deeply thoughtful book is its
attempt to construct a grammar for landscape that is as fixed as that offered by linguists.

5. Hooke, *The Landscape of Anglo-Saxon England*, 13–14.

6. Keith Basso, " 'Speaking with Names': Language and Landscape among the Western Apache," *Cultural Anthropology* 3 (1988), 99–130, at 102.

7. For a more gendered discussion of the gaze in Anglo-Saxon England, see Clare A.
Lees and Gillian R. Overing, *Double Agents: Women and Clerical Culture in Anglo-
Saxon England* (Philadelphia: University of Pennsylvania Press, 2001), 111–51.

8. Erich Auerbach, "Figura," in his *Scenes from the Drama of European Literature*
(Minneapolis: University of Minnesota Press, 1984; rprt. of 1959 ed.), esp. 53.

9. See further Ch. 4, "Rome as Capital of Anglo-Saxon England."

10. Thinking of Anglo-Saxon England as a postcolonial society carries with it a great
deal of terminological and historical baggage: the imperial center and the peripheral
province; the empire in decline and the development of a nationalist ethos; the shifting
status of paganism and Christianity; as well as the often contentious field of postcolonial
studies itself. For an examination of these issues, see Bruce W. Holsinger, "Medieval
Studies, Postcolonial Studies, and the Genealogies of Critique," *Speculum* 77 (2002),
1195–1227. My own thinking about the relation between Roman Britain and Anglo-

Saxon England has been influenced by David N. Dumville, "Sub-Roman Britain: History and Legend," *History* 62 (1977), 173–92; James Campbell, ed., *The Anglo-Saxons* (Oxford: Phaidon, 1982), esp. the chapters by the volume editor; C. J. Arnold, *Roman Britain to Saxon England* (Bloomington: Indiana University Press, 1984); and J. N. L. Myres, *The English Settlements*, Oxford History of England, Vol. 1B (Oxford: Clarendon Press, 1986).

11. Campbell, "The Lost Centuries," in Campbell, ed., *The Anglo-Saxons*, 20–44, at 20.

12. Elleke Boehmer, *Colonial and Postcolonial Literature: Migrant Metaphors* (Oxford: Oxford University Press, 1995), 1. She refers here to Marlow's famous words about the Thames Estuary as also having been "one of the dark places of the earth." The contemporary London psychogeographer Iain Sinclair has described this passage, with telling irony, as "the line they all quote"; see his *London Orbital: A Walk around the M25* (London: Granta, 2002), 375.

13. Boehmer, *Colonial and Postcolonial Literature*, 3.

14. Michael Winterbottom, ed. and trans., *Gildas: The Ruin of Britain and Other Works* (London: Phillimore, 1978), 24.3; see 98 for Latin, 27 for translation.

15. Jacques LeGoff, *The Birth of Europe* (Oxford: Blackwell, 2005), 27. For lithicization, see Richard Muir, *The New Reading the Landscape: Fieldwork in Landscape History* (Exeter: University of Exeter Press, 2000), 148; for the "reversion to timber" for building in post-Roman Britain, see Peter Salway, *A History of Roman Britain* (Oxford: Oxford University Press, 1993), 346–47. It should be added that wood and its many forms also provided a vivid set of metaphors to King Alfred for the preface to his translation of Augustine's *Soliloquies;* see Thomas A. Carnicelli, ed., *King Alfred's Version of St. Augustine's Soliloquies* (Cambridge, MA: Harvard University Press, 1969), 47–48.

16. See further A. C. Sutherland, "The Imagery of Gildas's *De Excidio Britanniae,*" in Michael Lapidge and David Dumville, ed., *Gildas: New Approaches* (Woodbridge, UK: Boydell, 1984), 157–68, esp. 164; for the British wine trade with the continent, see Salway, *A History of Roman Britain*, 475–77.

17. Robert W. Hanning, *The Vision of History in Early Britain from Gildas to Geoffrey of Monmouth* (New York: Columbia University Press, 1966), 52–53.

18. Bertram Colgrave and R. A. B. Mynors, ed. and trans., *Bede's Ecclesiastical History of the English People* (Oxford: Clarendon Press, 1969), I. xi.40–41.

19. The relation between empire and modes of transport is always revealing; as Boehmer, *Colonial and Postcolonial Literature*, 42, notes: "The Romans had laid roads; the British now [in the nineteenth century] built railroads and laid telegraph cables."

20. Robert Hardison, *Eccentric Spaces* (Cambridge, MA: MIT Press, 2000), 46. Le-Goff, *The Birth of Europe*, 11, speaks of Roman roads as "symbolic landmarks." See also Richard Hingley and David Miles, "The Human Impact on the Landscape: Agriculture, Settlement, Industry, Infrastructure," in Peter Salway, ed., *The Roman Era: The British Isles, 55 B.C.–A.D. 410* (Oxford: Oxford University Press, 2002), 141–71, esp. 156–57.

21. Muir, *The New Reading the Landscape*, 100.

22. For a very useful inventory of Roman stonework with inscriptions that was incorporated as spolia in Anglo-Saxon buildings, see Tim Eaton, *Plundering the Past: Roman Stonework in Medieval Britain* (Stroud, UK: Tempus, 2000), 59–66. Stone was not the

only form of Roman spolia used; see Terence Paul Smith, "Early Recycling: The Anglo-Saxon and Norman Re-Use of Roman Bricks with Special Reference to Hertfordshire," in Martin Henig and Phillip Lindley, ed., *Alban and St. Albans: Roman and Medieval Architecture, Art and Archaeology* (Leeds: British Archaeological Reports, 2001), 111–17. For inscriptions, see also Carlo Tedeschi, "Some Observations on the Palaeography of Early Christian Inscriptions in Britain," in John Higgitt, Katherine Forsyth, and David N. Parsons, ed., *Roman, Runes and Ogham: Medieval Inscriptions in the Insular World and on the Continent* (Donington, UK: Shaun Tyas, 2001), 16–25.

23. Muir, *The New Reading the Landscape*, 165–67; and further, as he notes, John Blair, ed., *Minsters and Parish Churches: The Local Church in Transition, 950–1200* (Oxford: Oxbow, 1988), Oxford University Committee for Archaeology, Monograph 17; also Salway, *A History of Roman Britain*, 420; and Eaton, *Plundering the Past*, 17–19, 56.

24. On the survival of Roman roads in Anglo-Saxon England, see David A. E. Pelteret, "The Roads of Anglo-Saxon England," *Wiltshire Archaeological and Natural History Magazine* 79 (1985), 155–163; Michael Reed, *The Landscape of Britain: From the Beginnings to 1914* (London: Routledge, 1997), 265–69; and Eaton, *Plundering the Past*, 42.

25. G. P. Krapp and E. V. K. Dobbie, ed., *The Anglo-Saxon Poetic Records*, Vol. III: *The Exeter Book* (New York: Columbia University Press, 1936), 136. All translations from Old English poetry are by the author. See R. M. Liuzza, "The Tower of Babel: *The Wanderer* and the Ruins of History," *Studies in the Literary Imagination* 36 (2003), 1–35.

26. E. V. K. Dobbie, ed., *The Anglo-Saxon Poetic Records*, Vol. VI: *The Anglo-Saxon Minor Poems* (New York: Columbia University Press, 1942), 55.

27. See Bosworth and Toller, *An Anglo-Saxon Dictionary and Supplement* (1921), *s. v. weallstan*. Eaton, *Plundering the Past*, 17, draws a distinction between *wercstan*, "dressed freestone," and *walstan*, "rubble," that does not seem to be maintained in the poetry.

28. See further Ch. 4, "Rome as Capital of Anglo-Saxon England."

29. Eaton, *Plundering the Past*, 127, suggests that "the work of giants" is meant at least partly to evoke the very large size of Roman stones.

30. For such a reading of the poem, see R. F. Leslie, ed., *Three Old English Elegies* (Manchester: Manchester University Press, 1961), 22ff.; and, in a more tentative statement, C. L. Wrenn, *A Study of Old English Literature* (New York: Norton, 1966), 154. Salway, *A History of Roman Britain*, 367, notes that any large town in Roman Britain, as well as many smaller ones, would have had public baths.

31. Peter S. Wells, *The Barbarians Speak: How the Conquered Peoples Shaped Roman Europe* (Princeton: Princeton University Press, 1999), 134.

32. Alain Renoir, "The Old English *Ruin*: Contrastive Structure and Affective Impact," in Martin Green, ed., *The Old English Elegies: New Essays in Criticism and Research* (Teaneck, NJ: 1983), 148–73.

33. Krapp and Dobbie, *ASPR* III:227.

34. Krapp and Dobbie, *ASPR* III:146.

35. Dobbie, *ASPR* VI:55.

36. Michael Hunter, "The Sense of the Past in Anglo-Saxon England," *Anglo-Saxon*

England 3 (1974), 29–50, at 36. On Roman remains in London, see Francis Sheppard, *London: A History* (Oxford: Oxford University Press, 1998), 69–71.

37. Erwin Panofsky, "The Ideological Antecedents of the Rolls-Royce Radiator," in Panofsky, *Three Essays on Style*, ed. Irving Lavin (Cambridge, MA: MIT Press, 1997), 155.

38. John Summerson, "The Past in the Future," in his *Heavenly Mansions and Other Essays on Architecture* (New York: Norton, 1998), 236.

39. M. R. Godden, "The Anglo-Saxons and the Goths: Rewriting the Sack of Rome," *Anglo-Saxon England* 31 (2002), 47–68

40. Salway, *A History of Roman Britain*, 338.

41. See further Reed, *The Landscape of Britain*, 60–87.

42. Bill Ashcroft, *Post-Colonial Transformation* (London: Routledge, 2001), 156.

43. W. G. Hoskins, *Local History in England*, 3rd ed. (London: Longman, 1984), 114–16.

44. H. P. R. Finberg, *Gloucestershire* (London: Hodder and Stoughton, 1955), 39.

45. Bede, *Historia ecclesiastica* V.xxiv, in Charles Plummer, ed., *Venerabilis Baedae Opera historica*, 2 vols. (Oxford: Clarendon Press, 1896).

46. Plummer, *Venerabilis Baedae Opera Historica*, I.v.368; J. F. Webb and D. H. Farmer, *The Age of Bede* (Harmondsworth, UK: Penguin, 1983), 189.

47. Eaton, *Plundering the Past*, 128.

48. Ibid.

49. In this respect, it is worth remembering Gregory the Great's injunction, in a letter to Abbot Mellitus, that Augustine of Canterbury should turn whatever pagan shrines and religious sites he found to Christian purposes (*Historia ecclesiastica* I. xxx, in Plummer, *Venerabilis Baedae Opera historica*). One might note as well the reuse of the Roman-built Church of St. Martin's in Canterbury by the first missionaries (*Historia ecclesiastica* I. xxvi). Such issues are discussed in illuminating detail in Richard Morris, *Churches in the Landscape* (London: Phoenix, 1997), 6–45. For the later Anglo-Saxon practice of building churches on what had been the sites of Roman forts, see Muir, *The New Reading the Landscape*, 152.

50. For a ground plan and dimensions of Escomb, see Harold M. Taylor and Joan Taylor, *Anglo-Saxon Architecture*, 3 vols. (Cambridge: Cambridge University Press, 1965), I:235–37. For a larger context, see Eric Cambridge, "The Early Church in County Durham: A Reassessment," *Journal of the British Archaeological Association* 137 (1984), 65–85.

51. For a perceptive study of Anglo-Saxon stone churches as stylistic homages to Rome, see Jane Hawkes, "*Iuxta Morem Romanorum*: Stone and Sculpture in Anglo-Saxon England," in Catherine E. Karkov and George H. Brown, ed., *Anglo-Saxon Styles* (Albany: SUNY Press, 2003), 69–99. For other photographs of such stones, see Eaton, *Plundering the Past*, 146–47.

52. Taylor and Taylor, *Anglo-Saxon Architecture*, I:235 and 236, respectively. For another photograph of the arch, see Eaton, *Plundering the Past*, 148.

53. Taylor and Taylor, *Anglo-Saxon Architecture*, I:236; Eaton, *Plundering the Past*, 16.

54. Salway, *A History of Roman Britain*, 396.

55. Muir, *The New Reading the Landscape*, 11–12. See also, Oliver Rackham, *Trees and Woodland in the British Landscape* (London: Weidenfeld and Nicholson, 2001), 19, who estimates that an abandoned field in Britain requires about thirty years to turn into mature woodland. See also, Ken Dark, "The Late Antique Landscape of Britain, A.D. 300–700," in Neil Christie, ed., *Landscapes of Change: Rural Evolutions in Late Antiquity and the Early Middle Ages* (Aldershot, UK: Ashgate, 2004), 279–316; and Stephen G. Upex, "Landscape Continuity and the Fossilization of Roman Fields, *Archaeological Journal* 159 (2002), 77–108.

56. Muir, *The New Reading the Landscape*, 5. The standard study for later periods is Hooke, *The Landscape of Anglo-Saxon England*.

57. Salway, *A History of Roman Britain*, 332, states that by the 440s at the latest a "distinctively 'post-Roman' society had emerged in Britain" — just in time, one might add, for the arrival of the Germanic tribes. He also states that "by the middle of the fifth century Britain was materially more impoverished and institutionally more primitive than it had been when Claudius' army landed in A.D. 43" (354). See also Martin Millett, *The Romanization of Britain: An Essay in Archaeological Interpretation* (Cambridge: Cambridge University Press, 1990), esp. 212–30.

58. This topic has been much discussed. See, most recently, Fred C. Robinson, "Retrospection in Old English and Other Early Germanic Literatures," *The Grove: Studies on Medieval English Language and Literature* 8 (2001), 255–76.

59. Muir, *The New Reading the Landscape*, 100.

60. For a brilliant inquiry into the psychological valences that ruins can have for those who observe or live amid them, see Summerson, "The Past in the Future," in his *Heavenly Mansions*, 219–42; and the engaging survey of the subject in Christopher Woodward, *In Ruins* (New York: Pantheon, 2002).

61. W. S. Merwin, *The Mays of Ventadorn* (Washington, DC: National Geographic, 2002), 77.

62. James Corner, "Preface," in Corner, ed., *Recovering Landscape: Essays in Contemporary Landscape Architecture* (Princeton Architectural Press, 1999), x.

63. W. G. Hoskins, *The Making of the English Landscape* (London: Penguin, 1985), 55.

64. D. W. Meinig, "Symbolic Landscapes: Some Idealizations of American Communities," in Meinig, ed., *The Interpretation of Ordinary Landscapes* (New York: Oxford University Press, 1979), 164.

Chapter 4: Rome as Capital of Anglo-Saxon England

1. Katherine O'Brien O'Keeffe, ed., *The Anglo-Saxon Chronicle: A Collaborative Edition*, Vol. 5: *Ms. C* (Cambridge: D. S. Brewer, 2001), 52. All translations are by the author unless noted otherwise. See the insightful study by Susan Irvine, "The *Anglo-Saxon Chronicle* and the Idea of Rome in Alfredian Literature," in Timothy Reuter, ed., *Alfred the Great: Papers from the Eleventh-Centenary Conferences* (Aldershot, UK: Ashgate, 2003), 63–77.

2. I quote from the C Text but the 815/816 entry in the other versions of the *Chronicle* is virtually identical.

3. See Veronica Ortenberg, *The English Church and the Continent in the Tenth and Eleventh Centuries* (Oxford: Clarendon Press, 1992), 132–34; and Bertram Colgrave, "Pilgrimages to Rome in the Seventh and Eighth Centuries," in E. Bagby Atwood and Archibald Hill, ed., *Studies in Language, Literature, and Culture of the Middle Ages and Later* (Austin: University of Texas Press, 1969), 156–72.

4. Quoted in Wilhelm Levison, *England and the Continent in the Eighth Century* (Oxford: Clarendon Press, 1946), 41.

5. Peter Clemoes, "Language in Context: *Her* in the 890 *Anglo-Saxon Chronicle*," *Leeds Studies in English* n.s. 16 (1985), 27–36. For the *Chronicle* more generally, see Thomas A. Bredehoft, *Textual Histories: Readings in the Anglo-Saxon Chronicle* (Toronto: University of Toronto Press, 2001), esp. 138–54. The question of *her* as it relates to Anglo-Saxon England leads to the further question of whether Englalond was an incipient nation. Exploring this question further is beyond the scope of this chapter, but the following studies should be noted: Patrick Wormald, "Bede, the *Bretwaldas* and the Origin of the *Gens Anglorum*," in Wormald with Donald Bullough, and Roger Collins, ed., *Ideal and Reality in Frankish and Anglo-Saxon Society: Studies Presented to J.M. Wallace-Hadrill* (Oxford: Blackwell, 1983), 99–129; Wormald, "*Engla Lond*: The Making of an Allegiance," *Journal of Historical Sociology* 7 (1994), 1–24; Nicholas Howe, *Migration and Mythmaking in Anglo-Saxon England* (Notre Dame: University of Notre Dame Press, 2001; Sarah Foot, "The Making of *Angelcynn*: English Identity before the Norman Conquest," *Transactions of the Royal Historical Society*, 6th ser., 6 (1996), 25–49; Kathleen Davis, "National Writing in the Ninth Century: A Reminder for Postcolonial Thinking about the Nation," *Journal of Medieval and Early Modern Studies* 28 (1998), 611–637; and the discussion of somewhat later conditions in R. R. Davies, *The First English Empire: Power and Identities in the British Isles, 1093–1343* (Oxford University Press, 2000), esp. 50–55 and 199–200.

6. Levison, *England and the Continent*, 41.

7. See Robert W. Hanning, *The Vision of History in Early Britain from Gildas to Geoffrey of Monmouth* (New York: Columbia University Press, 1966); and Michael Hunter, "Germanic and Roman Antiquity and the Sense of the Past in Anglo-Saxon England," *Anglo-Saxon England* 3 (1974), 29–50.

8. Charles Plummer, ed., *Two of the Saxon Chronicles Parallel* (Oxford: Clarendon Press, 1892), I:4.

9. J. W. Wallace-Hadrill, "Rome and the Early English Church: Some Questions of Transmission," in his *Early Medieval History* (Oxford: Blackwell, 1975), 131.

10. Pliny the Elder, *Natural History*, ed. and trans. H. Rackham (Cambridge, MA: Harvard University Press, 1969), II:196–97; *NH* IV.xvi.

11. Bertram Colgrave and R. A. B. Mynors, ed. and trans., *Bede's Ecclesiastical History of the English People* (Oxford: Clarendon Press, 1969), I.i.14–15.

12. See further Gregory Jusdanis, *The Necessary Nation* (Princeton: Princeton University Press, 2001), 23–39.

13. See the following chapter, "From Bede's World to 'Bede's World.'"

14. Michael Winterbottom, ed. and trans., *Gildas: The Ruin of Britain and Other Works* (London: Phillimore, 1978), 8.1, pp. 18 and 91, respectively.

15. Peter Brown has argued that Rome is "peripheral" to Gildas's story but does not

recognize that this position gave his work its rhetorical authority. See Brown, *The Rise of Western Christendom* (Oxford: Blackwell, 1997), 92.

16. Uppinder Mehan and David Townsend, " 'Nation' and the Gaze of the Other in Eighth-Century Northumbria," *Comparative Literature* 53 (2001), 1–26.

17. Colgrave and Mynors, *Bede's Ecclesiastical History*, II.i.134. For Gregory's ideas about place and how it is to be loved, see Éamonn Ó Carragáin, "The City of Rome and the World of Bede," Jarrow Lecture 1994, 26–27.

18. As Ortenberg, in *The English Church and the Continent,* writes of the papacy, "This link with England was a privileged one, and both parties saw it as such" (158).

19. See further Richard Morris, *Churches in the Landscape* (London: Dent, 1989), esp. "Roads from Rome," 6–45.

20. On local conditions in England and the *Libellus responsionum,* see Nicholas Brooks, "Canterbury and Rome: The Limits and Myth of Romanitas," in *Roma fra oriente e occidente,* Settimane di Studio del Centro Italiano di Studi Sull'alto Medioevo (Spoleto: Presso la Sede del Centro, 2002), 797–832, esp. 828.

21. See the fundamental discussion by Stephanie Hollis, *Anglo-Saxon Women and the Church: Sharing a Common Fate* (Woodbridge, UK: Boydell, 1992), esp. Ch. 1, "The Conversionary Dynamic: More Laws for Times like These."

22. Bede, *Historia ecclesiastica* I.xxvii.8, in C. Plummer, ed., *Venerabilis Baedae Opera historica,* 2 vols. (Oxford: Clarendon, 1896).

23. *Historia ecclesiastica* I.xxvii.

24. Bede's depiction of Gregory influenced, for example, Ælfric's portrayal of him as a Roman in his homily "Sancti Gregorii Pape. Urbis Romane Inclitus." For text, see Malcolm Godden, ed., *Ælfric's Catholic Homilies: The Second Series,* Early English Text Society, s.s. 5 (London: Oxford University Press, 1979), 72–80; for commentary, see Godden, *Ælfric's Catholic Homilies: Introduction, Commentary and Glossary,* Early English Text Society, s.s. 18 (London: Oxford University Press, 2000), 403–412; and Cynthia Wittman Zollinger, *Sanctifying History: Hagiography and the Construction of an Anglo-Saxon Christian Past* (Ph.D. dissertation, Ohio State University, 2002), 179–93.

25. See further Howe, *Migration and Mythmaking in Anglo-Saxon England,* 108–142; and for the politics of missionary work, N. J. Higham, *An English Empire: Bede and the Early Anglo-Saxon Kings* (Manchester: Manchester University Press, 1995), esp. Ch. 6, "An English Empire: Status and Ethnicity"; and Higham, "Dynasty and Cult: The Utility of the Christian Mission to Northumbrian Kings between 642 and 654," in Jane Hawkes and Susan Mills, ed., *Northumbria's Golden Age* (Stroud, UK: Sutton, 1999), 95–104.

26. For a similarly complex cultural triangle, see Michael Lapidge, "Byzantium, Rome and England in the Early Middle Ages," in *Roma fra oriente e occidente,* 363–99. The figure of Willibald, Anglo-Saxon traveler to Byzantium and missionary in northwest Europe, unites Lapidge's cultural triangle with the one I describe.

27. G. P. Krapp, ed., *The Anglo-Saxon Poetic Records,* Vol. II: *The Vercelli Book* (New York: Columbia University Press, 1932), 51. On the poem as geographical catalogue, see Nicholas Howe, *The Old English Catalogue Poems,* Anglistica 23 (Copenhagen: Rosenkilde and Bagger, 1985), 86–103.

28. On England's "emotional link with the cultus of St. Peter," see Wallace-Hadrill, "Rome and the Early English Church," 122.

29. In arguing this claim for Anglo-Saxon England, I would qualify Robert Bartlett's assertion that "one of the things that marks a distinction between the early Middle Ages and the High Middle Ages was the significance attached to such claims [about the centralized authority of the Roman papacy] and the degree of success in enforcing them." In this regard, England seems to have anticipated developments on the continent. See Bartlett, *The Making of Europe: Conquest, Colonization and Cultural Change, 950–1350* (Princeton: Princeton University Press, 1993), 243.

30. Walter Benjamin, *The Arcades Project,* trans. Howard Eiland and Kevin McLaughlin (Cambridge, MA: Harvard University Press, 1999), 3–26.

31. Colgrave and Mynors, *Bede's Ecclesiastical History,* I.xv.52; and V. xv–xvi.506–10. This topic is explored at length in the following chapter.

32. Colgrave and Mynors, *Bede's Ecclesiastical History,* V.xx.532.

33. Benjamin, *The Arcades Project,* 17.

34. See Bede's *Lives of the Abbots of Wearmouth and Jarrow,* in C. Plummer, ed., *Venerabilis Baedae Opera historica,* 2 vols. (Oxford: Clarendon Press, 1896), I:364–70.

35. Helmut Gneuss, *Handlist of Anglo-Saxon Manuscripts: A List of Manuscripts and Manuscript Fragments Written or Owned in England up to 1100* (Tempe, AZ: Arizona Center for Medieval and Renaissance Studies, 2001). See also the lucid survey of the subject by David Ganz, "Roman Manuscripts in Francia and Anglo-Saxon England," in *Roma fra oriente e occidente,* 607–647.

36. Wallace-Hadrill, "Rome and the Early English Church," 116.

37. Dorothy Whitelock, "The Prose of Alfred's Reign," in E. G. Stanley, ed., *Continuations and Beginnings: Studies in Old English Literature* (London: Nelson, 1966), 67–103, at 90.

38. Janet Bately, ed., *The Old English Orosius,* Early English Text Society, s.s. 6 (London: Oxford University Press, 1980), 126. A later passage in the text (142) relates Albinus's battles against the Britons, Picts, and Scots in Britain.

39. Bately, *The Old English Orosius,* 312.

40. Stephen J. Harris, "The Alfredian World History and Anglo-Saxon Identity," *JEGP* 100 (2004), 482–510.

41. Bately, *The Old English Orosius,* 18, for text, and 203 for commentary on sources.

42. Ibid., 19.

43. Colgrave and Mynors, *Bede's Ecclesiastical History,* I.i.14–15, for text and translation.

44. Ibid., 14.

45. Master Gregorius, *The Marvels of Rome,* trans. John Osborne (Toronto: PIMS, 1987), 17. The list of sights visited by Sigeric in Rome (as found in British Library, Cotton Tiberius B v) hardly qualifies as a travel account or narrative; see further the discussion of this list below, in Ch. 6.

46. The following discussion is heavily indebted to Ó Carragáin, "The City of Rome and the World of Bede." His discussion (9–11) of the ways in which the "stational processions" in Rome relate to the city's topography is fundamental and suggests in turn the ways in which Anglo-Saxon pilgrims to Rome, especially monks, could later reenact that topography on home ground. See also the fascinating conclusions advanced by Simon Keynes in "Anglo-Saxon Entries in the 'Liber Vitae' of Brescia," in Jane Roberts

and Janet L. Nelson with Malcolm Godden, ed., *Alfred the Wise: Studies in Honour of Janet Bately* (Woodbridge, UK: D. S. Brewer, 1997), 99–119.

47. For a sketch of Rome during this period, see Richard Krautheimer, *Rome: Profile of a City, 312–1308* (Princeton: Princeton University Press, 2000), Ch. 5, "Renewal and Renascence: The Carolingian Age," 109–142. See also Ortenberg, *The English Church and the Continent*, 134–46.

48. For methods of construction in Anglo-Saxon England, see the discussion in Ch. 2 above.

49. H. M. Taylor and Joan Taylor, *Anglo-Saxon Architecture*, 3 vols. (Cambridge: Cambridge University Press, 1965), I:89 and 235, respectively. All calculations are based on the external measurements of each church and are no more than approximations.

50. Richard Krautheimer, *Corpus Basilicarum Christianarum Romae* (Vatican City: Pontifical Institute of Christian Archeology, 1977), Vol. V, Plate V; see also 180. As Krautheimer notes, "Until the beginning of the sixteenth century, when construction of the new Renaissance basilica commenced, the fourth century church survived in remarkably little-altered form" (177). Thus one can safely generalize about its size and appearance throughout the centuries when it was visited by Anglo-Saxon pilgrims. For additional floor plans and elevations of Roman basilicas, see Sible de Blaauw, *Cultus et decor: Liturgia e architettura nella Roma tardoantica e medievale* (Vatican City: Biblioteca Apostolica Vaticana, 1994), Studi e Testi 356, 515–83; for very useful maps of Rome during this period, see Raymond Davis, ed., *The Book of Pontiffs (Liber Pontificalis): The Ancient Biographies of the First Ninety Roman Bishops to A.D. 715* (Liverpool: Liverpool University Press, 2000).

51. Elaine Treharne has reminded me that some Latin manuscripts, especially in Rouen and the Vatican, contain Old English and were probably produced on the continent. My identification of vernacular Old English with Anglo-Saxon England is not an absolute claim but an assertion of probabilities. I suspect, though, that anyone writing Old English in a Latin manuscript on the continent was likely to have been a linguistically nostalgic Anglo-Saxon.

52. This discussion owes much to conversations about *Elene* that I had with Cynthia Wittman Zollinger in the course of advising her dissertation at the Ohio State University. Her argument has now been published as "Cynewulf's *Elene* and the Patterns of the Past," *JEGP* 13 (2004), 182–96.

53. Krapp, *ASPR* II:67.

54. Robert Bartlett, in *The Making of Europe*, observes: "The images of exclusion and otherness available to those who formed and expressed opinions in twelfth-century western Europe included not only the dichotomy Christian/non-Christian, but also that of civilized/barbarian, and the two polarities were often mutually reinforcing" (23). Given the importance of Latinity for Christianity it is hardly surprising that non-Christians were seen as barbarians, in the strict sense of the term.

55. A similar resituating of the battle to the Danube occurs in the other major Old English work on the subject, *The Finding of the True Cross* (see *The Old English "Finding of the True Cross,"* ed. M.-C. Bodden (Cambridge: Brewer, 1987). This rewriting of history prompted Ælfric in his homily on the invention of the Cross to insist on the true location of the battle between Constantine and Maxentius. As Joyce Hill observes, this

version was "presented as a correction to an unhistorical popular version" of the battle as found in *Elene*. See her forthcoming "Preaching the Cross: Texts and Contexts from the Benedictine Reform." I am indebted to Professor Hill for sharing a prepublication copy of this study with me. For this homily, see Godden, ed., *Ælfric's Catholic Homilies: The Second Series*, 174–79, esp. 174–76.

56. Antonina Harbus in her *Helena of Britain in Medieval Legend* (Cambridge: Brewer, 2002), 36, observes that *Elene* has no interest "in the nationality of the protagonists" Constantine and Helena/Elene. She thus argues that Cynewulf is more interested in developing Elene's "saintly persona" than in "any issues of national identification" (37). As I have suggested, Cynewulf's interests in national identification are implicit in his use of language and geography to envision the Elene story within the terms of Anglo-Saxon cultural identity.

57. Peter Salway, *A History of Roman Britain* (Oxford: Oxford University Press, 1997), 233.

58. In this process, by which the powerful center makes a claim at once spiritual and political on its non-Christian borderlands, Elene assumes a heroic stature that is verbally reminiscent of Beowulf as he sets out from Geatland to do battle with Grendel in Heorot. And yet there are certain details in Cynewulf's description of Elene's departure for the Holy Land that suggest the poet's concern with matters of gender. For the ships commanded by Elene carry men and women ("werum ond wifum"; l. 236a) unlike the one that bears Beowulf and his fifteen male companions to Denmark (*Beowulf*, ll. 207b–9). Thus Cynewulf can say of Elene, echoing in our minds the coastguard's similar claim about the young Beowulf and yet also making it more encompassing: "Ne hyrde ic sið ne ær / on egstreame idese lædan, / on merestræte, mægen fægerre" (Never have I heard far or near of a woman leading a finer force across the seastream on the road of the ocean; ll. 240b–42). See *Beowulf*, ll. 244–49a for the comparable passage.

59. *Historia ecclesiastica* I.xxxii, in Plummer, *Venerabilis Baedae Opera historica*; Hollis, *Anglo-Saxon Women and the Church*, 17.

60. Horace, *The Odes and Epodes*, IV.iii.13, ed. and trans. C. E. Bennett (Cambridge, MA: Harvard University Press, 1946).

61. The most illuminating discussion of gender, including the use of *cwen*, in the poem is by Stacy Klein, "Reading Queenship in Cynewulf's *Elene*," *Journal of Medieval and Early Modern Studies* 33 (2003), 47–89.

62. Hollis, *Anglo-Saxon Women and the Church*, 7.

Chapter 5: From Bede's World to "Bede's World"

1. For the Latin spelling, see Bertram Colgrave and R. A. B. Mynors, ed. and trans., *Bede's Ecclesiastical History of the English People* (Oxford: Clarendon Press, 1981), 532, and also Bede, *Historia ecclesiastica* V. xxi, in C. Plummer, ed., *Venerabilis Baedae Opera historica*, 2 vols. (Oxford: Clarendon, 1896); for the Old English spelling, see Thomas Miller, ed., *The Old English Version of Bede's Ecclesiastical History of the English People*, Early English Text Society, o.s. 110 (London: Trubner, 1890), 468. For the etymology of *Jarrow* from the tribal name Gyrwe, from "an old word for 'mud' or 'fen' found in OE *gyr*, ON *gior* 'mud,'" that is, from the people who lived in fens or

muddy districts, see Eilert Ekwall, *The Concise Oxford Dictionary of English Place-Names* (Oxford: Clarendon Press, 1960), 268, *s. n.* "Jarrow."

2. Ellen Wilkinson, *The Town That Was Murdered: The Life-Story of Jarrow* (London: Victor Gollancz, 1939).

3. Quoted in the invaluable study by Tom Pickard, *Jarrow March* (London: Allison and Busby, 1982), 35. Additional information about the history of Jarrow and Northumbria in the nineteenth and twentieth centuries can be found in three fine volumes: Robert Colls and Bill Lancaster, ed., *Geordies: Roots of Regionalism* (Edinburgh: Edinburgh University Press, 1992); Norman McCord and Richard Thompson, *The Northern Counties from A.D. 1000* (London: Longman, 1998); and Neville Kirk, ed., *Northern Identities: Historical Interpretations of 'The North' and 'Northernness'* (Aldershot: Ashgate, 2000).

4. For a virtual tour of Bede's World, go to www.bedesworld.co.uk.

5. Among the numerous studies of Bede's historiography, see Gerald Bonner, "Bede and Medieval Civilization," *Anglo-Saxon England* 2 (1973), 71–90; R. A. Markus, "Bede and the Tradition of Ecclesiastical Historiography," Jarrow Lecture, 1975; and Jan Davidse, "The Sense of History in the Works of the Venerable Bede," *Studi Medievali* 23 (1982), 647–95.

6. See further on these issues the indispensable study by Walter A. Goffart, *The Narrators of Barbarian History (A.D. 550–800)* (Princeton: Princeton University Press, 1988), 235–328.

7. For Bede and the computus, see C. W. Jones, ed., *Bedae: Opera de temporibus* (Cambridge, MA: Medieval Academy of America, 1943); and Bede, *The Reckoning of Time*, trans. Faith Wallis (Liverpool: Liverpool University Press, 1999).

8. For Bede's narrative of the Synod of Whitby, see *Historia ecclesiastica* III.xxv, in Plummer, *Venerabilis Baedae Opera historica*; Colgrave and Mynors, *Bede's Ecclesiastical History*, 294–309.

9. *Historia ecclesiastica* III.xxv; Colgrave and Mynors, 296.

10. *Historia ecclesiastica* III.xxv; Colgrave and Mynors, 300–301.

11. *Historia ecclesiastica* I.xxvii; Colgrave and Mynors, 82–83.

12. *Historia ecclesiastica* I.xxvii; Colgrave and Mynors, 80–81.

13. *Historia ecclesiastica* I.xxvii; Colgrave and Mynors, 80–83.

14. Paul Meyvaert, "Diversity within Unity: A Gregorian Theme," *Heythorp Journal* 4 (1963), 141–62. See also, J. M. Wallace-Hadrill, *Bede's Ecclesiastical History of the English People: A Historical Commentary* (Oxford: Clarendon Press, 1993), 39–40.

15. J. M. Wallace-Hadrill, "Bede and Plummer," in Gerald Bonner, ed., *Famulus Christi: Essays in Commemoration of the Thirteenth Centenary of the Birth of the Venerable Bede* (London: SPCK, 1976), 366–85, at 373.

16. R. W. Southern, "Bede," in his *Medieval Humanism and Other Studies* (Oxford: Basil Blackwell, 1984), 1–8, at 1.

17. Among various studies of Bede and geography, see H. C. Darby, "The Geographical Ideas of the Venerable Bede," *Scottish Geographical Magazine* 51 (1935), 84–89; J. M. Wallace-Hadrill, "Bede's Europe," Jarrow Lecture, 1962; James Campbell, "Bede's Words for Places," in his *Essays in Anglo-Saxon History* (London: Hambledon Press, 1986), 99–119; and, more generally, Della Hooke, "The Anglo-Saxons in England in the

Seventh and Eighth Centuries: Aspects of Location in Space" and "Discussion," in John Hines, ed., *The Anglo-Saxons from the Migration Period to the Eighth Century: An Ethnographic Perspective* (Woodbridge, UK: Boydell, 1997), 65–99.

18. *Historia ecclesiastica* V.xxiv; Colgrave and Mynors, 566–67.

19. For studies of this ideal with reference to Anglo-Saxon England, see Christopher A. Jones, "Envisioning the *Cenobium* in the Old English *Guthlac A*," *Mediaeval Studies* 57 (1995), 259–91; and Roberta Frank, "Old English *Ancor* 'anchor': Transformation of a Latin Loanword," in K. E. Olsen, A. Harbus, and T. Hofstra, ed., *Germanic Texts and Latin Models: Medieval Reconstructions*, Germania Latina IV (Leuven, Belgium: Peeters, 2001), 7–27.

20. *Historia ecclesiastica* V.xxi; Colgrave and Mynors, 532–33.

21. For Bede and Benedict Biscop, see Patrick Wormald, "Bede and Benedict Biscop," in Bonner, *Famulus Christi*, 141–69; and Peter Hunter Blair, *The World of Bede* (Cambridge: Cambridge University Press, 1990), 155–83. Sister Benedicta Ward has usefully pointed, in this regard, to Bede's praise of Benedict Biscop for traveling so extensively. That he did so, Bede notes, freed others from that sort of work. See her "Preface" in Bede, *A Biblical Miscellany*, trans. W. Trent Foley and Arthur G. Holder (Liverpool: Liverpool University Press, 1999), p. xv. For Rome and the Anglo-Saxon Church, see J. M. Wallace-Hadrill, "Rome and the Early English Church: Some Questions of Transmission," in his *Early Medieval History* (Oxford: Blackwell, 1975), 115–37; and Éamonn Ó Carragáin, "The City of Rome and the World of Bede," Jarrow Lecture, 1994.

22. Robert W. Hanning, *The Vision of History in Early Medieval Britain from Gildas to Geoffrey of Monmouth* (New York: Columbia University Press, 1966), 64 and 65.

23. See further Nicholas Howe, *Migration and Mythmaking in Anglo-Saxon England* (Notre Dame: University of Notre Dame Press, 2001), 108–42.

24. *Historia ecclesiastica* I.i; Colgrave and Mynors, 14–15.

25. Pliny the Elder, *Natural History*, trans. H. Rackham (Cambridge, MA: Harvard University Press, 1969), II:196–97. *NH* IV.xvi.102.

26. See further F. W. Walbank, "The Geography of Polybius," *Classica et Mediaevalia* 9 (1947), 155–82; and Nicholas Howe, "In Defense of the Encyclopedia Mode: on Pliny's *Preface* to the *Natural History*," *Latomus* 44 (1985), 561–76.

27. W. M. Lindsay, ed., *Isidori Hispalensis episcopi Etymologiarum sive originum* libri XX (Oxford: Clarendon Press, 1911), XIV.vi.2.

28. See the numerous references to the *Etymologiae* in Helmut Gneuss, *Handlist of Anglo-Saxon Manuscripts: A List of Manuscripts and Manuscript Fragments Written or Owned in England up to 1100* (Tempe, AZ: Arizona Center for Medieval and Renaissance Studies, 2001), MRTS, 241; and William D. McCready, "Bede and the Isidorian Legacy," *Mediaeval Studies* 57 (1995), 41–73.

29. Michael Winterbottom, ed. and trans., *Gildas: The Ruin of Britain and Other Works* (London: Phillimore, 1978), 3.1; see 89 for Latin and 16 for translation.

30. Winterbottom, *Gildas: The Ruin of Britain*, 3.1; 91 for Latin and 18 for translation.

31. See Hanning, *The Vision of History in Early Medieval Britain*, 44–62; and Neil Wright, "Gildas' Geographical Perspective: Some Problems," in Michael Lapidge and David Dumville, *Gildas: New Approaches* (Woodbridge, UK: Boydell, 1984), 85–105.

32. Dorothy Bethurum, ed., *The Homilies of Wulfstan* (Oxford: Clarendon Press, 1957), 261–75; and Howe, *Migration and Mythmaking in Anglo-Saxon England*, 8–20.

33. *Historia ecclesiastica* I.vi; Colgrave and Mynors, 28–29.

34. Uppinder Mehan and David Townsend, " 'Nation' and the Gaze of the Other in Eighth-Century Northumbria," *Comparative Literature* 53 (2001), 1–26, at 7.

35. *Historia ecclesiastica* II.1; Colgrave and Mynors, 134–35.

36. For the Latin text, see *Itineraria et alia geographica*, Corpus Christianorum Series Latina 175 (Turnholt: Brepols, 1965), I:261; for the translation, see Bede, *A Biblical Miscellany*, 12. This CCSL volume also contains the text of Adomnan's *De locis sanctis*, 177–234. See also Denis Meehan, ed. and trans., *Adamnan's De Locis Sanctis* (Dublin: Dublin Institute for Advanced Study, 1958).

37. For these ground plans, see *Itineraria et alia geographica*, II.2–5, at 256 and 258.

38. Catherine Delano-Smith and Roger J. P. Kain, *English Maps: A History* (Toronto: University of Toronto Press, 1999), 8–12.

39. *Itineraria et alia geographica*, XVIII.4–5, at 279–80. For the role of Aldfrith, who traded an estate of land for a treatise on cosmography with the monastery at Wearmouth (as discussed in the Introduction to this book), in spreading Adomnan's work on the Holy Places throughout Northumbria, see Frank M. Stenton, *Anglo-Saxon England*, 3rd ed. (Oxford: Clarendon Press, 1971), 89.

40. Robert P. Bergman and Diane De Grazia, *Vatican Treasures: Early Christian, Renaissance, and Baroque Art from the Papal Collections* (Cleveland: The Cleveland Museum of Art, 1998), 31; for illustrations, see 30–31.

41. *Historia ecclesiastica* V.xxiv; Colgrave and Mynors, 570.

42. *Historia ecclesiastica* I.xv; Colgrave and Mynors, 50.

43. *Historia ecclesiastica* I.i; Colgrave and Mynors, 14–15.

44. In this same section, Bede includes a mention of the twenty-eight cities for which the island was once famous, presumably a reference to the major Roman settlements in the province of Britannia (*Historia ecclesiastica* I.i). See further Nicholas Howe, "Two Stories, Two Landscapes: Anglo-Saxon England and Contemporary America," in P. Squatriti, ed., *Natures Past: The Environment and Human History*, Comparative Studies in Society and History (Ann Arbor: University of Michigan Press, 2007).

45. *Historia ecclesiastica* I.i; Colgrave and Mynors, 16–17.

46. *Historia ecclesiastica* I.i; Colgrave and Mynors, 16–17.

47. Geoffrey of Monmouth, *The History of the Kings of Britain*, trans. L. Thorpe (New York: Penguin, 1988), 65.

48. *Historia ecclesiastica* I.xv; Colgrave and Mynors, 50.

49. For the denotative range of this word in Old English, see Bosworth and Toller, *An Anglo-Saxon Dictionary and Supplement* (1921), *s. v. utgang* (I).

50. For the use of a typical English landscape as a means of familiarizing the distant landscape of the Bible in Old English poetry, see George K. Anderson, *The Literature of the Anglo-Saxons* (Princeton: Princeton University Press, 1949), 117–19.

51. "Bede's World — Where History Was Made," printed brochure available at Bede's World.

52. Personal communication from Rosemary Cramp, August 2001, International Society of Anglo-Saxonists, Helsinki, Finland.

53. For the archaeology of Jarrow, see Rosemary Cramp, "Monkwearmouth and Jarrow: The Archaeological Evidence," in Bonner, ed., *Famulus Christi,* 5–18; and also her more general study "The Northumbrian Identity," in Jane Hawkes and Susan Mills, ed., *Northumbria's Golden Age* (Thrupp, UK: Sutton Publishing, 1991), 1–11.

54. "Bede's World — Where History Was Made," printed brochure available at Bede's World, 3–4.

55. Alan Plater, "The Drama of the North-East," in Colls and Lancaster, *Geordies: Roots of Regionalism,* 71–84, at 83.

56. Stuart Rawnsley, "Constructing 'The North': Space and a Sense of Place," in Kirk, ed., *Northern Identities,* 3–22, at 3.

Chapter 6: Books of Elsewhere: Cotton Tiberius B v and Cotton Vitellius A xv

1. On Latin encyclopedias in Anglo-Saxon England, see further Nicholas Howe, *The Old English Catalogue Poems* (Copenhagen: Rosenkilde and Bagger, 1985), Anglistica 23, 9–72; and William D. McCready, "Bede and the Isidorian Legacy," *Mediaeval Studies* 57 (1995), 41–73.

2. D. G. Scragg, "The Compilation of the Vercelli Book," *Anglo-Saxon England* 2 (1973), 189–207, at 190.

3. I refer to this manuscript throughout as Cotton Vitellius A xv rather than the *Beowulf* manuscript to avoid privileging its most famous work and thereby suggesting that the other works are somehow interesting only as they relate to it. See the classic study by Kenneth Sisam, "The Compilation of the *Beowulf* Manuscript," in his *Studies in the History of Old English Literature* (Oxford: Clarendon Press, 1953), 65–96. He concludes, "And if a cataloguer of those days had to describe it briefly, he might well have called it 'Liber de diversis monstris, anglice'" (96). The adverbial (*in*) *English* is meant to modify *book* rather than *monsters*. Sisam, it should be noted, excludes *Judith* from this description. The most recent large-scale survey of the subject is Andy Orchard's invaluable *Pride and Prodigies: Studies in the Monsters of the Beowulf-Manuscript* (Cambridge: D. S. Brewer, 1995). Other relevant studies include William E. Brynteson, "*Beowulf*, Monsters, and Manuscripts: Classical Associations," *Res Publica Litterarum* 5 (1982), 41–57; and Paul Beekman Taylor and Peter H. Salus, "The Compilation of Cotton Vitellius A xv," *Neuphilologische Mitteilungen* 69 (1968), 199–204.

4. P. McGurk, D. N. Dumville, M. R. Godden, and Ann Knock, ed., *An Eleventh-Century Anglo-Saxon Illustrated Miscellany: British Library Cotton Tiberius B.v., Part I* (Copenhagen: Rosenkilde and Bagger, 1983), EEMF 21. In subsequent notes, this title will be abbreviated as *An Eleventh-Century Miscellany.*

5. For the construction of the Exeter Book, see Patrick W. Conner, *Anglo-Saxon Exeter: A Tenth-Century Cultural History* (Woodbridge, UK: Boydell, 1993), 95–164.

6. W. B. Yeats, ed., *The Oxford Book of Modern Verse* (Oxford: Clarendon Press, 1936); and Philip Larkin, *The Oxford Book of Twentieth-Century English Verse* (Oxford: Clarendon Press, 1973).

7. Caroline Walker Bynum, *Metamorphosis and Identity* (New York: Zone Books, 2001), 26.

258   Notes to Pages 154–158

8. My readings of the two manuscripts are not meant to exclude other interpretations but rather are meant to complement existing ones, or, more exactly, to suggest how an Anglo-Saxon reader with an awareness of place might encounter and use each of these compilations.

9. Such is immediately apparent when one considers that several folios of Tiberius B v contain excerpted passages from Pliny's *Natural History:* ff. 49v–51r (*NH* XVIII.342–365) in McGurk, *An Eleventh-Century Miscellany,* 126–29; f. 52v (*NH* II.32–44), McGurk, *An Eleventh-Century Miscellany,* 132; f. 52v (*NH* II.83–84), McGurk, *An Eleventh-Century Miscellany,* 132; ff. 53r–53v (*NH* II.59–64), McGurk, *An Eleventh-Century Miscellany,* 133–34; ff. 53v–54r (*NH* II.62–77), McGurk, *An Eleventh-Century Miscellany,* 134–35.

10. See further Katherine O'Brien O'Keeffe, ed., *The Anglo-Saxon Chronicle: A Collaborative Edition,* Vol. 5: *Ms. C* (Cambridge: D. S. Brewer, 2001) for these texts and complete discussion.

11. Tiberius B v also contains an illustrated Latin text of *The Wonders of the East.* Oxford, Bodleian Library 614 (ff. 36r–48r) contains only the Latin text of *Wonders.* The appearance of this work in three different manuscripts and in two languages is quite unusual for Anglo-Saxon England and does suggest a deep cultural interest in it as well as rare luck in manuscript survival.

12. For the reordering of the manuscript, see McGurk, *An Eleventh-Century Miscellany,* 25–27; for seventeenth-century cartography and atlas making, see Walter A. Goffart, *Historical Atlases: The First Three Hundred Years, 1570–1870* (Chicago: University of Chicago Press, 2003).

13. See the judicious study by Peter J. Lucas, "The Place of *Judith* in the *Beowulf*-Manuscript," *Review of English Studies* 41 (1990), 463–78, esp. 467–71.

14. N. R. Ker, *A Catalogue of Manuscripts Containing Anglo-Saxon* (Oxford: Clarendon Press, 1957), 255. See also Helmut Gneuss, *Handlist of Anglo-Saxon Manuscripts: A List of Manuscripts and Manuscript Fragments Written or Owned in England up to 1100* (Tempe, AZ: Arizona Center for Medieval and Renaissance Studies, 2001), 69.

15. The overlap of materials in Cotton Tiberius B v and other Anglo-Saxon manuscripts has been studied in terms of the various relevant genres. Taken together, the evidence from the following studies clearly demonstrates that some sections of Tiberius B v circulated in booklet form: R. I. Page, "Anglo-Saxon Episcopal Lists, Parts I and II," *Nottingham Medieval Studies* 9 (1965), 71–95, and "Anglo-Saxon Episcopal Lists, Part III," *Nottingham Medieval Studies* 10 (1966), 2–24; David N. Dumville, "The Anglian Collection of Royal Genealogies and Regnal Lists," *Anglo-Saxon England* 5 (1976), 23–50, esp. 26–28; Dumville, "The West Saxon Genealogical Regnal List and the Chronology of Early Wessex," *Peritia* 4 (1985), 21–66; Dumville, "The West Saxon Genealogical Regnal List: Manuscripts and Texts," *Anglia* 104 (1986), 1–32; and Simon Keynes, "Between Bede and the *Chronicle:* London, BL, Cotton Vespasian B. vi, ff. 104–9," in Katherine O'Brien O'Keeffe and Andy Orchard, ed., *Latin Learning and English Lore: Studies in Anglo-Saxon Literature for Michael Lapidge* (Toronto: University of Toronto Press, 2005), I:47–67, esp. 57–61.

16. McGurk, *An Eleventh-Century Miscellany,* 107.

17. See Evelyn Edson, *Mapping Time and Space: How Medieval Mapmakers Viewed*

Their World (London: The British Library, 1997), 52–80; and Catherine Delano-Smith and Roger J. P. Kain, *English Maps: A History* (Toronto: University of Toronto Press, 1999), 12.

18. McGurk, *An Eleventh-Century Miscellany,* 51–54.

19. For these tables, see respectively in McGurk, *An Eleventh-Century Miscellany,* 45, 49, and 62.

20. Ibid., 59.

21. Ibid., 75.

22. For a full discussion of Sigeric's itinerary, see Introduction below.

23. McGurk, *An Eleventh-Century Miscellany,* 75.

24. For *gadrian,* see Heinrich Henel, ed., *Ælfric's De temporibus anni,* Early English Text Society, o.s. 213 (London: Oxford University Press, 1942), 2.

25. See, for example, *De temporibus* I.37, in McGurk, *An Eleventh-Century Miscellany,* 76.

26. McGurk, *An Eleventh-Century Miscellany,* 67–78.

27. Ibid., 78.

28. Ibid.

29. Ibid., 80.

30. McGurk, *An Eleventh-Century Miscellany,* 80; and Henel, ed., *Ælfric's De temporibus,* 50.

31. McGurk, *An Eleventh-Century Miscellany,* 80.

32. Ibid.

33. On the list technique of this manuscript, see further Jacqueline Stodnick, "'Old Names of Kings or Shadows': Reading Documentary Lists," in Catherine E. Karkov and Nicholas Howe, ed., *Conversion and Colonization in Anglo-Saxon England* (Tempe, AZ: Arizona Center for Medieval and Renaissance Studies, 2006), 109–31. My thanks to Professor Stodnick for allowing me to read a prepublication copy of her article.

34. David N. Dumville, "Kingship, Genealogies and Regnal Lists," in P. H. Sawyer and I. N. Wood, ed., *Early Medieval Kingship* (Leeds: University of Leeds Press, 1977), 72–104.

35. David Rollason, *Northumbria, 500–1100: Creation and Destruction of a Kingdom* (Cambridge: Cambridge University Press, 2003), 20–43.

36. As Dumville notes in "Kingship, Genealogies and Regnal Lists," this concern with legitimating royal power through genealogies appears among various early Germanic political cultures and was by no means unique to the Anglo-Saxons (74–75).

37. See Page, "Anglo-Saxon Episcopal Lists, Parts I and II," 85.

38. McGurk, *An Eleventh-Century Miscellany,* 66.

39. Ibid.

40. Ibid., 67.

41. Charles Plummer, ed., *Two of the Saxon Chronicles Parallel* (Oxford: Clarendon Press, 1892), 4 for A Text and 5 for E Text.

42. McGurk, *An Eleventh-Century Miscellany,* 68–69.

43. For this connection, see further Ch. 4, "Rome as Capital of Anglo-Saxon England."

44. McGurk, *An Eleventh-Century Miscellany,* 69–71.

45. Ibid., 71–73.

46. Ibid., 72.

47. For a text and discussion, see F. P. Magoun, "An English Pilgrim Diary of the Year 990," *Mediaeval Studies* 2 (1940), 231–52.

48. See F. P. Magoun, "The Rome of Two Northern Pilgrims: Archbishop Sigeric of Canterbury and Abbot Nikolás of Munkathverá," *Harvard Theological Review* 23 (1940), 267–77.

49. Plummer, *Two of the Saxon Chronicles Parallel*, 126 for A Text (994) and 129 for E Text (995).

50. McGurk, *An Eleventh-Century Miscellany*, 86–87.

51. G. P. Krapp, ed., *The Anglo-Saxon Poetic Records*, Vol. I: *The Junius Manuscript* (New York: Columbia University Press, 1931), 31.

52. McGurk, *An Eleventh-Century Miscellany*, 40–43.

53. Ibid., 16.

54. The secondary literature on this text and its tradition is large. In addition to the works cited in the following notes, the standard point of departure remains Rudolf Wittkower, "Marvels of the East: A Study in the History of Monsters," *Journal of the Warburg and Courtauld Institutes* 5 (1942), 159–97. See also John Block Friedman, "The Marvels-of-the-East Tradition in Anglo-Saxon Art," in Paul E. Szarmach, ed., *Sources of Anglo-Saxon Culture* (Kalamazoo, MI: Medieval Institute Publications, 1986), 319–41; and Mary B. Campbell, *The Witness and the Other World: Exotic European Travel Writing, 400–1600* (Ithaca: Cornell University Press, 1988). For a brief survey on maps and the *Wonders* tradition, see Naomi Reed Kline, *Maps of Medieval Thought: The Hereford Paradigm* (Woodbridge, UK: Boydell, 2001), 150–64.

55. For a reading of *Wonders* as anticipating "colonialist images" of India, see Andrea Rossi-Reder, "Wonders of the Beast: India in Classical and Medieval Literature," in Timothy S. Jones and David A. Sprunger, ed., *Marvels, Monsters, and Miracles: Studies in the Medieval and Early Modern Imaginations* (Kalamazoo, MI: Medieval Institute Publications, 2002), 53–66.

56. For a reading of *Wonders* as concerned with the order and diversity of those to whom God offers his salvific grace, see Greta Austin, "Marvelous Peoples or Marvelous Races? Race and the Anglo-Saxon *Wonders of the East*," in Jones and Sprunger, *Marvels, Monsters, and Miracles*, 25–51, at 43.

57. McGurk, *An Eleventh-Century Miscellany*, 10.

58. C. T. Lewis and C. Short, *A Latin Dictionary* (Oxford: Clarendon Press, 1969), 370, *s. v. colonia*.

59. See Alfred Hiatt, "Mapping the Ends of Empire," in A. J. Kabir and D. Williams, ed., *Postcolonial Approaches to the European Middle Ages: Translating Cultures* (Cambridge: Cambridge University Press, 2005), 48–76.

60. Quoted from McGurk, *An Eleventh-Century Miscellany*, 10; see also Orchard, *Pride and Prodigies*, 184; translation by author.

61. McGurk, *An Eleventh-Century Miscellany*, 10.

62. Quoted from McGurk, *An Eleventh-Century Miscellany*, 10; see also Orchard, *Pride and Prodigies*, 184; translation by author.

63. Quoted from McGurk, *An Eleventh-Century Miscellany*, 11; see also Orchard, *Pride and Prodigies*, 186; translation by author.

64. McGurk, *An Eleventh-Century Miscellany,* 11; see also the section on the river Copi (14) which repeats the gloss of *wælkyrian* for *gorgoneos.*

65. Quoted from McGurk, *An Eleventh-Century Miscellany,* 19–20; see also Orchard, *Pride and Prodigies,* 196; translation by author.

66. For a different reading of this episode, see Susan M. Kim, "The Donestre and the Person of Both Sexes," in Benjamin C. Withers and Jonathan Wilcox, ed., *Naked Before God: Uncovering the Body in Anglo-Saxon England* (Morgantown: West Virginia University Press, 2003), 162–80.

67. I acknowledge with pleasure how much I learned from directing Dana Oswald's dissertation, "Indecent Bodies: Gender and the Monstrous in Medieval English Literature" (Ohio State University, 2005); her subtle readings of the sites of erasure that appear in the images accompanying *Wonders* are especially notable.

68. Quoted from McGurk, *An Eleventh-Century Miscellany,* 23; see also Orchard, *Pride and Prodigies,* 200; translation by author.

69. Quoted from McGurk, *An Eleventh-Century Miscellany,* 24; see also Orchard, *Pride and Prodigies,* 200–202; translation by author.

70. McGurk, *An Eleventh-Century Miscellany,* 27.

71. Michelle P. Brown, *Anglo-Saxon Manuscripts* (Toronto: University of Toronto Press, 1991), 34, claims that this map "illustrates the advanced state of Anglo-Saxon cartography, culled from Antiquity and from a long tradition of pilgrimage and travel." For its place in the Orosian tradition, see J. B. Harley and David Woodward, *The History of Cartography,* Vol. I: *Cartography in Prehistoric, Ancient, and Medieval Europe and the Mediterranean* (Chicago: University of Chicago Press, 1987), 300–301. See also the more extended study by Martin Foys, "The Virtual Reality of the Anglo-Saxon *Mappamundi,*" *Literature Compass* 1 (2004): ME 016, 1–14. The map is frequently reproduced: Brown, *Anglo-Saxon Manuscripts,* 35, in black and white; P. D. A. Harvey, *Medieval Maps* (Toronto: University of Toronto Press, 1991), 26, in color; and Harley, *The History of Cartography,* Plate 22 in color but reversed right to left in some printings.

72. The conflation of Iceland and Thule continues, as in the film by Fridrik Thor Fridriksson entitled *Devil's Island* (1996), which is set at Camp Thule, a U.S. Army base converted into public housing for Reykjavik's poor in the 1950s.

73. For this etymology of *Angulus,* see Nicholas Howe, "An Angle on this Earth: Sense of Place in Anglo-Saxon England," *Bulletin of the John Rylands University Library of Manchester* 82 (2000), 1–25, esp. 1–4. This depiction of England as an angle on the earth has a later history in Boccaccio: "Britones angulo in occiduo positi et ab orbe fere ceteri separati"; see *De casibus virorum illustrium,* ed. Pier Giorgio Ricci ad Vittorio Zaccaria, in *Tutte le opere di Giovanni Boccaccio,* ed. Vittore Braca, Vol. 9 (Milan: Arnaldo Mondadori, 1983), VIII. Xix.728. In the French translation of this work done by Laurent de Premierfait, and used by Lydgate for his *Fall of Princes,* this statement reads: "En Europe qui est la tierce partie du monde est vne isle appellee bretaigne qui est situee en vn anglet du monde par deuers occidant." See John Lydgate, *The Fall of Princes,* ed. Henry Bergen, Early English Text Society, e.s. 121–24 (London: Oxford University Press, 1924–27), IV:329. I owe these references to Joseph Grossi's dissertation, "Uncommon Fatherland: Medieval English Perceptions of Rome and Italy" (Ohio State University, 1999).

74. On ideas of "cosmic liminality" in Anglo-Saxon England, see Nicole Guenther

Discenza, "A Map of the Universe: Geography and Cosmology in the Program of Alfred the Great," in Karkov and Howe, *Conversion and Colonization,* 83–108. My thanks to Professor Discenza for allowing me to read her study before its publication.

75. Fred C. Robinson, "Old English Literature in Its Most Immediate Context," in his *The Editing of Old English* (Oxford: Blackwell, 1994), 3–24.

76. McGurk, *An Eleventh-Century Miscellany,* 79. For an edition of that work, see Paul van de Woestijne, ed., *La Périégèse de Priscien* (Bruges: De Tempel, 1953); and Delano-Smith and Kain, *English Maps: A History,* 34–40.

77. Christian Jacob, "Mapping in the Mind: The Earth from Ancient Alexandria," in Denis Cosgrove, ed., *Mappings* (London: Reaktion Books, 2002), 24–49, at 48.

78. McGurk, *An Eleventh-Century Miscellany,* 66.

79. Meyer Schapiro, *Words, Script, and Pictures: Semiotics of Visual Language* (New York: George Braziller, 1996), 147 and 150.

80. Peter Clemoes, "Language in Context: *Her* in the 890 *Anglo-Saxon Chronicle*," *Leeds Studies in English* n.s. 16 (1985), 27–36.

81. Plummer, *Two of the Saxon Chronicles Parallel,* 194: A Text for 1066.

82. See Orchard, *Pride and Prodigies,* 12–18; and Joyce Tally Lionarons, "From Monster to Martyr: The Old English Legend of Saint Christopher," in Jones and Sprunger, *Marvels, Monsters, and Miracles,* 167–82.

83. Text from Stanley Rypins, ed., *Three Old English Prose Texts in MS. Cotton Vitellius A xv,* Early English Text Society, o.s. 161 (London: Oxford University Press, 1924), 68 and 71 for Christopher's height, and 70 for the king's insult.

84. Rypins, *Three Old English Prose Texts,* 72–3.

85. Ibid., 75.

86. Bertram Colgrave and R. A. B. Mynors, ed. and trans., *Bede's Ecclesiastical History of the English People* (Oxford: Clarendon Press, 1969), I.xviii: *quidam tribuniciae potestatis;* 58.

87. Colgrave and Mynors, *Bede's Ecclesiastical History,* I.xviii.58–59.

88. Bertram Colgrave, ed. and trans., *Two Lives of Saint Cuthbert: A Life by an Anonymous Monk of Lindisfarne and Bede's Prose Life* (Cambridge: Cambridge University Press, 1940), Ch. XLI, 288 and 90 for Latin, 289 and 91 for translation.

89. Orchard, *Pride and Prodigies,* 224–25.

90. In this regard, it should be noted that Alexander's military expeditions also had major scientific benefits, for which see Jacob, "Mapping in the Mind," in Cosgrove, ed., *Mappings,* 30–31. On Alexander as author-figure, see Margaret Bridges, "Empowering the Hero: Alexander as Author in the *Epistola Alexandri ad Aristotelem* and its Medieval English Versions," in M. Bridges and J. C. Bürgel, ed., *The Problematics of Power: Eastern and Western Representations of Alexander the Great* (Bern: Peter Lang, 1996), 45–59. For Alexander and the medieval mapping tradition, see Kline, *Maps of Medieval Thought,* 166–90.

91. For a reading of the text as a whole, see Brian McFadden, "The Social Context of Narrative Disruption in *The Letter of Alexander to Aristotle*," *Anglo-Saxon England* 30 (2001), 91–114.

92. Orchard, *Pride and Prodigies,* 226–27.

93. Ibid., 248–49.

94. Ibid.

95. Ibid., 250–51.

96. Ibid., 246–47.

97. Ibid., 250–51.

98. For a similar moment of overreaching, of going too far, consider the death of Thorvald in *Eirik the Red's Saga;* see Nicholas Howe, "Reading Places," *Yale Review* 81.3 (1993), 60–73, esp. 71–73.

99. Orchard, *Pride and Prodigies,* 250–51.

100. Ibid., 252–53.

101. Ibid., 184–85.

102. Ibid.

103. The technique appears elsewhere in *Wonders,* as at the start of its section on Hascellentia; Orchard, *Pride and Prodigies,* 186–87.

104. Ibid., 200–201.

105. Ibid., 200–202 and 201–3.

106. Ibid., 226–27.

107. Nicholas Howe, *Migration and Mythmaking in Anglo-Saxon England* (Notre Dame: University of Notre Dame Press, 2001), 143–80.

108. There is no discussion of this passage's geographical implications, for example, in the extended study by Frederick M. Biggs, "The Politics of Succession in *Beowulf* and Anglo-Saxon England," *Speculum* 80 (2005), 709–741.

109. Fr. Klaeber, ed., *Beowulf and the Fight at Finnburg,* 3rd ed. (Boston: D. C. Heath, 1950), 82. All quotations from *Beowulf* are taken from this edition.

110. Edward B. Irving, Jr., *A Reading of Beowulf* (New Haven: Yale University Press, 1968), 198.

111. For relevant studies of the poem, see Christopher Fee, "*Judith* and the Rhetoric of Heroism in Anglo-Saxon England," *English Studies* 78 (1997), 401–6; and Hugh Magennis, "Gender and Heroism in the Old English *Judith,*" in Elaine Treharne, ed., *Writing Gender and Genre in Medieval Literature: Approaches to Old and Middle English Texts* (Cambridge: D. S. Brewer, 2002), 5–18.

112. Mark Griffith, ed., *Judith* (Exeter: University of Exeter Press, 1997), 101.

113. See Howe, *Migration and Mythmaking,* 72–107; and Andrew P. Scheil, *The Footsteps of Israel: Understanding Jews in Anglo-Saxon England* (Ann Arbor: University of Michigan Press, 2004).

Chapter 7: Falling into Place: Dislocation in Junius 11

1. See further Ian Buruma, "The Romance of Exile," *The New Republic,* 2/12/2001: 33–38.

2. The *locus classicus* for this term is the opening line of *The Wanderer:* "Oft him anhaga are gebideð." Unless otherwise indicated, quotations from Old English poetry refer to G. P. Krapp and E. V. K. Dobbie, ed., *The Anglo-Saxon Poetic Records,* 6 vols. (New York: Columbia University Press, 1931–1953). This quotation is from *ASPR* III:134.

3. See Stanley B. Greenfield, "The Formulaic Expression of the Theme of 'Exile' in

Anglo-Saxon Poetry," *Speculum* 30 (1955), 200–206; reprinted in his *Hero and Exile: The Art of Old English Poetry,* ed. George H. Brown (London: Hambledon Press, 1989), 125–31.

4. E. T. DeWald, *The Illustrations of the Utrecht Psalter* (Princeton: Princeton University Press, n.d.), Plate CXIX for illustration, 59–60 for commentary. On the relation of the Utrecht Psalter to the illustrations in Junius 11, see H. R. Broderick, "Observations on the Method of Illustration in MS Junius 11 and the Relationship of the Drawings to the Text," *Scriptorium* 37 (1984 for 1983), 161–77; and Jessica Brantley, "The Iconography of the Utrecht Psalter and the Old English *Descent into Hell,*" *Anglo-Saxon England* 28 (1999), 43–63.

5. This illustration is reproduced most accessibly in Thomas H. Ohlgren, ed., *Anglo-Saxon Textual Illustration* (Kalamazoo, MI: Medieval Institute Publications, 1992), 241; for commentary, see 39.

6. *ASPR* V:132.

7. Yosef Hayim Yerushalmi, *Zakhor: Jewish History and Jewish Memory* (Seattle: University of Washington Press, 1982), 5–26.

8. On the recurrent presence of such historical moments in Junius 11, see the important study by Catherine Karkov, *Text and Picture in Anglo-Saxon England: Narrative Strategies in the Junius 11 Manuscript* (Cambridge: Cambridge University Press, 2001), CSASE 31, esp. 119. I am grateful to Professor Karkov for allowing me to read her book in proof.

9. For a description of the physical manuscript, see Karkov, *Text and Picture in Anglo-Saxon England,* Ch. 2; Barbara C. Raw, "The Construction of Oxford, Bodleian Library, Junius 11," *Anglo-Saxon England* 13 (1984), 187–207; and Katherine O'Brien O'Keeffe, *Visible Song: Transitional Literacy in Old English Verse* (Cambridge: Cambridge University Press, 1990), 179–86.

10. Thomas D. Hill, "The Fall of Angels and Man in the Old English *Genesis B,*" in Lewis E. Nicholson and Dolores W. Frese, ed., *Anglo-Saxon Poetry: Essays in Appreciation* (Notre Dame, IN: University of Notre Dame Press, 1975), 279–90.

11. Edward B. Irving, Jr., ed., *The Old English Exodus* (New Haven: Yale University Press, 1953; rprt. 1970); Irving, "New Notes on the Old English *Exodus,*" *Anglia* 90 (1972), 289–324; and Irving, "*Exodus* Retraced," in Robert B. Burlin and Edward B. Irving, Jr., ed., *Old English Studies in Honour of John C. Pope* (Toronto: University of Toronto Press, 1974), 203–23.

12. Elias Canetti, *Crowds and Power,* trans. Carol Stewart (New York: Noonday, 1984), 39.

13. Nicholas Howe, *Migration and Mythmaking in Anglo-Saxon England* (Notre Dame, IN: University of Notre Dame Press, 2001), Ch. 3. See also Patrick J. Geary, *The Myth of Nations: The Medieval Origins of Europe* (Princeton: Princeton University Press, 2002), 10 and 54.

14. See Paul Battles, "*Genesis A* and the Anglo-Saxon 'Migration Myth,'" *Anglo-Saxon England* 29 (2000), 43–66.

15. *Genesis:* 2936 lines; *Exodus:* 590 lines; *Daniel:* 764 lines; and *Christ and Satan:* 729 lines.

16. J. R. Hall, "The Old English Epic of Redemption: The Theological Unity of MS.

Junius 11," *Traditio* 32 (1976), 185–208; and Hall, " 'The Old English Epic of Redemption': Twenty-Five-Year Retrospective," in R. M. Liuzza, ed., *The Poems of MS Junius 11: Basic Readings* (New York: Routledge, 2002), 53–68. This volume also reprints Hall's 1976 article.

17. Karkov, *Text and Picture in Anglo-Saxon England*, 101. See also 46–47 for her reading of the Creation image that opens Junius 11 as uniting "Old and New Testaments just as the manuscript as a whole unites poems based on the Old and New Testaments in a narrative present. The reading of the book thus becomes a metaphor for the progress of time from Genesis to the Last Judgement."

18. Joyce Hill speaks usefully of that "moment in time, in the early eleventh century, when some Anglo-Saxons read these poems as an interlocking scheme" in various ways (morally, typologically, and liturgically); see her "Confronting Germania Latina: Changing Responses to Old English Biblical Verse," in Richard North and Tette Hofstra, ed., *Latin Culture and Medieval Germanic Europe* (Groningen: Egbert Forsten, 1992), 71–88, at 85.

19. O'Brien O'Keeffe, *Visible Song*, 180.

20. Among many the many studies of the manuscript's theological or liturgical unity, see Hall, "The Old English Epic of Redemption"; Hill, "Confronting Germania Latina"; Malcolm Godden, "Biblical Literature: the Old Testament," in Godden and Michael Lapidge, ed., *The Cambridge Companion to Old English Literature* (Cambridge: Cambridge University Press, 1991), 209–218; Richard J. Schrader, *Old English Poetry and the Genealogy of Events* (East Lansing: Colleagues Press, 1993), Ch. 2; Andy Orchard, "Conspicuous Heroism: Abraham, Prudentius, and the Old English *Genesis*," in Leo Carruthers, ed., *Heroes and Heroines in Medieval English Literature* (Woodbridge, UK: Boydell and Brewer, 1994), 45–58; Carol Braun Pasternack, *The Textuality of Old English Poetry* (Cambridge: Cambridge University Press, 1995), 179–95; and Richard Marsden, *The Text of the Old Testament in Anglo-Saxon England* (Cambridge: Cambridge University Press 1995), 441–43. For the manuscript's illustration program, see Barbara Raw, "The Probable Derivation of Most of the Illustrations in Junius 11 from an Illustrated Old Saxon *Genesis*," *Anglo-Saxon England* 5 (1976), 133–48; Thomas H. Ohlgren, "Some New Light on the Old English *Cædmonian Genesis*," *Studies in Iconography* 1 (1975), 38–73; and Karkov, *Text and Picture in Anglo-Saxon England*, esp. Ch. 6.

21. In this regard, I note but do not consider relevant for my reading the probable existence of *Genesis A* and *Genesis B*, as well as the composite nature of *Daniel* and of *Christ and Satan*. My concern is with the manuscript as it can be read in its current state rather than with what might have been the pieces used in its assembly. In this regard, I follow the argument of Pasternack, *The Textuality of Old English Poetry*, esp. "The Reader," 21–26.

22. Erich Auerbach, "Figura," in his *Scenes from the Drama of European Literature* (Minneapolis: University of Minnesota Press, 1984; rprt. of 1959 ed.), 53. See further Nicholas Howe, "The Figural Presence of Erich Auerbach," *The Yale Review* 85 (1997), 136–43.

23. Phyllis Portnoy, " 'Remnant' and Ritual: The Place of *Daniel* and *Christ and Satan* in the Junius Epic," *English Studies* 75 (1994), 408–22, at 410.

24. For the importance of Abraham in the Junius poems, see Hall, "The Old English Epic of Redemption," esp. 197. For the use of artful wordplay to underscore the theme of the covenant in Junius 11, see Roberta Frank, "Some Uses of Paronomasia in Old English Scriptural Verse," *Speculum* 47 (1972), 207–26, esp. 213–23.

25. Karkov, *Text and Picture in Anglo-Saxon England,* 1. See p. 17 for discussion of the relation between biblical and Anglo-Saxon history in the manuscript.

26. *ASPR* I:xxxix–xl.

27. R.T. Farrell, ed., *Daniel and Azarias* (London: Methuen, 1974), 32–33, suggests that only the person(s) who added *Christ and Satan* to the manuscript thought that the first three poems constituted a "first book." Even if true, this claim does not bear directly on how a reader of Junius 11 might interpret the reference to the "second book" at the end of the manuscript.

28. For a reading of *Daniel* as ending as "its author intended it to end," see Farrell, ed., *Daniel and Azarias,* 6. His argument is countered by Peter J. Lucas, "On the Incomplete Ending of *Daniel* and the Addition of *Christ and Satan* to Ms. Junius 11," *Anglia* 97 (1979), 46–59.

29. All quotations from *Genesis, Exodus, Daniel,* and *Christ and Satan* are from *ASPR* III.

30. See further Alessandro Scafi, "Mapping Eden: Cartographies of the Earthly Para- dise," in Denis Cosgrove, ed., *Mappings* (London: Reaktion, 2002), 50–70.

31. Pasternack, *The Textuality of Old English Poetry,* 183–85.

32. The *Genesis* poet offers a similar statement by Abraham himself about the many peoples he has visited during his lifetime; see ll. 2691–2703.

33. Howe, *Migration and Mythmaking,* 89–92. See also Richard North, *Heathen Gods in Old English Literature* (Cambridge: Cambridge University Press, 1997), 58–64.

34. See Peter J. Lucas, ed., *Exodus* (London: Methuen, 1977), 8–15. For a discussion of the illustrations in *Exodus,* see Karkov, *Text and Picture in Anglo-Saxon England,* 115–19.

35. See Daniel J. Elazar, "Judaism as a Theopolitical Phenomenon," in Jacob Neusner and Alan J. Avery-Peck, eds., *The Blackwell Companion to Judaism* (Oxford: Blackwell, 2000), 415–40, esp. 417–20.

36. Graham Caie, "The Old English *Daniel:* A Warning against Pride," *English Studies* 59 (1978), 1–9, esp. 3.

37. See, for example, Charles W. Kennedy, trans., *The Cædmon Poems Translated into English Prose* (Gloucester, MA: Peter Smith, 1965; reprt. of 1916 ed.), lxi. See also Portnoy, " 'Remnant' and Ritual," 413. For general readings of *Daniel,* see Robert E. Bjork, "Oppressed Hebrews and the Song of Azarias in the Old English *Daniel,*" *Studies in Philology* 77 (1980), 213–26; and Earl R. Anderson, "Style and Theme in the Old English *Daniel,*" *English Studies* 68 (1987), 1–23.

38. For the reading of l. 10 suggested here, as referring to the covenant with Abraham, see Farrell, *Daniel and Azarias,* 47 (notes to l. 10).

39. On the *Daniel* poet's use of the theme of *translatio imperii,* see Anderson, "Style and Theme," 17.

40. For this reading of ll. 193–94, see Farrell, *Daniel and Azarias,* 58.

41. Antonina Harbus, "Nebuchadnezzar's Dreams in the Old English *Daniel,*" *English Studies* 74 (1994), 489–508.

42. *ASPR* III:178–79.

43. Ruth Wehlau, "The Power of Knowledge and the Location of the Reader in *Christ and Satan*," *JEGP* 97 (1998), 1–12. See also Janet S. Ericksen, "The Wisdom Poem at the End of MS Junius 11," in Liuzza, *The Poems of MS Junius 11*, 302–26.

44. In this regard, one should note how quickly the poet of *Genesis* mentions hell as the destined home of the fallen angels in his creation story, namely, in a passage beginning at l. 34b.

45. See, for example, *Christ and Satan*, ll. 176–77; 187b–88; 256b–59a.

46. At the end of the poem, God explicitly banishes Satan to the *witescræf*, or pit of torment (ll. 690–91a).

47. For the "narrative or eternal present" of Junius 11, see Karkov, *Text and Picture in Anglo-Saxon England*, 142–44.

48. The most recent study of the manuscript dates it to c. 960–c. 990; see Leslie Lockett, "An Integrated Re-examination of the Dating of Oxford, Bodleian Library, Junius 11," *Anglo-Saxon England* 31 (2002), 141–73.

49. See especially his preface to the translation of *Genesis*, in Jonathan Wilcox, ed., *Ælfric's Prefaces* (Durham: Durham Medieval Texts, 1994), 116–19; and Mark Griffith, "Ælfric's Preface to *Genesis*: Genre, Rhetoric, and the Origins of the *Ars Dictamini*," *Anglo-Saxon England* 29 (2000), 215–34.

Conclusion: By Way of Durham

1. For the literary technique of the poem, see Calvin B. Kendall, "Let Us Now Praise a Famous City: Wordplay in the Old English *Durham* and the Cult of St. Cuthbert," *JEGP* 87 (1988), 507–521. I agree with D. R. Howlett's appraisal of the poem, though for quite different reasons than he offers: "There are no indications here that the poet thought 'Durham' was a last feeble gasp of an expiring tradition of verse composition. Nor is it. The work is more competent and craftsmanly than any modern critic has yet supposed." See "The Shape and Meaning of the Old English Poem 'Durham,'" in David Rollason, Margaret Harvey, and Michael Prestwich, ed., *Anglo-Norman Durham: 1093–1193* (Woodbridge, UK: Boydell, 1994), 485–95, at 495.

2. E. V. K. Dobbie, ed., *The Anglo-Saxon Poetic Records*, Vol. VI: *The Anglo-Saxon Minor Poems* (New York: Columbia University Press, 1942), 27.

3. For Anglo-Saxon lists of saints, see Robert M. Stein, "Making History English: Cultural Identity and Historical Explanation in William of Malmesbury and Laȝamon's *Brut*," in Sylvia Tomasch and Sealy Gilles, ed., *Text and Territory: Geographical Imagination in the European Middle Ages* (Philadelphia: University of Pennsylvania Press, 1998), 114–15.

4. The compiler of Cambridge, University Library MS Ff.i.27 recreated this sense of a "Cuthbert Circle" by including in his manuscript not simply the text of the Old English *Durham* but also Symeon's *Historia Dunelmensis ecclesiae*, various short items on the city, and the *Historia de sancto Cuthberto*; see *ASPR* VI:xliii.

5. Janet Backhouse, *The Lindisfarne Gospels* (Oxford: Phaidon, 1981), 87.

6. For a thoughtful reading of *Durham* as "politically and culturally nostalgic," see Seth Lerer, *Literacy and Power in Anglo-Saxon Literature* (Lincoln: University of Ne-

braska Press, 1991), 199–206, and, in somewhat altered form, Lerer, "Old English and Its Afterlife," in David Wallace, ed., *The Cambridge History of Medieval English Literature,* (Cambridge: Cambridge University Press, 1999), 7–34. See also, as Lerer suggests, Malcolm Baker, "Medieval Illustrations of Bede's *Life of St. Cuthbert,*" *Journal of the Warburg and Courtauld Institutes* 41 (1978), 16–49.

7. As David Rollason remarks: "The Anglo-Saxon saints had become part of England's heritage." See his *Saints and Relics in Anglo-Saxon England* (Oxford: Blackwell, 1989), 238. For the cult of St. Cuthbert, see 144–52.

8. Wilhelm G. Busse, "*Sua gað ða lareowas beforan ðæm folce, 7 ðæt folc æfter:* The Self-Understanding of the Reformers as Teachers in Late Tenth-Century England," in Ursula Schaefer, ed., *Schriftlichkeit im frühen Mittelalter,* Scriptoralia 53 (Tübingen: Gunter Narr Verlag, 1993), 58–106, at 65.

9. I do not mean to imply that this form of continuity was related to, or gave rise to, anti-Norman opposition during this period in any active sense. See further Rollason, *Saints and Relics in Anglo-Saxon England,* 220–22.

Index